CLARENDON LIBRARY OF LOGIC AND PHILOSOPHY
General Editor: L. Jonathan Cohen, The Queen's College,
Oxford

BLINDSPOTS

Also published in this series

Quality and Concept by George Bealer
Psychological Models and Neural Mechanisms: An Examination of Reductionism in Psychology by Austen Clark
The Probable and the Provable by L. Jonathan Cohen
The Diversity of Moral Thinking by Neil Cooper
The Metaphysics of Modality by Graeme Forbes
Interests and Rights: The Case Against Animals by R. G. Frey
The Logic of Aspect: An Axiomatic Approach by Antony Galton
Ontological Economy by Dale Gottlieb
Equality, Liberty, and Perfectionism by Vinit Haksar
Experiences: An Inquiry into some Ambiguities by J. M. Hinton
The Fortunes of Inquiry by N. Jardine
Metaphor: Its Cognitive Force and Linguistic Structure by Eva Feder Kittay
Metaphysics and the Mind-Body Problem by Michael E. Levin
The Cement of the Universe: A Study of Causation by J. L. Mackie
Divine Commands and Moral Requirements by P. L. Quinn
Simplicity by Elliott Sober
The Logic of Natural Language by Fred Sommers
The Coherence of Theism by Richard Swinburne
Anti-Realism and Logic: Truth as Eternal by Neil Tennant
The Emergence of Norms by Edna Ullmann-Margalit
Ignorance: A Case for Scepticism by Peter Unger
The Scientific Image by Bas C. van Fraassen
The Matter of Minds by Zeno Vendler
What is Existence? by C. J. F. Williams
Works and Worlds of Art by Nicholas Wolterstorff

BLINDSPOTS

Roy A. Sorensen

CLARENDON PRESS · OXFORD
1988

Oxford University Press, Walton Street, Oxford OX2 6DP
Oxford New York Toronto
Delhi Bombay Calcutta Madras Karachi
Petaling Jaya Singapore Hong Kong Tokyo
Nairobi Dar es Salaam Cape Town
Melbourne Auckland
and associated companies in
Berlin Ibadan

Oxford is a trade mark of Oxford University Press

Published in the United States
by Oxford University Press, New York

© Roy A. Sorensen 1988

All rights reserved. No part of this publication may be reproduced, stored in a retrieval system, or transmitted, in any form or by any means, electronic, mechanical, photocopying, recording, or otherwise, without the prior permission of Oxford University Press

British Library Cataloguing in Publication Data
Sorensen, Roy
Blindspots.—(Clarendon library of logic and philosophy).
1. Paradox
I. Title
165   BC199.P2
ISBN 0-19-824981-0

Library of Congress Cataloging in Publication Data
Sorensen, Roy A.
Blindspots.
(Clarendon library of logic and philosophy)
Bibliography: p.
Includes index
1. Knowledge, Theory of. 2. Logic. 3. Moore, G. E.
(George Edward), 1873–1958. I. Title. II. Series.
BD161.S63   1988   165   87-28236
ISBN 0-19-824981-0

Set by Pentacor Ltd., High Wycombe, Bucks
Printed in Great Britain by
Biddles Ltd., Guildford and King's Lynn

This book is dedicated to my parents,
Omar Arnold Sorensen
and
Judith H. Sorensen

Acknowledgements

THE list of those who have improved this book through conversation and correspondence would not fit on this page. If it would, Julia Driver, Christopher Boorse, and Douglas Stalker would be found at the top. Had I the space, the list would still be incomplete because of the anonymity of journal referees who labour for motives that must constitute a mystery for economists. My gratitude toward them must therefore be left diffuse and shadowy. However, I can specifically thank the editors and publishers of *The Australasian Journal of Philosophy. The Philosophical Quarterly, Synthese, Philosophical Studies, Philosophia, American Philosophical Quarterly,* and *The Canadian Journal of Philosphy* for permission to reprint material from my articles in those journals.

Roy A. Sorensen
New York University

Contents

Introduction   1

1. *An Analysis of Moore's Problem*   15
   I.   Moore's Problem   15
   II.   Adequacy Conditions and Past Proposals   16
         A. Defining Moorean Propositions   16
         B. Avoiding Doxastic Logic   19
         C. Distinguishing between Moorean Inconsistency
            and Other Types   23
         D. Accommodating Non-obvious Examples   28
         E. Accommodating Impure Cases   33
   III. Criticizing Believers   34
   IV.   A More Formal Account of Belief Criticism   40
   V.   A Classification of Moorean Sentences by Time and Role   44
   VI.   Other Propositional Attitudes and Mooreanness   47
   VII. Blindspots   50
   VIII. Summation and Conclusions   55

2. *Belief Blindspots and Truth*   57
   I.   Blindspots and Truth   57
   II.   Validity and Arguments Containing Blindspots   65
         A. Ellis's Epistemic Semantics and General Moorean
            Propositions   66
         B. Ellis on Relevance and a Precedent   69
         C. Van Fraassen on Theoretical Scepticism about
            Belief and Belief *de se*   70
         D. Are the Alleged Counter-examples Arguments?   75
   III. Ramsey's Proposal and Conditional Blindspots   77

3. *Limits on Agreement*   85
   I.   The Case for Agreement   85
   II.   Basic Disagreement   88
   III. Two Types of Blindspot Disagreement   91
         A. Simple Blindspot Disagreement   92
         B. Complex Blindspot Disagreement   92

		IV. Misjudgement Theories	96
		A. Hetero-referential Misjudgement Theories	98
		B. Self-referential Misjudgement Theories	102
	V.	Pre-commitments and Blindspot Disagreement	115
4.	*Knowledge Blindspots, Anti-realism, and the Argument from Ignorance*		117
	I.	Degrees of Epistemological Optimism	118
	II.	Personal Limits	118
	III.	Impersonal Limits and Anti-realism	121
	IV.	Variations of the Argument from Ignorance	129
		A. The Simple Form	130
		B. The Falsity Form	140
		C. The Gappy Form	143
		D. The Unbreakable Tie Form	144
	V.	Logical Analogies	151
		A. Hypertasks and Symmetrical Blindspots	151
		B. Mystery Numbers	154
		C. Applications to the Modal Appeals to Ignorance	157
5.	*Blindspot Predicates*		160
	I.	Unlimited Blindspot Predicates	160
		A. Best-explanation Blindspots	161
		B. Incompleteness Blindspots	177
		C. Incomprehensibility Blindspots	183
		D. Causality Blindspots	185
	II.	Limited Blindspot Predicates	186
		A. Temporally Limited Blindspots	186
		B. Agent-limited Blindspots	188
		C. Three Misadventures with Personal Blindspot Predicates	189
	III.	Blurry Predicates	199
		A. Defining Blurry Counterparts to Vague Predicates	206
		B. Dispensability or Identity?	213
6.	*Rival Responses to the Sorites*		217
	I.	Reversibility and Non-standard Sorites Arguments	217
	II.	Rejecting the Argument's Validity	219
		A. The Invalidity Approach	219
		B. Validity Gaps	224
	III.	Rejecting a Premiss	226
		A. Rejecting the Base Step	226
		B. Rejecting the Induction Step	230
	IV.	The Untenability of the Limited Sensitivity Thesis	246

Contents

7.	*History of the Prediction Paradox*		253
	I. Early Commentary on the Prediction Paradox		255
	A. Assimilation to the Pragmatic Paradoxes		256
	B. Surprise as Unprovability		258
	C. Assimilation to Logical Fatalism		260
	D. Quine's Accusation of *Argumentum ad Ignorantiam*		262
	II. Emergence of the Sentential Self-reference Approach		264
	A. Shaw's Seminal Contribution		264
	B. Lyon's Charge of Equivocation		266
	C. The Kaplan–Montague Analysis		267
	D. Assimilation to Godel's Sentence		269
	E. Assimilation to the Langford Visiting Card Paradox		272
	F. Further Refinements and Criticisms of the Approach		273
	III. Game-theoretic self-reference		280
	IV. Emergence of the Epistemic Approach		283
	A. Misgivings about the Propriety of the Announcement		283
	B. Assimilation to Moore's Problem		284
	C. Rejection of the Temporal Retention Principle		286
	D. Assimilation to the Lottery Paradox		288
	V. The KK-rejectors		289
	VI. Assimilation to the Sorites		292
	VII. The Rise of the Prediction Paradox		295
8.	*Appraisal of Past Proposals*		297
	I. Criticisms of the Self-referentialists		298
	A. Knowability, Deducibility, and Gratuitous Self-reference		298
	B. Pseudo-Scotus and the Self-referentialists		299
	C. Reduction to the Liar		301
	D. Pseudo-Scotus and the Prediction Paradox		303
	II. Criticisms of the Clarifiers		310
	III. Criticisms of the Epistemological Approach		310
	IV. Criticisms of the KK-rejectors		312
	A. Relevance of the Alleged Counter-examples to KK		313
	B. The Dispensability of the KK principle		317
	V. A Further Puzzle for the Temporalists		320
	VI. Criticisms of the Game-theoretic Approach		322
	VII. Criticisms of the Sorites Assimilators		324
9.	*Consequential Blindspots and the Existential Premiss*		328
	I. Consequential Blindspots and the Prediction Paradox		328

	II.	Reduction of the Bottle Imp	333
	III.	A Strengthened Prediction Paradox	336
	IV.	The Reduction of the Bottle Imp Reconsidered	343
10.	*Agency, Super-games, and Blindspotting*	344
	I.	The Super-games	344
		A. The Iterated Prisoners' Dilemma	345
		B. The Chain Store Paradox	348
		C. Hodgson's Paradox of Punishment	349
		D. Iterated Chicken	351
		E. The Iterated Pricing Game	352
		F. Super-games and Emergent Threat Potential	352
	II.	Criticisms of Davis and Hardin	353
	III.	Blindspotting	355
	IV.	Isolated Agents and Common Causes	361
	V.	The Vagueness of 'Knowledge'	365
	VI.	Blindspotting in the Booth Paradox	368
	VII.	Appeals to the Similarity Principle	369
11.	*Stability and Anti-expertise*	371
	I.	Newcomb's Problem	371
	II.	The Case of the Infallible Predictor	375
	III.	Instability Cases	378
	IV.	Analogues	382
	V.	Anti-expertise and Moore's Problem	386
		A. The Hidden Moorean Implication	386
		B. Overshadowed Hypotheses	390
		C. 'Anti-expert' as a Personal Blindspot Predicate	392
	VI.	Conclusions about the Instability Cases	396
12.	*The Slippery Slope Fallacy*	398
	I.	Hypothetical v. Categorical Slippery Slope Arguments	398
	II.	Joint Probabilities	403
		A. Improbable Antecedents and Vacuous Slopes	405
		B. Redundant Slopes	407
		C. Certain Slopes and the Statistical Concept of Fallacy	408
		D. Explanation, Chain Reaction, and Speculation	411
		E. Validity Illusions	413
	III.	Counter-example Resistance and Mendacious Generalizations	414
		A. Recipe for Mendacious Mathematical Inductions	415
		B. Universally Resistant Slopes	420

		Contents	xiii
		C. Local Resisters	430
	IV.	Deviancy v. Unity	436

Bibliography 439

Subject Index 451

Name Index 454

Introduction

WITTGENSTEIN 'once remarked that the only work of Moore's that greatly impressed him was his discovery of the peculiar kind of nonsense involved in such a sentence as "It is raining but I don't believe it" '.[1] This book might be considered an anti-Wittgensteinian study of this kind of 'nonsense'.

What Moore discovered were propositions I call 'blindspots'. The ordinary meaning of 'blind spot' is rooted in opthalmology. The blind spot of an eyeball is the spot in the retina where the optic nerve passes through the inner coat of the eyeball. Since there are no photoreceptors in this spot, there is no sensitivity to light and hence no vision. Since this spot is so tiny, it poses no practical handicap (although baseball players sometimes blame their failed catches on blind spots). Indeed, many people never learn of their blind spots. The reader can locate his blind spot by means of the following pair of dots:

●   ●

Hold this page about twelve inches from your eyes. Close your left eye. Now look steadily at the left-hand dot while moving the page first slowly away from you and then slowly back toward your face. The right-hand dot will disappear from your field of vision when its image falls on your blind spot.

Notice that when the dot disappears it becomes 'completed'. Instead of merely becoming an empty region in your subjective visual field, the region is 'filled in' in accordance with its surroundings. If the dots were white and its surroundings were black, the right-hand dot would be replaced by blackness. If the dots rested on a line within a striped background, the dot would be replaced by the 'missing' segment of the line.[2] Your blind spot differs from the blind spots of other people whose curiosity you

[1] Norman Malcolm, *Ludwig Wittgenstein: A Memoir* (Oxford: Oxford University Press, 1984), 56.
[2] Those who wish to verify these claims about the completion effect can inspect the illustrations on p. 23 of Mark Fineman's *The Inquisitive Eye* (New York: Oxford University Press, 1981).

might have aroused through this experiment. Whereas we are all equally 'blind' in the dark, our varying blind spots make us blind in an individual fashion. Our common structures create personalized ranges of vision.

The reader may have detected that I have begun to slide to another reading of 'blind spot'. Instead of talking about a certain internal structure, a spot on the retina, I have begun to talk about a spot in an external field of vision that is invisible because of the internal structure. I have turned from why we cannot see to what we cannot see.

This equivocation between two opthalmological senses of 'blind spot' leads us to a secondary sense of the term. Generalizing, we can speak of a blind spot as being any 'area in which one fails to exercise understanding, judgement, or discrimination'.[3] For example, Senator John Glenn accused Attorney-General Edwin Meese of an 'ethical blind spot' during Meese's controversial confirmation hearings. Meese enjoyed the friendship of many wealthy men who gave him a number of loans on very generous terms (some of which were interest-free and unsecured). While in office, Meese helped some of his creditors receive government jobs. During his confirmation hearings, Meese was asked whether the question of a conflict of interest arose when he enhanced the employment prospects of his friends. Meese responded that the question never occurred to him. If we were to accept the truth of Meese's response, then I think we should agree with Senator Glenn that Meese failed to see an obvious moral issue, and that this failure is evidence of an underlying area of ethical insensitivity. My second example is from one of Alistair Cooke's introductions to an episode of *The Jewel in the Crown*. In order to explain Winston Churchill's imperialistic stance toward India, Cooke maintained that Churchill had a blind spot when it came to India. According to Cooke, Churchill's attitude toward India was formed by experiences as a young man witnessing glorious military battles. These unrepresentative samples of Great Britain's involvement with India coloured Churchill's perspective, making him unable to see what the incoming reports were making plain to others.

The application of 'blind spot' to the case of Meese and

---

[3] This definition is from *Webster's Third New International Dictionary* (Springfield, MA: Merriam-Webster, 1981).

Introduction

Churchill is natural in light of the extended use of 'see' to cover judgements. Since we also 'see' things by mirrors, radio, and radar, it might also be expected that talk of blind spots will be found in describing equipment that enhances our perceptions. New drivers are taught to look over their shoulder before changing lanes because of the blind spot not covered by their side-view and rear-view mirros. Pilots who wish to avoid radar detection fly close to the ground because low altitudes are in the blind spots of radars. Likewise, the localities in which radio reception is markedly poorer than the surrounding areas are called blind spots.

What binds these different senses of 'blind spot' together is a notion of idiosyncratic inaccessibility. The eye cannot receive the image that falls on that one particular spot on the retina. It cannot 'reach out' to process the right-hand dot. Likewise, Glenn thinks Meese has no special problems with most judgements but does have a problem in reaching the correct judgements about the requirements of impartiality imposed by public office. And Cooke believes Churchill does well enough with most of his political appraisals but falls dramatically short in the matter of India. Automobile rear-view mirrors permit us to see almost everything behind us; we only lack access to a special spot. Likewise with radio and radar; our range of pick-up is structured in such a way that there is a peculiar discontinuity.

Something is inaccessible if it cannot be reached. What we can and cannot do is determined by an implicit set of constraints. I cannot reach Australia by car but can by aeroplane. The relevant constraints are often most clearly formulated in terms of laws and initial conditions. The statement 'I cannot float in thin air' can be spelled out as something like 'Given the law of gravity and the initial condition that I am a 165–pound object on earth in its undisturbed orbit, I will not float in air.' In general, our claims about inaccessibility are relative to our destination, means of conveyance, and further constraints. Blind spots can be classified by specifiying these values.

The destinations that will interest me in this book are propositions. The means of conveyance are propositional attitudes. And I am interested in weak constraints, the weakest 'constraint' being the laws of logic. I will call propositions that are inaccessible under weak constraints 'blindspots'. (The deletion of the space is intended to differentiate my technical use of the term.) Although the genus of blindspots is vaguely defined, its species and subspecies can be more precisely defined by specifying the type of propositional attitude and the laws constituting the constraints.

The philosophical interest of a concept is usually established by exhibiting its relevance to theses that are already acknowledged to be of philosophical interest. Blindspots will not run contrary to this pattern. However, the book has been planned so that this parasitic sort of legitimization emerges as a welcome byproduct of achieving another goal that reflects my main motivation for studying blindspots. For my discussion of blindspots shall be organized around the solution of a family of paradoxes that has fascinated me for the past seven years or so. Included in this family is a collection of defective mathematical inductions: the sorites, the prediction paradox, and the iterated prisoners' dilemma, and variations of these three.

The best-known of the bunch is the sorites. Most people are introduced to the puzzle in the same way that the ancient Greeks were. It is first observed that any (suitably arranged) collection of one million grains of sand is a heap. Next we note that removing one grain of sand from a heap leaves it a heap. Yet if we have the patience to continue the minute subtractions, the heap eventually disappears. The paradox lies in the fact that these three claims cannot be all true. We can show that the first two assumptions rule out the third by means of a mathematical induction.

1. A collection of one million grains of sand is a heap.
2. If a collection of n grains of sand is a heap, then so is a collection of $n-1$ grains.
3. A collection of 1 grain of sand is a heap.

At first blush, many people are tempted to reject the second premiss. But that would force us to say that there is a counter-example to the generalization. In other words, we would have to say that one grain can make the crucial difference between whether something is a heap or not a heap. This seems far-fetched because our usage of 'heap' seems too rough to be compatible with sensitivity to such small changes.

The prediction paradox came into circulation during World War II. Logic students usually hear it in the form of a story featuring a teacher who announces that there will be a surprise test next week.

Introduction

One of his students first points out that if the test is given on the last day, Friday, it will not be a surprise. Since they know that the test cannot be given on Friday, the students also know that the test cannot be given on Thursday. For if no test were given by Wednesday, only two alternatives would remain, and the previous argument eliminates one of them. Having ruled out Thursday and Friday, a similar argument can be used to rule out Wednesday, Tuesday, and Monday. So the clever student concludes that the surprise test cannot occur. Like the sorites, this argument can be couched as a mathematical induction:

1. The students know that the test cannot be given on the last day.
2. If the students know that the test cannot be given on day n, then they also know that the test cannot be given on day $n-1$.
3. The students know that the test cannot be given on any day.

Since most people believe that the teacher can give a surprise test, they reject the conclusion. As with the sorites, most people regard the first step as unassailable and so suggest that the second must be false. But once again, they face the embarrassing issue of specifying the counter-example.

The iterated prisoners' dilemma emerged in the 1950s with the growth of interest in game theory. The most intensively studied type of game is the prisoners' dilemma. An example of this type of game can be obtained by supposing that Row and Column are two rationally self-interested agents who will receive dollar pay-offs in accordance with Table 0.1. (Row receives the left-hand values, Column the right-hand.)

TABLE 0.1

		Column	
		Co-operate	Compete
Row	Co-operate	(100, 100)	(0, 101)
	Compete	(101, 0)	(1, 1)

There is a consensus that this game will result in mutual competition even though mutual co-operation affords a far higher reward for both parties. The reasoning is that competing *dominates* co-operating, that is, the compete option guarantees rewards that are never worse than the co-operate option would have given and which are sometimes better. Regardless of Column's choice, Row gets a higher pay-off by competing. The iterated prisoners' dilemma arises as a 'supergame' in which the prisoners' dilemma is played repeatedly. For example, suppose Row and Column are certain that they will be playing the above game exactly 100 times, each being informed of the other's move after each play. Since it now seems possible that Row's choice will influence the choices of Column, and vice versa, one would expect that they would try to influence each other by co-operating. If the players competed on all 100 plays, we would be inclined to regard them as irrational. Those impressed by the dominance argument might argue that a one-play prisoners' dilemma differs from a $n + 1$ play prisoners' dilemma because the dominance principle only applies when one is sure that one's choice will not have any further influence on one's interests. If there are $n + 1$ plays, then this requirement is not met; one must take into account the possibility of future retaliation and reward. So the co-operation displayed by players in an iterated prisoners' dilemma does not show that co-operation will occur in the one-play prisoners' dilemma.

However, the prisoners are certain that their choice on the last play of the prisoners' dilemma is equivalent to a one-play prisoners' dilemma. So if the argument from dominance is correct, the prisoners will compete on the last play. But given that the prisoners know that they will compete on the last play regardless of the previous course of the game, they should also compete on the second to last play. And given that they will compete on the second to last play, they should compete on the third to last. The same reasoning requires competition on the fourth to last, fifth to last, and so on. We are thus driven to the conclusion that rationally self-interested players will compete on every move of the iterated prisoners' dilemma.

The paradox of the iterated prisoners' dilemma can be compactly expressed as an apparently sound mathematical induction leading to an absurd conclusion.

1. The players know they will compete at play 100.

2. If the players know they will compete at play n, then they know they will compete at $n-1$.
3. The players know they will compete on every play.

Although some theorists accept this conclusion, most reject it as absurd. As was true for the sorites and the prediction paradox, the majority also accept the base step but cannot mount a reasonable objection to the induction step.

My direct objective is to show how study of blindspots provides a unified solution to these three paradoxes. The path I make in pursuit of this target is designed to reveal the general nature and importance of blindspots as explanatory entities. The first few chapters cultivate the background for my later deployment of blindspots. I begin by developing the notion of blindspots from an analysis of Moore's problem: the problem of explaining what is odd about sentences like 'It is raining but I do not believe it.' My solution to the problem is couched in terms of the desiderata of belief formation. These desiderata give rise to structural requirements which 'pure Moorean propositions' violate in a unique way. Desiderata for other propositional attitudes give rise to similar requirements which account for a wide class of peculiar yet non-Moorean sentences. Thus pursuit of a solution to Moore's problem leads to a large class of positions which might be true but which cannot be held. Our vision of reality contains blindspots. Of course, the blindspots do not logically preclude us from seeing the whole truth. In a friendly universe, our 'completions' of the gaps in our fields of vision might be entirely veridical. Filling gaps in accordance with surroundings is good induction. But it is also good induction to believe that some good inductions will go bad. Since the best we can count on is an indifferent universe, we are left with the conclusion that some truths may well have been placed out of reach by the rules of representation.

Blindspots create considerable difficulties for those who hold that truth must be analysed in terms of belief. And in Chapter 2 considerable energy is spent driving this point home. The implications blindspots have for truth carry over to validity. These implications make themselves felt when we consider arguments featuring blindspots as premises or conclusions. These arguments can be valid and even sound without having the power to persuade rationally. This creates difficulties for subjective theories of validity, such as Brian Ellis's epistemic semantics, in which an argument is deemed valid if and only if no one rationally accepts the premisses and rejects the conclusion. Blindspots produce parallel peculiarities when they serve as the antecedent or consequent of conditionals. These 'conditional blindspots' are counter-examples to Ramseyian theories of evaluating conditionals. For such theories counsel us to test the acceptability of conditionals by hypothetically adding the antecedent to our stock of beliefs and checking whether the consequent would be believed.

Since study of blindspots shows that we have unique ranges of open positions, irresolvable disagreement can arise when one party's evidence prompts him to take a position that is off limits to the other. Species of the resulting sort of disagreement are studied in Chapter 3. The emphasis is shifted from belief to knowledge in Chapter 4. After noting how knowledge blindspots reinforce traditional epistemological limits and suggest new ones, I turn to semantic anti-realism; the view that truth conditions cannot transcend assertion conditions. Since consistent but unknowable propositions are excluded by semantic anti-realism, I argue that knowledge blindspots are counter-examples to this thesis.

One down-to-earth way of viewing the issue of semantic anti-realism is through an investigation of modal arguments from ignorance. Inferences from contingent ignorance are familiar enough. Textbook writers regularly dismiss them as fallacious. As long as we adopt the traditional conception of fallacy as an invalid argument that looks valid, I doubt that an adequate account of *argumentum ad ignorantiam* is possible. So I advance a statistical concept of fallacy that pictures fallacious argument forms as akin to partially functional tools. Under this view, many instances of the fallacious form can be good arguments. In particular many appeals to contingent ignorance are cogent effect to cause inferences. In the case of appeals to necessary ignorance, however, the traditional and statistical conceptions dovetail. For the modal appeals are sound only if valid, thereby committing the arguer to holding that his argument satisfies deductive standards. Since the anti-realist denies the possibility of unknowable truths, he is committed to the validity of certain forms of this argument. For example, he must deem valid 'It cannot be known whether or not everything doubled in size last night, therefore, it is neither true nor false that everything doubled in size last night.' A variety of such modal appeals to ignorance are considered. My objection is that we always have inductive evidence for the invalidity of these arguments. Although there is no formal way to deduce their invalidity, the validity of modal appeals to ignorance can be rendered improbable by showing how such appeals can be systematically paired with defeating logical analogies. The demonstration begins with the observation that certain quasi-mathematical propositions are symmetrical blindspots: blindspots whose negations are also blindspots. An infinite stock of these blindspots is used to derive the 'mystery numbers': numbers whose identities are unknowable. The structural features of modal appeals to ignorance can be precisely imitated by obviously invalid arguments about the properties of mystery numbers. Thus the analogy between each argument and its invalid mimic undermines the original's claim to validity.

Appeal to mystery numbers is also made in Chapter 5 concerning predicates whose application systematically yields blindspots. Some of these uniformly yield predications that are blindspots for everyone. 'Flat', 'fair die', and 'four metres long' all count as examples as long as the highest standards of precision are in force. Hume's scepticism about miracles, Price's scepticism about paranormal events, and Quine's scepticism about illogical cultures can be construed as claims that 'miracle', 'paranormal event', and 'illogical culture' are blindspot predicates. The same interpretation is possible for other types of local epistemological specticism. A second species of blindspot predicates uniformly yields predicates that are blindspots for only the subject of the predication. If someone applies 'modest' to Mother Teresa, we obtain a proposition that Mother Teresa cannot know but which others can. Study of these personal blindspots reveals flaws in some objections to materialism and determinism. The last group of predicates, called 'blurry predicates', only sometimes yields blindspots. Usually a blurry predicate can be associated with a sequence of individuals yielding a progression of increasingly inaccessible predications. This shading-off phenomenon is also characteristic of vague predicates. The simplest way to account for the resemblance is via the hypothesis that vague predicates are identical to blurry predicates. The identity claim is backed by the fact that the mystery numbers permit us to define blurry predicates in a way that leaves them functionally indistinguishable from vague predicates.

Further support for the identity thesis comes from an appeal to the sorites paradox. I argue that once we commit ourselves to common-sense realism, the sorites forces us to view vague predicates as having unlimited sensitivity to changes. In other words, I maintain that unqualified belief in the existence of everyday things–heaps, flowers, and people–commits us to the view that removing one grain of sand from a heap can turn it into a non-heap. Thus I maintain that the sorites must be solved by flatly rejecting the induction step. Rival positions are surveyed and criticized in Chapter 6. The criticisms are intended to be general ones, ones that give us reason to believe that rival approaches must fail in principle. My analysis is also intended to stand as a positive theory of vagueness. For I am committed to optimism about the results of extending probability theory into philosophy of language and psycholinguistics.

Just as blurry predicates prove crucial to my solution of the sorites, personal blindspot predicates play a pivotal role in the resolution of the prediction paradox. Like 'modest', predicates such as 'surprise', 'secret', and 'anonymous' induce blindspots tailored to certain individuals or groups. These blindspots contour the 'inferential space' of each agent in idiosyncratic ways that play havoc with our intuitions about reason's indifference to who we are and when we are.

Some of this havoc is nicely illustrated by the history of the prediction paradox. Thus one motive for describing the puzzle developmentally is that its history buttresses my opinion of the explanatory power of blindspots. A second motive for proceeding historically is that the prediction paradox nicely illustrates how curiosities can evolve into problems of philosophical importance. Thirdly, the historical approach provides an opportunity to study an example of progress in contemporary analytic philosophy. The literature on the prediction paradox constitutes a paradigm of piecemeal philosophy. It is a history of journal articles, discussion notes, and asides. As a child observing ants band together to carry large morsels to their nest, I used to wonder how they co-ordinated their movements to reach their goal. Eventually I was told that the ants actually do not all co-ordinate. Indeed the motion of the morsel is the outcome of a many-sided tug of war.

Food tends to reach the nest because of a central tendency of the group. No ant leads the journey. Some have great positive influence, some less so, and a few even hamper the project. And of course, the involved ants only constitute a small subpopulation of the colony: the vast majority are preoccupied with other projects. Since many of our collective projects are imperfectly co-ordinated and are pursued amidst the indifference of the majority, an analogy with the ants can frequently be drawn. Such is the case with philosophers and the prediction paradox. For although large strides were made by a few commentators, our understanding of the puzzle was chiefly forwarded by the small and inharmonious steps of many commentators. Although the literature on the prediction paradox displays a disturbing amount of redundancy and error due to ignorance of the work of others, it also displays the fertility of the problem. The prediction paradox has been assimilated to pragmatic paradoxes, logical fatalism, the liar, Godel's theorem, Moore's problem, the lottery paradox, the sorites, and other puzzles.

Although some of the strengths and weaknesses of these assimilations naturally arise in a discussion of the history of the paradox, their appraisal only begins in earnest in Chapter 8. Much weight is assigned to recalcitrant variations of the paradox. Many of the proposals advanced in the past forty years are objections to assumptions that are not essential to all variations of the paradox. An adequate solution must be a complete solution. The completeness condition encourages us to seek out new variations of the puzzle in question. For these new variations are our data. Paradoxes are manifestations of inconsistencies amongst our central beliefs. Proper diagnosis of the inconsistency requires a good sample of its manifestations. As with all good samples, the collection of paradoxes must be neither too small nor biased. Once we have the representative sample, we can make the inductive inference that the original population of paradoxes contains no members that resist our solution.

Chapter 9, 'Consequential Blindspots and the Existential Premiss', deals with the sort of analysis I have promoted as a solution to the prediction paradox. The approach is demoted to the status of an instructive failure by a variation of the paradox that also reveals the incompleteness of most past proposals. For the variation is a strengthened version of the prediction paradox that manages to avoid making an assumption generally thought to be essential to the prediction paradox. It does this by making 'intention' the crucial concept instead of 'surprise'. Since the notion of intention is connected to the concept of rational choice, the strengthened prediction paradox reveals the relevance of certain puzzles associated with decision and game theory.

Chapter 10 concentrates on these puzzles. The strengthened prediction paradox bridges the gap between weak versions of the puzzle and the iterated prisoners' dilemma. This paradox will in turn be shown to be part of a large family of 'super-game puzzles'. They differ from traditional versions of the prediction pardox because they involve the notion of agency. I argue that much of my old analysis of the prediction paradox can be salvaged by study of the phenomenon of 'blindspotting'. Blindspotting is a matter of manipulating the epistemic states of others (and sometimes oneself) by exploiting semi-blindspots. A proposition is a knowledge semi-blindspot of another if and only if they are co-possible but not co-knowable. Given that you do not like the fact that your adversary knows a semi-blindspot, you can force him to lose this knowledge by feeding him new information favouring its mate. Since the semi-blindspot need only be a semi-blindspot for one's adversary, others might find the information helpful enough to achieve knowledge of both propositions. The blindspotee, on the other hand, finds the semi-blindspots competing for scarce credence. The result is lost knowledge without forgetfulness.

To handle common cause variations of the blindspotting puzzles, I assume that rational choices must be stable. Stability forbids rational agents from choosing options they know to be inferior. This assumption has been the target of a surprisingly strong challenge in the literature on Newcomb's problem. After reviewing the stability requirement's role in defence of the two box solution, I concentrate on 'instability cases' that have been presented as counter-examples to the principle. These decision problems always feature the chooser as an 'anti-expert', namely, someone who is reliably wrong about a certain field of propositions. By showing that 'anti-expert' is a personal blindspot predicate, the ostensible counter-examples are revealed to be impossible situations. This legitimates the appeal to stability.

The concluding chapter generalizes the lessons learned from the separate analyses of the mathematical inductions. The generalization proceeds through a study of the slippery slope fallacy. Since at least a large percentage of these arguments are valid, I once again call upon the statistical notion of fallacy. My account concedes that many instances of the fallacious form are good arguments–even predictably so, as is illustrated by the wealth of good slippery slope arguments found in mathematics. However, outside hospitable environments, the argument form has to be handled with great care. For the fact that slippery slope arguments have many premisses, and the fact that almost all of these premisses are conditionals, combine to make their evaluation treacherous. By taking many small steps, we obtain a valid argument whose premisses are individually undeniable and thereby create an illusion of cogency. Often arguers try to take a shortcut by taking fewer steps of larger scale and thereby leave a premiss open to challenge. But with the help of mathematical induction, we can compress the slope into a single generalization. By choosing generalizations that cannot be refuted by counter-example, we obtain especially strong slippery slope arguments. Study of blindspots reveals the structure of this counter-example resistance. So in addition to placing the sorites, prediction paradox, and iterated prisoner's dilemma on a continuum with more simple-minded slippery slope arguments, the blindspot analysis also allows us to create new slippery slope arguments. Some of these novel arguments are comparable in power to the originals that prompted this investigation. Thus blindspots illuminate a type of reasoning that inspires a queer sort of fascination in philosophers and non-philosophers alike.

The various analyses and subanalyses that fill this book are intended to draw support from one another by displaying a unified diagnosis of apparently disparate problems. Although one cannot hope to have escaped error in philosophical theorizing, one can hope to have developed a fertile account. The falsehoods of such an account are viewed in the same way as we view the bad branches of a good tree: worth removing to make way for new growth from the same structure. So my efforts have been directed to the formation of an account that can be viewed as 'basically on the right track'.

1

An Analysis of Moore's Problem

THIS chapter is devoted to a solution to Moore's problem.[1] After explaining the problem, I will formulate conditions that a solution to the problem should satisfy. These adequacy conditions will chiefly come as lessons learned from past proposals. My solution will emanate from a discussion of how the desiderata of belief give rise to structural requirements for our beliefs.

I. MOORE'S PROBLEM

Moore's problem is the problem of explaining why sentences like the following are odd.

(1) It is raining but I believe it is not raining.
(2) It is raining but it is not the case that I believe it is raining.

Many people are tempted to dismiss (1) and (2) as contradictions. But if, for example, (2) were a contradiction, it would be a necessary falsehood and hence its negation would be a necessary truth. However, 'Either it is not raining or I believe it is raining' fails to be a necessary truth even in the mouths of our most marvellous meteorologists. (1) and (2) could be true. After all, (1) merely describes a commissive error and (2) merely describes an omissive error. We often have a practical interest in conditionals whose antecedents are Moorean sentences. A person who believes 'If I eat this mushroom and it is, contrary to my belief, poisonous, then I will die' will probably not eat the mushroom unless he has great confidence in his judgement that the mushroom is edible. But if the antecedent were a contradiction, the conditional would have no more practical interest than 'If some mushrooms are not mushrooms, then I will die.'

Commentators on Moore's problem have also noted that the

[1] Portions of this chapter are taken from 'Pure Moorean Propositions', *Canadian Journal of Philosophy*, 153 (Sep. 1985), 489–506.

oddity of (1) and (2) is not present in their future and past tense counterparts.

> (3) It is raining but I will believe otherwise in the future.
> (4) It is raining but it is not the case that I believed so in the past.

Sentence (3) is a clumsy way of predicting a change of mind. (4) is an equally clumsy way of saying that the rain was not expected. Nor is the peculiarity present in the third person counterparts of (1) and (2).

> (5) It is raining but he believes that it is not raining.
> (6) It is raining but it is not the case that he believes it is raining.

However, the first person plural and second person counterparts of (1) and (2) are peculiar.

> (7) It is raining but we believe that it is not raining.
> (8) It is raining but it is not the case that we believe it is raining.
> (9) It is raining but you do not believe that it is raining.
> (10) It is raining but it is not the case that you believe it is raining.

Although the oddity of (7) and (8) is the same as the oddity of (1) and (2), (9) and (10) are odd in a different way. In the first person examples, the speaker seems to be contradicting himself. In the second person examples, the speaker is saying something that is self-defeating.

II. ADEQUACY CONDITIONS AND PAST PROPOSALS

A. *Defining Moorean Propositions*

A complete solution to Moore's problem should show how one, in some sense, contradicts oneself when one utters a Moorean sentence and should also answer the question 'What is a Moorean sentence?' Optimally, this answer should be a definition. Commentators have concentrated on constructing proposals that satisfy the self-contradiction condition. Their interest in the definitional condition has been slight. Although they are content to characterize Moorean sentences with the open sentence '*p* but I do not believe it', there are Moorean sentences that do not conform to this characterization.

(11) God knows that we are atheists.
(12) Although you do not agree with me about anything, you are always right.

Neither (11) nor (12) bears any significant *grammatical* resemblance to the open sentence. Nevertheless, whatever tempts us to call (1) and (2) contradictions also tempts us to call (11) and (12) contradictions. So the definitional condition of providing criteria for what counts as a Moorean sentence cannot be satisfied with the open sentence characterization. Any proposal that does not satisfy the definitional condition is incomplete since one is left without a way of determining which sentences are 'like' sentences (1) and (2). The first adequacy condition is not entirely independent of the second. So although little attention has been given to the definitional condition, proposals that satisfy the self-contradiction condition often have implications concerning the second. So it is not the case that all previous proposals are inadequate simply because they fail to supply criteria for being a Moorean sentence. Nevertheless, I think that those proposals which do not contain omissive errors concerning the definitional condition, contain commissive errors. As we shall soon see, past proposals satisfying the self-contradiction condition usually imply definitions of 'Moorean sentence' that are either too narrow or too broad.

As an example of the attempt to satisfy the self-contradiction condition, consider L. Jonathan Cohen's account of pragmatic paradoxes. Cohen argues that pragmatic paradoxes are consistent propositions which are falsified by their own utterance.[2] The idea is to reconcile the consistency of the odd sentences with the intuition that the speaker is contradicting himself by showing how the normally irrelevant act of utterance undermines their truth. Cohen's definition was made with three examples in mind:

[2] Cohen's account is presented in 'Mr O'Connor's "Pragmatic Paradoxes"', *Mind*, 64 213 (Jan. 1950), 85–7.

> (13) I remember nothing at all.
> (14) I am not speaking now.
> (15) I believe there are tigers in Mexico but there aren't any there at all.

Given that (13) is understood as concerning a total lack of habit memory, a person's utterance of (13) would constitute excellent inductive evidence for its falsity. But since mindless parroting of the sentence is logically possible, the falsification would not be deductively conclusive. A *spoken* token of (14), given normal indexing of the indexicals, does constitute deductive refutation of the proposition it expresses. No charitable qualifications are needed to make

> (16) There are no sentence tokens.

fit Cohen's definition. For the existence of any token of (16) is a sufficient condition for the falsity of the proposition it expresses. But even charitably interpreted, (15) does not conform to Cohen's definition. Suppose there are no tigers in Mexico but Jane believes that there are some there. Further suppose that she utters a token of (15) to make her point about pragmatic paradoxes. Her token would then express a true proposition.

Is the Jane example fishy? Technically, Jane did produce a true *utterance*. But one might insist that a charitable interpretation of Cohen's definition would require the speaker to *assert* the pragmatic paradox. Since Jane did not believe what she was saying, the 'counter-example' is disqualified. Encouraged by this result, we clarify (or perhaps revise) Cohen's definition to read: a pragmatic paradox is a consistent proposition that is falsified by its own *assertion*. This definition is suited to unobtrusive self-falsifiers such as 'Since thirteen is an unlucky number, I never use sentences containing thirteen words.' But obvious self-falsifiers tend to elude it. It is difficult to *assert* an obvious falsehood. You can only assert what you can give the appearance of believing. Given the audience's reluctance to attribute obvious errors to people, they will interpret obviously false utterances non-literally. Thus the audience's charity makes it difficult to assert an obvious self-falsifier. Since lists of paradigm cases of pragmatic paradoxes are heavily populated with obvious self-falsifiers, the new version of

Cohen's definition is too narrow. In particular, 'It is raining but I do not believe it' will fail to qualify in light of its unassertibility. So despite its promise as a satisfier of the self-contradiction condition, Cohen's account violates the definitional condition.

B. *Avoiding Doxastic Logic*

The problem with the last proposal was the unassertibility of Moorean sentences. A group of commentators suggest that we turn this problem into the solution. Why not define a Moorean sentence as one which expresses a consistent and yet unassertible proposition?[3] Since the unassertibility of 'It is raining but I do not believe it' issues from its unbelievability, the group of those who try to solve Moore's problem by an appeal to unassertibility overlaps with another group who appeal to unbelievability. The unbelievability group would appear to have a definition that captures the essence of Moore's problem closer to its source: a Moorean sentence is a sentence which expresses a consistent yet unbelievable proposition. However, a purist of this persuasion would be sacrificing some premises that are useful to unassertibilists in derivations of 'self-contradictions'. For instance, A. P. Martinich employs the maxim of Quality: do not knowingly participate in a speech act for which the conditions of successful and non-defective performance are not satisfied. For an assertion to be non-defective, the assertor must believe what he is saying. The belief is *conversationally* implied. Martinich explains

In particular, a speaker who says 'It is raining and I do not believe that it is raining' asserts in part

   (A) It is raining

and, by the maxim of quality, conversationally implies

   (B) I believe it is raining.

But (B) contradicts the other part of what he asserts, namely,

   (B′) I do not believe that it is raining.

---

[3] The unassertibilist approach can be traced back to Max Black's 'Saying and Disbelieving', *Analysis*, 13 (Dec. 1952), 28–31.

And hence the content of what the speaker means is contradictory; and, in this straightforward way, logically odd.[4]

If Martinich had merely maintained that Moorean sentences are unbelievable he would not be in a position to employ conversational implications. The contradiction is derived from the assumption that the Moorean sentence is non-defectively asserted; not from the assumption that it is merely believed.

Besides illustrating one advantage of the unassertibilist approach. Martinich's derivation of a contradiction illustrates some of the difficulties of such derivations. Why does Martinich apply the maxim of Quality to only the first conjunct of 'It is raining but I do not believe it'? Shouldn't it apply to the whole utterance? If it is applied to the whole utterance, won't we have appeal to the doxastic principle $B(p \& q) \supset (Bp \& Bq)$ to reach step (B)? (Read 'Bp' as 'It is believed that p.') Should this principle be considered a principle of logic? Or are we to reach (B) from the assumption that what the speaker asserted was *true*? In that case, Moorean sentences are to be defined as sentences expressing consistent propositions whose truth is incompatible with their assertibility. In answering these questions, we should also disambiguate (B').[5] If it is read as '$-Bp$', it contradicts (B). If it is read as '$B-p$', it does not contradict (B). The first reading gives us the prospect of deriving a standard contradiction: $Bp \& -Bp$. The second reading only allows us to infer directly inconsistent beliefs $Bp \& B-p$. If we are seeking a standard contradiction, then Martinich's derivation can only explain Moorean sentences of the form $p \& -Bp$; those of the form $p \& B-p$ would remain unexplained.

Martinich's appeal to Gricean principles of conversation puts some flesh on the claim that Moorean sentences *cannot* be asserted. For the 'cannot' must refer to the violation of some constraint. The way that we cannot assert Moorean sentences must be distinguished from the way we cannot assert that pigs fly.

Constraints must also be specified by those who wish to say that Moorean sentences cannot be believed. A rigorous way of specifying constraints on belief is through doxastic logic — a logic of belief. The best known example of this approach is Jaakko

---

[4] A. P. Martinich, 'Conversational Maxims', *Philosophical Quarterly*, 30 120 (July 1980), 224.

[5] The significance of this ambiguity is stressed in J. N. Williams, 'Moore's paradox: one or two?' *Analysis*, 39 3 (June 1979), 141–2.

Hintikka's analysis of Moore's problem in *Knowledge and Belief*. Hintikka explains the peculiarity of Moorean sentences in terms of *doxastic indefensibility*. Roughly, a statement is doxastically indefensible if and only if the speaker cannot consistently believe it. Uttering a Moorean sentence is self-defeating since it gives its hearers all they need to overthrow the statement.[6] Hintikka explains that when someone makes a statement there is a presumption that it is at least possible for the speaker to believe what he is saying. This presumption is violated in the case of Moorean sentences because it is obvious to the speaker and his audience that he cannot consistently believe what he is saying. To demonstrate the doxastic indefensibility of (1) and (2), Hintikka uses a logic of belief that is a doxastic interpretation of the modal system deontic S4. Most philosophers are reluctant to accept Hintikka's analysis because they believe his logic of belief is too strong, even for ideal thinkers. For example, in his proofs of the unbelievability of Moorean sentences, Hintikka appeals to the rule that belief in p implies belief that one believes p, and the rule that belief collects over conjunction: $(Bp \,\&\, Bq) \supset B(p \,\&\, q)$. Further evidence that his logic of belief is too strong lies in its distortion of our ordinary notion of indefensibility. For it can be demonstrated that my belief that someone else believes an inconsistent proposition counts as an indefensible belief in Hintikka's system.[7] Lastly, the analysis makes a problematic appeal to what is obvious to speakers and their audiences. Thus his analysis evokes admiration without acceptance.

Some philosophers are reluctant to accept any logic of belief because they are sympathetic to the view that belief is 'crazy as hell'. Sympathy to the view that anything can be believed, call it gullibilism, has been expressed by Haskell Fain and A. Phillips Griffiths.

There is no proposition so transparent in its falsehood that all of mankind could see through it. There is no proposition so compactly true that no one could miss it. The most trivial of tautologies can be believed false; the most blatant of contradictions can be believed true. Even that most venerable proposition 'I exist' — which, Descartes claimed is 'necessarily

---

[6] For the exact definition of doxastic indefensibility, see *Knowledge and Belief* (Ithaca: Cornell University Press, 1962), 71.

[7] Leonard Linsky presents the proof in 'On Interpeting Doxastic Logic', *Journal of Philosophy*, 65 (17 Sept. 1968), 500–2.

true each time that I pronounce it, or that I mentally conceive it—can be falsely believed to be false. For what is to prevent some lunatic from believing that he does not exist?[8]

Perhaps gullibilist intuitions underlie some of our scepticism about appeals to charity, self-evidence, innate ideas, and incorrigibility. Citing Hume, the gullibilist could defend his thesis by maintaining that since believing and the objects of beliefs are distinguishable, they are therefore separable, and so credence can be distributed over objects of belief in any fashion. In any case, the incompatibility of gullibilism and doxastic logic is best exposed through a distinction between strong and weak gullibilism.

(SG) Strong gullibilism: $(p) \Diamond (x) Bxp$.
(WG) Weak gullibilism: $(p) \Diamond (\exists x) Bxp$.

Hintikka's claim that the utterer of a standard Moorean sentence could not possibly believe the proposition his token expresses is incompatible with (SG). Presumably, Hintikka would also claim that no one could ever believe

(18) It is raining but at no time does anyone believe it.

This would make Hintikka's position incompatible with even weak gullibilism.

Hintikka's anti-gullibilism should come as no surprise. Anyone who believes there is a non-trivial logic of belief is committed to the view that belief is orderly. The order is standardly described in terms of belief expanding rules and belief restricting rules. For example, the principle that belief distributes over conjunction, $B(p \& q) \supset (Bp \& Bq)$, enables us to expand our list of beliefs given that the antecedent is on the list. On the other hand, the rule proscribing direct inconsistency, $Bp \supset -B-p$, restricts lists of beliefs. Since gullibilism asserts that belief can be distributed over propositions in any fashion, it denies the legitimacy of all rules of belief.

---

[8] Haskell Fain and A. Phillips Griffiths, 'On Falsely Believing that One Doesn't Know', in Nicholas Rescher (ed.), *Studies in the Philosophy of Mind* (Oxford: Basil Blackwell, 1972), 10.

C. *Distinguishing between Moorean Inconsistency and Other Types*

My conjecture is that sympathy with gullibilism has prevented many philosophers from accepting substantive systems of doxastic logic. In any case, interest in doxastic logic has dwindled, so much so that it is not feasible to erect a convincing analysis on this kind of foundation. An alternative is to simply diagnose the oddity of Moorean sentences in terms of the impossibility of their utterers being right. Max Deutscher has tried to solve Moore's problem by pointing out that (1) and (2) resemble contradictions because their tokeners can believe them only at the expense of having inconsistent beliefs.

to assert that *p* is to present '*p*' to the audience as a view to which the speaker subscribes. Since the speaker presents '*p* but I don't believe that *p*' to the audience as a view to which he subscribes, he presents to the audience a set of views such that it is logically necessary that one of them is false. This is what is wrong with asserting '*p* but I don't believe that *p*'.[9]

Deutscher is certainly correct in stressing the desirability of consistency amongst belief. But consistency is just one desideratum amongst a set of competing desiderata. Though consistency is highly prized, competition with other desiderata sometimes leads to permissible types of inconsistency. For example, we treasure completeness amongst beliefs and so are willing to take a small risk of commissive error in order to avoid the certainty of omissive error. The probability of a given belief being wrong might be quite low. But we realize that these small probabilities accumulate to make it virtually certain that we now harbour some errors. So completeness requires us to believe this virtual certainty. Thus reasonable people will assent to

(19) I believe at least one false proposition.

Belief in (19) precludes the possibility of all of one's beliefs being true. For one's belief in (19) can be true only if one harbours a false belief. This seems to make belief in (19) infallible. The supposition that one's belief in (19) is mistaken leads straight to contradiction.

Well, maybe not *straight* to contradiction: contradiction is easy

[9] Max Deutscher, 'Bonney on Saying and Disbelieving', *Analysis*, 27/6 (June 1967), 184–6.

enough to derive given the current state of logic, perhaps too easy. Suppose that my beliefs other than (19) are all true. Although this is a slender possibility, it is a possibility. What then is the truth value of (19)? If (19) is true, none of my beliefs are false and so (19) is false. But if (19) is false, then one of my beliefs is false which makes (19) true. Thus the supposition that my 'first order' beliefs might all be true leads to a contradiction. We are driven to the paradox that my second order belief in (19) makes it logically necessary that I have a false belief distinct from my belief in (19). This is the sophisticated preface paradox.[10] In order to make the point about rational inconsistent belief without the paradox, one must avoid the self-referential reading of (19). Belief in (19) is a second order belief; a belief about beliefs. If we read it as only asserting that a first order belief is false, there is no paradox of self-reference.

(19′) At least one of my first order beliefs is false.

If this proposition is false, one of my second order beliefs is false. If it is true, one of my first order beliefs is false. So belief in (19′) precludes the possibility of all of my beliefs being true. Therefore, my belief in (19′) saddles me with an inconsistent set of beliefs. The price of avoiding the self-referential paradox is that one must give up the infallibility claim. But the price is happily paid since the objective is merely to obtain an example of rational inconsistent beliefs.

The quest for another counter-example to Deutscher's analysis might lead one to consider the omissive counterpart to (19):

(20) I fail to believe at least one true proposition.

However, Deutscher only intends to rule out inevitable *commissive* error. Another candidate for counter-example is:

(21) There is a proposition which I both believe and disbelieve.

[10] This paradox has been the focus of J. J. MacIntosh's attention in a number of articles. His most recent analysis is presented in 'Some Propositional Attitude Paradoxes', *Pacific Philosophical Quarterly*, 65 1 (Jan. 1984), 21–5. The simple form of the puzzle was first introduced by D. C. Makinson in 'The Paradox of the Preface', *Analysis*, 25 (1965) 205–7.

Moore's Problem

Belief in (21) can only be true if I have a false belief. Here we do not have to rely on self-reference to guarantee the impossibility of all of my beliefs being true. For the truth of (21) and my remaining beliefs would only unparadoxically imply that I both believe and disbelieve (21). I could come to believe (21) on the basis of an induction from past discoveries of directly inconsistent beliefs (or at least my interpretation of certain belief conflicts as direct inconsistencies).

Deutscher might take issue with the claim that (21) is a counter-example on the grounds that the asserter of (21) would not be *specifying* the set of views. One reply is that the set of all of my beliefs is a specified set of views. Another reply is that a smaller set could be specified. Consider an individual's views about the local lottery. He believes it is a fair lottery featuring 1000 tickets and a single prize. Prior to the draw, the man denies that ticket number 1 will be the winning ticket on the grounds that its probability of winning is only 0.001. He issues similar denials on similar grounds for tickets 2, 3, 4 and so forth until he has denied of each ticket that it is the winning ticket. Nevertheless, he also believes that there will be a winning ticket because he believes that the lottery is fair. Thus he has advanced the following views:

    L1. Ticket number 1 is not a winning ticket.
    L2. Ticket number 2 is not a winning ticket.
    L3. Ticket number 3 is not a winning ticket.

    L1000. Ticket number 1000 is not a winning ticket.
    L1001. There is a winning ticket i.e. one of (L1)–(L1000) is false.

Although this set of views is inconsistent, it is at least arguably rational. As the number of beliefs required to obtain the inconsistency increases, the inconsistency becomes more tolerable. The same sort of scale effect holds for circularity. Small circles are bad, big circles are tolerable. Of course, bigger is not always better when it comes to scale effects. For example, small slippery slope arguments are better than mountainous ones.

Since the set of views (L1)–(L1001) is arguably rational, it is assertible. 'I believe ticket number 1 is not a winning ticket and I believe ticket number 2 is not a winning ticket and . . . and I believe there is a winning ticket' might be too long to practically assert. But it would be the length, not the inconsistency that made it resistant to assertion. Since the individual could make his views explicit, there would be no impugnable lack of specificity in his assertion:

> (22) Although I believe of each ticket that it is not a winner, I believe that at least one of them is a winner.

The beliefs expressed by (22) are *indirectly* inconsistent. Although there is no proposition such that I both believe and disbelieve it, my beliefs cannot all be true. Contrary to Deutscher's proposal, the fact that (22) is logically consistent and yet could not be consistently believed, does not make it a Moorean sentence.

Further evidence that Deutscher's implicit definition of 'Moorean sentence' is too broad comes in the form of direct inconsistencies and patent inconsistencies.

> (23) I believe it is both raining and not raining.
> (24) I believe it is raining and I believe it is not raining.

Sentence (24) records a direct inconsistency because the inconsistent beliefs are directly opposed to one another across the same proposition: (Bp & $B-p$). Patent inconsistencies are beliefs in flat contradictions: $B(p$ & $-p)$. The case for attributing direct and patent inconsistencies is strengthened by our fallibility in judgements of contradictoriness. Some propositions look like contradictions but are not. For example, most people balk at 'Alaska is both the easternmost and westernmost state.' That Alaska is the westernmost can be quickly gleaned from inspection of a globe. That it is easternmost follows because some of the Aleutian Islands extend beyond the 180th meridian, the global dividing line between East and West. Other propositions look consistent but are really contradictory. For instance, Raymond Smullyan reports seeing a sign outside a restaurant that read as follows,[11]

---

[11] Raymond Smullyan, *What is the Name of this Book?* (Englewood Cliffs, N. J.: Prentice-Hall, 1978) 185–6.

GOOD FOOD IS NOT CHEAP
CHEAP FOOD IS NOT GOOD

No doubt many of those reading the sign did not detect the equivalence. Among this group some agreed with one claim and disagreed with the second. This subgroup contained people with directly inconsistent beliefs. Some philosophers are inclined to doubt that people ever believe flat contradictions. They think that charitable attribution of belief always saves us from this blackhole of incoherence. Yet the charity will have to be extended to those who spurn it. In *Song of Myself*, Walt Whitman is undaunted by the hobgoblin of little minds; 'Do I contradict myself? Very well then I contradict myself (I am large, I contain multitudes).' Hegel almost begs to be interpreted as contradicting himself: 'Something moves, not because at one moment it is here and at another moment there, but because at one and the same moment it is here and not here, because in this "here", it at once is and is not.'[12] Some proponents of paraconsistent logics, such as Graham Priest, defend the Hegelian view that motion realizes contradictions. According to Priest, true contradictions should not be multiplied beyond necessity, but the logical and semantical paradoxes show that some are necessary.[13] In the face of such sophisticated interpretees, the practice of charitable interpretation strikes some as unproductively paternalistic. Better to view the natives as having gone to hell in their own way.

Many people are inclined to regard all patent inconsistencies as direct inconsistencies. The most direct way to support this conclusion is through an appeal to the principle that belief distributes over conjunction: $B(p \& q) \supset (Bp \& -Bq)$. Some people may also be inclined to view all direct inconsistencies as patent inconsistencies. The most direct path to this conclusion is by an appeal to the principle that belief collects over conjunction: $(Bp \& Bq) \supset B(p \& q)$. Those who accept both doxastic principles should thus maintain that the distinction between direct and patent inconsistencies collapses upon close scrutiny. But since I seek an

[12] This is A. V. Miller's translation of a sentence from Hegel's *Science of Logic* (New York: Humanities Press, 1969), 440.

[13] Graham Priest, 'The Logic of Paradox', *Journal of Philosophical Logic*, 8 (1979), 219–41.

analysis of Moore's problem free of commitment to doxastic logic, I shall continue to draw the distinction.

How do indirect, direct, and patent inconsistencies differ from the Moorean sentences we began with?

(1) It is raining but I believe it is not raining.
(2) It is raining but it is not the case that I believe it is raining.

By themselves, sentences (1) and (2) fail to imply that utterers are inconsistent. Only once we suppose that the speakers believe their utterances does an inconsistency arise. On the other hand, sentences (21)–(24) alone suffice to imply that their utterers are inconsistent. The supposition that their utterers believe (21)–(24) plays no essential role in establishing the inconsistency.

D. *Accommodating Non-obvious Examples*

Commentators on Moore's problem tend to dwell on the obvious examples, such as 'It is raining but I do not believe it.' The existence of non-obvious Moorean sentences is suggested by the fact that some definite descriptions employing indexicals are difficult to decipher. Recall the riddle of the man viewing a portrait. A woman asks him whose picture he is looking at. He answers 'Brothers and sisters have I none, but this man's father is my father's son.' Many people wrongly infer that the man is looking at a picture of himself (in fact he is looking at a picture of his son). Taking this riddle as our inspiration, we could construct non-obvious Moorean sentences. Suppose a lone explorer's diary records his discovery of a huge flat valley. He adds the comment that this news would surprise the unbelieving explorer that would be reached by travelling 30 kilometers north, 60 kilometers east, 30 kilometers south, and 60 kilometers west of him. Since this path leads back to himself, the explorer's diary contains a complicated Moorean sentence. Another example can be concocted from a mixture of kinship and doctrinal terms.

(25) The atheism of my mother's nieceless brother's only nephew angers God.

This implies 'My atheism angers God', which in turn implies 'God exists but I believe that God does not exist.' Suppose Jerry has little analytical talent but has a good memory and a healthy respect for authority. He overhears an authority assert that the atheism of his mother's nieceless brother's only nephew angers God. Since, contrary to the authority, Jerry is a God-fearing but gossipy Christian, he believes the authority and tells his friend (25). One might object that Jerry does not really understand (25) and so does not believe it. But this objection rests on two dubious assumptions. First, it assumes that believing that p implies understanding p. Yet people certainly seem to believe many things they do not understand. For example, most people with casual contact with physics believe $e = mc^2$ and believe that space is curved. Second, even if believing implies understanding, one cannot require that one believes only if one believes all of the logical consequences of what one believes. Since the truths of logic are logical consequences of any belief, and no one believes all of these, it would follow that no one believes anything. Yet, nothing short of this condition for understanding will guarantee that no one believes the proposition expressed by a non-obvious Moorean sentence. Once one grants that some Moorean sentences are believable and assertible one must reject the commonly held view that incredibility and unassertibility are essential features of all Moorean sentences.

A major source of the view that Moorean sentences are unassertible or (absolutely) unbelievable is the mistaken thesis that 'I' is referentially transparent. Proponents of the transparency of 'I' maintain that users of the word 'I' cannot be mistaken about its referent. The thesis 'No user of "I" can be mistaken about the referent of the word' has a vacuous and a non-vacuous interpretation. Holders of the non-vacuous interpretation maintain that the user of 'I' has a guaranteed referent and that he can always know that 'I' refers to him.[14] Proponents of the vacuous interpretation use the apparent guaranteed self-reference as evidence against the thesis that the question of error arises in the first place.[15] This point is sometimes given a Wittgensteinian twist

[14] Proponents of the view that 'I' is non–vacuously incorrigible include C. S. Pierce, Gilbert Ryle, and Maithili Schmidt-Raghavan in 'On "I" as an Index', *Pacific Philisophical Quarterly*, 61 4 Oct. 1980), 39–46.

[15] The vacuous variation can be traced back to Wittgenstein. G. E. M. Anscombe has defended this version in 'The First Person' appearing in Samuel Guttenplan (ed.) *Mind and Language* (Oxford, 1975), 45–65. D. S. Clarke arrives

in which it is denied that 'I' refers to anything in the paradigm of an incorrigible utterance 'I am in pain.' The occurrence of 'I' is sometimes compared to the pseudo-referential occurrence of 'it' in 'It is raining' and is sometimes compared to the 'O' in 'Ouch!' and other avowals. Regardless of whether the vacuous or non-vacuous interpretation is adopted, proponents of the referential transparency of 'I' agree that the speaker cannot mistakenly believe that the word refers to someone else. This incorrigibility provides a contrast between 'I' and proper names. Amnesia may prevent Ronald Reagan from knowing the referent of 'Ronald Reagan wears white socks' but it would not prevent him from knowing the referent of his assertion of 'I wear white socks.' One might object that impairment of Reagan's knowledge of English could prevent him from knowing the referent of 'I' just as those ignorant of French do not know the referent of '*je*'. However, proponents of the incorrigibility thesis could challenge the claim that one can make *assertions* in a language one is incompetent to speak. Alternatively, they could restrict the incorrigibility thesis to those having competency in the language in question. A decisive counter-example to the incorrigibility thesis must be one in which the speaker *uses* the word 'I' in a sentence without being able to tell to whom the word refers. Thus the counter-example should not be one based on the speaker's linguistic ignorance or the fact that he is mentioning, translating, or unintentionally uttering the word.

Causal ambiguity provides a basis for the proper sort of counter-example. Suppose Ronald Reagan and Jimmy Carter each type 'I am in pain' into terminals connected to a single screen. If the terminals are secretly arranged so that only one of them causes a token of the sentence to appear, then neither Reagan nor Carter will know the referent of 'I'. To know the referent of 'I' in this situation one must know who produced it. Users of 'I' normally know that it refers to them because they normally know that they are causing the production of the word token. This causal ambiguity can arise closer to the source. For example, through the wonders of radio–physiology, Reagan rents Carter's mouth. In

---

at Anscombe's conclusion through a different argument in 'The Addressing Function of "I" ', *Analysis*, 38 2 (Mar. 1978), 91–3. Zeno Vendler has offered yet a third argument for this position in 'A Note to the Paralogisms' in Gilbert Ryle (ed.) *Contemporary Aspects of Philosophy* (Stocksfield 1977), 111–21.

Washington his throat and jaw are wired to send radio messages to Carter's throat and jaw, enabling him to talk through Carter's mouth. Out of Carter's mouth comes the utterance 'I am Ronald Reagan speaking to you from Washington'. Since he would be speaking the truth, the first person statements issuing from Carter's mouth need not refer to Carter even though the sentences are being used rather than mentioned (as in quoting or translating first person statements). I am not sure how far back the causal ambiguity can be. For example, suppose the message is sent from Reagan's brain to Carter's brain so that Carter has first person thought tokens authored by Ronald Reagan. Do they refer to Reagan? If so, Descartes's *cogito* becomes dubious. For how does Descartes know that he is tokening 'I exist' in the transitive as opposed to the intransitive sense? The transitive reading of 'The missionary is cooking' imputes agency to the missionary while the intransitive reading makes him a patient (or dinner!). The verb 'token' is like 'move'. Just as I can move actively or passively (move or be moved), I can token sentences and perhaps thoughts actively or passively. Thus Descartes's thoughts might not be linked with himself in the active way he supposes. This is important. For suppose the evil demon sends a signal that will later produce the thought 'I am now thinking' in Descartes. By the time Descartes thinks the thought, the evil demon has committed suicide. Since 'I' was produced by the evil demon, it refers to him. Further suppose that the evil demon indexed 'now' to the time of reception rather than the time of production (as owners of dictaphones do when they record the message 'I am not here now'). Then Descartes's thought 'I am thinking now' would be false because the evil demon would not be thinking at the time of the thought. So Russell might be right to recommend an impersonal *cogito* as a replacement: there is some thinking occurring.

In addition to doubts about the reference of 'I' engendered by ignorance of the cause of 'I', doubts can also be prompted by conceptual difficulties about causation. For the production of 'I' can be overdetermined. For example, if the screen is hooked to the terminals of Reagan and Carter in such a way that either of them typing 'I am in pain' causes the sentence to appear, then the fact that they both type the sentence overdetermines the production of 'I am in pain.' It is not clear that Reagan produced the sentence since it would have appeared without his typing. Likewise, the sentence was not dependent on Carter's typing. Here 'I' inherits an indeterminacy of 'cause'. Unlike the causal ambiguity case, new empirical information cannot resolve the referential question raised by causal overdetermination. Thus there are both empirical and conceptual sources for the failure of referential transparency.

Only extraordinary circumstances could render the referent of 'I' doubtful. But only similarly extraordinary circumstances could make me seriously doubt who it is I am referring to when I utter my name. Extraordinary circumstances establish the opacity of both expressions. So there is no reason to assign 'I' a special status. Moorean sentences could be formed in a language free of the first person singular.

Once it is conceded that 'I' is not referentially transparent, the only reason for supposing it or other indexicals to be essential to Moorean sentences disappears. Our reluctance to describe 'It is raining but Ronald Reagan does not believe it' as a Moorean sentence is based on the possibility that Reagan might reasonably believe this sentence because of ignorance of what 'Ronald Reagan' denotes. But since the same possibility holds for 'It is raining but I do not believe it', paradigm Moorean sentences can be reasonably believed as well. Since the rarity of referent errors does not afford a principled way of distinguishing Moorean from non-Moorean sentences, almost all contingent sentences implying current error should count as Moorean. Some of these sentences will contain referring expressions that the speaker can easily be mistaken about. For example, a seamstress overhears her boss say 'My fastest worker does not believe she is my fastest worker.' She spreads the story to her son not knowing that she is the fastest worker. The reasonableness of her belief seems to undermine any connection between her Moorean belief and the paradigm cases. However, the feature Deutscher stressed still remains. Her belief in the story combined with the fact that she is denoted by the definite description ensures that she has an inconsistent set of beliefs.

Lastly, it should be noted that there are risky Moorean sentences. If George Bush says 'The next thing Reagan says is true', and Reagan then says 'Nancy smokes but George Bush does not believe it', Bush has indirectly asserted a Moorean sentence.

Had Reagan said 'Voodoo economics worked', there would have been no Mooreanness for Bush. So in addition to slipping into a Moorean bind through ignorance of *who* you are talking about, you can also slip into the bind through ignorance of *what* you are asserting.

E. *Accommodating Impure Cases*

Besides their tendency to use obvious Moorean sentences commentators also tend to use examples describing error about contingencies. They shy away from examples such as

(26*a*) Although my brother is an only child, I believe he has a sibling.
(26*b*) All bachelors are males but I believe some bachelors are not males.
(26*c*) There are infinitely many twin primes but I believe there are finitely many twin primes.

because the sentences fail to highlight the elusiveness of the speaker's inconsistency. Analytical errors can be met with familiar kinds of criticisms. In (26*a*) the first conjunct is a contradiction making the whole statement logically false. There is no problem of criticism here. Unlike (26*a*), (26*b*) is a contingent statement. However, its second conjunct describes belief in a contradiction. Once again, we understand what's wrong and know how to proceed. Contemporary ignorance about whether there are infinitely many twin primes leaves us in ignorance as to whether (26*c*) is necessarily false or contingent. But we know that in either case, belief (26*c*) will share the analytical defectiveness of either (26*a*) or (26*b*). Although (26*a*)–(26*c*) are Moorean, their overdetermined defectiveness enables us to criticize them without understanding how Moorean sentences in general ought to be criticized. They are impure cases. In addition to being criticizable in the same way that a tokener of (1) or (2) is, a tokener of (26*a*)–(26*c*) can be criticized in other ways.

There is another, more controversial class of impure Moorean sentences. They are controversial because the class will only be regarded as non-empty if one accepts the existence of self-intimating or incorrigible propositions. A proposition *p* is self-intimating just in case it is consistent and is true only if believed: $\Diamond p \ \& \ -\Diamond \ (p \ \& \ -Bp)$. Propositions about one's own pain are standard examples of self-intimating propositions. Belief itself is sometimes claimed to be self-intimating. If it were, it would be of great interest to doxastic logicians since the self-intimating claim for belief is equivalent to the BB principle: $Bp \supset BBp$. According to the BB principle, 'I believe it is raining but it is not the case that I believe that I believe it is raining' is a contradiction. Likewise, proponents of the self-intimating nature of pain should regard

(27a) I am in pain but it is not the case that I believe I am in pain.

as a contradiction. Yet it would still be admitted to have a Moorean flavour. The Moorean flavour can also be detected in incorrigibility examples, such as

(27b) I am not in pain but I believe that I am in pain.

Those who deny that any propositions are incorrigible or self-intimating should regard (27a) and (27b) as pure Moorean sentences. But believers in incorrigibility and self-intimation should see a double-vulnerability in examples (27a)–(27b). For in addition to being criticizable along Moorean lines, these sentences are also criticizable as contradictions.

III. CRITICIZING BELIEVERS

It is said that Niels Bohr used to have a horseshoe over his door. When asked whether he believed horseshoes bring good luck, Bohr answered 'No, but I am told that they bring luck even to those who do not believe in them.'[16] How could we criticize Bohr if we viewed his position as more than a joke? Only superficial symbolization is needed to reach the gist of his remark. Let 'b' denote Bohr. Let 'Hx' read 'x has a horseshoe', and 'Lx' read 'x has good luck brought by his horseshoe'.

---

[16] E. Segre tells this story in his *From X-rays to Quarks* (San Fransisco: Freeman, 1980).

(P) Hb & Bb(x) − Lx & (x)((Hx & Bx − Lx) ⊃ Lx)

Position (P) makes Bohr's stock of 'information' explicit in the form of a single statement 'Bohr has a horseshoe but believes that horseshoes do not bring good luck even though they bring good luck to those who do not believe horseshoes are lucky.' We must first note that (P) is logically consistent. Furthermore, (P) does not even imply that Bohr has inconsistent beliefs. This becomes clear if you imagine someone other than Bohr asserting the sentence. Thus we cannot criticize the holder of position (P) by showing that it leads to a contradiction. Nor can we criticize (P) on the grounds that (P) itself implies that the holder has inconsistent beliefs. We must criticize (P) differently from the way we would criticize the position 'I believe horseshoes bring good luck and I believe that horseshoes do not bring good luck' or any of (22)–(24). Successful criticism requires the additional premiss that *Bohr believes* the position. (P) is a bad position for *Bohr* to believe in a way that it is not a bad position for *Ed Koch* to believe. For we expect Bohr beliefs to strongly cohere with other Bohr beliefs; we do not expect Ed Koch beliefs to strongly cohere with Bohr beliefs. Beliefs are like citizens of a nation. Their status as compatriots imposes rights and duties towards each that do not apply to foreigners. Foreign beliefs, like foreign people, have some normative status but to a diminished degree. My beliefs should show some sensitivity to your beliefs. But not as much as to its kin. That's what makes disagreement bad news and inconsistency worse news. Sensitivity must also be accorded to one's past and future beliefs. But once again, not to the same degree as my present beliefs. But is a change of mind more important than a disagreement with another person? The uncertainties surrounding this question parallel the uncertainties surrounding the comparative importance of my non-contemporary compatriots and foreigners.

To say that all compatriots *ought* to have higher sensitivity is not to say that all do. Most do, but some don't. Those that don't are criticized as unpatriotic, or uncomradely, or in extreme cases as traitors. Treachery is a provincial wrong. The Russian official who betrays his country for his love of England is castigated in Moscow but not in London. The fact that he has acted against *his* country makes his deed worse, in Russian eyes, than had the traitor merely been a foreign spy. To understand what is lamentable about treachery, we have to view the traitor from his victim's vantage point with partisan standards of behaviour.

We might criticize Bohr for believing (P) on the grounds that it is superstitious and hence irrational to believe that horseshoes bring luck to certain individuals. However, the same criticism would apply to Ed Koch if he agreed with Bohr. It is not the superstitiousness of (P) that piques our interest. We are interested in the internal disharmony.

In describing the nature of the disharmony, we are apt to say that Bohr's beliefs *commit* him to conflicting beliefs. We are tempted to spell out the commitment along the following lines. Given that he believes he has a horseshoe and believes that horseshoes fail to bring good luck, how can he also believe that sceptics get good luck from their horseshoes? Since he professes to be a sceptic, he should believe that his horseshoe brings him good luck. Yet his belief that horseshoes do not bring luck commits him to the belief that his horseshoe does not bring him good luck. So Bohr is committed to both believing and disbelieving that his horseshoe brings him good luck. This strikes most of us as a good criticism of the Bohr belief. But why does it strike us as good? By claiming that Bohr is committed to the direct inconsistency, we are not attributing a direct inconsistency to him. In order to arrive at the undesirable commitment, we began with Bohr's bizarre belief and deduced further beliefs. These deductions are not plausible if they are intended to be psychologically accurate. Construing the reasoning as something he *ought* to do saves us from empirical disconfirmation. But even this normative interpretation seems strained by the fact that it sets the standards of responsible belief quite high. Following through *all* of the consequences of our beliefs would be a practical impossibility. Since logical truths are consequences of any proposition, absolute thoroughness (given that we believed something) would entail logical omniscience. Apart from the fact that we cannot meet such high standards, it also seems a waste to try. Our limited intellectual resources should instead be assigned to the more interesting consequences of our beliefs. If we back away from the demand that believers believe all of the consequences of what they believe, what do we back down to? Believers could trivially satisfy the request to believe *some* of the consequences. Requiring them to believe *most* or even the vast majority would raise embarrassing questions about how the beliefs are to be counted. Besides, the believer could disown any particular chain of reasoning leading to an unwelcome commitment by declaring that group of consequences to be in the tiny minority of beliefs untouched by his high degree of thoroughness. Given that the goal of absolute thoroughness is unattainable and wasteful even to approximate, and given that anything less than absolute thoroughness is ineffective in supporting commitment verdicts, what entitles us to focus the full light of logic on Bohr's queer belief?

The answer is that absolute thoroughness is a *test* of the completeability of our beliefs. Although incompleteability is not inconsistency, incompleteable belief structures carry the danger of collapsing into inconsistent ones. Just as buildings can stand on cracked foundations, the potential for inconsistency need not constitute disaster for the belief structure. The potential harm need never actualize. And even if it does actualize, the damage may not merit repair. Where actual inconsistencies are tolerable, so are potential ones. Nevertheless, incompleteability is a clear type of structural flaw. It prevents our beliefs from growing in a certain direction, enforcing neutrality, and thus limiting our freedom. The crimp it puts into belief formation can be compared to the crimp chess players suffer from when an enemy knight becomes embedded in their half of the board. The regularity with which such a formation leads to setbacks makes this a *kind* of position to avoid.

The key elements of my analysis of Moore's problem can be traced to the doxastic goals of getting truth and avoiding error. The quick answer to why inconsistency is bad is that it inevitably saddles us with error. Those who like to accentuate the positive reply that although patent inconsistency, $B(p \& -p)$, gives us only error, direct inconsistency, $Bp \& B -p$, compensates for the inevitable error by inevitably providing a true belief. The rejoinder is that this is a lopsided exchange. The amount false beliefs harm us exceeds the amount true beliefs benefit us. Better therefore to abstain from belief than to suffer an inevitable net loss. This double standard parallels those discussed in ethics. Just as letting evil happen is thought preferable to actively promoting it, omissive error is less bad than commissive error. Likewise the man who does nothing is better than the man who alternately does good and evil. Badness seems to be weighted more heavily than goodness; the same impression is given by falsehood and truth. What is the weighting? How many true beliefs are needed to balance a given number of false beliefs? Even once a convention for counting beliefs is adopted, no precise answer can be given. However, evidence for the fact that false beliefs are weightier than true beliefs can be found in the various proposals for an adequate acceptance rule. Simple acceptance rules will just specify the probability a statement must have in order to merit belief. Common proposals are 0.90, 0.95, and 0.99. Of course, the proposals are made with an admission of some arbitrariness, but they do indicate that the ratio of true beliefs to false beliefs cannot be 1:1 and indeed must be fairly high. What can be conceded to the critic is that indirect inconsistencies can be acceptable as long as the trade-off between true and false beliefs is favourable. The goal of maximizing true beliefs explains why we seek completeness even at the cost of indirect inconsistency.

Our commitment talk can thus be viewed as a way of appraising the structural merits of a belief (these merits being reducible to the goals of getting truth and avoiding error). We ferret out the relevant features by examining the supposition that the position has a given set of merits. In the case of Bohr, we check whether he could have completeable true belief in (P). A belief is completeable just in case the believer's absolute thoroughness would not lead to any direct inconsistencies. So to check whether Bohr could have a completeable true belief in (P) we need only check the consistency of the supposition that:

(P) is true, and
Bohr believes (P), and
Bohr is absolutely thorough, and
Bohr is free from direct inconsistencies.

Since this supposition leads to a contradiction, we conclude that Bohr lacks a completeable true belief in (P). Either Bohr does not believe (P), or he has a false belief in (P), or Bohr's true belief in (P) is incompleteable. Thus we can say that if Bohr really believes (P), his belief is flawed either by falsehood or incompleteability. This explains why the most charitable response to Bohr's utterance is to view it as a joke rather than as a serious assertion. It also explains our reaction to utterances such as 'Miss America is a lesbian–I don't believe it!'. 'Luke ate an incredible number of eggs', and 'George Washington sired over fifty illegitimate children; I still can't believe it.' Rather than attribute *obviously* flawed beliefs to the utterers, we assume the speakers are exaggerating, that they are expressing their surprise in a colourful way. But since the principle of charity is constrained by psychological realism, we are willing to attribute beliefs that are more subtly flawed.

At this point we are in a position to account for the intuition that the utterer of a Moorean sentence is contradicting himself. In uttering the sentence, he gives the appearance of believing the proposition expressed by the sentence. Anyone who believes a Moorean sentence is vulnerable to a form of criticism which proceeds through a demonstration of the believer's commitment to directly inconsistent beliefs. Since simultaneous belief in p and belief in $-p$ is a paradigm of 'contradicting yourself', and the commitment to these opposed beliefs is so obvious in standardly discussed Moorean sentences, the appearance of self-contradiction is strong. However, the Moorean speaker has only contradicted himself through a *commitment* to directly opposed beliefs; he need not actually have inconsistent beliefs. Nevertheless he is *pinned* by the prospect of inconsistency. The impression that he is contradicting himself springs from a structural flaw induced by the belief.

But what about the definitional condition? To distinguish Moorean sentences from sentences reflecting other types of doxastic demerit, we can draw a distinction between two closely related types of doxastic criticism. In scrutinizing Bohr's position, we employed belief-based criticism. The truth and completability of the position could not be sustained given that *Bohr believed* the position. Other positions can be criticized without the belief assumption. A direct criticism shows that the truth of the position is incompatible with completability. For example, 'I believe it is raining and I believe it is not raining' can only be true at the expense of completeability. Doxastic demerit follows from the truth of the proposition alone. Pure Moorean sentences can be defined as those which are vulnerable to belief-based criticism but are immune to direct criticism.

The adjective 'pure' is needed to exclude cases in which the speaker is vulnerable to additional forms of structural criticism.

Sometimes the object of belief is a contradiction, as with (26a) and (26b). 'Triangles are either equilateral or not, but I believe some are neither' strikes us as Moorean because *if we were to ignore the contradiction* it is vulnerable to belief-based criticism but not direct criticism. The contradiction could be ignored by deliberately translating the object of belief in such a way as not to reveal its contradictoriness. For example, 'Some triangles are neither equilateral nor not equilateral' could be superficially translated in terms of the disjunctive predicate 'Fx' for 'x is either equilateral or not'. The larger sentence then takes on the appearance of a standard Moorean sentence: $(x)Fx \ \& \ B-(x)\overline{F}x$. When the contradiction is obvious, one may well doubt the wisdom of ignoring the more grievous offence of believing a contradiction in order to convict the utterer of the lesser Moorean misdemeanour. But when the contradiction is obscure or uncertain, waiving the charge of contradiction can be the best course of action.

The same strategy can be applied to reports of errors about incorrigible and self-intimating propositions, such as (27a) and (27b). Ignoring the alleged fact that pain is self-intimating and incorrigible would make the utterer vulnerable to belief-based criticism but not direct criticism. Indeed the strategy is a general solution to the problem of impure cases because all impure cases feature overdetermined vulnerability to structural criticism. A sentence such as 'I am directly inconsistent but I do not believe it' owes its Moorean appearances to the fact that we can ignore the content of the object of belief. We realize that there is something wrong regardless of the content.

IV. A MORE FORMAL ACCOUNT OF BELIEF CRITICISM

The picture of Moorean sentences drawn in broad strokes above should be supplemented with a detailed description of the types of criticism crucial to the definition of 'pure Moorean sentence'. This can be done with the help of some technical definitions. To reach a precise definition of 'direct doxastic criticism' first let 'Ba_tp' read 'a believes at time t that p'. A *direct doxastic* criticism of agent a at time t with respect to q on the basis of p is a criticism which attempts to show that p is a consistent proposition that implies that a has an incompleteable belief structure with respect to q. Agent a

at t has an imcompleteable belief structure with respect to q just in case: if a is absolutely thorough at t, then he is directly inconsistent with respect to q at t. Agent a is *directly inconsistent* at t with respect to q if and only if he believes and disbelieves q at t, i.e. $Ba_t q$ & $Ba_t -q$. Agent a is *absolutely thorough* at t just in case his beliefs are deductively closed and distribute over material conditionals at t. His beliefs are *deductively closed* at t if and only if he believes all of the logical consequences of what he believes at time t; $(q)(r)(Ba_t q \ \& \ \Box (q \supset r)) \supset Ba_t r)$. Lastly, a's beliefs distribute over material conditionals at t just in case $(q)(r)(Ba_t(q \supset r) \supset (Ba_t q \supset Ba_t r))$. If a uttered a token of

(28) I believe I am taller than myself.

or any of (23), (24), (26a), (26b), he would be susceptible to a direct doxastic criticism. If he uttered (1), (2), or (25), he would be immune to this type of criticism. However, he would be susceptible to a belief-based criticism. A *belief-based* criticism of agent a at time t with respect to q on the basis of p is a criticism that attempts to show that p is a consistent proposition such that p & $Ba_t p$ implies that a at t has an incompleteable belief structure with respect to q. Let the proposition expressed by (1) be q & $Ba_t -q$ and the one expressed by (2) be q & $-Ba_t q$. One is now in a position to prove that anyone who utters (1) is susceptible to a belief-based criticism. This can be done by showing that the supposition that a has a true belief that (1) which does not lead to a direct inconsistency and does not prevent him from being absolutely thorough (see line 1 below), is inconsistent. So anyone who utters 'It is raining but I believe it is not raining' either does not correctly believe the proposition expressed by his utterance, is directly inconsistent about whether it is raining, or is not absolutely thorough. So he is susceptible to a certain kind of criticism even if he is immune to direct doxastic criticism. In the proof below, notice that line 2 is justified by the fact that a's absolute thoroughness at t, abbreviated Ta_t, implies that his beliefs distribute over conjunction; $(q)(r)(Ba_t(q \ \& \ r) \supset (Ba_t q \ \& \ Ba_t r))$.

1. $[(q \ \& \ Ba_t -q) \ \& \ Ba_t (q \ \& \ Ba_t -q)] \ \& \ [-(Ba_t q \ \& \ Ba_t -q) \ \& \ Ta_t)]$
2. $Ba_t q \ \& \ Ba_t Ba_t -q$ 1, TF, UI

3. $Ba_tq \ \& \ Ba_t-q$ 1, 2, TF
4. $(Ba_tq \ \& \ Ba_t-q) \ \& \ -(Ba_tq \ \& \ Ba_t-q)$ 1, 3, TF

This demonstrates that a is susceptible to belief-based criticism concerning q at t if he utters (1). Notice that Ba_tp played an essential role in the criticism. The same holds for the criticism of $(q \ \& \ -Ba_tq)$.

1. $[(q \ \& \ -Ba_tq) \ \& \ Ba_t(q \ \& \ -Ba_tq)] \ \& \ [-(Ba_tq \ \& \ Ba_t-q) \ \& \ Ta_t)\ ]$
2. $Ba_tq \ \& \ Ba_tBa_t-q$ 1, TF, UI
3. Ba_tq 1, 2, TF

A pure Moorean proposition for a at t with respect to q is a proposition which cannot serve as a basis for a direct doxastic criticism of a at t with respect to q but which can serve as a basis for a belief-based criticism of a at t with respect to q. One can be inconsistent without being susceptible to either kind of criticism. Thus (19), (21), and (22) do not express propositions which are pure Moorean propositions. Jerry's utterance of (25) does express a pure Moorean proposition. His friend could show him that he has contradicted himself concerning the existence of God by first assuming that Jerry's belief is a true belief. Second, his friend could show Jerry that a consequence of his belief is that Jerry is an atheist who angers God. Third, he could show that this in turn implies that God exists but Jerry believes that God does not exist. So Jerry is committed to believing that God exists and to believing that God does not exist, and so he is contradicting himself. Of course, Jerry does not actually both believe and disbelieve that God exists. Jerry has merely failed to be absolutely thorough. His friend's criticism forces Jerry to give up his belief (given that Jerry wants to avoid contradicting himself).

Those who believe that (1) and (2) could not possibly be believed might object that my account does not explain this unbelievability. Given that they also believe that people cannot believe obvious contradictions, one could answer that there are different ways of contradicting oneself and so different ways in which one can obviously contradict oneself. Thus the unbelieveability of (1) and (2) would be explained as on a par with, but not reducible to, the unbelievability of obvious contradictions like (28).

The definition of 'pure Moorean proposition' offered above can be equivalently expressed in terms of a conjunction of modal statements. A proposition p is a pure Moorean proposition for agent a (at time t) if and only if:

$$[\Diamond(p \ \& \ Ta_t \ \& \ -(\exists q)(Ba_tq \ \& \ Ba_t-q))] \ \&$$
$$[-\Diamond(p \ \& \ Ba_tp \ \& \ Ta_t \ \& \ -(\exists q)(Ba_tq \ \& \ Ba_t-q))].$$

Although this definition is rather cumbersome, it does have the virtue of suggesting a way of distinguishing between three grades of Mooreanness. The grades can be classified in terms of the superfluousness of elements in the second big conjunct of the above definition. A first grade Moorean proposition only satisfies the second conjunct with the help of all of the conjunct's elements. Such a proposition would be expressed by the utterance of

(1) It is raining but I believe it is not raining.

In contrast to (1), the omissive version of Moore's sentence satisfies the following condition: $-\Diamond(p \ \& \ Ba_tp \ \& \ Ta_t)$.

(2) It is raining but it is not the case that I believe it.

The mere supposition that I have a true and thorough belief in (2) leads to contradiction. The *reductio* can proceed without the assumption that I am free of direct inconsistency. We can also distinguish a third grade of Mooreanness in which both the thoroughness and consistency conditions are superfluous. For example, 'It is not the case that I believe something' is incapable of being the object of a true belief: $-\Diamond(p \ \& \ Bp)$.

It is important to note, at this point, that I am not committed to any doxastic logic. I am committed to the thesis that there are forms of criticism which employ doxastic principles as *tests* for the presence of structural flaws. So when I appeal to principles like the deductive closure of belief and the distribution of belief over material conditionals, I am doing so in a hypothetical fashion. The appeals have the form: given that a's belief that p does not make him susceptible to criticism C, the assumption that doxastic principle D applies to him will not lead to contradiction. My proposal's lack of commitment to a doxastic logic distinguishes it

44   *Moore's Problem*

from an approach such as Hintikka's which does involve a commitment to a doxastic logic. My proposal is compatible with there being no adequate doxastic logics.

V. A CLASSIFICATION OF MOOREAN SENTENCES BY TIME AND ROLE

So far I have concentrated on classifying types of Moorean *propositions*. The next task is to define Moorean *sentences* in terms of those propositions. The goal is to reflect the varying properties of Moorean sentences. For example, it would be nice to have an explanation of the difference in peculiarity between 'It is raining but I do not believe it' and 'It is raining but you do not believe it.' Grammar provides a poor means of grouping sentences together in accordance with types of oddity. For instance, the peculiar first person singular sentence 'Only I have beliefs' resembles the peculiarity of the second person singular 'You do not have beliefs' more closely than it resembles the first person singular sentence 'I do not have beliefs.' Superficial grammatical features of Moorean sentences are too arbitrary to serve as an instructive guide.

My analysis makes Mooreanness a relative affair; what is Moorean for me need not be Moorean to you. In addition to making *who* you are relevant to Mooreanness, the analysis also makes *when* you are relevant. This relativity suggests the possibility of classifying Moorean sentences in terms of time and speaking roles.

Pure Moorean sentences can be defined in terms of pure Moorean propositions. An omnitemporal, universal, pure Moorean sentence is a sentence-type such that all of its tokens express propositions that are purely Moorean for everyone at every time. Consider

(29) No one has believed, believes, or will believe anything.

If an agent, *a*, believes this, he is committed to the direct inconsistency of both believing and disbelieving (29). The sentence

(30) No one believes anything now.

expresses propositions which are purely Moorean for everyone at the time of tokening but not before or after, and thus is universal but not omnitemporal.

A *user*, pure Moorean sentence is a sentence-type such that each of its tokens expresses a proposition which is a pure Moorean proposition for the user of that token at the time of use. For example,

(31) I have no beliefs now.

along with (1), (2), (7), (8), and (25), are user, pure Moorean sentences. Sentences like

(32) Ronald Reagan has no beliefs now.

are not user, pure Moorean sentences since people other than Ronald Reagan can use tokens of them without thereby expressing propositions which are pure Moorean propositions for them.

One might object that it is possible for a tokener of (31) to have expressed a proposition that was not Moorean for him. Various kinds of cases can be imagined.

(i) Smith dies on 1 January 1985. The next day, Jones writes (31) on Smith's forehead thereby expressing the proposition that Smith has no beliefs on 1 January 1985.
(ii) Smith writes (31) into his will, to be read after he dies.
(iii) In order to have a typewritten copy of Smith's will, his secretary types (31) along with the rest of the will.
(iv) Having only a French copy of Smith's will, Smith's lawyer translates the French counterpart of (31) into the English sentence (31).

Case (i) is constructed by exploiting the fact that first person pronouns can be used in an extended sense to merely denote the bearer of the sentence token containing the pronoun. In this sense, personal pronouns can denote inanimate objects, as when someone puts the label 'Please eat me' on a piece of cake. Case (ii) exploits the fact that temporal indexicals can be indexed to the time the token is produced or the time it is received. For example, motorists in England encounter 'Slow down now' signs. When, as usual, times of production and reception are the same, the two ways of indexing yield the same result. Case (iii) takes advantage of the fact that sentence tokens which are quotations need not have their indexical elements indexed to the quotation token; usually they are indexed to the original token. Case (iv) takes advantage of the parallel lack of dependency for tokens which are translations.

The use/mention distinction can be drawn to handle cases such as (iii) and (iv). Cases like (i) are avoided by the understanding that I am only concerned with tokens which are read in the unextended sense. Finally, cases such as (ii) are avoided by limiting my claims to tokens in which there is no divergence between the results of production and reception indexing.

An *addressee*, pure Moorean sentence is a sentence-type such that each of its tokens expresses a pure Moorean proposition for the addressee of the token at the time that token is used. For example,

(33) Christmas is closer than you believe,

along with (9) and (10), is an addressee, pure Moorean sentence. In *Meaning*, Stephen Schiffer claims that a speaker tells his audience that p only if he intends to produce in the audience the activated belief that p. Although there are counter-examples to this principle, the intention is common enough to explain why addressee, pure Moorean sentences seem self-defeating. The user of such a sentence can fulfill his intention only if the adressee contradicts himself. A *user-specific*, pure Moorean sentence is a user, pure Moorean sentence which is neither universally nor addressee Moorean. An *addressee-specific*, pure Moorean sentence is an addressee, pure Moorean sentence which is neither universally nor user Moorean. A *user-addressee-specific*, pure Moorean sentence is a sentence which is both a user and an addressee pure Moorean sentence but which is not universally Moorean. For example, 'You and I are solipsists', along with (7) and (8) (given the inclusive sense of 'we'), is a user-addressee-specific, pure Moorean sentence.

Interestingly enough,

(34) I do not exist,

can be shown to be a third grade Moorean sentence for the user. If *a* uses (34), he expresses the proposition that it is not the case that *a* exists. However, if *a* believes something, then *a* exists. Since the absolute thoroughness condition can be satisfied vacuously, uttering (34) does not make one susceptible to direct doxastic criticism. Once belief in (34) is assumed, the thoroughness cannot be vacuous, so the utterer is vulnerable to belief-based criticism. The possibility of vacuous satisfaction of the thoroughness condition also qualifies 'All of my beliefs are false' as a third grade Moorean sentence. One of the nice features of the 'I do not exist' example is that it shows that a sentence can be Moorean even though the sentence does not mention any propositional attitudes. The sentence qualifies by its preclusion of a necessary condition for belief, as does 'Nothing exists' and 'Sentience is impossible.'

VI. OTHER PROPOSITIONAL ATTITUDES AND MOOREANNESS

Given certain assumptions concerning the analytical connections between belief and various other propositional attitudes, sentences such as the following can be shown to be pure Moorean sentences.

(35) It is raining but I doubt whether it is raining.
(36) It is raining and I guess that it is raining.
(37) You know that it is raining but I do not agree with you.

For example, to doubt that *p*, is to disbelieve *p*. To doubt whether *p* is equivalent to neither believing nor disbelieving *p*; one is in a state of suspended judgment. So doubting whether *p* implies neither believing nor disbelieving *p*. But then (35) implies

(2) It is raining but it is not the case that I believe it is raining.

Since (35) cannot serve as a basis for a direct doxastic criticism and (2) is a second grade Moorean sentence, it follows that (35) is a second grade Moorean sentence. Given that guessing implies lack of belief, (36) also implies (2), making it Moorean. Likewise, the thesis that knowledge implies belief and disagreement implies lack of shared belief, ensures that (37) implies (2) as well. Anti-subjectivists should be heartened by the fact that 'Infanticide is impermissible but I approve of it' can also be shown to be

Moorean given the plausible assumption that approving of x implies believing x to be permissible.

Examples (35)–(37) illustrate how sentences describing propositional attitudes other than belief can nevertheless be Moorean because of the beliefs (or lack of belief) implied by those propositional attitudes. However, propositional attitudes can also be relevant to Mooreanness by virtue of the fact that they are implied by belief. Consider

(M) Most of my beliefs are false.

Philosophers who believe massive error to be impossible might maintain that (M) is necessarily false. For instance, Donald Davidson maintains that the principle of rational accommodation requires interpreters to maximize their agreement with the interpretee. Since this principle must also be followed by an omniscient interpreter, it follows that most of our beliefs are true. Since most of Davidson's readers either find the principle of rational accommodation too strong or deem question-begging the assumption that an omniscient interpreter could interpret our beliefs, most of my readers should be inclined to view (M) as a contingent sentence. Given that it is contingent, it satisfies the first condition for being Moorean. No directly inconsistent beliefs can be deduced from (M) alone under the supposition that I am thorough. So saying (M) does not expose me to direct doxastic criticism. To check whether it exposes me to belief-based criticism, we add the assumption that I believe (M). Now there is something wrong. If most of my beliefs are false, I must attach a probability of less than 0.5 to each of my beliefs. This probability assignment would not follow if I could find a narrower reference class for the belief in question. For example, suppose that my high proportion of false beliefs is due to the fact that nearly all of my beliefs about baseball are false. Learning this would enable me to assign a high probability to some of my beliefs that are not about baseball. But learning that nearly all of my beliefs about baseball are false would mean that they are no longer my beliefs–which would undercut the plausibility of (M). After all, (M) is only problematic when understood as about my *current* beliefs. It is self-defeating to search for a narrower reference class for (M). Therefore, believing (M) does commit me to:

Moore's Problem

(M') My subjective probability of (M) is less than 0.5.

But given that I believe (M), I must think it more likely to be true than false. So I am committed to:

(M″) It is not the case that my subjective probability of (M) is less than 0.5.

In other words, absolute thoroughness dictates that I both believe and disbelieve (M'). Thus my utterance of (M) does make me vulnerable to belief-based criticism but not to direct criticism. Therefore, (M) qualifies as a Moorean sentence. But in order to get this result, I must invoke analytic connections between belief and propositional attitudes associated with subjective probability. Thus we have an example of how other propositional attitudes can be relevant to Mooreanness even when they do not imply or preclude belief.

It is also interesting to note that (M) reveals the vagueness of 'Moorean sentence'. Granted some reasonable criteria for counting beliefs, as was tacitly assumed in the above discussion of (M), borderline cases of Mooreanness will be found in the following list of sentences.

(M0) 0% of my beliefs are false.
(M1) 1% of my beliefs are false.
(M2) 2% of my beliefs are false.
(M3) 3% of my beliefs are false.
.
.
.
(M100) 100% of my beliefs are false.

Clearly (M0) is not Moorean because it is equivalent to 'None of my beliefs are false.' Nevertheless believing (M0) is inductively unreasonable, reminding us of those who 'are not always right, but never wrong'. It is more reasonable to believe that 'Some of my beliefs are false' even though this commits one to indirect inconsistency. Since one is not committed to any direct inconsistency by believing 'Some of my beliefs are false', it is not Moorean. The same goes for 'A small percentage of my beliefs are false.' This shows that the early members of the sequence (M1), (M2), (M3), . . . are non-Moorean. But since (M51) implies 'Most of my beliefs are false', (M51) is Moorean as are all of its successors. (M50) can also be shown to be Moorean because belief in p carries commitment to a degree of confidence greater than 0.5. Since one's degree of confidence must actually be much higher than 0.5, we are also in a position to show that (M49) and many of its predecessors are Moorean. But since there is no way to non-arbitrarily precisify 'much higher', there is no way to tell where the earliest Moorean sentence is. Thus 'Moorean sentence' is a vague predicate. Is the vagueness of my definition bad news? No, it is good news. For the vagueness of my definientia is coordinated with the vagueness of the definiendum just as the vagueness of 'immature dog' is coordinated with the vagueness of 'puppy'.

VII. BLINDSPOTS

None of the following sentences count as Moorean under my present definition of 'pure Moorean proposition':

(38) It is raining but I do not know that it is raining.
(39) It is raining but you do not know that it is raining.
(40) No one knows anything.

Nevertheless, they have much in common with the previous examples of pure Moorean sentences. The oddity of (38) and (39) is not displayed by their past tense, future tense, and third person counterparts. Although the temptation is not quite as strong, one is still inclined to dismiss (39) and (40) as contradictions. Like (9) and (10), (39) seems self-defeating.

In *Knowledge and Belief*, Hintikka notes that the primary purpose of addressing a statement to an individual is to inform him of something. So it seems to follow that if one addresses

(41) *p* but you do not know that *p*

to *a*, it must be possible for *a* to know that (41) is true. Assuming that (41) is not intended to convey something like 'p but you did not know that p', (41) appears to be equivalent to

(42) You know that the case is as follows: p but you do not know that p.

Hintikka comments:

Of course, what [(41)] expresses may very well be true. It may even be known to be true. But it can remain true only as long as it remains *sotto voce*. If you know that I am well informed and if I address the words [(41)] to you, these words have a curious effect which may perhaps be called antiperformatory. You may come to know that what I say was true, but saying it in so many words has the effect of making what is being said false. In a way, this is exactly the opposite to what happens with some typical utterances called performatory. In appropriate circumstances, uttering the words 'I promise' is to make a promise, that is, to bring about a state of affairs in which it is true to say that I promised. In contrast, uttering [(41)] in circumstances where the speaker is known to be well informed has the opposite effect of making what is being said false.[17]

So according to Hintikka, (39) is an antiperformatory sentence. It should be noted that that antiperformatory effect will only be achieved under a narrower set of circumstances than Hintikka intimates. Hintikka correctly requires that the audience know that the speaker is well-informed. If a wild-eyed drunk tells you 'Lima is east of Miami but you do not know it', the drunk would have uttered a truth. But in addition to knowing that the speaker is well-informed, we must also know that he is sincere. For instance, one of Kierkegaard's parables features a clown who discovers a fire and comes on stage to warn the audience. The audience's belief that the warning is part of the show leads to disaster. Had the clown said 'There is a fire in the theatre but you do not know it', he would have uttered a truth despite the audience's belief that the clown is well-informed about theatre conditions.

These kinds of sentences have aroused the interest of some philosophers. For example, in 'Meaning and Knowledge'[18] David Cole lists the following sentences in order to show that there is no

---

[17] Jaakko Hintikka, *Knowledge and Belief* (Ithaca: Cornell University Press, 1962), 90–1.
[18] Cole's article appeared in *Philosophical Studies*, 36/3 (Oct. 1979), 319–21.

logical connection between knowing the meaning of a proposition and knowing how one would in principle determine its truth value:

(43) No one has any self-knowledge,
(44) Everyone is unconscious,
(45) No one knows that p, yet p.

Sentence (40) fits in well with Cole's examples. Cole considers them counter-examples to the view that one can only know the meaning of a proposition if one knows how one would in principle determine its truth. We know what it would be like for (43)–(45) to be true even though they could not possibly be known to be true. This is because (43)–(45) imply that they are not known to be true.

The similarity between pure Moorean sentences and (38)–(40) can be brought out by parallel definition. Agent a is epistemically, absolutely thorough at t, abbreviated $T^e a_t$, just in case a knows all of the logical consequences of what he knows and his knowing distributes over material conditionals. Proposition p is a *knowledge blindspot* for a at t if and only if p is consistent and the following condition is met: $-\Diamond\,(p\ \&\ Ka_t p\ \&\ T^e a_t)$. In this case a is susceptible to *knowledge-based criticism*. Definitions for the various kinds of epistemic blindspot sentences are obtained by substituting 'epistemic blindspot' for 'pure Moorean proposition' definitions of the various kinds of pure Moorean sentences.

One might object that the definition of knowledge blindspot contains a redundancy since knowledge implies truth. My reply is that I wish, for the time being, to define these propositions without committing myself to an epistemic logic and presupposing this implication would commit me to an epistemic logic (albeit a very plausible one).

What has been done for knowledge can be done for other propositional attitudes. For there are many propositional attitudes that have scopes smaller than the class of all consistent propositions. I propose the term 'blindspot' for the inaccessible propositions in question. Thus a proposition p is a blindspot relative to a given propositional attitude A and a given individual a (at time t) if and only if p is consistent but a cannot have attitude A toward p. The exact meaning of the 'cannot' is to be specified by background constraints. These constraints can range from merely the rules of logic (make 'cannot' equivalent to 'logically impossible') to a more substantial set of constraints such as the laws of physics, the principles of psychology, or immunity from structural criticisms like those described for belief. Pure Moorean propositions are a species of belief blindspots. Given the constraints imposed by certain desiderata of belief, I cannot believe that 'It is raining but I do not believe it' even though it is a consistent proposition. Although all pure Moorean propositions are belief blindspots, some belief blindspots are not pure Moorean propositions. Relative to the constraints embodied by direct doxastic criticism, I cannot believe 'I believe it is raining and I believe it is not raining' although it expresses a consistent proposition. So it is a belief blindspot but not a pure Moorean proposition. Impure Moorean propositions such as 'Some opthalmologists are not eye doctors but I don't believe it' are not belief blindspots because they are not consistent. So the class of Moorean propositions is both broader and narrower than the class of belief blindspots. Nevertheless, the theme of inaccessibility provides an intimate bond between the two notions.

Since belief is such a central concept, belief blindspots have greater philosophical interest than any other kind of blindspot (with the possible exception of knowledge blindspots). The role of belief in the performance of speech acts, especially assertion, was responsible for the discovery of belief blindspots by Moore. But now Moore's discovery puts us in a position to unearth less salient kinds of blindspots.

Many belief blindspots are also blindspots for other propositional attitudes. I can neither believe nor guess that 'Turnips are carnivorous but I guess that they are not.' But others are not belief blindspots. For example, I can believe and know that

(46) It is raining but I do not guess that it is raining.

but there is something queer about guessing that (46) is true. It is a guessing blindspot but neither a belief blindspot nor a knowledge blindspot. Although I can believe that

(47) Nothing is obvious,

it cannot be obvious to me.

Other blindspots reveal interesting features of propositional attitudes. I can neither remember nor forget 'I have never learned anything.' The fact that this proposition is both a forgetting and a remembering blindspot shows that forgetting and remembering are only contraries not contradictories. Both require prior knowledge. Also consider 'Twenty years from now I will not know that I wrote this sentence on a cold morning in January.' Regardless of the quality of my memory, I cannot retain knoweldge of this proposition. For twenty years from now it will be a knowledge blindspot : something I cannot know and hence cannot remember. Since there need not be a cessation of belief or any sort of internal breakdown, I cannot be said to have forgotten. Thus it is a counter-example to Lemmon's definition of knowledge as having learned p without forgetting it.[19]

Are there blindspots for every propositional attitude? It might be suggested that pro and con attitudes have unlimited scope, that nothing lies beyond desire, hope, or hate. Objections to this suggestion can be extrapolated from the literature on masochism. Can I (intrinsically) like the fact that I am in pain? If not, then there are like blindspots. If there are like blindspots, they point us toward blindspots for the more complex pro and con attitudes. Contemplative propositional attitudes offer greater promise as examples of blindspot-free attitudes. 'Imagine', 'assume', 'suppose', 'conceive', and 'entertains the proposition that' are contemplative attitudes given their weak readings. The property of being free from blindspots would justify abstraction principles for these attitudes. That is, we could say that any consistent state of affairs can be imagined, assumed, or supposed. These abstraction principles are of philosophical interest. Many philosophers appeal to the abstraction principle for imagination as a test of consistency. For if all consistent propositions are imaginable, unimaginability implies inconsistency. Fictional discourse is sometimes analysed as a set of instructions as to what should be supposed. The abstraction principle for supposition would guarantee that any consistent set of propositions could constitute a story. This accords with the intuition that anything can happen in fiction. If there were supposition blindspots, there would be limits to fiction. The fact that some theories limit fiction this way counts as an objection against them. Consider David Lewis's view that storytelling is a

[19] Lemmon defends this definition in 'If I Know, Do I Know that I Know?', in Avrum Stroll, *Epistemology* (New York: Harper & Row, 1967), 54–82.

matter of pretending to inform people of certain facts. 'The author purports to be telling the truth about matters he has somehow come to know about, though how he has found out about them is left unsaid. That is why there is a pragmatic paradox akin to contradiction in a third-person narrative that ends ". . . and so none were left to tell the tale".'[20] Is it really a pragmatic paradox? The fact that, in the story, no one tells the story, does not imply that the story is not actually told. If the story were told in the first person, there would be a pragmatic paradox but only within the story. If Lewis' theory were correct we wouldn't be able to tell consistent stories about universes forever devoid of storytellers. Yet we can tell dull stories about the collisions between chunks of granite clunking about in elsewise empty space. Thus the absence of supposition blindspots constitutes an objection to Lewis's theory of fiction.

VIII. SUMMATION AND CONCLUSIONS

In addition to avoiding commitment to doxastic logic, my solution to Moore's problem does not appeal to the obviousness of certain inferences and it is not limited to explaining the oddity only for perfect logicians. My solution does not require idealization; it is completely at home in the ordinary world. Direct doxastic and belief-based criticisms are just two ways people criticize one another. The two kinds of criticisms are quite similar; in fact pure Moorean propositions are the only counter-examples to the thesis that they are the same. Crucial to my solution is the reconciliation of the fact that neither (1) nor (2) is a contradiction with the intuition that anyone who said (1) or (2) would be contradicting himself. The reconciliation is brought about by denying the conditional 'If someone contradicts himself, he must believe a contradiction'. The sense in which the sayer of (1) or (2) is contradicting himself is specified by my definitions of direct doxastic and belief-based criticisms. By defining 'pure Moorean proposition' in terms of immunity to direct doxastic criticism and susceptibility to belief-based criticism, the similarities between pure Moorean propositions and their cousins are illuminated. By

[20] David Lewis, 'Truth in Fiction', *American Philosophical Quarterly*, 15 1 (Jan. 1978), 40.

distinguishing between user, addressee, and universal pure Moorean propositions, the Moorean sentences I first had to classify according to their grammatical features of person and number can now be distinguished without appeal to their grammatical features. Thus a sentence like

(48) No one, except for me, has any true beliefs

can be put into the same class as second person Moorean sentences like (9) and (10) even though it is not in the second person. Further generality is obtained by means of the parallel definitions of knowledge blindspots. Thus, in addition to explaining how utterers of (1) and (2) contradict themselves, my solution satisfies the definitional condition of explaining what a (pure) Moorean sentence is. Since my proposal satisfies the previously stated adequacy conditions, my proposal is indeed a solution to Moore's problem.

2
Belief Blindspots and Truth

IN the first chapter I described Moore's problem as a difficulty about accounting for the oddity of certain sentences. I now turn to the task of showing its general significance. My point of departure is its impact on an influential theory that truth depends on the concept of belief. The second section shows how this theory makes Moore's problem relevant to the notion of validity. Much of the discussion concerns an inadequacy it reveals in epistemic semantics. In the last section, the topic changes from evaluating arguments to the evaluation of conditionals. 'Conditional blindspots' are introduced and are shown to resist the Ramsey approach to conditionals.

I. BLINDSPOTS AND TRUTH

Moore's problem is epistemologically interesting because it reveals a way in which truths can be inaccessible. The inaccessibility of these truths is not mysterious. For they are truths which imply their inaccessibility by implying that certain desiderata of belief fail to be satisfied. So, almost as a matter of brute stipulation, they exhibit the independence of truth and belief.

Although the independence of truth and belief accords with common sense, it is a fertile source of philosophical problems. For it underpins the classic appearance/reality distinction. Given the independence, it is natural to wonder how well appearance fits reality. How do we find out? Direct comparison is impossible since we can only compare appearances with other appearances. Indirect comparison is only possible on the basis of some prior direct comparisons. So we lack positive evidence that the world is as it appears. But then why suppose there is an external world at all? Why suppose that we know anything at all? Indeed, why suppose there is a 'we' to begin with? After all, the only experiences I've had are my own. How can the fact that *one* human has experiences constitute grounds for supposing that virtually all humans have experiences? For all I know, there could just be me and my experiences.

Berkeley showed us how a denial of the independence of appearance and reality derails this sceptical train of thought. Given that reality is analysed in terms of appearances, we can obtain the sort of intimacy with the real world that common sense demands. But common sense can only be served this way if it gives up what it shared with the sceptic; the independence of appearance and reality.

Berkeley's incipient verificationism was passed to Hume and Kant, down through the German idealists and American pragmatists, finally receiving careful elucidation in the hands of the logical positivists. Logical positivism was taken to its outer limits– and beyond, by Wittgenstein. Wittgenstein ultimately broke with positivism to develop a looser type of philosophy centred on the study of ordinary language. Yet he retained the verificationism in the form of a use theory of meaning that still has influence. Its impact on theories of truth can be gleaned from the writings of philosophers such as P. F. Strawson.

Of course there are many ways in which one can say something which is in fact true, give expression, if you like, to a true proposition, without thereby expressing belief in it, without asserting that proposition: for example when the words in question form certain sorts of subordinate or co-ordinate clauses, and when one is quoting or play-acting and so on. But when we come to try to explain in general what it is to say something true, to express a true proposition, reference to belief or to assertion (and thereby to belief) is inescapable. Thus we may harmlessly venture: Someone says something true if things are as he says they are. But this 'says' already has the force of 'asserts'. Or, to eschew the 'says' which equals 'asserts', we may harmlessly venture: Someone propounds, in some mode or other, a true proposition if things are as anyone who believed what he propounds would thereby believe them to be. And here the reference to belief is explicit.

Reference, direct or indirect, to belief expression is inseparable from the analysis of saying something true (or false).[1]

Against this background theory of truth, Moore's problem is especially perplexing. Sentences such as 'I went to the pictures on Tuesday but I do not believe it' and 'No one has, had, or ever will have beliefs' seem like flat counter-examples to the thesis that

[1] P. F. Strawson, *Logico Linguistic Papers* (London: Methuen, 1971), 189.

truth depends on belief. For the doctrine seems to demand that unbelievability dovetail with contradiction. Contradictions, according to this theory, amount to a conflict between belief and disbelief in a sentence. Yet, as Elizabeth Wolgast observes,

This conflict is precisely what characterizes Moore's paradoxical sentence: one cannot assert it because one cannot believe both the things it expresses. For on the one hand it expresses the conviction that the speaker went to the pictures and on the other hand it expresses disbelief about the same matter. We have just the features necessary to make a sentence contradictory; all that is lacking is the form 'p and $-p$'.

How, then, can we explain the fact (which is stressed by Moore) that the sentence might all the same be true? Surely something that might be true is no contradiction! Our discussion of truth, however, showed that truth is related to belief–to suppositions, hypotheses, beliefs. And the issue of the 'truth' of Moore's sentence cannot arise, because that sentence cannot express a belief. It is self-vitiating.[2]

The strange consequences that follow from the supposition that Moorean sentences are contradictions are rivalled by the peculiar results of the supposition that they lack truth values. If Moorean sentences lack truth values then so do their negations. So my utterance of 'It is false that it is both the case that I went to the pictures on Tuesday and I do not believe it' would not be true. Likewise it would not be true that 'Someone at some time believes something.' Solipsism could not be said to be false. Brooke Shields's utterance of 'I am dominated by my mother but I do not believe it' would lack a truth value but her friend's sentence 'Brooke Shields is dominated by her mother but she does not believe it' would have a truth value.

These consequences are reminiscent of the oracular assertions of the later Wittgenstein. This is some evidence that Wittgenstein reacted to Moore's problem along the lines that Wolgast suggests. They both seem to find the consequences tolerable and indeed might consider them insights of considerable philosophical importance. I regard the peculiarity of these consequences as a symptom of a conflict with common sense. It is an old conflict, the one Berkeley opened with the slogan 'To be is to be perceived.' Common sense takes truth and belief to be *logically* independent. Of course this is not a denial of the possibility that there may be a

---

[2] Elizabeth H. Wolgast, *Paradoxes of Knowledge* (Ithaca: Cornell University Press, 1977), 198–9.

non-logical, yet law-like dependency of truth on belief. After all, it is a piece of common sense to say that we know a great many facts, and it is difficult to see how we could have this knowledge without beliefs being formed in a reliable, hence, largely truth–preserving way. But had the universe been different, massive error could be the rule. We *could* be the victims of a grand illusion. We can imagine how massive error could be generated by an evil demon or a playful neuro–surgeon stimulating our brains. The problem posed by the sceptic is how do we reconcile the first piece of common sense with the second? Once we give up a logical dependence of truth on belief, how do we retain the non-logical dependence? Berkeley agreed with the sceptic about the incompatibility of giving up one and not the other, but disagreed with the sceptic's insistence that we give up the logical dependence to begin with. But isn't the sceptic right to insist? If the universe were entirely uninhabited, there would still be truths about the universe. It would either contain helium or it would not contain helium despite the fact that no one was around to form beliefs about helium.

When faced with the objection that 'To be is to be perceived' is wrong because we can imagine an unperceived tree. Berkeley took the objector to be contradicting himself. For the unperceived tree which the objector fancies he imagines is being perceived by him through his very act of imagination. There are two ways to construe Berkeley's reply. First, we can interpret Berkeley as subscribing to the principle that to imagine x is to imagine oneself perceiving x. The objection is then reminiscent of an argument employed by Goethe and Freud to support the view that no one can imagine his own death. Suppose that I imagine my wriggling body being tossed into a giant blender and being churned into dog food. Offhand, it seems that I have successfully imagined myself die a remarkable death. Yet didn't I picture the scene from a particular angle with typical stereoscopic vision? Doesn't this show that what I was actually imagining was myself seeing my *body* being pulpified? Given that I have to imagine myself *witness* my death in order to imagine my death, it follows that I did not successfully imagine my death. For I must have still existed in order to have observed the blending. If this is the sort of reasoning Berkeley had in mind, then his point is that when I imagine an 'uninhabited' universe, I am surreptitiously planting myself in the universe in order to peruse its emptiness. Call this the implant argument.

The implant argument has been used as a rejoinder to a type of objection used against subjectivist theories. The anti-subjectivist objection is an appeal to imagination. The audience is called upon to perform a thought experiment in which the alleged subjective source of the property in question is removed from the scene while the property remains. Our success in imagining such a scene is presented as a counter-example to the subjectivist's thesis. Moore made such an appeal in response to Sidgwick's theory that value can only reside in the conscious states of sentient beings. Moore asked his readers to perform a thought experiment.[3] The reader is first to imagine an exceedingly beautiful world filled with well proportioned mountains, rivers, stars, and so forth. The one sort of thing we cannot add is sentient life. At no time is natural beauty appreciated in this world. Second, the reader is to imagine an exceedingly ugly world. Once again, without any sentient creature that would be revolted by its surroundings. Wouldn't it be better that the first world exist rather than the second? Opponents of aesthetic objectivism refuse to answer affirmatively. Some diagnose the persuasiveness of the thought experiment by claiming that converts surreptitiously import themselves into the imagined worlds. The converts imagine that they are in the world in question observing the objects of that world. This is the familiar implant argument discussed above.

Others object that the thought experiment cannot be carried out because imagining oneself observing *p* is observing *p*. Here, the role of the adverb 'imaginatively' in 'He imaginatively observed the uninhabited world' is patterned after 'He slowly observed the uninhabited world'. 'Imaginatively' is being modelled after veridical adverbs such as 'carefully', 'suddenly', 'quietly', and 'ostentatiously'. Veridical adverbs allow us to infer 'He G-ed' from 'He F-ly G-ed.' For example, Oliver Johnson objects that if the thought experimenter imaginatively contemplates Moore's pair of worlds, he thereby violates the requirement that the worlds be unobserved. Since the thought experimenter must imaginatively contemplate the two worlds in order to justify a judgement that one is better than the other, the thought experiment must fail to establish the

---

[3] Moore's thought experiment is described in his *Principia Ethica* (Cambridge: Cambridge Univerity Press, 1903), 83–4.

objectivity of aesthetic qualities. Johnson argues that the basic difficulty cannot be evaded by having the chooser imagine worlds that will come into existence at a time later than his last imagination of them.

The world of his choice, when it comes into being later, either will or will not have the qualities that he imaginatively pictures in it. If it has the qualities, then it is a world that has been viewed by an observer, even though only by means of imagination. If it does not have these qualities, then we have no grounds on which to attribute any value to it at all, since we have no idea what it is like.

. . . the root difficulty with Moore's two-world illustration is that he asks the person who is to choose between the worlds to perform a task he simply cannot accomplish–to imagine the unimaginable, to visualise two worlds with certain aesthetic qualities and at the same time to choose between these worlds without allowing that visualisation to affect his choice.[4]

If Berkeley is interpreted along these lines, then his objection is that when I imagine an uninhabited universe, I am perceiving it in a special way–imaginatively. Call this the special perception argument.

The basic flaw of the special perception argument is that 'imaginatively' is not a veridical adverb. From the premise that I imaginatively sailed the seven seas, it does not follow that I sailed the seven seas. Likewise I can imaginatively smell tuna without smelling tuna, imaginatively believe my cat to be a lion without believing it to be a lion, and imaginatively observe Halley's comet without observing Halley's comet. The phrase 'in my imagination' works like 'in my heart' and 'in the mind's eye'. A man can commit adultery in his heart without committing adultery. A unicorn can be placed before the mind's eye without there being any unicorn. The mind's eye is an eye only in the way a plastic flower is a flower, and a toy soldier is a soldier. Observation by means of imagination is not like observation by means of a telescope. Although 'telescopic observation' has the same surface grammar as 'imaginative observation', they have different depth grammars. Once the disanalogy is noted, there is little positive reason to view imaginative perception as a special type of perception.

The above criticism only seeks to remove an apparent positive

[4] Oliver Johnson, 'Aesthetic Objectivity and the Analogy with Ethics', Godfrey Vesey (ed.), in *Philosophy and the Arts* (New York: St. Martin's Press, 1973), 168.

Belief Blindspots and Truth

reason for viewing imagination as a type of perception. To show that imagination is not a type of perception, the criticism must be supplemented with reasons for believing that the special perception thesis is false rather than merely unsupported. This supplemental line of criticism will be equally applicable to the implant argument. We begin by noting that even if it is self-defeating to imagine an unperceived object, it does not follow that there are none. If the two arguments were taken seriously, they would equally well establish the conclusion that all objects can be perceived by *me*, and for that matter, can be perceived by me *now*. Consider Russell's integer; it equals n where $n-1$ is the largest integer ever thought of. You cannot refute its existence by pointing out that it cannot be specified. By logical analogy, we conclude that the special perception and implant arguments are defective.

The implant argument can also be criticized on the grounds that it fails to distinguish between personal and impersonal imaginings. To imagine myself as the lone observer of a tree is one matter, to imagine the tree is another. This distinction cannot be explained away in terms of degrees of unobtrusiveness. However muted my presence is supposed to be, I can distinguish between that low degree of obtrusiveness and my total absence from the scene. Compare imagination to photography. The photograph is taken from a particular angle by a particular individual. But this does not mean that the photographer is in the photograph.

Although 'There are skyscrapers in Hanoi but I do not believe it' is a belief blindspot, neither of the following are imagination blindspots:

(1) There are skyscrapers in Hanoi but I imagine there are none.
(2) There are skyscrapers in Hanoi but it is not the case that I imagine it.

I can imagine that (1) is true by imagining that I am flying over Hanoi marvelling at its skyscrapers and picturing how that city would look without those giant buildings. To imagine that (2) is the case, I just suppose myself asleep while making my flight over the skyscrapers. Little, if anything, resists imagination. Hume is clearly committed to the nonexistence of imagination blindspots.

'Tis an establish'd maxim in metaphysics, *That whatever the mind clearly conceives includes the idea of possible existence,* or in other words, *that nothing we imagine is absolutely impossible.* We can form the idea of a golden mountain, and from thence conclude that such a mountain may actually exist. We can form no idea of a mountain without a valley, and therefore regard it as impossible.[5]

Hume is not alone in taking the scope of imagination to be so large that it encompasses all consistent propositions. Contemporary literature on personal identity, the ontological argument, and philosophy of mind, reveals many proponents of the view that possibility implies imaginability. Actually, Hume accepts an even stronger thesis than

(H1) If p is possible, then p is imaginable.

For he also accepts the converse:

(H2) If p is imaginable, then p is possible.

As it stands, (H2) is vulnerable to Thomas Reid's objection that we can imagine the truth of many propositions that have been proved necessarily false by mathematicians. For example, we can imagine that there is a largest prime or that a number has the same ratio to another as the side of a square has to its diagonal.[6] However, I do not know of any clear counter-exmples to (H1). There are psychological limits on what I can *distinctly* imagine. I can imagine that there is a chiliagon on my desk only in a blurry fashion. What makes my indistinct image of a chiliagon a thousand-sided figure rather than a 999-sided figure is that I intend it to be a thousand-sided figure. It's *my* image. I have the same sort of authority over my imaginings as an artist has over his paintings. Even if an artist's painting of a boat bobbing in foggy waters no more resembles a boat bobbing in foggy waters than a buoy bobbing in foggy waters, his intentions settle the question of what the painting is a picture of. Although I do not know of any clear counter-examples to (H1), there are some difficult cases that might be counter-examples. For example, it seems impossible to imagine that an object is yellow all over and blue all over. Yet it is difficult

---

[5] David Hume, *A Treatise of Human Nature*, ed. Selby-Bigge, 32.
[6] Albert Casullo argues that (H2) can be revised to meet Reid's objection in 'Reid and Mill on Hume's Maxim of Conceivability', *Analysis*, 39 4 (Oct. 1979), 212–19.

to show that 'The object is yellow all over and blue all over' is analytically false. If the proposition is really consistent and if it is really impossible to imagine it being true, colour incompatibility propositions would be imagination blindspots and so counter-examples to (H1). But I am inclined to believe that one of the conjuncts is false and so am sceptical about imagination blindspots. In any case, it is clear that imagination is not limited in the way Berkeley requires.

Berkeley's influence is most keenly felt in contemporary theories of truth. The fact that common sense balks at the interdependency of belief and truth is sometimes conceded and is sometimes cast as a temptation spawned by bad theory. Wolgast writes:

It seems very natural to say that a sentence or proposition can be true even though it is never thought or formulated—that truth is something apart from the practices or beliefs of any society. On my view, however, this issue exemplifies the confusion introduced by supposing that propositions are the objects of belief. It follows from my account that the issue whether a belief-expressing sentence is true arises only upon treating it as an expression of belief. To ask whether something is true is to raise the question whether such a belief would be true. There is no abstract issue of truth apart from this. This is not to say that someone must hold a particular belief in order for its truth to come into question. It is only to say that the sentence must be treated *as a belief-expressing one*, and its truth dealt with as the truth of someone's belief.[7]

If truth and belief are as intimately connected as Wolgast suggests, we should also expect an intimate connection between belief and validity. Since valid arguments are truth-preserving ones, they should also be credibility preserving. However, it can be shown that this natural extension of the Berkeleian theme leads to further counter-intuitive results when the arguments contain Moorean sentences. These counter-intuitive results are best appreciated against the background of an actual theory of belief-based validity.

II. VALIDITY AND ARGUMENTS CONTAINING BLINDSPOTS

Brian Ellis's 'epistemic semantics' contains one of the clearest and most sophisticated developments of a belief-based notion of validity. His logical theory is representative of a variety of

[7] Elizabeth Wolgast, *Paradoxes of Knowledge*, 190.

subjective theories of logic which seek to avoid problems associated with truth conditions by instead focusing on assertion or acceptance conditions. Since belief 'aims at truth', we should not be surprised to find a high degree of convergence between approaches which emphasize truth conditions and those emphasizing acceptance conditions. But in light of Moore's problem, we should also predict divergences when either the premisses or the conclusion of an argument are acceptance blindspots. In general we will find that subjective semantics will compare poorly with classical semantics in these divergence cases.

A. *Ellis's Epistemic Semantics and General Moorean Propositions*

Crucial to Ellis's account is the concept of a rational belief system. Essentially, a rational belief system is one that is 'ultimately defensible before an audience of competent speakers'. By 'ultimate defensibility', Ellis means that the believer could take a position on every issue expressible in the language without being guilty of linguistic incompetence. According to Ellis, the rules of the language require consistency from speakers. If a speaker accepts and rejects the same proposition or rejects a disjunction while affirming both disjuncts, he is not abiding by the conventions of the language.

Although Ellis does not believe that epistemic semantics is significantly superior to classical logic in the case of sentential and first–order predicate languages, he does believe that epistemic semantics does a better job with modal and conditional languages. For classical logic handles the latter with highly problematic appeals to possible worlds. Epistemic semantics does not require the postulation of new entities to express modalities. To say something is possible is to say that it is compatible with something else. The type of possibility depends on what type of thing the something else is. Compatibility with tautologies is logical possibility, compatibility with the laws of nature is physical possibility, and so on. Ellis analyses the claim that p is compatible with q as a claim that p and q are both believed in some rational belief system. So to say that 'It is physically possible that diamonds melt' is to say that there is some rational belief system in which 'Diamonds melt' is believed along with all and only those beliefs thought to express laws of nature. Iterated modalities, such as 'It is possible that it is possible that diamonds melt', although peculiar to assert, are intelligible as statements about the compatibility of compatibility claims. These statements are in turn analysed as beliefs about beliefs generating a hierarchy of languages featuring ever-higher order meta-beliefs.

Thus epistemic semantics can handle modality without the artificial air induced by the classical ontic escalation to possible worlds. Ellis manages to convey his dissatisfaction about this artificiality by quoting Duhem's reaction to Oliver Lodge's theory of electricity. Duhem writes

> Here is a book (O. Lodge, op. cit.) intended to expound the modern theories of electricity and to expound a new theory. In it there are nothing but strings which move around pulleys, which roll around drums, which go through pearl beads, which carry weights; and tubes which carry water while others swell and contract; toothed wheels which are geared to one another and engage hooks. We thought we were entering the tranquil and neatly ordered abode of reason, but we find ourselves in a factory.[8]

If we had nothing better than possible worlds, then we might have to tolerate the artificiality. But Ellis maintains that epistemic semantics explains everything that possible worlds explain. Since epistemic semantics explains the phenomena more economically and with far less artificiality, Ellis concludes that we are left without a reason to believe or even to pretend to believe that possible worlds exist.

Ellis concedes that his formal languages and rational belief systems are artificial in the sense that they are idealizations. But he points out every science contains idealizations. Possible worlds are not saved by this observation because they are not idealizations of anything. Rational belief systems are idealizations of ordinary belief systems.

The appeal to idealization can be used to explain a number of artificialities. For example, epistemic modesty seems to demand that any rational human believe that he has at least one false belief. Thus epistemic modesty convicts rational humans of (indirect) inconsistency. Ellis could handle this problem by maintaining that inductive grounds for supposing that some of our beliefs are mistaken are grounds for not fully believing the

---

[8] P. Duhem, *The Aim and Structure of Physical Theory* (Princeton: Princeton University Press, 1954), trans. P. P. Wiener, 70–1.

positions in question. In this way consistency is achieved at the expense of the complexity accompanying the switch from 'belief' to 'degree of belief'. Since Ellis treats probability in terms of degrees of belief, full belief is portrayed as the limiting case of partial belief, as a matter of having a probability of 1. Understood in this way, full belief should be a rare phenomenon amongst rational humans. The fact that it is not rare might be explained as the result of pressures for simplification induced by scarce intellectual resources. Thus, adopting full beliefs instead of high degrees of belief displays a rationality of economy. Ellis's talk of full belief could then count as an idealization in which the economic constraints are ignored. Since 'rational' is a broad, vague, ambiguous, and context–dependent word, manœuvres like the one above can assimilate many apparent counter-examples to the class of idealization–induced artificialities.

The classical definition of validity states that an argument is valid if and only if there is no interpretation of its non-logical terms in which its premises are true and its conclusion is false. According to Ellis's account, an argument is valid if and only if there is no rational belief system in which its premises are accepted and its conclusion rejected. Truth conditions have been exchanged in favour of acceptance and rejection conditions.

As a proponent of psychologism, Ellis pictures the limits of enriched belief to be the limits of logic. Reason for thinking the limits are not the same is available in the form of general propositions about belief.[9]

(a) Someone has a belief.
(b) No one has a belief.

Anyone who rejects (a) necessarily has a false belief. Since anyone who has beliefs that cannot possibly all be correct is inconsistent, and consistency is a necessary condition for a rational belief system, no rational belief system rejects (a). So (a) qualifies as a tautology in Ellis's epistemic semantics, although it is not a classical tautology. Therefore, any argument having (a) as its

---

[9] I first discussed the significance of Moorean sentences for Ellis's semantics in 'Epistemic and Classical Validity', *Journal of Philosophical Logic*, 19 (Nov. 1982), 458–9.

conclusion counts as a valid argument in Ellis's system.[10] Just as (a) counts as a tautology, (b) qualifies as a contradiction because it is not accepted in any rational belief system. Therefore any argument that has (b) as its sole premiss is valid in epistemic semantics. For example, we can validly argue from (b) to

(c) Birds sing.

Or we can argue from (c) to (a). This counter-intuitive result casts doubts on the adequacy of Ellis's semantics. In effect, Ellis treats inconsistency as a special case of universal indefensibility. This makes the limits of logic the limits of belief and ensures peculiar results when we try to transcend the limits of belief.

B. *Ellis on Relevance and a Precedent*

Ellis has responded to this criticism by comparing it to the peculiar fact that arguments with contradictory premises or necessary conclusions are always classically valid.[11] For instance, the argument from 'Skunks stink and skunks don't stink' to 'Birds sing' is classically valid. If we accept the validity of this silly argument, why not accept the validity of the arguments I complain of? Ellis also suggests that part of our reluctance to accept the validity of the arguments used in my criticism may be due to the irrelevance of the premises to the conclusion.

However, there are epistemically valid arguments whose intuitive validity is not due to the failure to satisfy a relevance requirement, pragmatic conventions, or whatever. For example,

(A) i. If no one has a belief, then no one knows anything.
 ii. <u>No one has a belief.</u>
 iii. Someone knows something.

Although (A) is epistemically valid, it is classically and intuitively

---

[10] The predicate 'have a belief' does not occur in the languages that Ellis explicitly considers. So it should be noted that my criticism has to do with an extension of these languages.

[11] Ellis's response to this criticism appears in 'Reply to Sorensen', *Journal of Philosophical Logic*, 19 (Nov. 1982), 460–2.

invalid. But it would be intuitively and classically valid if we had substituted the negation of (iii) for (iii). Call this revised argument (A'). Since (A') satisfies all the needed requirements of relevance, pragmatic propriety, etc. and negating its conclusion cannot alter the fact that these requirements are satisfied, (A) must also meet the needed requirements.

Epistemic semantics trivializes arguments that are not intuitively trivial. Argument (A') is valid by *modus ponens*, not by the fact that (ii) is a universal Moorean proposition. An adequate semantics should not treat (A) and (A') alike.

C. *Van Fraassen on Theoretical Scepticism about Belief and Belief* de se

Bas van Fraassen has offered an alternative defence of epistemic semantics.[12] According to van Fraassen, a rational and competent speaker of English could have theoretical grounds for scepticism about beliefs, and so could believe 'No one has a belief.' After all, we do have examples of people who are rational in the ordinary sense of the word and who do adopt the position that belief is a defunct concept like phlogiston. The sociologist George Lundberg has argued that the evolution of mental concepts into physical concepts is still incomplete.[13] Just as the concept of 'phlogiston' belongs to an immature stage of chemistry, mental concepts belong to an immature stage of social science. The philosopher Paul Churchland has argued for a similar thesis in a more intricate fashion.

Just as I would not wish to say that Churchland's claims in his book *Scientific Realism and the Plasticity of Mind* show him to be irrational or linguistically incompetent, I would not wish to attribute irrationality or linguistic incompetence to the many philosophers who have differed with me on the meaning of 'exist', 'and', 'or', and 'not', nor even to those who have denied the validity of inference rules I deem obviously valid.[14] We can all be

---

[12] Van Fraassen's initial response appears in 'Epistemic Semantics Defended', *Journal of Philosophical Logic*, 19 (Nov. 1982), 463–4.

[13] Lundberg takes this position in 'The Postulates of Science and Their Implications for Sociology', in M. Natanson (ed.), *Philosophy of the Social Sciences* (New York, Random House, 1963), 33–72.

[14] My impression is that every standard rule of inference has been challenged in

open-minded. What is at issue is whether those who believe 'No one has a belief' are rational *as Ellis defines it*. So producing examples of people who believe 'No one has beliefs' who are also rational in the ordinary sense of the word is irrelevant.

Recall that my reason for thinking that belief sceptics do not satisfy Ellis's definition issues from his completeability requirement. Ellis requires rational believers to never form beliefs in such a way as to preclude the possibility of being right on every issue. He does not require the believer to *actually* complete his beliefs. Potential completeness suffices. The function of the completability requirement is to preserve tautologies and contradictions. My objection is that the requirement displays overkill since it preserves these at the expense of counting as tautologies and contradictions some statements which are neither classically nor intuitively tautologies or contradictions.

Now consider an individual who believes there are no beliefs. How is he to take a position on every issue without falling victim to the charge of linguistic incompetence (as Ellis conceives it)? We ask him whether he believes 'No one has beliefs' and he answers 'No one has beliefs but it is not the case that I believe it.' We ask him whether he believes 'Either seven is prime or seven is not prime.' He asserts that he does not believe it. Yet he will assent to 'Either seven is prime or seven is not prime.' In general, the man *systematically* assents to omissive Moorean sentences. How are we to interpret what he says? Do we credit him with the same concept of belief that we hold? If the individual were to reject a disjunction while affirming both disjuncts, Ellis would have us conclude that the man was not abiding by the conventions of the language. Here, an appeal is made to linguistic competence in order to preserve the key notion of disjunction. Ellis would dismiss scepticism about disjunction as a non-starter. To translate someone as a sceptic about disjunction is to mistranslate him. But how can sceptics about disjunction be dismissed without also dismissing sceptics about belief?[15] Like disjunction, belief is a central *logical* concept

print by some philosopher or other. Even *modus ponens* has been rejected by Vann McGee in 'A Counterexample to *Modus Ponens*', Journal of Philosophy, 82/9 (Sep. 1985) 462–71.

[15] The analogy between belief and logical connectives in epistemic semantics was first brought to my attention by Tyler Burge (personal correspondence, 1983).

for Ellis. Thus van Fraassen's suggestion that Ellis be defended by an appeal to the possibility of sceptics about belief is incompatible with Ellis's appeals to linguistic competence. Of course, those who are not followers of epistemic semantics might be able to find a relevant difference between scepticism about disjunction and scepticism about belief. Indeed, the classical logician's ability to make sense of the sceptic about belief might be counted as an advantage of classical semantics.

Second, we should consider the sceptic's modal beliefs. When he is asked whether 'Some dogs are brown' is believed in at least one rational belief system, he answered negatively. He will thus be counted as not believing that it is possible that some dogs are brown. Yet he will assent to 'It is possible that some dogs are brown.' So those who believe that 'No one has beliefs' will have inconsistent modal beliefs. This result is due to the fact that Ellis analyses modal beliefs as beliefs about beliefs. Since validity judgements are just a species of modal belief for Ellis, they too will force the sceptic about belief into inconsistencies.

My third objection to van Fraassen's appeal to theoretical scepticism about belief is that it is an incomplete defence. Even if the rational credibility of 'No one has beliefs' could be defended by an appeal to theoretical scepticism, the defence could not be extended to commissive universal Moorean propositions:

(3) Penguins fly but everyone believes they do not.

Even those sceptical about belief cannot believe (3) because (3) commits one to the attribution of beliefs.

Van Fraassen responds to commissive Moorean propositions by raising the problem of belief *de se*.[16] Van Fraassen maintains that an agent could believe (3) if he believes himself to be a Martian and believes 'everyone' only ranges over humans. The point of his answer is that he believes that self-reference is involved. One might object that the problem will arise, apart from self-reference, once we consider languages containing unrestricted quantifiers which must range over all agents. Van Fraassen replies that this extra condition would ensure that the ensuing 'validity' of the

---

[16] My presentation of van Fraassen's position on commissive Moorean propositions is based on personal correspondence received in 1983.

negation of (3) would not be logical validity. After all, in classical semantics we can stipulate that all models must have more than one million entities in the domain, or that each must contain a model of set theory in its domain, and so on. Such stipulations would ensure the validity of $(\exists x)(\exists y)\, x \neq y$. But this is not logical validity since it is not a fact of *logic* that something exists rather than nothing. The domain of the quantifier can logically be any set at all. Stipulations as to which set is the domain, namely, absolutely all agents, are illegitimate in the quest for logical validity. Van Fraassen concedes that epistemic semantics should be extended to self-referential languages but notes that the difficulties raised by self-reference are not peculiar to epistemic semantics.

It should first be noted that if the appeal to belief *de se* succeeds in establishing the rationality of believing (3), it also establishes the rationality of direct and patent inconsistencies:

(4) Everyone believes that penguins fly and everyone believes that penguins do not fly.
(5) Everyone believes that penguins fly and do not fly.

As van Fraassen points out, one can use the expression 'everyone' without believing that it includes you. But the same goes for 'absolutely everyone', 'absolutely everyone with positively no exceptions', 'everyone unrestrictedly', and I think 'everyone, including me'. As I argued in the previous chapter, 'I' and 'me' are not referentially transparent. In extraordinary circumstances involving causal ambiguity or causal overdetermination of the production of the word 'I', I can be mistaken about who is referred to in my utterance of 'I am in pain'. The same goes for all other 'quasi-indicators'. No verbal expression carries epistemological magic. If we agree that reference error establishes the Ellisian rationality of believing (4), we should accept the Ellisian rationality of both of the following.

(6) I believe penguins fly and I believe that penguins do not fly.
(7) I believe penguins fly and do not fly.

Having gone this far, it's a short step to 'Anything goes.' For if it is rational for me to believe that I believe a particular flat contradiction, how can it be irrational to believe that contradiction? Once we allow errors about the domain of discourse to establish the rationality of believing (3), why not allow errors about the domain of discourse to invalidate inferences such as 'Exactly 80 per cent of cats are fat, therefore, some cats are fat'? A rational person who thought that the quantifiers governed different domains of discourse could believe the premiss without believing the conclusion. In the same fashion, he could form a rational belief in 'Most women snore and most women do not snore.' But this does not change the contradictions into contingencies.

As in the appeal to theoretical scepticism about belief, van Fraassen's appeal to the problem of belief *de se* is intended to make universal Moorean propositions rationally credible. But in order for either appeal to work, the concept of rationality must meet Ellis's theoretical requirements. As long as an agent is in the domain of discourse of (3), the fact that he does not believe himself to be in the domain of discourse fails to save him from inconsistency. For his belief in (3) will then only be true if he falsely believes that penguins fly. In other words, belief in (3) precludes the possibility of all of the agent's belief's being true. If the agent is unaware of his belief in (3), he may be unaware of the inconsistency. But ignorance of inconsistency does not produce the ostrich-effect of preserving one's rationality. Aware or not, one's beliefs are incompleteable. The possibility of being right on every issue has been precluded. Ellis's concept of a rational belief system does not tolerate such a preclusion. For rational belief systems are the counterparts of possible worlds. The issue of whether someone could rationally, in the non-technical sense, believe (3) because of an erroneous belief *de se* is irrelevant.

If the agent does not believe himself to be in the domain of discourse of (3), then it might finally be suggested that it is uncharitable to interpret him as believing (3) in light of the ensuing inconsistency. It would be more charitable to attribute to him a belief in a proposition resembling (3) but having a smaller domain of discourse. However, the price of this charity is the failure to come up with an example of a rational belief system containing (3).

D. *Are the Alleged Counter-examples Arguments?*

A Wittgensteinian might maintain that the above discussion is flawed by the fact that the alleged arguments are not really arguments. The objection proceeds by conjoining the view that Moorean sentences are unassertible with a requirement that the components of an argument must be asserted. All of my alleged counter-examples to subjective semantics are 'arguments' featuring a Moorean sentence or belief blindspot as either a premiss or a conclusion. Therefore, the objection continues, all of the examples contain an unassertible component which guarantees that the examples fail to meet one of the requirements for being an argument.

One of the consequences of this view is that many philosophical arguments are no more arguments than wooden Indians are Indians. Consider the case of nihilists. Peter Unger has 'argued' that he does not exist.[17] If we take the view that the unasssertibility of a proposition implies the unassertibility of its negation, the unassertibility of 'I do not exist' would render 'I exist' unassertible. So assigning Unger's utterances the status of necessary non-argument would also mean assigning 'I think, therefore, I exist' the status of non-argument. Wittgensteinians might be gratified by this result. For they tend to view philosophy as a degenerate activity, a product of linguistic confusion. Good philosophy is the correction of bad philosophy; corrections completed, philosophy vanishes. What deeper a correction than to show that a group of philosophers are not even arguing? As pessimistic as the group might have been about resolving their differences, they at least agreed that they were arguing.

Non-philosophical arguments might also turn out to be non-arguments. For as previously noted, sociologists as well as philosophers have argued for the thesis 'There are no beliefs.' Developments in cognitive psychology and neuro–science could produce other advocates of the position. Since Wittengensteinians wish to grant legitimacy to fields outside philosophy, they would not want to say that the sociological, psychological, and neurological arguments were non-arguments. They would have to respond by either gerrymandering the fields so that the arguments, despite

---

[17] See his paper 'I Do Not Exist' in *Perception and Identity* (Ithaca, NY: Cornell University Press, 1979), 235–51.

appearances, count as philosophical or by denying that the thesis in the mouth of a scientist means the same as 'There are no beliefs' means in the mouth of a philosopher.

I have already argued that, at most, only obvious Moorean sentences are unassertible. So I believe many arguments with Moorean components could satisfy the requirement set by the objector. But I also find the requirement unacceptable. It is certainly inappropriate for *reductio ad absurdum* arguments. Here, we assume what we do not believe. Some arguments are advanced in a completely speculative spirit. They are advanced as a device to figure out what follows from what. The assumption that the premises or conclusion might be believed plays no role in working out the consequences. Nor should it play a role, since it would interfere through the introduction of superfluous information.

Rather than producing further argument against the requirement that the components of an argument be asserted, our time will be more efficiently spent by changing the topic to conditionals. For it is generally agreed that one can assert a conditional without asserting its antecedent. The assertibility of conditionals containing blindspots can be illustrated with one of William Lycan's criticisms of Cartesian foundationalism.

> There is an idea that we are *obligated* to start from an epistemic position of zero: holding no beliefs and trusting no epistemic methods that have not been epistemically guaranteed in advance. But this idea, taken literally as it stands, is a contradiction. If you have no beliefs and no epistemic methods to start with, you can't epistemically justify or guarantee anything, or perform any other doxastic act. If that is what the Epistemologist is demanding of the Scientist-Laborer, we may ignore him: we can't be obligated to perform contradictory tasks.[18]

Notice the blindspot in Lycan's counterfactual 'If you have no beliefs and no epistemic methods to start with, you can't epistemically justify or guarantee anything, or perform any other doxastic act.' Despite the unbelievability of the antecedent, the conditional is still eminently assertible. Since the antecedents of conditional play much the same role as the premises of arguments, concentrating on conditionals will enable me to make my point without the hindrance of the assertibility requirement.

[18] William G. Lycan, 'Epistemic Value', *Synthese*, 64 2 (Aug. 1985), 145.

III. RAMSEY'S PROPOSAL AND CONDITIONAL BLINDPOTS

I can assert 'If the moon was just obliterated, then the tides will be disrupted' without believing either the antecedent or the consequent of the conditional. Of course, I can imagine someone believing the components of the conditional. According to a philosopher like Wolgast, the fact that we can imagine someone expressing belief in the components enables the antecedent and consequent to have truth values. But how is the truth or acceptability of the conditional to be explained?

One of Frank Ramsey's many interesting suggestions was that beliefs could be explained on analogy with maps. Our beliefs about particular matters of fact are maps by which we guide our actions. They are dispositions to act. General beliefs, on the other hand, are dispositions to change our maps. They help us move from particular belief to particular belief.[19] Since general beliefs are conditional beliefs, Ramsey's picture of belief suggests an approach to conditional propositions.

The general approach is to evaluate conditionals by hypothetically adding the antecedent to one's stock of beliefs and determining whether one would then be bound to also believe the consequent. Some proponents of the approach, such as Stalnaker, view it as a means of determining the truth values of conditionals. Others, such as Ellis, only seek acceptance conditions.[20] I will couch my discussion in terms of acceptance conditions but my comments will be equally applicable to the truth condition approach. I will be concentrating on a kind of conditional that is peculiarly resistant to both varieties of the epistemic approach to conditionals.

Informally, the conditionals in question will be those containing blindspots. For example

(8) If I have no beliefs, then I am not a Republican.
(9) If the Pope thinks I have all the virtues, then I am modest.
(10) If I do not exist, then I do not have any beliefs.

[19] Ramsey's map metaphor is given an excellent development in David M. Armstrong's *Belief, Truth and Knowledge* (Cambridge: Cambridge University Press, 1973).
[20] For a general account of the approach see Kenneth Warmbrod's 'Epistemic Conditionals', *Pacific Philosophical Quarterly*, 64 3, 249–65.

The antecedent of (8) is a blindspot to me, as is the consequent of (9) and both the antecedent and consequent of (10). Although (8)–(10) contain blindspots, they are not themselves blindspots. They are quite believable. So it would be an instance of the fallacy of composition to argue that since the parts of a conditional are blindspots, the conditional as a whole is a blindspot. Sometimes the blindspot is contained in the conditional as the negation of the antecedent or consequent.

(11) If I have mastered a language, then I have some beliefs.

The contrapositive of (11) explicitly contains a blindspot. No doubt blindspots could be 'contained' in subtler ways than (11). To avoid the unnecessary vagueness of 'contain' I shall introduce the term 'conditional blindspot'. A proposition is a *conditional blindspot* if and only if it is a consistent non-blindspot that is equivalent to a conditional whose antecedent or consequent is a blindspot. Thus (11) is a conditional blindspot by virtue of the fact that it is equivalent, by contraposition, to the following conditional blindspot.

(12) If I have no beliefs, then I have not mastered a language.

Conditionals whose antecedents are blindspots, call them 'antecedental blindspots', have the interesting property of resisting *modus ponens*.

If all of my beliefs are false, I cannot be a competent teacher.
<u>All of my beliefs are false.</u>
I cannot be a competent teacher.

The second premiss of this argument is a blindspot for me. Assent to it would render me vulnerable to belief-based criticisim. So the above argument could not be used to expand my beliefs in a manner that would leave me unexposed to criticism. Despite the argument's validity, it is a poor persuader.

Conditionals whose consequent are blindspots, consequential blindspots, also resist *modus ponens* but for a different reason.

If the dinosaurs had not been killed off by a cosmic

catastrophe millions of years ago, no intellegent life would exist today.
The dinosaurs were not killed off by a cosmic catastrophe millions of years ago.
No intelligent life exists today.

Unlike the previous argument, both premisses of the above argument are believable. Either premiss can be believed even though their conjunction is a blindspot. It would be an instance of the fallacy of division to conclude that the parts of a conjunction must be blindspots on the grounds that the conjunction as a whole is a blindspot. Nevertheless this argument shares its predecessor's status as a poor persuader.

Now consider the following conditional blindspots.

(13) If I have no beliefs, then I have no knowledge.
(14) If no one believes anything, then no one knows anything.
(15) If I do not exist, then I do not think.
(16) If no one exists, then no one thinks.

These conditional blindspots do not pose a special problem for the advocate of possible world semantics. For we need only locate the closest world in which the antecedent is true and then check whether the consequent is true in that world. However, a special problem does arise for Ramsey's subjective approach. To add the antecedent of any of (13)–(16) to one's stock of beliefs is to add a belief that behaves much like a contradiction. If one takes the position that one cannot add a blindspot to one's stock of beliefs, then one has to leave conditional blindspots unevaluated. This is unfortunate because (13)–(16) are intuitively evaluated as acceptable. Even proponents of the Ramsey approach assert conditional blindspots. For example, Brian Ellis writes

If there were no creatures with beliefs, there would be nothing that is true or false, probable or improbable. The universe would not be so very different. It would consist of the same galaxies, stars, planets, rocks, crystals, molecules, atoms and sub-atomic particles, arranged in more or less the same way, i.e. reality would not be greatly changed. It is just that in such a world there would be no beliefs, and hence nothing to be judged true or false. But would it not be true that the sun is hot, even if no one believed it, or no one was around to believe anything? Of course, I agree that the sun would be hot. The temperature of the sun is independent of human existence. That is something I certainly believe. 'If no one were around the sun would be hot', is a sentence that expresses something that I believe, and if there were an objective physical relationship of truth between belief states and reality, then this would surely be a candidate for a true belief.[21]

Those suspicious of philosophical discourse might be willing to reject the intuition that the antecedental blindspots, (13)–(16), are acceptable because of their philosophical appearance. However, this willingness to run contrary to intuition should weaken in light of consequential blindspots that might be offered by non-philosophers. For example, Ludwig Buechner's 'Without phosphorus there would be no thoughts' or any of the following:

(17) Had there been an all out nuclear war in 1984, none of us would be alive today.
(18) If we didn't have brains, we could not think.
(19) Without chemicals life itself would be impossible.

Adding the antecedents of these conditionals to our stock of beliefs can only be done by those who reject the conditionals. For adjusting our beliefs in such a way as to produce the acceptance of a blindspot renders us vulnerable to belief-based criticism. Thus, if (17)–(19) are evaluated, they are evaluated as unacceptable. Indeed, all consequential blindspots would be unacceptable. This is the wrong result. Since conditionals such as (17)–(19) cannot be dismissed as philosophical nonsense, weight must be assigned to the intuition that they are acceptable. In the case of antecedental blindspots, such as (13)–(16), it is difficult to see how the evaluation can proceed. One might take the position that anything follows from a 'pragmatic contradiction'. But this yields a counter-intuitive pattern of evaluations. All antecedental blindspots would become trivially acceptable. This would include those whose consequents are the negations of the consequents of (13)–(16):

(13') If I have no beliefs, then I have knowledge.
(14') If no one believes anything, then someone knows something.

[21] Brian Ellis, 'Truth as a Mode of Evaluation', *Pacific Philosophical Quarterly*, 61 1–2 (Jan.–Apr. 1980), 91–2.

(15′) If I do not exist, then I think.
(16′) If no one exists, then someone thinks.

Although (13)–(16) are intuitively acceptable, (13′)–(16′) are not. So counter-intuitive evaluations follow from the attempt to treat conditional blindspots as trivially acceptable. One might suggest that we bite the bullet and accept the counter-intuitive results in the same spirit that classical logicians accept the 'paradoxes' of material implication and the validity of arguments that violate principles of relevance. However, the classical logician can appeal to a host of pragmatic principles to explain away the apparent conflict between his theory of logic and common sense. The advocate of the epistemic approach to conditionals cannot make use of the pragmatic waste basket because there are conditional blindspots which satisfy all pragmatic preconditions. The explanation for why we assent to (13)–(16) and dissent from (13′)–(16′) is semantic rather than pragmatic. Background commitments such as 'Knowledge implies belief' are responsible for our judgements.

Another possible approach to conditional blindspots can be gleaned from Robert Stalnaker's discussion of

(20) If my employees dislike me, then I will never know it.

Stalnaker maintains that conditionals such as (20) fail to show a divergence between conditional belief and dispositions to change one's beliefs.[22] He points out that when we learn the antecedents of conditionals we also learn peripheral facts that sometimes prevent us from going on to believe the consequent. Usually these peripheral facts can be ignored. But in the case of (20) we cannot ignore the peripheral fact that when we learn, we also learn that we have learned. This prevents us from believing the consequent (20) when we learn its antecedent.

But given this account, why do we have such conditional beliefs? If the role of conditional beliefs is to change our dispositions to act, and conditionals such as (20) can never succeeed in doing this, they are pointless.

One way of meeting this objection is to amend the Ramsey approach by insisting that conditionals can represent dispositions

[22] Stalnaker's discussion appears in his book *Inquiry* (Cambridge: MIT Press, 1984), 184–5.

to change propositional attitudes besides belief. One could certainly *assume* or *suppose* that the consequence of (20) is true. For

(21) My employees dislike me but I will never know it.

is not an assumption or supposition blindspot. In order to state the amended Ramsey thesis more simply, one might take 'acceptance' to be a general term encompassing belief, assumption, and an assortment of other propositional attitudes. The thesis can then be stated as 'Conditional propositions represent dispositions to change what one accepts.' I might be moved to assert (20) upon learning that my employees have concealed their dislike of preceding employers. Prior to learning of their past prevarication, my confidence in their frankness ensured that suppositions that my employees disliked me tended to be accompanied by the supposition that I learn of their dislike. This disposition could be observed in my conversations about worker productivity. In these conversations with other employers, no one challenges my belief that my employees love and respect me. But to illustrate a point about the causes of worker sabotage, I am asked to suppose that my workers disliked me. Mightn't they take out their frustration on my equipment? 'No' used to be my reply. 'The workers' dislike of me would not lead to frustration because they would openly voice their complaints and the matter would be resolved openly.' But having learned that my employees have been secretive about their dissatisfaction in the past, I am no longer inclined to reply that way. Now the supposition of dislike leads to the supposition of concealment rather than the supposition of open discussion.

By using the generic concept of acceptance, one will be able to avoid counter-examples that are only belief blindspots. But what about the following 'generic blindspots'?

(22) Chain stores existed in seventeenth century Japan but no one accepts it.
(23) Undertows do not exist but everyone accepts their existence.

To know whether these are avoidable, we must have a better idea of what counts as an acceptance propositional attitude.

According to Stalnaker, acceptance of a position is a matter of treating is as true: one ignores the possibility that it is false. Acceptance can be motivated by a variety of reasons and can be done with various degrees of tentativeness, justification, and self-consciousness. Acceptance attitudes can be (roughly) distinguished from the rest by the appropriateness of applying the notion of correctness and error to them. So although beliefs, assumptions, and suppositions can be said to be acceptance attitudes, pro attitudes such as wishes, wants, and hopes do not qualify.[23] The correctness requirement also rules out non-partisan propositional attitudes such as contemplation, consideration, wondering whether p, and being puzzled by p. However the most informative clue is that acceptance must resemble belief. As Stalnaker says elsewhere, 'the cluster of propositional attitudes which were grouped under the label *acceptance* share a common structure with belief'. The structure Stalnaker alludes to is specified by three conditions which are much stronger than Ellis's:

1. If P is a member of a set of accepted propositions, and P entails Q, then Q is a member of that set.
2. If P and Q are each members of a set of accepted propositions, then $P \& Q$ is a member of that set.
3. If P is a member of a set of accepted propositions, then not–P is not a member of that set.[24]

Of course, Stalnaker does not present these conditions as a description of everyday acceptance. They are normative, embodying an ideal of rationality which we imperfectly approximate.

Stalnaker is certainly correct in supposing that 'assume', 'suppose', and 'posit' have strong readings in which they resemble belief. Witness the preceding sentence. Or consider the lyric 'Moses supposes his toeses are roses but Moses supposes erroneously.' But given that 'assume', 'suppose', 'posit', 'presuppose', and 'presume' are given this strong interpretation in which they satisfy conditions (1)–(3), they all have blindspots. For the conditions guarantee that there are consistent propositions that

---

[23] Stalnaker's characterization of acceptance appears in *Inquiry* (Cambridge: MIT Press, 1984), 79–80.
[24] Ibid., 82.

cannot be accepted. So Stalnaker's revision fails in light of generic blindspots mentioned above. Conditionals such as

(24) If no one exists, then no one accepts anything.

are non-trivially true or acceptable but are not so under the Stalnaker analysis. The original problem returns this time in the language of acceptance blindspots.

Blindspots pose a general problem for subjectivist theories. For subjectivist theories require all truths to be accessible to belief. If incompatibilities of propositions were the only sort of incompatibilities that beliefs could manifest, subjectivism might work. But since beliefs can be incompatible in other ways, a distinction must be drawn between inconsistencies in what is believed and inconsistencies between beliefs. So there is a divergence between the range of the believable and the range of the possible. Some positions are unoccupiable even though they describe a way the world might be. Thus blindspots reinforce the position upon which classical scepticism and common sense converge.

3
Limits on Agreement

THE impersonality of the limits imposed by blindspots is a product of the overlap between personal limits. Since we have an interest in what is inaccessible to all of us, these overlap areas arouse our curiosity in the same way that traditional epistemic limits do. However, the non-overlapping areas are also interesting. The fact that blindspots provide personalized ranges of believable propositions suggests that irresolvable disagreement could arise. For couldn't you have evidence that one of my blindspots is true? If so, your evidence could not rationally persuade me into believing the blindspot. I could only accept the evidence by reasoning around my blindspot.

Everyone agrees that practical limitations and imperfections of ordinary people will ensure that some disagreements are left unresolved. But different positions emerge once we agree to ignore these problems by considering ideal thinkers in epistemologically ideal environments. The first section of this chapter is devoted to a survey of this range of positions. Next, views about basic disagreement are considered. In the third section, I discuss two types of 'blindspot disagreement' which support the thesis that idealized thinkers can have irresolvable disagreements. The artifical examples of blindspot disagreement are followed in the fourth section with a general discussion of misjudgement theories. Misjudgement theories can only be right if someone is wrong and are thus liable to generate substantive blindspot disagreements. A subclass of misjudgement theories, 'error theories', would be excluded a priori by a consensus requirement for scientific beliefs. Since this pre-commitment is unacceptable, I conclude that the requirement should be rejected.

I. THE CASE FOR AGREEMENT

A variety of grounds exists for supposing that ideal thinkers in ideal epistemological environments must agree. When we picture reason as a complete guidance system, it is natural to suppose that two people can never disagree in a way that eliminates the possibility of them retracing their steps to the crucial error. They are guaranteed a common point of departure and a common means of transport. Since reason never gives conflicting directions, the two parties will be led to the same beliefs.

This argument is rather Cartesian. According to S. V. Keeling, Descartes believed that irresolvable disagreement about p is a sufficient condition for ignorance about p on the part of the disagreers.

> Now the existence of this disagreement is conclusive evidence, Descartes argues, that neither disputant really has knowledge respecting the point in dispute. For both parties cannot be in the right, and neither need be. Nor in fact can either of them be possessed of knowledge, for its possession presupposes it to have been reached by clear and cogent reasoning. But neither disputant could have reached it by this means, for if he had, he could have expounded the reasoning point by point, convinced his colleague at each step, and so in the end have compelled his agreement. Thus, from the fact of their eventual disagreement alone, we may infer an absence of relevant knowledge in both disputants.[1]

Perhaps the characterization of this line of reasoning as Cartesian is unduly narrow.[2] It seems that any Rationalist should be optimistic about agreement under idealization assumptions. The Rationalists maintained that knowledge is a matter of intuiting self-evident first principles and then drawing deductive inferences from them. Since the first principles are a priori, they are accessible to all who are free of internal intellectual flaws and free from external interference. Kant is also committed to agreement amongst ideal thinkers in ideal epistemological environments. All those for whom experience is possible have the same forms of intuition and the same system of a priori concepts. A commitment to consensus can be traced back to Plato. Our ideal thinkers will have a vision of the forms, including the form of forms, and so know the essences of all things. For that matter, we should also expect empiricists to assent to the consensus thesis. The ideal nature of the thinkers ensures that their senses are functioning

[1] S. V. Keeling, *Descartes* (London: Oxford University Press, 1968), 65.
[2] My claims about the breadth of philosophical support for the thesis that ideal thinkers in ideal environments must agree are based on correspondence (1985) with Charles J. McCracken.

properly. The ideal nature of their environment will ensure that there will be sufficient sense experience to yield the set of protocol sentences which agree in a general way with that of other ideal perceivers. Each perceiver will proportion his belief in the sentences of others to the exact degree of their evidential warrant.

Dewey characterized his rationalist and empiricist predecessors as embarked on a quest for certainty. Such a quest presupposes the possibility of achieving certainty. If one can obtain certainty, then it is counter-intuitive to suppose that others could not share that certainty even in ideal circumstances. So if one accepts Dewey's characterization of his predecessors, one should expect a consensus about consensus. But foundationalism is not the only grounds for expecting ideal thinkers to agree. The necessity of agreement is also accepted by Peirce as far as science is concerned. For Peirce argues that scientists converge towards truth and thus, in the long run, all scientists must agree.

We need not appeal to the guidance system picture in order to generate arguments for inevitable agreement. We could instead appeal to the principle of sufficient reason. By idealizing our thinkers and their conditions, we have ruled out all extraneous variables. Since there is no reason why they should form different beliefs, we should conclude that they will form the same beliefs. Picture the matter experimentally. If disagreement arose wouldn't we suppose that conditions were not really ideal? To suppose that disagreement could arise would make the divergence of opinion inexplicable.

A recent technical argument for agreement can be found in the work of Keith Lehrer.[3] The Lehrer–Wagner argument appeals to the epistemic respect experts have for one another. When an expert learns that another well-informed expert assigns a different probability to a proposition, then he should revise his probability assignment. And should he learn of disagreement about the proper weight to accord a third expert, new weights are in order. The degree of revision varies with the magnitude of the difference and the initial weight he assigns to the other expert's opinion. After this first revision, the experts should once again compare

---

[3] Lehrer first presented his basic argument in 'When Rational Disagreement is Impossible', *Nous*, 10/3 (Sep. 1976), 327–32. The argument has been refined and its consequences elucidated in a book co-authored with Carl Wagner, *Rational Consensus in Science and Society* (Dordrecht: Reidel, 1981).

probability and weight assignments. In the absence of agreement, further revisions will be made until a consensus is reached.

II. BASIC DISAGREEMENT

The Cartesian argument presupposes that reason is a two-stage guidance system. First, reason guides the selection of our basic beliefs, beliefs not based on other beliefs. Second, it guides the selection of our non-basic beliefs given our set of basic beliefs.

Many contemporary philosophers instead maintain, in effect, that reason is a single-stage guidance system. The first stage is eliminated. Reason only guides the selection of our non-basic beliefs given our set of basic beliefs. This is a popular position amongst contemporary ethicists. According to Hare, basic beliefs are chosen as ultimate decisions of principle.[4] According to R. W. Beardesmore, our enculturation is responsible for our basic beliefs.[5] Despite their disagreement as to how we acquire our basic beliefs, Hare and Beardesmore agree that reason does not determine their acquisition. Since people can acquire different sets of basic beliefs, they can have basic disagreements. Basic disagreements cannot be rationally resolved because basic beliefs are not, by definition, based on reasons (other beliefs). Although the single-stage model permits basic disagreements to be irresolvable, it suggests that there are no irresolvable non-basic disagreements. Given that the parties agree on their basic beliefs, they will agree on everything under ideal conditions.

The issue of basic disagreement in ethics tends to be complicated by the fact that proponents of basic ethical disagreement tend to be opponents of basic empirical disagreement. Thus they must rely on a problematic fact/value distinction in order to produce examples of basic ethical disagreement. A further complication is introduced by the fact that they tend also to be proponents of basic aesthetic disagreement. So given that two people disagree about whether people ought to be taxed to pay for a particular public sculpture, we have to eliminate two possibilities in order to show that the disagreement is purely ethical. First, we must eliminate the possibility that the disagreement is based on an empirical disagreement. For example, both might agree that tax

[4] See Hare, *Language of Morals* (London: Oxford University Press, 1960), 68–9.
[5] W. V. Quine, 'Epistemology Naturalized', *Ontological Relativity and Other*

dollars should only go to a work of art if it will be viewed by many people, but differ on the empirical prediction that the work in question will be viewed by many people. Second, we must eliminate the possibility that the disagreement rests on an aesthetic disagreement. For instance, both might agree that only great art merits tax dollars, but differ as to whether the piece in question is great art. Lastly, we have to make sure that the disagreement does not issue from a logical error or divergences in the disputant's data base. These problems make the issue of basic ethical disagreement difficult to resolve.[6]

The issue of basic disagreement can also arise for degrees of belief. Objective Bayesians diverge from the subjective or personalist theory of probability on the issue of assigning prior probabilities. E. T. Jaynes declares

Surely the most elementary requirement of consistency demands that two persons with the same relevant prior information should assign the same prior probabilities. Personalistic doctrine makes no attempt to meet this requirement, but instead attacks it as representing a naïve 'necessary' view of probability, and even proclaims as one of his fundamental tenets that we are free to violate it without being unreasonable.[7]

In effect, personalists permit basic probabilistic disagreement. Objective Bayesians disallow it and seek to provide criteria that will uniquely determine appropriate degrees of rational belief for everyone sharing the same information.

The theme of basic disagreement receives an interesting twist by the historian of science, Thomas Kuhn. Kuhn maintains that scientists sometimes fall into basic disagreement when they adopt different paradigms. Since paradigms constitute the standards by which scientific questions are raised and appraised, divergence in paradigms cannot be reconciled with impartiality. Furthermore, these divergences can alter the meanings of key scientific terms since the meanings of these terms depend on background

---

[6] The difficulties surrounding basic ethical disagreement are discussed in greater depth in Wayne Wasserman, 'What is fundamental ethical disagreement?', *Analysis*, 45/1 (Jan. 1985), 34–9.

[7] E. T. Jaynes, 'Prior Probabilities', *IEEE Trans. Sys. Sci.,* Cyb. SSC–4. 1968, 228. Rosenkrantz quotes Jaynes's statement with approval in *Inference, Method and Decision* (Dordrecht: D. Reidel 1977), 53. A third example of an Objective Bayesian is H. Jeffreys in his *Theory of Probability* (London: Oxford University Press, 1961), 3rd edn.

assumptions which have fallen into dispute. Thus diverging positions can be incommensurable.

A type of basic disagreement must also be countenanced by methodological conservatives. They maintain that the mere fact one believes a proposition confers some (albeit slight) warrant upon it. Interestingly, some students extend this conservatism to guesses. Their theory is that one's first impressions tend to be somewhat reliable even without any awareness of the evidence that might be responsible for the impression. So they will stick to their first impressions unless significant evidence for an alternative comes to mind. Methodological conservatives tend to provide naturalistic defences of their position. For example, it is sometimes observed that evolutionary pressures have favoured creatures who form beliefs in a reliable fashion. So the mere fact that I believe something is reason to suppose that it was formed in a reliable fashion. Since two methodological conservatives may well begin with different sets of initial beliefs, and the principle only instructs you to be conservative about your own beliefs, they can respond to the same evidence differently. Theoretically at least, there could be disagreement amongst ideal thinkers given the same evidence. D. Goldstick has cited this consequence as an objection to methodological conservatism:

Imagine two individuals, A and B, of whom A believes and B disbelieves that p. Suppose that A knows all the facts which are available to him, and B knows all the facts which are available to *him*. Suppose further that A knows all the (relevant) facts that B knows and B knows all the (relevant) facts that A knows–other than the facts as to whether or not p and as to whether or not q (for every q knowable by A or B only on the basis of inference from the correct answer to the question whether or not p). Surely it is *not* logically possible that in some situation obtaining under these conditions A should be justified in believing that p and B should be justified in disbelieving that p. Yet A and B might both be methodological conservatives, each of them justifying his own opinion on whether or not p by reference to the mere fact that held it and to nothing else at all.[8]

Unlike Kuhn, methodological conservatives have not subsumed any historical disagreements under the category of irresolvable disagreement. Indeed, some of them might take the position that various naturalistic forces pressure us toward agreement. For

[8] D. Goldstick, 'Methodological Conservatism', *American Philosophical Quarterly*, 8/2 (April. 1971) 187.

example, the need for co-ordination and epistemic respect. Nevertheless, William Lycan has displayed an open mind to the possibility that these forces may favour some disagreement. He speculates in a footnote, 'The evolution of epistemic mechanisms has to be viewed sociobiologically as well as psychobiologically. For example, it may be epistemically and selectively advantageous that a population of Scientist-Laborers contain a certain small percentage of cranks and ratbags of various kinds. Let a hundred ratbags blossom'.[9] The advantage Lycan alludes to is epistemic. It is also possible to make the case for pluralism on utilitarian grounds. Sidgwick suggested that the utilitarian might deal with moral disagreement by observing,

> though two different kinds of conduct cannot both be right under the same circumstances, two contradictory opinions as to the rightness of conduct may possibly both be expedient; it may conduce most to the general happiness that A should do a certain act, and at the same time that B, C, D should blame it . . . it may be best on the whole that there should be conflicting codes of morality in a given society at a certain stage of its development.[10]

Given that moral disagreement has the best consequences, the utilitarian would have the peculiar obligation to sustain and foment disagreement with his own moral position. Indeed, some critics of utilitarianism have argued that belief in utilitarianism has worse consequences than not believing it and so have concluded that utilitarianism implies that it should not be believed. Coupling this conclusion with a requirement that belief in a true moral theory cannot be (morally) wrong, the critics conclude utilitarianism is self-defeating.

III. TWO TYPES OF BLINDSPOT DISAGREEMENT

Blindspots give us reason to believe that irresolvable disagreement is possible. For they display idiosyncratic inaccessibility. By choosing issues involving propositions that are blindspots for one thinker but not the other, we can expect to find diverging responses to the same evidence. One thinker will be forced

---

[9] William G. Lycan, 'Epistemic Value', *Synthese*, 64/2 (Aug. 1985), 160.
[10] Henry Sidgwick, *Methods of Ethics* (London: Macmillan 1907), 7th edn., 491.

to reason around his blindspots while the other will be unconstrained.

A. *Simple Blindspot Disagreement*

Simple blindspot disagreement arises when the object of disagreement is a blindspot.

Suppose Art and Bob are twin ideal thinkers. In addition to knowing this, they know that Dr Knowart is a great expert on the correctness of Art's beliefs. One day Dr Knowart tells the twins:

(M) It is raining but Art does not believe it.

Despite Art's epistemic respect for Dr Knowart, Art cannot believe (M). There is a conflict between Art's evidence and his consistency. However, there is no conflict for Bob. Bob can believe (M). And Bob should believe (M) by virtue of the fact that Dr Knowart is an authority on the matter. Bob should not be worried by the fact that Art arrives at a different conclusion on the basis of the same evidence. For Art's failure to agree with Bob is due to a limitation on what Art can believe. One might object that Bob should worry about the possibility that Art will resolve his conflict by simply ignoring the second conjunct of (M) and believing the first conjunct 'It is raining.' But this selectiveness would be arbitrary. Art has epistemic respect for Dr Knowart as a reliable indicator of Art's errors. Art has no more reason to suppose that Knowart is right about the first conjunct than he does to suppose that Knowart is right about the second conjunct.

Art and Bob realize that there is no point in arguing about (M). For each realizes that the other has argued just as an ideal thinker should. Their disagreement is irresolvable. However, it is not interminable. Given that we interpret (M) as attributing only a current error to Art, Art can later believe (M). For there is no problem in believing that one made a particular error in the past.

B. *Complex Blindspot Disagreement*

Complex blindspot disagreement arises when the object of disagreement is a 'semi-blindspot'. Roughly, a semi-blindspot is a part of a complex blindspot. A more precise definition requires a distinction between holistic blindspots and superblindspots. Both of these types of blindspots are conjunctions. Superblindspots are blindspots that contain a (proper) conjunct that is a blindspot. For example,

(1) I have no beliefs and I am proud of it.
(2) You are modest but I am not.
(3) Everyone is unconscious but will soon wake.

Each of these has a 'sub-blindspot' as its first conjunct. If the propositional attitude in question distributes over conjunction, its blindspots must be compositional. That is, any consistent conjunction containing a sub-blindspot will itself be a blindspot. Holistic blindspots are conjunctive blindspots that lack sub-blindspots. Although the whole is a blindspot, none of its parts are:

(4) It is raining but I believe it is not raining.
(5) Although everyone is optimistic about the launch, it will be a disaster.
(6) The hypothesis is *ad hoc* yet true.

Each conjunct of a holistic blindspot will be called a 'semi-blindspot' with respect to the conjunction of the remaining conjuncts. Thus the conjunction of two propositions which are mutual semi-blindspots must be a blindspot. Although semi-blindspots are each accessible, they are not co-accessible when the propositional attitude collects over conjunction. Thus I can know that the identity of my benefactor is being kept a secret from me and I can know that my benefactor is Bo Derek but I cannot know both. The two semi-blindspots are epistemic contraries, either can be known but not both. Once a semi-blindspot is incorporated into one's body of beliefs, its mate behaves much like a regular blindspot. Relative to that body of beliefs, it is a consistent but inaccessible proposition. Since everyone accepts a great number of semi-blindspots, it follows that each person has an equal number of 'relative blindspots'.

In light of the lottery and preface paradoxes, I doubt that belief collects over conjunction. But notice that the conjunctions in these counter-examples are enormous. Small conjunctions composed of just two conjuncts never make convincing counter-examples. This is not to say there are no small scale counter-examples. Indeed, there must be small scale counter-examples if there are large scale counter-examples. The pairwise collection principle states:

(P) If one believes p and believes q, then one believes both p and q.

Since p and q can themselves be conjunctions, repeated application of (P) yields the large scale collection principle. Belief in r and belief in s, implies by (P) belief in $(r \& s)$. Belief in $(r \& s)$ and belief in t, implies by (P) belief in $((r \& s) \& t)$. And so on. Eventually we reach an unacceptable consequence about what is believed. But the conjunction grows too slowly to ever allow us to draw a sharp line between the last acceptable conjunction and the first unacceptable one. 'Belief' is too vague for such pairwise discriminations. Thus we are never *warranted* in attributing a pair of beliefs to a person without attributing belief in the corresponding conjunction. Analogously, we are never warranted in asserting that a person arriving at 12.11 arrived noonish while denying that another who arrived at 12.12 arrived noonish. Nevertheless, both claims could be correct.

A further factor that tends to make applications of (P) fruitful is that debaters are vying for the best explanation of the available evidence. This imposes, at least at the pragmatic level, a requirement of overall coherency. This in turn requires beliefs to collect over conjunction. So although (P) does not hold as a purely logical principle, additional constraints can require us to form beliefs as (P) requires in 'small-scale' situations.

The upshot of all this is that belief semi-blindspots will crowd each other out. My belief that 'It is raining' will prevent me from believing 'I do not believe it is raining.' Since a pair of propositions can be semi-blindspots to me but not to you, the scarcity of doxastic space may be restricted to just me. I will have to cope with a constraint that you do not. This will create divergences in how we respond to the same evidence. The resulting disagreement can concern a semi-blindspot.

We can illustrate this second type of disagreement by placing Art and Bob in a new situation.[11] Suppose Art and Bob each

---

[11] The following example of complex blindspot disagreement is given a more detailed presentation in my 'Disagreement Amongst Ideal Thinkers', *Ratio*, 23/2, (Dec. 1981) 136–8.

regard Harry Higher and Larry Lower as authorities on matters concerning the national song-writing contest. They also agree that Higher is more reliable than Lower. On Monday, Higher informs Art and Bob that:

(7) Winners of the last contest will not believe they won until Thursday.

So the twins believe (7). On Tuesday, Lower tells them:

(8) Art is the winner of the last contest.

Notice that for Art, (7) and (8) are semi-blindspots. Given the conditions of the story, we cannot suppose that Art manages to believe each of the two propositions by failing to collect his beliefs over the blindspot 'Winners will not believe they won until Thursday and Art is a winner.' We must instead suppose that Art will not believe one of the semi-blindspots. In particular, Art will believe (7) but not (8) because (7) is the proposition supported by the more authoritative source, Harry Higher. Bob, on the other hand, is not forced to choose between authorities. He is free to believe both of Art's semi-blindspots. Bob should not be worried by the fact that Art disagrees about (8). If anything, Art's lack of belief enhances the probability of (8) by ensuring that a necessary condition of Art winning the contest is satisfied. Even though (8) is not a blindspot, we once again have ideal thinkers disagreeing.

Although the range of consistent positions is the same for all thinkers, the range of defensible positions differs from thinker to thinker. The disparity between sets of available positions creates the potential for irresolvable disagreement. For we can present ideal thinkers with evidence in favour of holding a position that is in only one of their sets of defensible positions. Given that we picture reasoning as a matter of changing positions in response to evidence, we can make sense of the claim that blindspots influence reasoning. Blindspots are obstacles which force us to manœuvre around them. Since no two people entirely share their blindspots, individuals have varying epistemic terrains.

Awareness of these differences should not lead us to overlook the similarities between thinkers. Only some blindspots are personal. Shared blindspots will not force divergence in reasoning. When we bump into them, we can all react in the same way.

However, the resulting uniformity in our pattern of reasoning does not eliminate the partisanship of our system of representation. We are still precluding the occupation of some synthetic positions a priori. For no rational being can be *completely* open-minded. (As the late Alan Ross Anderson was fond of saying, we should be open-minded but not so open-minded that our brains fall out.)

My thesis has been that *some* blindspot disagreements are irresolvable. Many other blindspot disagreements are resolvable. For example, a person can overlook the fact that his position is a blindspot even to himself. Bringing this fact to his attention resolves the disagreement a priori.

IV. MISJUDGEMENT THEORIES

The blindspot disagreements concocted in the doxastic adventures of Art and Bob are rather artificial. Occasionally, we do find blindspot sentences in ordinary life. Merchants tell shoppers 'Christmas is closer than you think.' Senator John Glenn 'informs' Attorney General aspirant Ed Meese that he has an ethical blindspot. And we accuse others of not being able to face the truth. But in order to be considered as something more than mere curiosities, blindspot disagreements should be shown to arise over interesting theses.

Before beginning our search, let us remind ourselves of what we are looking for. A blindspot disagreement arises when and only when agreement is precluded by the issue's status as a blindspot or semi-blindspot. This suggests that theories which imply the existence of blindspots will breed the desired sort of disagreement between the blindspotees (people to whom the proposition is a blindspot) and the non-blindspotees. So a natural place to look for blindspot disagreement is amongst misjudgement theories.

A misjudgement theory is a theory that implies the existence of misjudgements. Misjudgement consists of a defect in either the process or product of judgement. The process can be defective without harm to the product as in the case of an unjustified but true belief. In the case of a justified but false belief we have a good process and a bad product. In practice, the quality of the judgement process is strongly correlated with the quality of the judgement product. If we define 'error theory' to be a theory that implies the existence of (either omissive or commissive) errors, we can say that any error theory is a misjudgement theory but not vice versa. For a misjudgement theory might merely imply that we are unjustified or have been 'gettiered'. As Barbara Winters has emphasized, sceptical counter-possibility hypotheses need not imply massive error.[12] The possibility that most of my beliefs owe their truth to a cosmic coincidence is just as damaging to my knowledge claim as the possibility that bad luck has rendered most of my beliefs false.

We can classify misjudgement theories by classifying the implied statements concerning misjudgements. Along one dimension we can classify in accordance with the type of propositional attitude. Along another, we can distinguish between process and product and subdivide in terms of justification problems, Gettier problems, and perhaps Harman problems[13] under the process branch, with omissions and commissions under the product branch. We can also consider variations in detail. At one end of the spectrum, we find exact specification of who makes the misjudgement, what the inappropriate propositional attitude is, and which proposition is the object of the misjudgement.

(9) On January 1, 1982, David Stockman falsely believed the Reagan administration would balance the budget by 1985.

At the other end of the spectrum lie highly indefinite claims. At this outer limit we find:

(10) Someone at some time commits an error.

Theories that imply highly indefinite misjudgement statements are unlikely to spawn blindspot disagreement. For although the misjudgement statements are semi-blindspots, their mates are too improbable to create competition. Consider the following pair of semi-blindspots:

(11) Someone will be struck by lightning in August 1999 but he will not believe it beforehand.

---

[12] Winters makes this point in 'Sceptical Counterpossibilities', *Pacific Philosophical Quarterly*, 62/1 (Oct. 1981), 30–8.

[13] I refer to Gilbert Harman's social knowledge cases presented in *Thought* (Princeton: Princeton University Press, 1973).

(12) With the possible exception of Roy Sorensen, no one will be struck by lightning in August 1999.

Although belief in (12) would drive out belief in (11), it is extremely unlikely that I could obtain the evidence that would prompt belief in (12).

In addition to the specificity of the misjudgement statement, we can also inquire about its topic. For our purposes, it will suffice to distinguish between misjudgement theories that take themselves as topics and those that take other propositions as the objects of error.

A. *Hetero-referential Misjudgement Theories*

Most misjudgement theories are hetero-referential. They do not predict that people will disagree with the theory itself. An error theory can be quite non-commital about the nature of the error. For all it need do is to imply some disagreement. This will suffice because the parties to the disagreement cannot both be correct.

It should be further noted that the implied disagreement need not be direct disagreement. People directly disagree just in case there is a proposition such that one believes it and the other disbelieves the proposition. With direct disagreement the parties directly contradict each other. People indirectly disagree just in case they lack direct disagreement but have beliefs that cannot all be true. In other words, if we were to pool their beliefs together, it would necessarily be the case that some of the beliefs were false beliefs. For example, my beliefs about the influence of expected grades on enrolment leads me to the hypothesis that a majority of my students believe that they will finish in the top half of the class. This hypothesis predicts indirect disagreement amongst my students. Since only half my students can finish in the top half, some of my students are mistaken. But the theory does not imply a specific proposition of the form 'Student s will not finish in the top half but he believes he will.'

Indirect disagreement is also present in chain-letter schemes. A standard chain letter scheme runs as follows. You receive a letter requesting that you send a dollar to each person on an enclosed list. You are then to cross out the name of the first person on the list, add your own, and send the list with the same set of instructions to five other people. If all goes well with your segment of the chain, you will receive ($5 + $25 + $125 + $625 + $3125) = $3905. Even if only a small percentage of the people below you respond, you will have a handsome return on your $5 investment. But as with all pyramiding schemes the mere fact that there is only a finite number of people will ensure that the chain eventually breaks and some people have paid more than they have 'earned'. What makes the chain grow is the belief that you will not be amongst the members of this unfortunate group. Everyone can agree that some will make the error which places them in this group as long as no one believes that he will make the error.

Chain-letters clogged the US Postal Service during the Depression, a Depression preceded by a similar sort of speculative snowballing in the American stock market. The steady rise of stock prices in the 1920s inspired great confidence in traders, which in itself inspired still greater confidence. For as long as one believes that others believe prices will continue to climb, one can buy with the belief that one will soon be able to sell at a higher price. As this optimistic process continued to feed upon itself, traders began to realize that the price of a stock was no longer a function of its expected dividend. The price was instead principally a function of the belief that one could find some 'other fool' to whom one could sell. As long as no one believed that he would be the 'last fool', prices would continue to rise. As traders came to fear that they might be the last fools, they began to sell. The fall in prices created more fear of falling prices, which in itself was the grounds for yet more fear.

Error theories implying indirect disagreement can be held by all parties to the disagreement. Such theories are only semi-blindspots with respect to propositions that eliminate a great many others as victims of error.

It is also possible for theories predicting direct disagreements to win a complete consensus. For example, hypotheses to the effect that certain concepts are 'essentially contested' can be believed by all parties to the dispute. For such theories only predict disagreements. They don't take sides as to who is right. Well, almost never. The hypothesis that 'essentially contested concept' is itself an essentially contested concept is a self-referential error theory. For it implies that others will disagree with the hypothesis itself.

In ordinary usage 'fallacy' means either a commonly held false belief or a common error of reasoning. The ambiguity is encouraged by our difficulties in distinguishing between propositions and inference rules. I shall abide by the logician's convention and reserve 'fallacy' for the second sense, making all fallacies bad inference rules. I will adopt the term 'myth' to cover commonly held false beliefs. Any theory to the effect that a certain belief is (currently) a myth is a self-referential error theory because 'unbelieved myth' is a contradiction in terms. There could be no myth that ship captains can perform marriages, that lemmings commit suicide *en masse*, and that the Russians invented vodka, if no one subscribed to the myths. However, theories to the effect that a certain type of transition between beliefs is a fallacy can be hetero-referential. For people can make inferences without realizing that they are instances of argument forms they regard as fallacious. Those with knowledge of a rule can break it unwittingly through errors about whether the rule's execution condition is satisfied.

The usual point of describing something as a myth or a fallacy is to change people's minds. We at least wish the myth to be less popular and the fallacy committed less frequently. However, the misjudgements are sometimes described as nearly irremediable. Hume often took this line in explaining the unpersuasiveness of sceptical arguments. We can also find theories of recalcitrant misjudgement emanating from the distinction between subjective and objective properties. The distinction centres on the observation that while some properties seem independent of us (being cracked, a rock, heavier than air), others appear dependent on beliefs (being stalemated, president, costing five dollars). As shown by interest in the difference between primary and secondary qualities, the subjective/objective distinction is generally thought to have ontological implications. The subjective properties are thought to be less real than the objective ones because only the objective properties inhere in the objects themselves. The subjective ones are projected on to external things. The thoroughness of the projection misleads us into thinking that the external things really have the properties that careful study discloses to be only subjective. Thus proponents of the distinction amaze others by claiming that 'The world isn't really coloured'. 'Time is unreal', and 'Beauty is in the eye of the beholder.'

Consider Michael Wreen's recent analysis of the distinction between conventional and natural properties. According to

Wreen, some properties and words exhibit a 'world/word wedge', that is, the property fails to correspond to the meaning of the word. His principal example is vagueness and 'vague'. According to Wreen, a word is vague only if a significant number of people (of the appropriate sort) believe it to have a large number of borderline cases. A second example is 'being spelled with two "m"s'; 'accommodate' is spelled with two 'm's only if a significant number of people believe that it is spelled that way. Or consider the claim 'Studio 54 is *the* place to be seen at'. This property also seems dependent on a number of people believing Studio 54 to have the property. As a final illustration of Wreen's distinction, we might add Daniel Boorstin's definition of 'celebrity': someone known for his well-knownness. Wreen calls properties exhibiting the world/word wedge 'conventional properties' and defines them as follows:

X-ness is a conventional property if and only if (a) an adequate analysis of *x*-ness differs from an adequate definition of '*x*', and (b) the difference is that the proper analysis of *x*-ness is or includes being believed by a significant number of *Y*s . . . where *Y*s are people, or some subclass of people, and where the dots represent the property elements expressed in the definition of '*x*'.[14]

Nonconventional properties are then dubbed 'natural properties'. According to Wreen, concepts associated with conventional properties are ontologically laden:

to believe that a word is vague is, *ipso facto*, to believe something about the way the world is.

The reason this is so is that conventional properties, as defined above, are properties we, on most occasions, systematically but benignly fool ourselves about. Using them, we cannot but take them as natural and objective properties, else the point and purpose of having the corresponding terms and concepts would be largely lost. . . . That is to say, under most conditions, in order for us to find our way about, we take, and have to take, the roadmaps of our own invention, the conventional objects and properties of our own creation, as objective and natural objects and properties, that is, as things existing in their own right, and not, with their corresponding terms, exhibiting the world/word wedge.[15]

Wreen is pointing to practical pressures that make us abrogate the

---
[14] Michael Wreen, 'Vagueness, Values, and the World/Word Wedge', *Australasian Journal of Philosophy*, 63/4 (Dec. 1985), 454.
[15] Ibid., 454–5.

distinction he has drawn in a cool hour of contemplation. Since it is difficult to break our habitual ontological stance toward conventional objects, Wreen should expect resistance to his theory. But unless the resistance is implied by the theory itself, it will remain a hetero-referential error theory.

Similar resistance should be expected by the author of *Inventing Right and Wrong*. For J. L. Mackie maintains that moral language is structured in such a way as to foment a recalcitrant misconception about the objectivity of morality. Kant speaks similarly of the lure of transcendental illusion. Even after understanding how the antinomies arise, Kant believes that we are still tempted to extend concepts appropriate to phenomenal reality to noumenal reality.

Misjudgement theories can vary in the degree of recalcitrance they assign to the defect. However, there is an upper limit. To describe a universal error as perfectly recalcitrant is self-defeating. For perfect recalcitrance would imply the undetectability of the error. So at this extreme, recalcitrant error theories become self-referential.

B. *Self-referential Misjudgement Theories*

A self-referential misjudgement theory implies misjudgement about the theory itself. Since every theory implies its own truth, any theory that implies that people will fail to believe the theory is predicting error about itself. If an error description specifies those in error, it will spawn a simple blindspot disagreement between proponents of the theory and the persons implied to be unbelievers.

1. *Unlimited Versions*

Some theories imply that no one will believe them. Consider the theory that there are no beliefs. This type of metaphysical scepticism can be generated in a number of ways. Recall that George Lundberg argued that mental concepts evolve into physical concepts, and since 'belief' has yet to mature in this way, it is an obsolete concept akin to 'phlogiston'.[16] Churchland developed the phlogiston theme in defending a version of eliminative materialism that implies that there are no beliefs. If Lundberg and Churchland are correct in maintaining that their

---

[16] Lundberg takes this position in 'The Postulates of Science and Their Implications for Sociology', in M. Natanson (ed.), *Philosophy of the Social Sciences* (New York, Random House, 1963), 33–72.

theories imply that no one has beliefs, their theories are incapable of being correctly believed. Since their thesis 'There are no beliefs' is a belief blindspot for everyone, it is an example of simple blindspot disagreement.

Scepticism about justified belief is more common than scepticism about belief. I. T. Oakley commits himself to such scepticism with the first sentence of his article 'An Argument for Scepticism Concerning Justified Belief': 'I shall argue that no beliefs are justified (or reasonable, or rational). . . . So in this paper, I shall be arguing that no one is justified in any beliefs even to the most minimal degree.'[17] Epistemological anarchism, the view that no belief is better justified than any other, has had adherents throughout the history of philosophy. For example, Seneca attributes to Protagoras the view that every side of an issue, including this one, can be equally well supported. Some epistemological anarchists might deny that this implies scepticism about justified belief. For they might claim that their notion of justification allows belief in p and belief in not-p to simultaneously enjoy a positive degree of justification. In any case, the tradition is kept alive by the likes of Paul Feyerabend and Peter Unger. Sympathy to the position is not restricted to professional philosophers. For example, the literary critic John Unterecker espouses epistemological anarchism in order to show why we we should not dismiss James Merrill's ouija board poetry:

What I am trying to suggest is that all systems, once they lose favor, are as metaphoric and mythic as the actions of discarded gods–and that our systems will soon crumble into the metaphors from which they were made. We study failed systems and faiths with interest, pleased to speculate about the ways in which they must have satisfied certain fundamental human needs. Too often we forget that our accurate analysis both of those failed systems and of 'reality'–our best science and our most devoutly held faiths in any truths–are equally mythic and amusing. Every scrap of truth and fact that I believe in, including this statement of my current convictions, is bound, undoubtedly sooner or later, to be recognized as the invention–the unintended tissue of satisfying fiction– that it has always been, one that in its most convincing way satisfied for me an essential human need.[18]

---

[17] I. T. Oakley 'An Argument for Scepticism Concerning Justified Belief', *American Philosophical Quarterly*, 13/3 (July 1976), 221.
[18] From the foreword of Judith Moffett, *James Merrill* (New York: Columbia University Press, 1984), xvii.

The proponent of epistemological anarchism has a blindspot disagreement with others because his position is expressed by a universal justification blindspot. The statement 'Epistemological anarchism is correct but it is no more justified than its negation' cannot be justifiably believed. Thus the position is made inaccessible by its denial of unique justification rather than by an implied restriction as to who holds the position. Although this is a blindspot disagreement, it is not irresolvable. For epistemological anarchism is as inaccessible to its proponent as it is to prospective converts. One can only hold the position through a prior sin. There are no epistemological anarchists in an intellectual utopia.

Since epistemological anarchism cannot be justifiably believed, any proposition that implies epistemological anarchism cannot be justifiably believed. This is the basis for a popular strategy against a variety of doctrines. By showing that the theory precludes the possibility of justified belief, one shows that it is self-defeating. Epicurus, for instance, sought to refute determinism in this fashion: 'He who says that all things happen of necessity cannot criticize another who says that not all things happen of necessity. For he has to admit that the assertion also happens of necessity.'[19] The general idea is that a justified judgement is a kind of free choice between alternatives. Supplementing this volunteeristic conception of belief with the view that determinism is incompatible with free will yields the conclusion that determinism rules out the possibility of justified belief. Voltaire does not shirk this consequence: 'I necessarily have the passion for writing this, and you have the passion for condemning me; both of us are equally fools, equally the playthings of destiny. Your nature is to do harm, mine is to love truth and to make it public in spite of you.' But Voltaire should also admit that he is destined to believe that some beliefs are justified. For indeed he must believe this in order to decide what is true. He must picture some of his beliefs as arising because of their truth. As Kant says, 'we cannot possibly conceive a reason consciously receiving a bias from any other quarter with respect to its judgements, for then the subject would ascribe the determination of its judgement not to its own reason, but to an impulse. It must picture itself as the author of its principles independent of foreign influences.'[20] Supporting Kant is the oddity

---

[19] Epicurus, Aphorism 40 of the Vatican Collection.
[20] Immanuel Kant, *Grundlegung*, 81.

of 'I believe *p* because *x* biases me in its favour.' Bias is irrelevant influence. By tracing the history of your belief to causes independent of the truth value of *p*, you undermine the belief. After all, to believe *p* is to believe *p* is true. By disallowing the possibility that beliefs are formed by processes relevant to the truth value of *p*, one attempts an impossible separation of belief in *p* and belief in the truth of *p*. Consider the peculiarity of trying to persuade others that beliefs are only formed irrationally or that every change of mind is due mostly to an exchange of biases.[21] This sort of misgiving has also been voiced about mechanism. Norman Malcolm writes, 'my acceptance of mechanism as true for myself would imply that I am incapable of saying or doing anything for a reason . . . it would also imply that I am incapable of having rational grounds for asserting anything including mechanism.'[22] Similar criticism is also popular against materialism. For example, we find Haldane dismissing the view on the grounds that it casts belief formation as a blind process: 'if materialism is true, it seems to me that we cannot know that it is true. If my opinions are the result of chemical processes going on in my brain, they are determined by the laws of chemistry, not of logic.'[23] Karl Popper has maintained that materialism is self-defeating because it lacks the ontology necessary for justification. For justification requires logic, and logic is an abstract system requiring abstract entities.[24] Psychologism, the view that logic is reducible to psychology, has also been criticized for undermining the possibility of justification. For if logical laws are just descriptions of how we think, they lack the normative status necessary for warranting beliefs.

Experimental studies supporting the significance of experimenter bias are sometimes criticized as self-defeating.[25] The

---

[21] Barbara Winters has provided an excellent defence of the principle that 'it is impossible to believe that one believes p and that one's belief of p originated and is sustained in a way that has no connection with p's truth'. See her 'Believing at Will', *The Journal of Philosophy*, 76/5 (May 1979), 243–56.

[22] Norman Malcolm, 'The Conceivability of Mechanism', *The Philosophical Review*, 77/3 53.

[23] J. B. S. Haldane, *The Inequality of Man* (London: Chatto and Windus, 1932), 132.

[24] Popper presents this argument in *The Self and its Brain*, co-authored with John C. Eccles (New York: Springer-Verlag, 1977), 75–81.

[25] I have in mind the experimental literature following Robert Rosenthal's early work. A discussion of this literature and a reply to the objection that it is self-

objection is that the results of such experimenters discredit the experiments themselves. For those conducting the experiments are just as vulnerable to the charge of bias as those whom they study. The sociologists, historians, and philosophers who cite this experimental work in their attacks on the objectivity of science have been criticized by Israel Scheffler along this line:

> And indeed there is a striking self-contradictoriness in the effort to persuade others by argument that communication, and hence argument is impossible; in appeal to the facts about observation in order to deny that commonly observable facts exist, in arguing from the hard realities of the history of science to the conclusion that reality is not discovered but made by the scientist. To accept these claims is to deny all force to the arguments brought forward for them.[26]

Recent studies of peer review suggest an interesting offshoot of the bias controversy. Psychologists such as Douglas Peters and Stephen Ceci have argued that journal editors and referees are biased against authors affiliated with low prestige institutions.[27] Some experimental support for the bias hypothesis was gathered by resubmitting articles to journals that had already published them. Since the resubmitted articles only differed from the originals in carrying a low prestige affiliation (in addition to some cosmetic changes), Peters and Ceci appealed to prestige bias to explain the fact that all but one of the nine refereed articles were rejected. Peters and Ceci submitted their article to a journal with a blind review policy, *The Behavioral and Brain Sciences*, so they are not committed to explaining its acceptance in terms of prestige bias running against competing submissions. Interestingly, eight of the sixty-one commentators on the Peters and Ceci article preferred to account for their results in terms of randomness.[28]

---

defeating appears in Michael Martins', 'The Philosophical Importance of the Rosenthal Effect', *Journal for the Theory of Social Behaviour*, 7 1 (Apr. 1977), 81–97.

[26] Israel Scheffler, *Science and Subjectivity* (Indianapolis: Bobbs-Merrill, 1967), 44.

[27] Their article 'Peer-review practices of psychological journals: The fate of published articles, submitted again' first appeared along with peer commentary in *The Behavioral and Brain Sciences*, 5/2. My references are from a reprint Steven Harmad (ed.), *Peer Commentary on Peer Review* ed. (New York: Cambridge University Press, 1982).

[28] Peters and Ceci cover the randomness thesis in their response 'Peer–review research: Objections and obligations', 65.

Should one of these commentators go on to write an article defending the thesis that all article acceptance is a chance phenomenon, submission of the article would present a peculiar dilemma for a referee who found the article convincing. For if the referee recommends the article for publication on the grounds that it succeeds in showing that article acceptance is a random affair, he commits himself to discounting the informativeness of his own referee report.

What we find above are attempts to show that a seriously held theory is actually an unlimited error theory. This strategy has also been applied against frivolous theories that we cannot otherwise dispose of. For instance, consider Don Locke's attack on Russell's hypothesis that the world popped into existence five minutes ago complete with fossil records, 'memories', etc.

If there has been no past then we have no past history, and if we have no past history we have never acquired any information nor any reason for believing anything, not even about the present. Without a past, I could not have learned what tables are, and so could have no reason for thinking this to be a table I am writing on. And since, if Russell's hypothesis were correct, we could have no reason for regarding anything as correct, it follows that we would then have no reason for regarding the hypothesis itself as correct. It is, in short, not something that can rationally be believed, for to believe it would mean we had no reason for believing it.[29]

2. *Group Universal Versions*

Since unlimited misjudgement theories are self-defeating, they are resolvable blindspot disagreements. In order to avoid the disaster of self-defeat, a misjudgement theory must allow itself to be non-defectively judged by some people. Group universal theories manage to do this by restricting the error to all the members of a particular group.

To obtain our first example, note that scepticism about belief need not be global. One could advance local scepticism about belief which merely limits the range of possible believers. For instance, Donald Davidson's theory of belief excludes the possibility of dogs having beliefs. So if Fido could form an opinion about Professor Davidsons's theory and also believed himself to be a dog, Fido would have a blindspot disagreement with Davidson. Since the thesis 'Dogs do not have beliefs' is only unbelievable to

[29] Don Locke, *Memory* (New York: Doubleday, 1971), 129–30.

those who believe they are dogs, this is an example of complex blindspot disagreement. Should we ever develop robot philosophers, the disagreement could become heated. Human philosophers who believe 'Machines cannot think' can hardly hope to persuade their mechanical counterparts.

An example related to global and local scepticism about belief was the object of one of Bertrand Russell's favourite anecdotes. After Russell had finished a lecture on solipsism, he was greeted by an enthusiastic member of the audience who declared herself a solipsist and relieved to know that 'there are at least two of us'.

The woman in Russell's story occupies a position that is a blindspot for Russell and herself. Since occupation of this position is vulnerable to criticism, the disagreement is not irresolvable. Were her solipsism coherent, she would not expect to find any other solipsists. Her belief, 'I am a solipsist' is a semi-blindspot with respect to 'You are a solipsist.' Acceptance of the first belief makes the second inaccessible. Although normal people can believe that the woman is a solipsist, other solipsists cannot. Thus 'I am a solipsist' creates a complex blindspot disagreement between solipsists.

The acquisition of certain kinds of beliefs often receives developmental explanations that do not allude to the truth value of the beliefs. We can see why this tends to happen with religious, political, ethical, and aesthetic beliefs. Beliefs about natural properties can usually be explained as effects of the states of affairs they purport to represent. Since evaluative beliefs do not appear to be about natural properties, we are drawn to explanations that do not imply the truth of the belief. For example, we will appeal to the principle that people tend to be 'infected' with the beliefs of those to whom they are most heavily exposed. Thus children tend to have the same religious and political affiliations as their parents. Appeals to group interests are also popular. Since the difference between fact and value is sometimes murky or at least easily clouded, non-cognitivist explanations of beliefs can be extended to areas that did not initially appear promising. In particular, they can be extended to yield predictions about a theory's own reception. For example, Marx explained the political beliefs of capitalists in terms of a group interest that was sufficiently strong to guarantee their rejection of his economic theory. Freud appears to have believed that some of the defence mechanisms described in his psychology guaranteed that his theory would not be fully accepted by his peers. It is fairly common for theorists to explain the unfavourable reception of their theories by attributing bias to their audience. What is unusual about Marx and Freud is that the bias attribution is implied by the theory itself. Thus enthusiastic reception of their theories by individuals belonging to the groups in question would disconfirm them.

Although error theories usually suggest that the unbelievers are unjustified, some error theories are more open-minded. Proponents of cognitive pluralism maintain that there is more than one legitimate set of cognitive values. Since justification can only take place *within* such a system, people with different systems might both be justified and fully informed and still disagree. Once one accepts the existence of alternative cognitive value systems, it is natural to expect disagreement. For example, Nicholas Rescher has argued that lack of philosophical agreement is inevitable due to the pluralistic nature of underlying cognitive values. He further argues that this essential disagreement will also occur with the thesis itself.[30]

3. *Statistical Versions*

Although some error theories may imply that *everyone* in a particular group will reject the theory in question, it is more common for such theories merely to imply that a certain *portion* of thinkers will fail to agree. In other words, they imply that some people will disagree with the theory, but they do not imply that any given individual will disagree. For example, in *A Discourse on Method* Descartes asserts 'that no opinion, however absurd and incredible, can be imagined, which has not been maintained by some one of the philosophers'. Since the negation of Descartes's claim is itself an opinion, his theory implies that some philosopher disagrees with it. But it does not imply that any particular philosopher will disagree.

Rather than multiply briefly described examples of statistically self-referential error theories, I wish to describe an especially interesting one in some detail. Like the 'last fool' theory, it concerns the stock-market.

Most stockbrokers maintain that you do not have to rely on a

[30] Rescher comments on this consequence in 'Philosophical Disagreement', *Review of Metaphysics* 32/1 (Sept. 1978), 250–1.

process of self-feeding speculation to make profits in the stock-market. There are other ways of making profits. Proponents of 'technical' analysis maintain that profitable predictions of stock prices can be made on the basis of historical sequences of prices. To take a rather primitive example, 'bottom fishers' look for stocks that have fallen to a stable low price. The reasoning is that the stock's past high price shows that it has the potential to return to that level. A more popular approach is 'fundamental' analysis. Here one attempts to predict the price of a stock by the economic features of the firm. So the relevant information includes facts about the performance of established products, the development of new products, corporate leadership, competition and so on. Another basis for prediction is insider information. Government and corporate officers have access to information unavailable to the investment community as a whole. Stock-market transactions made on the basis of this information are called 'insider trading'. Although insider trading is illegal, the belief that it occurs creates a lively interest in the transactions of people suspected of it. By buying what the insider buys, one can share the wealth.

All of these stock-market strategies assume that one's prospects for profit are better if one tries to predict prices than if one merely chooses stocks at random. The efficient market hypothesis (EMH) denies this assumption.[31] According to the EMH, the stock-market is over-researched. The hope of making profits through price predictions lures so many capable people into a study of the market that any information relevant to the future price of the stock is promptly reflected in the price of the stock. This makes the market an efficient user of information. Given the absence of 'wasted' information, the data available to researchers fails to determine the price of stocks in any way sufficient to generate *profitable* predictions. A profitable prediction must provide a higher expected return than a chance prediction *and* the disparity between the two must be large enough to cover transaction costs. Of course, it is easy enough to predict that nominal stock prices will rise in the long run due to inflation if nothing else. And it is easy to make conditional predictions such as 'Weapon industry stocks will rise if we go to war', 'Automobile supplier stocks will rise if automobile stocks rise', and 'The stock-market will slump if

[31] Burton G. Malkiel provides an entertaining introduction to the efficient market hypothesis in *A Random Walk Down Wall Street* (New York: Norton 1985).

interest rates on government securities rise.' But you cannot expect that such predictions will make you richer than you would have been if you had selected your stocks by throwing darts at the *Wall Street Journal.* Since advocates of the EMH maintain that no profitable predictions can be made about stock-market prices, they describe the price behaviour of stocks as random.

In describing the price behaviour as random, proponents of the EMH are not claiming that the prices lack reasons or causes. The defender of the efficient market hypothesis could be a determinist. The EMH does not preclude explanations of price behaviour, only (profitable) predictions. The explanations of price changes will either allude to changes in the perceived earning potential of the firm in question or changes in the expected return from alternative investments. However law-like these changes might be, supporters of the EMH deny that they provide a basis for profitable prediction. The asymmetry between explanation and prediction arises from the fact that past events are not influenced by our speculations.

There are three main versions of the EMH. The weak version states that stock prices are random with respect to information about historical sequences of stock prices. This version expresses scepticism about technical analysis. The semi-strong version of the EMH states that stock prices are random with respect to all public information. This variation implies scepticism about fundamental analysis as well as any eclectic combination of methods based on information available to the investment community as a whole. The strong version of the EMH relaxes the constraint on information even further, so that all kinds of information are permitted, public and private. It states that even with the benefit of all of this information, prices are random.

There is strong academic support for the semi-strong version of the EMH. Statistical studies of the portfolios managed by security brokers and analysts fail to reveal any supernormal (above-chance) profit. Indeed, random investments tend to be more profitable than researched investments because those who research tend to engage in more buying and selling, thus incurring higher transaction costs. In the light of this result, the practical advice generated by the EMH is to follow a simple buy and hold strategy. Most investors prefer stable returns; they want the variance of their expected returns to be low. Those investors who wish to lower the variance beyond that afforded by the dart-throwing technique might wish to hire an investment counsellor who can employ more sophisticated statistical techniques to reach and maintain a given level of risk. Such a counsellor might also provide useful advice about lowering one's tax burden and transaction costs. However, most security analysts do not conceive of themselves as counsellors limited to advice on risk, taxes, and transaction costs. Most consider their role to be price predictors. If the truth of the EMH were conclusively established, most security analysts would be exposed as financial quacks and their theories of investment might be classified as pseudo-scientific. Yet the theories would be an odd sort of pseudo-science. Given the prevalence of fundamental analysis, the theories seem to be applied economics. How can this sort of applied economics be pseudo-scientific and yet economics be the healthiest social science?

One might suppose that supporters of the EMH would argue that the detractors of the EMH are biased or ignorant, or at least that the EMH will come to be accepted by nearly everyone in the long run. But actually, consensus about the EMH would disconfirm the EMH.

In order for the [efficient market] hypothesis to be true, it is necessary for many investors to disbelieve it. That is, market prices will promptly and fully reflect what is knowable about the companies whose shares are traded only if investors seek superior returns, make conscientious and competent efforts to learn about the companies whose securities are traded, and analyze relevant information promptly and perceptively. If that effort were abandoned, the efficiency of the market would diminish rapidly.[32]

If everyone believed in the EMH, no one would try to predict stock prices. The stock-market would no longer be over-researched. Its subsequent transformation into an inefficient user of information would make profit through price prediction feasible. So the EMH would be false. In order for the EMH to be true, a substantial portion of the investment community must disagree with it.

Since the EMH is public information, the semi-strong version of

---

[32] James H. Lorie, Peter Dodd, and Mary Hamilton Kimpton, *The Stock Market*, 2nd edn. (Homewood, Ill. Irwin, 1985) 80.

the EMH predicts that it will be rejected by experts on the stockmarket fully familiar with the evidence supporting the EMH. Since we must assign significant weight to the opinion of dissenting experts, we should have at least a slight reservation about the truth of the EMH. To have full confidence in the EMH would be tantamount to ignoring evidence. Believers in the EMH should be somewhat unnerved by the fact that their theory says that equally knowledgeable people can very well disagree with the theory. In light of the essential nature of the disagreement, there is an essential reservation about the EMH.[33] In contemporary economics, the EMH is the most prominent theory about the stockmarket. Its status as a well supported null hypothesis makes it the theory to beat. The EMH is a substantive economic theory. It is also an example of an error theory. Thus the semi-strong version of the EMH is a substantive example of complex blindspot disagreement. As such, it is a counter-example to most of the theories about consensus discussed earlier in this chapter.

Contrary to the Cartesian two-stage model, the proponent of the EMH cannot hope to persuade dissenters by clearly and carefully retracing the line of reasoning that leads to the EMH. For the goal of total consensus could only be achieved if the EMH is false.

Nor does it seem plausible to blame the disagreement on a divergence of basic beliefs. Most supporters and opponents of the EMH do not differ on the foundations of neo-classical economics in any systematic way. One might claim that there is an attitudinal difference between the parties. For example, one might maintain that opponents of the EMH are more acquisitive, risk-loving, Neitzschean, or whatever. These attitudes might then be contrasted to the attitudes of supporters of the EMH. For example, it might be maintained that supporters of the EMH are sceptics at heart, risk-averse, retiring, etc. Even if there were a correlation in attitudes, the question of whether the divergence in attitudes causes the disagreement would remain. One would have to rule out the possibility that the disagreement about the EMH causes the attitudes, as well as the possibility of a common cause.

Contrary to Peirce, we cannot expect that progressively more

---

[33] I develop the thesis that the EMH carries an essential reservation in 'An "Essential Reservation" about the EMH', *The Journal of Portfolio Management*, Summer 1983.

enlightened thinkers will converge on the EMH. Awareness of this convergence would undercut it. Likewise, we cannot expect that the epistemic respect experts have for each other would force an idealized investment community to reach a consensus that the EMH is true. Of course, they could reach a consensus that the EMH is false. If all true theories are theories upon which total agreement can be reached (in ideal circumstances), then it follows that the EMH is false. The fact that we wish to leave the truth of the EMH as at least an open, empirical question, commits us to a rejection of the ideal consensus requirement.

Although the EMH is the best supported error theory about the stock-market, it is not the only error theory. For example, some investors profess to be 'contrarians' who select unpopular stocks because they are unpopular. They regard the received opinion about the value of stocks as inversely correlated with their true value. In effect, they make the majority an anti-expert; someone who is reliably wrong. Others choose small or 'odd-lot' traders as their anti-experts. Still others profess great confidence in the anti-expertise of physicians and dentists. Indeed, anyone who believes that there is a method of getting rich in the stock-market is committed to the unagreeableness of the method. For if everyone believed the method worked, most would use it and thereby undermine its efficacy. After all, the typical stock transaction of a fortune-seeker presupposes a disagreement about its value. In such a transaction, either the buyer believes that the stock is worth more than its price or the seller believes that the stock is worth less than its price. Otherwise, the transaction costs could not be justified. Of course agreement is possible if various external conditions obtain. For example, the fortune seeker may need cash, a tax loss or be required to divest. But in the typical speculative transaction, there is disagreement, and where there is disagreement, there must be error. In an efficient market, the attribution of error to others is rampant. Thus a theory of how to obtain supernormal profits in the stock-market is a theory which implies that many people err in their transactions.

V. PRE-COMMITMENTS AND BLINDSPOT DISAGREEMENT

Those who view consensus as a scientific ideal take themselves to be propounding a non-partisan requirement. However, this ideal would rule out error theories. What appeared to be a formal requirement is revealed to have substantive implications as to which theories are worthy of acceptance.

This phenomenon has a precedent in political theory. Voting schemes were initially construed as policy-neutral decision procedures. But as political scientists have noted, how we decide does influence what we decide. Consider the political system defined by W. A. McMullen:

> An *extreme participatory democracy* I define as an organization in which all (adult) members participate in all decision-making of the organization; and an *informed* extreme participatory democracy I define as one in which all the members have access to all the information relevant to all the decisions that the organization has to take.[34]

McMullen notes that this type of organization is widely viewed as an ideal that practical considerations place out of reach. But despite the apparent openness of such a system, it actually precludes some policies that do not seem inherently objectionable. For example, censorship of pornography would be self-defeating because citizens would have to examine the questionable material in order to be informed. Hence, whatever harm follows from exposure to pornography would have already taken place. Also, state secrets would have to be known by all citizens. Thus one traitor could turn over everything. So without the sort of universal loyalty we associate with totalitarian states, an informed extreme participatory democracy cannot have state secrets. Thus the adoption of the decision rules of this kind of democratic state would commit us to substantive policies.

Likewise, adoption of the consensus requirement would commit us to substantive theories. Perhaps all error theories will be ultimately revealed as scientifically unacceptable. However, it would be dogmatic to exclude them a priori. Their fate should be settled piecemeal, not by building their unacceptability into our concept of science.

---

[34] W. A. McMullen, 'Censorship and Participatory Democracy: A Paradox', *Analysis*, 32/6 (June 1972), 207.

Once we drop the consensus requirement, we admit the possibility of irresolvable scientific disagreement. This disagreement need not have its origins traced to a divergence in basic beliefs. For we are now tolerating the possibility of blindspot disagreement in science.

In summary, blindspot disagreement is a type of disagreement that can arise even from an initial state of complete agreement amongst ideal thinkers. This shows that irresolvable disagreement need not be basic disagreement. Since the operative blindspots can be temporary, we can also draw a distinction between irresolvable disagreement and interminable disagreement. And since blindspots can concern any topic, we can further conclude that the possibility of irresolvable disagreement is not confined to any particular field such as ethics or aesthetics. Blindspot disagreement also reveals a limit on the transmissibility of knowledge. If the issue has a blindspot structure, knowledge of the correct position on the issue can only spread so far. Thus the impossibility of obtaining a consensus about a theory does not refute it. What is also suggested is that there are epistemic borders between people and even between the temporal parts of an individual. We are not always in a position to pool our information and come to occupy the same position. Thus, there is a structural variety to rational belief.

4
Knowledge Blindspots, Anti-realism, and the Argument from Ignorance

In this chapter I continue the anti-subjectivist theme by means of knowledge blindspots instead of belief blindspots.[1] Knowledge blindspots are of direct importance to epistemology. For epistemology is the study of the scope and limits of knowledge; the epistemologist wants to provide a general description of what we can know and what we cannot know. Knowledge blindspots are directly relevant to this enterprise because they can be used to reinforce traditional limits and uncover new ones. After distinguishing between degrees of epistemological optimism in the first section, I go on to discuss the significance of personal limits. The third section concerns impersonal epistemic limits and their relevance to semantic realism, the view that truth conditions can transcend assertion conditions. In my terminology, semantic realism amounts to the claim that there are verification blindspots of the strongest sort. Since there is a straightforward proof of these blindspots, there is a simple refutation of semantic anti-realism. After defending this refutation against some recent objections, I consider another way of viewing the issue of realism. Since anti-realists deny the existence of unknowable truths, they are committed to the validity of certain modal appeals to ignorance. A statistical concept of fallacy is introduced to show why ordinary arguments from ignorance are fallacious. After illustrating appeals to *necessary* ignorance, I argue that these modal versions of *argumentum ad ignorantiam* are also fallacious. For the derivation of 'mystery numbers' enables each of the modal appeals to be paired with invalid arguments that precisely mimic the structure of their counterparts. The logical analogies block knowledge of the validity of modal appeals, thereby undermining their cogency.

---

[1] Portions of this chapter are taken from 'Vagueness, Blurriness, and Measurement', *Synthese*, forthcoming.

I. DEGREES OF EPISTEMOLOGICAL OPTIMISM

The most optimistic answer to the question 'What can be known?' is 'Everything.' We are then pictured as having complete access to all truths. The world is envisioned as epistemically open.

The most pessimistic answer to the question is 'Nothing.' This is the familiar position of universal scepticism. In effect, the universal sceptic maintains that all consistent propositions are epistemic blindspots.

Almost all thinkers have adopted positions between these two extreme positions. Virtually everyone is an epistemological pessimist about some kinds of propositions and an optimist about others. Even outside philosophy one can detect varying epistemological views about politics, religion, morality, and aesthetics.

But of course, the most sophisticated sceptical theories tend to be formulated by the people who have a professional interest in them: philosophers. Moses Maimonides does not merely appeal to widespread disagreement to support his view that positive propositions about God cannot be known. He bases his scepticism on a theory about the role of analogy in the formation of knowledge. Kant's scepticism about propositions which describe things-in-themselves is rooted in a general theory of how we make judgements. Hume's scepticism about reports of miracles is based on a principle of weighted certainties backed up by a theory of rational belief formation.

II. PERSONAL LIMITS

Epistemologists have generally been interested in impersonal epistemic limits. The principal exception to this generalization is the issue of privileged access. I can know that I have a toothache merely by feeling it. Since no one else can feel my toothache, no one else can know that I have a toothache by feeling it. They must learn about my toothache in other ways (by being told, by seeing me hold my jaw, and so on). Likewise, I cannot know that others have toothaches by feeling their toothaches. Here we have a limit about the *way* one can know a proposition. It is a personal limit because the limit depends on who you are.

But interest in this personal limit on the way one can know

certain propositions is largely derived from its apparent implications about *what* can be known about other minds. My ways of knowing about the psychological states of others are, broadly speaking, either behavioural or structural. But how can behavioural or structural statements be evidence for the ascription of psychological states to others? Behavioural and structural statements do not logically imply psychological statements. As far as logical possibility is concerned, people can painlessly writhe, complain, and scream as we nail their feet to the floor. We want to say 'That is logically possible but it is wildly improbable.' This commits us to saying that the behavioural and structural statements inductively support the psychological statements. The argument by analogy spells out this support as follows. My psychological states correlate with kinds of behaviour, so it is reasonable to assume that when structurally similar beings manifest those kinds of behaviour, they have psychological states similar to my own. Judged by the standard criteria for evaluating analogical arguments, this argument for other minds is inadequate. First, the sample is small (containing only me). Second, the conclusion is very strong. To do its job, the argument has to justify my conviction that virtually all living humans have psychological states. Since the strength of inductive arguments varies inversely with the strength of their conclusions, this strong conclusion makes the argument from analogy weak. Finally, the conclusion of the argument is unverifiable. With the failure of the argument by analogy, we appear to lack justification for the high degree of confidence with which we ascribe psychological states to others. The solipsistic scepticism suggested by our difficulties with other minds is a personal sort of scepticism. For the propositions under the scope of the scepticism would vary from person to person. Whereas statements about your psychological states would be unknowable to me, they would be knowable to you, and vice versa.

This position, concerning the asymmetric knowability of psychological statements, is epistemological solipsism. The epistemological solipsist can be viewed as a proponent of the view that psychological statements are knowledge blindspots for everyone except the person who is the topic of the statements. Since blindspots are consistent 'propositions, this sort of solipsist concedes the logical possibility of the existence of other people.

Only the *metaphysical solipsist* denies this possibility. Metaphysical solipsism can only be deduced from epistemological solipsism given optimistic epistemological principles. If we assume that all psychological truths must be available to us, then we can validly infer metaphysical solipsism from our inability to learn psychological truths about others. Since most philosophers are not strong epistemological optimists, the general view is that this assumption is false; hence there is a viable distinction between epistemological and metaphysical solipsism.

Although the question of personal limits has been chiefly raised as an issue in the philosophy of mind, the existence of such limits can be established with humdrum blindspots such as 'It is raining but Ronald Reagan does not know it.' Reagan cannot know it but we can. No special assumption need be made about Reagan to see that he is limited in a way we are not. Since such statements can be personalized to any individual, we can draw the general conclusion that every person has a unique range of knowable propositions. We can also personalize the blindspots for groups. 'It is raining but the Democrats do not know it.' In this way it can be shown that no two groups have the same epistemic range. Thus one form of cultural relativism is easily established. What one can know is partly determined by one's membership in a culture. But one's interest in this result is likely to wane once it is realized that blindspots can equally well establish relativism concerning any group, however outrageously gerrymandered. The group of purple tie-owners cannot know 'It is raining but purple tie-owners do not know it,' yet others can. But this fails to be an interesting sociological fact because it fails to reveal any theory-laden connection between a group and what it can know. The blindspot is a trivial one; it can be established with standard assumptions.

Substantive blindspots require substantive analyses. Charles Robert Richet, a Nobel Laureate for medicine, once said 'I possess every good quality, but the one that distinguishes me above all is modesty.' A theory of modesty is needed to show that this position is a blindspot.[2] Some people deny that

(1) I am modest.

[2] Julia Driver provides such a theory in 'Can Modesty be a Virtue?', (unpublished manuscript). The ensuing comments on modesty borrow points from her paper.

expresses a blindspot because they take modesty to be a matter of not bragging. I side with those who take it to be a matter of underestimating one's self-worth. A person who is far below normal in achievements and talents would not be bragging if he sincerely told others that he was somewhat below normal, yet on this account he would be immodest. One way analyses can qualify as substantive is by challenging other substantive theories. The underestimation theory of modesty does this through its incompatibility with some respected theories of virtue. Given that modesty is a virtue, it is a virtue of ignorance. So contrary to Plato, it would not be a matter of self-knowledge. The repugnance of this conclusion causes modesty to be spurned in some circles:

'My dear Watson', said he, 'I cannot agree with those who rank modesty among the virtues. To the logician all things should be seen exactly as they are, and to underestimate one's self is as much a departure from truth as to exaggerate one's own powers. When I say, therefore, that Mycroft has better powers of observation than I, you may take it that I am speaking the exact and literal truth.'[3]

Those who persist in regarding modesty as a virtue will also have to abandon Aristotle. For modesty cannot be a matter of steering a moderate course between extremes. The underestimation account also serves to exacerbate the implausibility of the unity of virtues thesis (having one virtue requires having them all). For given that modesty is a virtue and one's modesty cannot be known, the more general claim

(2) I have all the virtues.

is a blindspot. But when we further assume the unity of the virtues, every self-attribution of a virtue becomes a blindspot.

III. IMPERSONAL LIMITS AND ANTI-REALISM

In addition to providing evidence for personal limits, blindspots have been used to establish impersonal limits. The simplest and most general way that blindspots have served this purpose are as

---

[3] From Conan Doyle, 'The Greek Interpreter', *Memoirs of Sherlock Holmes* (New York: Harper & Brothers, 1894), 180.

counter-examples to 'anti-realism'. There is considerable variance in the meanings philosophers attach to 'anti-realism'. As its prefix suggests, one way of understanding the term is through an understanding of what it denies. In ontological contexts, a person who believes that universals exist is a realist about universals. A person who believes that sets exist is a realist about sets. This usage suggests that a realist about x is just someone who believes x's exist. I shall consider this formula a definition of 'ontological realism'. Two frequently discussed forms of ontological realism are scientific realism and common-sense realism. Roughly, the scientific realist believes that the entities invoked by mature science exist. This view is to be contrasted with a position like instrumentalism which regards talk of such entities as only serving the purpose of enhancing our power to predict and control nature. Likewise the common-sense realist is committed to the existence of common-sense entities; trees, chairs, people, and so forth. Of course, neither the scientific nor the common-sense realist would feel comfortable with the claim that *all* of the entities exist. However, they are confident that most of these things exist. A weaker position is that those who engage in scientific and common-sense discourse *intend* that their terms be construed as referring to the entities in question. This is a variety of *intentional* realism. Whereas the ontological realist commits himself to successful reference, the intentional realist confines himself to attempted reference. Lastly, we can speak of *semantic* realism. The semantic realist believes that 'truth conditions transcend verification conditions', that is, he holds that some statements can be true even if there is no way for them to be verified.

The semantic realist asserts that the realm of verifiable facts is smaller than the realm of truths. Michael Dummett objects: 'But even the most thoroughgoing realist must grant that we could hardly be said to grasp what it is for a statement to be true if we had no conception whatever of how it might be known to be true; there would, in such a case, be no substance to our conception of its truth condition.'[4] Unverifiable truths are insubstantial to the anti-realist because he believes that evidence and meaning are intimately connected. Quine emphasizes this connection: It is no shock to the preconceptions of old Vienna to say that epistemo-

---

[4] Michael Dummett, 'What is a Theory of Meaning (II)?', in Gareth Evans and John McDowell (eds.), *Truth and Meaning* (Oxford: Clarendon Press, 1976), 100.

logy now becomes semantics. For epistemology remains centred as always on evidence, and meaning remains centred as always on verification; and evidence is verification.'[5] Sympathy to the view that verification conditions somehow make up the meaning of a proposition breeds antipathy to the possibility of an uncheckable proposition. For it would be no genuine propositon at all. 'A "possibility" which, when specified, could in no way ever be discovered, is not a possibility, but merely an empty form of words.'[6] Prima-facie intolerance of verification blindspots is exhibited by many positions. Intuitionists maintain that the meaning of a statement is given by its assertion conditions. Since a true but unknowable proposition lacks assertion conditions, the intuitionist regards such as statements as meaningless. Pragmatism identifies truth with warranted assertibility so it excludes unknowable truths in the same fashion as intuitionism. The idealist maintains that everything is reducible to thinkers and their thoughts. Reality is wide open to inquiry. This consequence was especially cherished by the post-Kantian idealists. They wanted to move away from the picture of thinkers being trapped within their own circle of ideas; so they dumped noumenal reality, removing any 'outside' to escape to. With this removal came the need for a coherence theory of truth. Statements are true to the degree they harmoniously fit together. If a statement is unknowable, its degree of fit can be no greater than its negation's degree of fit. So the degree of fit of an unknowable statement cannot be high enough for it to qualify as true.

These anti-realist theories have a common tendency to shrink the domain of truth down to the domain of the knowable. There is a variety of motivations for identifying the true with the knowable. One major motivation is that it undermines scepticism. Sceptics are semantic realists. Sceptics assert that there are truths that cannot be known. Indeed, global sceptics maintain the unknowability of all truths. One manifestation of the sceptic's realism emerges from the classical argument from counter-possibilities. Here the sceptic produces an unknowable statement whose negation is implied by a statement we believe we know. For example, if I

---

[5] W. V. Quine, 'Epistemology Naturalized', *Ontological Relativity and Other Essays* (New York: Columbia, 1969), 89.

[6] Terry Forest, 'P-Predicates', in Avrum Stroll (ed), *Epistemology* (New York: Harper & Row, 1967) 91.

know that I am typing, then I am not dreaming that I am typing. Given that knowledge distributes over conditionals, I can only know that I am typing if I know that I am not dreaming. But how can I know that I am not dreaming? There is no test. Even if there were a testable difference between dream experiences and waking experiences, I would still have to ensure that I was not dreaming that I correctly performed the test. By adopting anti-realism one can rule out these sceptical hypotheses as meaningless. After all, the sceptical hypotheses are designed to be unknowable. In so far as the hypotheses satisfy the requirements of the sceptic's counter-possibility arguments they fail to satisfy the anti-realist's semantic requirement.

Since anti-realism rules out unverifiable statements, it is an epistemologically optimistic theory of meaning. The relevance of blindspots to anti-realism is easy to grasp because they are prima-facie counter-examples to semantic anti-realism. Since a variety of interesting philosophical positions are anti-realist, blindspots raise the possibility of a simple refutation of a large family of interesting philosophical positions.

The possibility that verificationism is vulnerable to a knock-down refutation was first broached by W. D. Hart in 1979.[7] Hart's point of departure was an article by F. B. Fitch that had lain dormant for twenty years. An anonymous referee had led Fitch to study the conflict between a group of individually plausible principles about factive sentential operators. The conflict has been generalized by J. J MacIntosh.[8] Consider an arbitrary sentential operator 'D' governed by the following principles:

*Distrib*ution Principle: $D(p \,\&\, q) \supset (Dp \,\&\, Dq)$
*Fact*ive Principle: $Dp \supset p$
*Poss*ibility Principle: $p \supset \Diamond Dp$

From these three, we can derive a 'modal collapse', that is, we can show that they imply $p \supset Dp$.

---

[7] Hart's argument appears in 'The Epistemology of Abstract Objects', *Aristotelian Society Supplementary*, 53 (1979).
[8] The generalization appears in MacIntosh 'Fitch's Factives', *Analysis*, 44/4(Oct. 1984), 153–8.

1. $D(p \& -Dp) \supset (Dp \& D-Dp)$ *Distrib*
2. $D-Dp \supset -Dp$ *Fact*
3. $-D(p \& -Dp)$ 1,2 Propositional Logic
4. $\Box -D(p \& -Dp)$ 3, Necessitation
5. $-\Diamond D(p \& -Dp)$ 4, Definition of $\Box$
6. $(p \& -Dp) \supset \Diamond D(p \& -Dp)$ 5, *Poss*
7. $p \supset Dp$ 5,6, Propositional Logic

MacIntosh points out that if 'D' is read a '*a* knows that', '*a* brought it about that', 'is conserved by God', 'is caused to obtain', we cannot accept that modal collapse at step 7. About the only sentential operator for which the collapse is acceptable is Diodorean possibility, which treats '$\Diamond$' as 'either is or will be the case'. Perhaps just for this reason, Diodorean possibility is of little interest. MacIntosh concludes that when we consider interesting factive operators, *Poss* is always the principle to reject. The argument 'points to a worthwhile moral about possibility, namely, that we must beware of agreeing too readily that things are *possible*'.[9]

Bernard Linsky further generalizes the argument by noting that the second step can be reached with a principle weaker than *Fact*.[10]

*Ref*lection Principle: $D-Dp \supset -Dp$

Linsky goes on to point out that MacIntosh's scepticism about *Poss* amounts to an argument for blindspots. The direct argument for knowledge blindspots begins with the observation that there are consistent propositions of the form '$p \& -Kp$' such as 'The number of stars is even but it is not known that the number of stars is even.' We then proceed to establish the unknowability of such propositions:

1. $K(p \& -Kp)$ Assumption
2. $Kp \& K-Kp$ 1, *Distrib*
3. $Kp \& -Kp$ 2, *Fact*
4. $-K(p \& -Kp)$ 1,3 Propositional Logic
5. $\Box -K(p \& -Kp)$ 4, Necessitation

---

[9] Ibid., 157.
[10] Linsky makes the point in 'Factives, Blindspots and Some Paradoxes', *Analysis*, 46/1 (Jan. 1986), 10–15.

Hart's attack on verificationism proceeds by having us dwell on the existence of unknowable truths while evaluating the following argument:

(A) All true statements are meaningful statements.
(B) All meaningful statements are verifiable statements.
(C) <u>All verifiable statements are knowable statements.</u>
(D) All true statements are knowable statements.

According to Hart, verificationists are committed to all three premises of the argument, so they are committed to (D). Yet Fitch's original study provides counter-examples to (D). Since the essence of verificationism, (B), is the most controversial premise in the valid argument, Hart concludes that it should be rejected. Thus verificationism is refuted by knowledge blindspots.

R. G. Swinburne has objected that Hart has only succeeded in refuting a very strong form of verificationism. Some verificationists could escape refutation by maintaining that 'verify' is not a factive. In other words, they could maintain that falsehoods could be verified. Under this construal, verification is only a matter of acquiring justification. Since people can have false beliefs that are none the less justified, this nonfactive interpretation of 'verify' would enable the verificationist to deny (C).

The relevance of Linsky's generalization can be appreciated by considering J. L. Mackie's reply to Swinburne.[11] Mackie maintains that even modest forms of verificationism are susceptible to refutation because we can switch to other sorts of blindspots. Reinterpret K as 'It is justifiably believed at t_1 that . . . '. One might expect that although this operator distributes over &, the argument will fail at step 3 because the new K is not truth entailing. However step 3 still goes through because if it is justifiably believed that p is not justifiably believed, p is indeed not justifiably believed. In Linsky's language, *Ref* holds for the new operator. One can block step 3 by instead interpreting K as 'It is justifiably believed at some time that . . . '. For it could be justifiably believed at t_1 that 'p is never justifiably believed', but justifiably believed at t_2 that 'p is justifiably believed'.

This block is of only temporary comfort to the verificationist,

[11] Mackie's reply appears in 'Truth and Knowability', *Analysis*, 40/2 (Mar. 1980), 90–2.

however. For Mackie points out that the weakened operator runs foul of 'p but it is never verified that p'. There is no time at which this modified statement can be verified. Verification of a conjunction requires simultaneous verification of each conjunct. If the statement were verified, there would have to be a time at which both p and 'p is never verified' receive verification. But this is impossible even though we are interpreting the operator non-factively. So by slightly deviating from the Fitch recipe, Mackie is able to get the desired result. Since semantic anti-realism implies at least the weak sorts of verificationism that Mackie criticizes, the Hart attack is ultimately fatal to anti-realism.

Nevertheless, the decisiveness of Hart's attack has been questioned. I know of four objections to the blindspot refutation of semantic anti-realism. The first sort of objection appeals to the utility of verificationism in explaining linguistic behaviour. For example, Dorothy Edgington begins her critique of the argument by asking

Could there be truths which are, in principle, inaccessible to us? Anyone but an extreme metaphysical realist will answer 'No'. For the items to which truth can be ascribed are not *in rerum natura*. They are the products of human thought—linguistic items, or what is conveyed by linguistic items, or beliefs. They involve the application of concepts, which requires that there be criteria for their application, and beings who can apply them.[12]

The second objection is that the argument is too simple to be sound. (No pain, no gain?) This initially struck me as a rather queer transvaluation of argumentative standards. After all, wasn't simplicity supposed to be a virtue? But rather than suppose that the critics are engaged in some sort of Black Mass of analytic philosophy, I decided that they must be making an appeal to tradition. They must be saying that it is unlikely that our predecessors could have missed such a simple objection if it were a good objection. But this interpretation also seems uncharitable. For this would force the critics to say that our ancestors enjoyed some epistemic advantage over us. For only that will explain why the critics cannot point out the flaw that our progenitors must have found so obvious as to be unworthy of comment. Then I

---

[12] Dorothy Edgington, 'The Paradox of Knowability', *Mind*, 94/376 (Oct. 1985), 557.

considered the possibility that they were advancing some statistical argument about the high failure rates of simple arguments in philosophy. But this too seemed an improbable attribution. For who would claim that 'simple argument' identifies a class of arguments with an abnormally high proportion of bum inferences? This leaves me at a loss to specify the details of the simplicity objection. So it is best that I pass on to a third objection raised by T. Williamson.

According to Williamson, 'the argument fails because it uses principles of logic that anti-realists need not — should not — accept.'[13] In particular, anti-realists should abide by intuitionist logic. According to Williamson, this will block the refutation. For when the argument is fully fleshed out, we will find that it relies on principles the intuitionist rejects, such as double-negation.

Dorothy Edgington, on the other hand, believes that the verificationist's best prospects lie in a rather tortuous detour from familiar modal logics.[14] The point of the detour is to summon up a new notion of actuality that we can use to amend the old principle. Rather than the old $p \square\!\!\!\rightarrow \Diamond Kp$, we are to embrace

$$Ap \square\!\!\!\rightarrow \Diamond KAp.$$

'A' is an actuality operator that is not equivalent to the ordinary language 'actually'. With its help, Edgington believes she can 'justify the claim that in certain cases, while it is not possible to know that p, it is possible to know that actually p'.[15] She maintains that this distinction can be drawn once a string of background assumptions are made. First, we are to agree with David Lewis that 'actual' is an indexical, but we are to disagree with his claim that individuals are world-bound. Second, we assume that verificationists can accommodate knowledge of counterfactual situations. This includes those that are 'essentially counterfactual' such as 'If I had not observed the supernova, no one would have known that it took place'. Third, '$\Diamond$' is to be interpreted in terms of 'possibilities' rather than possible worlds.

---

[13] Williamson advances this criticism in 'Intuitionism Disproved?', *Analysis*, 42/4 (Oct. 1982) 203–7.

[14] George Schlesinger outlines a response similar to Edgington's in the last chapter of *The Range of Epistemic Logic* (Aberdeen: Aberdeen University Press, 1985).

[15] Dorothy Edgington, 'The Paradox of Knowability', *Mind*, 94/376 (Oct. 1985), 563.

My own difficulties in detecting a difference between possibly knowing that p and possibly knowing that actually p may be due to an insufficient grasp of Edgington's technical sense of 'actual'. If her assumptions are jointly coherent, perhaps I could be educated and come to agree with her formula. However, Edgington does not make it clear how this would constitute a conversion to verificationism. Although there is a syntactic resemblance between the old $p \:\Box\!\!\rightarrow\: \Diamond Kp$ and the new $Ap \:\Box\!\!\rightarrow\: \Diamond KAp$, there has been a semantic upheaval in the background that jeopardizes the claim that the new doctrine is just a slight modification of the old. In any case, one wonders why all the changes are necessary. Edgington motivates them by presenting the blindspot refutation of verificationism as a paradox. In order for there to be a paradox there must be a conflict between beliefs that are quite dear to us. However, the only reason Edgington gives for believing that all truths are accessible is its utility in explaining language and thought. But since our explanations are pretty widely conceded to be poor ones, this does little to show why verificationism should be antecedently preferable to its negation. To motivate the changes by describing the stimulus as a paradox just begs the question against the semantic realist.

Williamson's claim that the argument is invalid in intuitionistic logic may be correct. We certainly cannot run the reasoning through in the familiar way. But this does not prove that there is no alternative path. There is (almost) never any way to formally prove invalidity. But even if Williamson is right, the argument remains significant. For if it really shows that anti-realists must be intuitionists, it shows that anti-realists must adopt a logic that almost no one accepts. The intuitionist is only of philosophical interest in the same way that the solipsist, the anarchist, and the pacifist are of philosophical interest. Almost no one considers it a live option.

IV. VARIATIONS OF THE ARGUMENT FROM IGNORANCE

The heartier one's semantic realism, the more apt one is to view anti-realism as a product of *argumentum ad ignorantiam*. For the anti-realist draws conclusions about truth values from premises about our ignorance of those truth values. If it could be shown that all arguments from ignorance were fallacious, the anti-realist could be easily refuted. However, as with many kinds of argument that are described as fallacious, we encounter interesting difficulties in pinpointing just what is wrong with them.

A. *The Simple Form*

The term *argumentum ad ignorantiam* appears to have been coined by Locke. Although discussion of the fallacy can be traced as far back as Spinoza's *Ethics*, neither Aristotle nor Bacon's *Novum Organon* mentions it.[16] The fallacy is standard fare in contemporary logic textbooks. Illustrations of the fallacy are almost always intended to fit the following simple forms (reading 'Kp' as 'It is known that p' or 'There is evidence that p');

$$\text{Simple Forms:} \quad (A1) \ \frac{-Kp}{-p} \qquad (A2) \ \frac{-K-p}{p}$$

Irving Copi claims that the fallacy of *argumentum ad ignorantiam* frequently occurs in contexts in which there is no clear-cut evidence either way and cites parapsychology as an example. Arguments from ignorance concerning God, UFOs, and the dangers of disease, drugs and departures from the status quo are popular examples amongst other writers. It is taken to be fallacious to conclude that God does not exist from the absence of proof that God exists. This illustrates (A1). One of Copi's exercise examples provides an illustration of (A2):

On the Senate floor in 1950, Joe McCarthy announced that he had penetrated 'Truman's iron curtain of secrecy.' He had 81 case histories of persons whom he considered to be Communists in the State Department. Of Case 40, he said, 'I do not have much information on this except the general statement of the agency that there is nothing in the files to disprove his Communist connections.'[17]

John Woods and Douglas Walton have suggested that there are three subfallacies that lead people to overlook the invalidity of *argumentum ad ignorantiam*.[18] First, we may fail to distinguish

---

[16] Richard Robinson briefly discusses these historical points in 'Arguing from Ignorance', *Philosophical Quarterly*, 21/83 (Apr. 1971), 108.

[17] Richard H. Rovere, *Senator Joe McCarthy* (New York: Harcourt, Brace, 1959).

[18] Woods and Walton present their analysis in 'The Fallacy of "Ad Ignorantiam"', *Dialectia*, 32/2 87–99.

between unconfirmed and disconfirmed hypotheses.[19] Second, there may be a syntactic confusion between 'K$-p$ therefore $-p$' and '$-$Kp therefore $-p$', and between 'K$--p$ therefore p' and '$-$K$-p$ therefore $-p$'. Lastly, there may be dialectical misdeed where the onus of proof is shifted illegitimately. Although the onus of proof falls on the person who asserts p, he may succeed in winning acceptance of p by demanding evidence against it and construing the lack of counter-evidence as warranting the presumption that p.

Fallacy attribution is a problematic affair. It should first be noted that some examples of *argumentum ad ignorantiam* are valid arguments. Logic textbooks standardly illustrate *argumentum ad ignorantiam* with mathematical examples:

No one has ever proved Goldbach's conjecture.
Goldbach's conjecture is false.

No one has ever disproved Goldbach's conjecture.
Goldbach's conjecture is true.

Since one of these two arguments has a necessarily true conclusion, one of them is valid. But this does not make us withdraw the charge of fallacy. For the arguer's belief that the argument is valid would be right for the wrong reason. In the light of this example, we might retreat to the position that the fallacy is not a matter of mistaking an invalid argument for a valid one, but rather a matter of unjustifiably believing that the argument is valid.

However, this position may still be too strong. For perhaps the arguer is being 'gettiered'. Suppose someone believes the following argument is valid by the KK principle (if you know then you know that you know):

No one knows that he knows that Fermat's last theorem is true.
No one knows that Fermat's last theorem is true.

---

[19] George Schedler takes the equivocation between unconfirmed and disconfirmed to be crucial to the arguments from ignorance. Upon this basis he argues that *argumentum ad ignorantiam* is a fallacy of equivocation rather than a fallacy of relevance in 'The Argument from Ignorance', *International Logic Review*, 11/1 (June 1980), 66–71.

This argument has the form '$-KKp$ therefore $-Kp$' (which conforms to (A1)). Since the application of the KK principle does not require more finely grained interpretation than this, it is a specialized appeal to ignorance. Since KK has only recently fallen out of favour amongst philosophers, it is not far-fetched to suppose that our arguer's belief in KK is justified but false. Given that Fermat's theorem is false, the conclusion of his argument is necessarily true. Since the arguer's reasons for believing that the argument is valid did not include the fact that the conclusion is a necessary truth, he would have justified true belief that the argument is valid without having knowledge of its validity. Since his acceptance of the validity of the argument is caused by the error of believing that KK validates it, his reasoning would count as fallacious. So in order to attribute the fallacy of *argumentum ad ignorantiam*, we must make psychological inferences about how the arguer arrived at the belief that his argument is valid. Of course this bit of psychology must be preceded by a prior psychological judgement as to whether the arguer believes the argument to be deductive or inductive.

Since there is considerable slack in the attribution of beliefs, our evidence that someone has committed a fallacy tends to be soft. Furthermore, there are methodological considerations that militate against attributions of logical errors. For virtually everyone recognizes a principle of charity is needed in order to make sense of what a person says. By requiring us to minimize attributions of irrationality, the principle creates a presumption against fallacy attribution. For example, we should not dismiss the following appeal to ignorance as invalid.

> It is not known that everything is known.
>
> It is false that everything is known.

Rather than translating the argument as '$-Kp$ therefore $-p$', we should use the more detailed '$-K(p)Kp$ therefore $-(p)Kp$' to reveal that it is valid via quantifier negation and existential generalization. Similar care is in order for arguments such as

> I do not know that it is common knowledge that Nancy Reagan smokes.
>
> It is not common knowledge that Nancy Reagan smokes.

Under some analyses of 'common knowledge', common knowledge that p requires everyone (in the relevant group) to know that p is common knowledge. Whereas these analyses would validate the inference, rival analyses would not. Our inability to find a validating translation may be due to a deficit of ingenuity rather than the argument's invalidity. Consider

> Dan does not know he is in pain.
> Dan is not in pain.

Is our inability to find a validating translation of this argument due to its invalidity or due to our ignorance about the logical structure of 'pain'? Perhaps an analysis of 'pain' will one day be proposed which validates this argument in the same way that analysis of 'omniscience' validates 'No one knows that someone is omniscient, so no one is omniscient'.

Should the quest for a validating interpretation appear clearly unpromising, the principle of charity encourages us to treat the argument as inductive rather than deductive. For example, some philosophers are inclined to infer the non-existence of F s from the absence of evidence for Fs.[20] There is no hope of finding a validating interpretation for 'There is no evidence that there are planets made of golf balls, therefore, there are none.' So it should not be treated as a deductive argument.

Some textbook writers concede that there can be good appeals to ignorance. For example, Copi qualifies his condemnation of *argumentum ad ignorantiam* as follows:

In some circumstances it can safely be assumed that if a certain event had occurred, evidence of it could be discovered by qualified investigators. In such circumstances it is perfectly reasonable to take the absence of proof of its occurrence as positive proof of its nonoccurrence. Of course, the proof here is not based on ignorance but on our knowledge that if it had occurred it would be known. For example, if a serious security investigation fails to unearth any evidence that Mr X is a foreign agent, it would be wrong to conclude that their research has left us ignorant.[21]

---

[20] Defenders of this inference include Norwood Russell Hanson in the title essay of Stephen Toulmin and Harry Woolf (eds.), *What I Do Not Believe and Other Essays* (Dordrecht 1972), Michael Scriven in *Primary Philosophy*, (New York 1966), 103, and most recently Robert McLaughlin in 'Necessary Agnosticism?', *Analysis* 44/4 (Oct. 1984), 198–202.

[21] Irving Copi, *Introduction to Logic*, 6th edn. (New York: Macmillan, 1982), 102.

Generalizing from this concession, it might be maintained that appeals to ignorance are justified in circumstances where one's evidence supports the conditional 'If p, then it would be known that p.' Indeed, those with a distaste for inductive logic might maintain that such circumstances prompt us to interpret the appeal to ignorance as an enthymatic *modus tollens*. According to this analysis, arguments from ignorance tend to be fallacious because this background conditional tends to go unsupported by the arguer's evidence. In advancing an argument from ignorance, one assumes a burden of proof. One's evidence must also support the existence of an epistemic link.

This analysis has the virtue of encouraging us to check whether the arguer has evidence for the conditional 'If p, then it would be known that p.' Consider recent allegations of discrimination against victims of acquired immune deficiency syndrome (AIDS). People are worried that casual contact with AIDS victims is dangerous. The AIDS virus has been detected in bodily fluids such as tear drops and saliva, so some officials have prevented AIDS children from attending school. Critics complain that the exclusion is unjustified because there is no scientific evidence that AIDS can be contracted through casual contact. Since these critics want to show that the fear of contracting AIDS through casual contact is unfounded, they should be interpreted as advancing an argument from ignorance:

1. There is no scientific evidence that AIDS can be contracted through casual contact.
2. No one can contract AIDS through casual contact.

Rather than dismissing the argument out of hand, the missing epistemic link analysis renders a qualified verdict. That is, the argument is fallacious *unless* the arguer is also in a position to assert 'If AIDS can be contracted through casual contact, then there would be scientific evidence that it can.' To the credit of CNN news, one AIDS researcher was allotted almost a full minute to defend this conditional. He first noted that researchers have interviewed a large number of AIDS victims. Most of these victims have had casual contact with many people (which includes saliva transmission through kissing and sharing marijuana cigarettes). So if AIDS can be contracted through casual contact, some of those interviewed should have had only casual contact with an AIDS victim. This would have provided scientific evidence that AIDS can be contracted through casual contact. Yet all of those interviewed had more than casual contact with an AIDS victim. So we are invited to conclude that the best explanation of the non-appearance of this evidence is the falsity of the hypothesis that AIDS can be contracted by casual contact. Although one might raise objections to the researcher's one minute defence of the conditional, he is not vulnerable to the charge of a fallacious *argumentum ad ignorantiam*. Even if it should turn out that the conditional is false, the researcher was in a position to justifiably assert it.

The burden of proof requirement suggests that whether an argument from ignorance is fallacious is relative to the arguer. Consider a standard example of *argumentum ad ignorantiam*; 'There is no evidence for God's existence, so God does not exist.' When presented by theologically naïve people, the argument is fallacious. They cannot give a good defence of the conditional 'If God exists, there would be evidence for God's existence.' However, familiarity with theology could put one in a position to assert the conditional. Recall that Bertrand Russell's atheism sometimes provoked the question of what he would say were he to confront God in the hereafter. Russell's response was that he would ask God why He made his existence such a mystery. An explanation alluding to the importance of faith would be unpersuasive to Russell since he saw no point in rewarding irrationality. For Russell, 'If God exists, His existence would be known' was probable, constituting the epistemic link necessary for a good argument from ignorance. Copi's parapsychology examples illustrate the same sort of relativity. Those unfamiliar with parapsychology are not in a position to infer the absence of paranormal phenomena from the absence of positive evidence. However, those who learn that over fifty years of enthusiastic parapsychological research has failed to produce any serious evidence of paranormal phenomena are in a position to make the inference. One might object that this is not *disproof* of the paranormal. But this objection rests on an equivocation between the relative and absolute senses of 'disproof'. In the relative sense, 'disproof' amounts to evidence meriting disbelief. In this sense, it is possible for one body of evidence to be greater disproof than another. In the absolute sense, 'disproof' requires absolute certainty and so does not permit the possibility of one claim being more disproved than another. The sense of 'disproof' relevant to discussions of the argument from ignorance is the relative sense.

Leaving the above analysis as it stands would invite the charge of triviality. After all, confrontation with any ostensibly invalid argument should arouse curiosity about whether it is an enthymeme. The virtues of the above analysis are just the virtues of general policy of charitable interpretation. Whenever someone argues 'not-p therefore not–q', we should check whether his evidence also supports 'If q then p.'

If the analysis were understood as a claim that all appeals to ignorance are enthymematic *modus tollens* arguments, it would no longer be trivial. It would be false. We are only entitled to consider something to be an enthymeme if we are entitled to view it as the abbreviated expression of an intended argument. We are not normally entitled to view appeals to ignorance this way. First of all, if the argument is an enthymeme, it could be an enthymeme of another form. This point can be illustrated by an appeal to ignorance made by diplomats in Libya. Prior to the American raid on Libya, Khadafy claimed that he had moved a thousand foreigners into surrounding military bases. Diplomats claimed that this was unlikely because they lacked any evidence for it. If this was an enthymeme, only further facts about the circumstances attending the diplomat's utterance will disambiguate between the alternatives. For example, the facts may lead us to spurn the simple *modus tollens* construal in favour of an argument with richer structure:

1. If the foreigners were moved, most would have realized they had a serious problem with the Libyan government.
2. Most foreigners try to inform their embassies when they realize they have a serious problem with their host government.
3. The Libyan government would lack either the motive or the ability to thwart all the ensuing attempts to inform the diplomats.
4. The diplomats have no evidence of the movement of foreigners.
5. There was no movement of foreigners.

Knowledge Blindspots

The second objection to viewing appeals to ignorance as *modus tollens* enthymemes is that it is unnecessary. The mere fact that the arguer uses '−Kp' to support '−p' commits him to holding that '−Kp' is reason for inferring '−p'. Any evidence relevant to 'If p then Kp' is already evidence relevant to the propriety of inferring '−p' from '−Kp'. Introduction of the conditional merely exchanges one topic for an evidentially equivalent topic. So nothing is gained by claiming that there is a hidden conditional premiss. And something is lost: simplicity.

One might nevertheless insist that good appeals to ignorance must be regarded as enthymemes of some sort or other. For unless they are enthymemes, we cannot distinguish the good from the bad arguments by form alone.

This objection rests on a misconceived requirement. Although a fallacy is a formal flaw of an argument, it does not follow that every instance of that form must be a bad argument. It is enough that the population of instances contain an abnormally large percentage of bad argument tokens. Compare fallacies with other malfunctioning tools. Leaky buckets, bent nails, and warped cutting boards do not *invariably* yield defective results. Sometimes the results are just fine. Indeed, in special environments they systematically perform as well as their perfectly operational counterparts. If the leaky bucket is taken to Maine to collect rocks, we can predict that it will do just fine. Likewise, a fallacious argument form will have some instances that are good arguments. Knowing that an argument token instantiates a fallacious argument form does not permit us to deduce with one hundred per cent certainty that the token is bad. Rather, we have to make an inductive inference. A fallacy is an argument type that has an abnormally large percentage of bad instances. So information that a token instantiates a fallacious type is of interest to the logician in the same way that information that a patient has high blood pressure is of interest to a physician. The information serves as a premiss in a statistical syllogism. As is typical of inductive reasoning, adding extra premisses affects the strength of the argument. Learning that an instance of *argumentum ad ignorantiam* was propounded by a logician, or appeared in a scientific journal, or concerned the speaker's own pain, will enhance the strength of the argument. Learning that the argument was propounded by a politician, or appeared in an advertisement, or concerned a crime, will weaken the argument. Thus information going beyond the form of the argument is incorporated when knowledge of fallacies is applied.

There are two ways to support statistical claims about the frequency of a property within a population. First, one can directly sample the population. Second, one can appeal to other regularities that invite the conclusion that the property will have the frequency in question. Best is to do both. The analyses of fallacies found in textbooks and journal articles concentrate on evidence of the second sort. They support the view that a particular error is common in a variety of ways. Two of the most popular are appeals to misleading similarities between fallacious and non-fallacious argument forms, and appeals to error paths, by which the commission of more basic errors is shown to lead to the fallacy in question. Recall that Woods and Walton point out the resemblance between 'K$-p$ therefore $-p$' and '$-$Kp therefore $-p$' and emphasize that overlooking the difference between disconfirmation and lack of confirmation makes appeal to ignorance a tempting inference.

Since Woods and Walton assume that appeals to ignorance are intended to be deductive arguments, they criticize them for failing to satisfy a necessary condition of a good (deductive) argument: validity. However, some instances of *argumentum ad ignorantiam* satisfy this condition. More disturbing is the fact that many instances of *argumentum ad ignorantiam* cannot be charitably interpreted as deductive arguments. Indeed, most appear to be attempts at inference to the best explanation. After all, the falsity of 'p' provides a simple explanation of our lack of evidence for its truth. The reasoning is from effect to cause. Falsity can be inferred from ignorance in the same way as fire can be inferred from smoke. Of course, the hypothesis may score low on other criteria for a good explanation. And in some types of cases, there are even simpler explanations. If there just is no flow of information toward me or if it is blocked (as in censorship), the simpler explanation is an appeal to these facts about my epistemic access.

Inference to the best explanation also underlies the appeal of other fallacies. *Ad populum* inferences offer us a common cause explanation of widespread belief in p. Each belief is being caused by the state of affairs described by p. *Post hoc ergo propter hoc* arguments have the form:

1. Events of type A always come before events of type B.
2. Events of type A cause events of type B.

As a limiting case, the types can have just one token. The premiss is then equivalent to the description of a particular event preceding another particular event. As the types come to encompass large numbers of tokens, the inference becomes more attractive. For the hypothesis 'A causes B' will account for the strong regularity in a straightforward fashion. Although the coincidence explanation is a live option when the number of tokens is small, its prospects fade as the number increase. However, common-cause explanations do not drop out of the competition. People tend to overlook these rivals. This leads them to propound *post hoc* arguments on the basis of evidence that can be equally well explained by other hypotheses. Likewise, *ad populum* arguments tend to be deployed when the pervasiveness of the belief can be explained by alternate hypotheses which do not imply that the beliefs are *independent* effects of a single cause.

Appeals to ignorance also have a tendency to falter because of competition from rivals. In claiming that the $-p$ state of affairs is responsible for our ignorance of p, we are postulating a causal chain featuring $-p$ as a remote cause. This explanation can be intercepted by finding an intermediate cause in this chain that is compatible with p and compatible with $-p$. Absence of arson causes absence of evidence of arson. However, the intensity of the fire can also cause absence of evidence by destroying traces. Sirius's having less than ten planets will prevent us from obtaining evidence that it has ten. But so will the faintness of the light cast from that portion of the universe. Absence of blackmail causes absence of evidence of blackmail; but only through the absence of blackmail complaints which can also arise from victims not wishing to risk prosecution and disgrace. Rival explanations will rest content with an intermediate cause that has an ambiguous proximate cause. Causal explanation is problematic for mathematical knowledge because mathematical propositions are not made true by any contingent state of affairs. However, the impossibility of a task can still be a cause of its non-performance. If 'There are infinitely many twin primes' is false, mathematicians will be unable to prove it true, which will leave them in ignorance about its truth value. But inability to prove the hypothesis may be due to insufficient ingenuity. So the explantory chain is once again interrupted.

B. *The Falsity Form*

The possibility that our ignorance about a mathematical proposition is due to insufficient ingenuity can be eliminated by substituting a stronger premiss. For if the premiss states that it is *necessarily* unknown that p, insufficient ingenuity cannot explain our ignorance. But the necessary falsehood of p straightforwardly explains it.

$$\text{Falsity Form:} \quad \frac{\Box - Kp}{\Box - p}$$

The conclusion implies the premiss, so the explanatory connection could hardly be tighter. Furthermore, if the conclusion is true, the argument is trivially valid. For the conclusion would be a necessary truth, and any argument whose conclusion cannot be false cannot be invalid. However, this still leaves us short of the verdict that all instances of the form are valid.

The question of validity is more crucial to modal appeals to ignorance than to their simpler brethren. An extensional appeal to ignorance can be a good argument even if it is invalid. For it may be good according to the standards appropriate to explanatory inferences. However, an arguer can only believe that his modal appeal to ignorance scores well on non-deductive criteria if he believes that it is also valid. For the arguer has to believe the conclusion is true. But if the conclusion is true, the argument is valid. Hence, those who make modal appeals to ignorance are committed to defending their validity.

This defence would be straightforward if it could be shown that there are no invalid instances of the argument form. Sympathy to the view that all instances of the form are valid can be expected from those who believe that all truths are knowable. Consider James B. Pratt's criticism of epiphenomenalism. Since the epiphenomenalist believes that his psychological states are only effects and never causes, he denies that one thought can cause another. Thus consciousness of logical relations is never responsible for one thought leading to another. Therefore, the epiphenomenalist cannot claim that his beliefs are based on logic. But this makes epiphenomenalism unknowable: 'The hopeless contradiction of such a position is obvious. With one breath the [epiphenomenalist] asserts that his doctrine is logically demonstrable and that there is no such thing as logical demonstration. As Bradley has put it, no theory can be true which is inconsistent with the possibility of knowing it to be true.'[22] Those writing under the influence of idealism exhibit their allegience to the enriched version of the appeal to ignorance by their quick transition from unknowability to self-contradictoriness. McTaggart argues, 'If materialism is true, all our thoughts are produced by purely material antecedents. These are quite blind, and are just as likely to produce falsehood as truth. We thus have no reason for believing any of our conclusions—including the truth of materialism, which is therefore a self-contradictory hypothesis.'[23] If the falsity form of the modal appeal to ignorance is valid, all consistent propositions are knowable—there are no knowledge blindspots. It must be conceded to the idealists that some propositions imply their own knowability. So there are instances of the form that are non-trivially valid.

1. Necessarily, no one knows that there is an omniscient being.
2. Necessarily, there is no omniscient being.

Nevertheless, there are also invalid instances.

1. Necessarily, no one knows that nothing is known.
2. Necessarily, something is known.

Although the premiss is true, the conclusion is false. Had the universe been devoid of knowers, nothing would have been known. The same point can be made with 'Everyone is modest' and Russell's hypothesis that the universe popped into existence

---

[22] James B. Pratt, *Matter and Spirit* (New York: MacMillan, 1922) 21.
[23] J. E. McTaggart, *Philosophical Studies* (London: Longman, Green and Co.,1934) 193.

five minutes ago complete with fossil records, 'memories' and other 'traces'. Any universal knowledge blindspot suffices to show that the falsity form of the argument from ignorance has invalid instances.

The finitude of reliable measurement suggests particularly compelling examples. Consider the claim that there are perfect cubes. A cube must have flat surfaces. A surface is flat only if it has no bumps, curves, or irregularities. Since what counts as a bump, curve, or irregularity is context dependent, 'flat' is also context dependent. Practical purposes are usually best served by not allowing small deviations to defeat the claim that a surface is flat. However, theoretical purposes are often served by allowing any deviation to defeat the claim. Teachers of solid geometry signal this standard for flatness with adjectives such as 'absolutely' and 'ideally'. According to this standard, almost all of the objects that we normally consider flat are not really flat. They may look flat but microscopic examination will almost always reveal a tiny bump or dent. If one microscope fails to reveal a bump, more powerful instruments would almost surely show that the surface is not truly flat. Should even the most powerful of our microscopes fail to defeat the surface's claim to flatness, we would not have thereby proved that it is indeed flat. However minute our inspections, there is always the possibility that a very tiny bump has gone undetected. If there are any absolutely flat surfaces, we cannot know that they are absolutely flat. Since a perfect cube is composed of perfectly flat sides, it follows that we cannot recognize perfect cubes. If there are any, we cannot know it. A census of all ostensible cubes might enable us to conclusively falsify 'There are perfect cubes in the universe' but the claim cannot be conclusively verified. Thus it is a knowledge blindspot. Since 'Are there perfect cubes?' is a question of physics, it is particularly inappropriate to infer a negative answer from the impossibility of knowing that an affirmative answer is true.

Someone who conceded that the falsity form has invalid instances could nevertheless maintain his argument was a valid instance. His concession would only deprive him of one way of establishing the argument's validity. However, his alternatives are few. In practice, the validity of the form has been assumed. Piecemeal defences aren't found.

C. *The Gappy Form*

The falsity form of the argument from ignorance is related to the gappy form:

Gappy form: $\underline{\Box -Kp \ \& \ \Box -K-p}$
$\Box(p$ lacks a truth value$)$

Here we are licensed to infer a truth-value gap from the symmetric unknowability of a proposition. The gappy form of argument was a favourite of the logical positivists. They attempted to forge an epistemic link by means of the verificationist criterion of meaning. By demanding that meaningful statements be either analytic or verifiable, the logical positivists could use the irresolvability of issues as grounds for declaring them non-issues. Thus the problem was made the solution. What was bothersome about a question like 'Did the universe double in size last night?' was its unanswerability. But with the verificationist criterion of meaning this unanswerability exposed the issue as a pseudo-question. In addition to its efficiency in disposing of metaphysical, moral, and aesthetic problems, the verificationist criterion of meaning was an excellent weapon against scepticism. Most sceptical arguments appeal to non-analytic, unverifiable counter-possibilities. For example, if I claim to know that I walked into my office an hour ago, the sceptic is apt to raise the possibility that the universe sprang into existence five minutes ago complete with fossil records, 'memories', and so forth. I can produce no evidence which will show that this hypothesis is false. The sceptical counter-possibilities are designed to be impossible to rule out. But when armed with the verificationist criterion of meaningfulness, I can use this very feature to rule them out–as meaningless rather than false.

Even those who are not attracted to anti-realism as a response to scepticism are sometimes attracted to the gappy form of the argument from ignorance. Consider the Heisenberg uncertainty principle: one cannot know the exact position and the velocity of a subatomic particle. Even philosophers with realist leanings will often accept the physicist's inference that therefore there is no fact of the matter as to what is an electron's position *and* velocity. The unknowability of conditionals such as 'If I had flipped this coin one minute ago, it would have landed heads' is sometimes used as grounds for denying it a truth value. And when the issue of vagueness comes up, many philosophers are inclined to use the fact that it is impossible to check the truth value of a borderline proposition to conclude that 'there is no fact of the matter'. This is also a popular conclusion in the case of fictional statements such as 'Tom Sawyer has type O blood.'

The popularity of the gappy form of the appeal to ignorance has survived despite the current philosophical consensus that an adequate verification criterion cannot be formulated. Despite the ingenuity of the logical positivists, every formulation of the criterion was revealed to be either too narrow or too broad. The anti-realist's inability to specify their verification requirement should raise doubts about how effectively it can be deployed.

Further doubts about this form of argument can be deferred until section V. For the gappy form of the argument from ignorance is a special case of an argument from ignorance that enjoys even wider appeal.

D. *The Unbreakable Tie Form*

The previous variations of the argument from ignorance only concern one or two propositions. So they only apply to large ranges of alternatives when applied repeatedly. The following variation deals with these ranges of alternatives directly.

> Unbreakable Tie Form: $(p) \Box - Kp$
> $\Box(p)$ p is not true
> (where p ranges over some designated class of propositions)

Whereas the previous two arguments had conclusions that were specific about whether we should infer falsity or a truth-value gap, the above had been left unspecific for the sake of generality. We can consider the previous two appeals to be special cases of the above form. The domain of discourse of the falsity form of the modal appeal to ignorance is a single proposition which we conclude to be false. The domain of discourse of the gappy form is a proposition and its negation which we conclude to lack truth values. Although unbreakable tie arguments tend to be more persuasive, they only differ in the scale and structure of their range of alternatives.

Most unbreakable tie arguments have falsity and gappy variations, so we could have classified them as having a complex falsity form or a complex gappy form. Controversy about the reduction of numbers to sets provides a nice illustration. Whether one follows von Neumann in stipulating that $2 = \{0\} \cup \{\{0\}\}$ or one follows Zermelo in stipulating that $2 = \{\{0\}\}$ is generally considered irrelevant to the reduction of number theory. Both are equally adequate for the generation of important mathematical results. Indeed, there are infinitely many adequate definitions. Aside from stylistic advantages, they only diverge in the way they answer peculiar questions such as 'Is 3 a member of 5? But since these questions are 'don't cares', the divergence does not seem to undermine the egalitarianism in discernible mathematical virtues of the competing definitions of numbers. Thus there is no objective basis for preferring one definition over its competitors. Paul Benacerraf regards this as an embarrassment of riches.

> I have argued that at most one of the infinitely many different accounts satisfying our conditions can be correct, on the grounds that they are not even extensionally equivalent, and therefore at least all but one, and possibly all, contain conditions that are not even necessary and that lead to the identification of the numbers with some particular set of sets. If numbers are sets, then they must be *particular sets*, for each set is some particular set. But if the number 3 is really one set rather than another, it must be possible to give some cogent reason for thinking so; for the position that this is an unknowable truth is hardly tenable.[24]

Since it is impossible to know that, say, Zermelo's definition of '3' is true, Benacerraf infers that the definition is false. Since this argument applies equally well to all set theoretic definitions of number, it follows that they too are false.

Other philosophers, such as Crispin Wright and Gilbert Harman, take the view that there is no fact of the matter. Once we have outstripped all possible evidence, there is no issue to be decided. They compare this situation with the one Quine's anthropologist faces when confronted with the task of radical translation. Although new evidence may eliminate some rival

---

[24] Paul Benacerraf, 'What numbers could not be', in Paul Benacerraf and Hilary Putnam (eds.), *Philosophy of Mathematics*. 2nd edn. (Cambridge: Cambridge University Press, 1983), 284.

translation manuals, no amount of evidence will uniquely determine the correct manual. So we face a large range of alternatives of the form 'Manual *m* is the correct manual' knowing only that they cannot all be correct. Quine concludes from this that none of the claims is correct or incorrect. For Quine is enough of a positivist to only concede the existence of an issue when there is the prospect of settling it.

One of the oldest unbreakable tie arguments serves as a subargument designed to show that we can only be directly aware of sense data. The classic argument from perceptual relativity begins with the observation that in certain non-standard conditions, things look different from the way they are. To see is to see something. So the things we are seeing in these non-standard situations are not identical to the physical objects in view. Therefore, the only things we directly see in non-standard situations are non-physical representations of the physical things. These are called sense data. To show that we only directly perceive sense data in *standard* conditions, an unbreakable tie argument is deployed. George Pitcher provides a particularly perspicacious presentation of it.

It cannot be maintained that although in non-standard conditions, one is directly aware of the qualities of sense-data, nevertheless in standard conditions, one is directly aware of the qualities of the (physical) thing itself; for non-standard conditions shade imperceptibly into standard ones, and it would be absurd to claim that at some arbitrary point, one stops being directly presented with the qualities of sense-data and starts being directly presented with the qualities of the physical thing itself. For example, if one approaches the distant hills and they gradually stop looking purple and begin to look green, it would be ridiculous to claim that at some point, one stopped sensing the colour of a sense-datum and began to perceive the colour inhering in the hills themselves directly.[25]

The ultimate conclusion of the perceptual relativity argument follows promptly. For if only sense data are directly perceived in non-standard situations, and if only sense data are directly perceived in standard situations, we are never directly aware of anything except sense data.

In addition to varying the conditions of the observer and the surrounding environment, one can also appeal to differences

---

[25] George Pitcher, *A Theory of Perception* (Princeton: Princeton University Press, 1971), 29. Pitcher goes on to criticize the first stage of the relativity argument leading up to the unbreakable tie stage.

between species. When it is further supposed that these different modes of perceptions are incompatible, we obtain another type of unbreakable tie argument. This argument has been discussed in Stuart Katz's and Stephen Wilcox's 'Do Many Private Worlds Imply no Real World?'[26] Since evolutionary processes have led different species to represent the world in radically different ways, and humans are just another species, there is no reason to accord our representation privileged status. But without this privileged status, there is no more reason to believe that our representation is correct than there is reason for supposing that alternative representations are correct. For this premiss it is concluded that none of the representations are correct. In particular, the human representation is not correct. Given that we retain the idea that there is an external world which serves as the standard of correctness, we are forced into *epistemological* scepticism about the *nature* of the external world. That is, we say that there is an external world ('noumenal reality') but deny that we can know anything about it. If we give up the notion of an external world, we either embrace *ontological* scepticism about the external world (deny that it exists) or *semantic* scepticism about the external world. Semantic scepticism about the external world denies the meaningfulness of 'There is an external world.' So strictly speaking, they neither affirm, deny, nor suspend judgment about its existence.

One might try to solve the above problem by denying that animals really represent the world. Following Descartes, one might deny they have beliefs. Interestingly, there is another unbreakable tie argument which has this outrageous claim as its conclusion. Suppose Fido sees his master bury a bone in his backyard. Fido then begins to paw at the very spot the bone is buried. David Armstrong observes,

It is entirely natural to explain the dog's action by attributing certain beliefs to him. And if the explanation is so natural, that is already some argument for thinking it an intelligible explanation (whether or not it is a true explanation). Against this, however, it is argued that this 'natural' explanation of the observed facts becomes suspect when it is asked exactly what it is that the dog believes. Has the dog got concepts of 'burying', of 'bone' . . . ? It is sufficiently obvious that he does not have our concepts

[26] This article appears in the *Journal for the Theory of Social Behaviour*, 9/3 (Oct. 1979), 289–301.

of these things. But if he lacks our concepts, what can it mean to say that 'he believes that he has a bone buried there' . . . ? We want to say that the dog believes something—but we do not seem able to say what! Is our attribution of beliefs to the dog really intelligible after all? Perhaps it is concealed nonsense.[27]

The dog's conceptual poverty yields a disturbingly large range of alternative belief attributions. This plethora of alternatives undermines any precise attribution. Some epistemologists believe that this difficulty drives us toward the conclusion that animals lack belief.[28] Whereas the Benacerraf argument involves an infinite class of definitions which are mutually exclusive, the above argument concerns an infinite class of belief attributions which are non-exclusive. Another difference is that Benacerraf's propositions are plainly equi-evident; the animal belief attributions vary in plausibility.

It is also possible to interpret the continuity argument against dualism as an unbreakable tie argument. Keith Campbell presents the argument as follows:

Evolutionary theory asserts that complex modern forms, such as man, are the remote descendants of earlier species so much simpler that like the amoeba they show no signs of mental life. If minds are spirits they must have arrived as quite novel objects in the universe, some time between then and now. But when? We see only a smooth development in the fossil record. Any choice of time as the moment at which spirit first emerged seems hopelessly arbitrary.

In the embryonic development of man, the same problem arises. The initial fertilized cell shows no more mentality than an amoeba. By a smooth process of division and specialization the embryo grows into an infant. The infant has a mind, but at what point in its development are we to locate the acquisition of a spirit? As before, any choice is dauntingly arbitrary.[29]

---

[27] David Armstrong, *Belief, Truth and Knowledge* (Cambridge: Cambridge University Press, 1973), 25. Armstrong goes on to defend the coherency of belief attributions to animals against this argument.

[28] Stephen Stich discusses this position in 'Do Animals Have Beliefs?', *Australasian Journal of Philosophy* (March 1979), 19.

[29] Keith Campbell, *Body and Mind* (Garden City, N. Y: Anchor Books, 48–9. Another example of the argument can be found in D. M. Armstrong, *A Materialist Theory of Mind* (London: Routledge and Kegan Paul, 1968), 30–1. Derek Parfit employs a science-fiction type argument from continuity in *Reasons and Persons* (New York: Oxford University Press, 1984), 239. Criticism of the argument from continuity can be found in Eric Russert Kraemer and Charles Sayward, 'Dualism

Knowledge Blindspots 149

This argument can be construed in strictly metaphysical terms if we suppose that there is a suppressed premiss to the effect that non-physical things can only be introduced by physical discontinuities. However, Campbell's talk of the arbitrariness of any choice as to when minds arrive on the scene encourages the epistemic interpretation. Since the dualists believe that minds were introduced at some time, they are committed to the possibility of explaining how they arose for the first time. However, evolutionary theory shows that any such explanation would be defeated by the arbitrariness objection. The virtues of any particular explanation would be matched by a competing explanation. Since no explanation can be the winner, they are all losers. So dualism cannot fulfill its explanatory obligation and is therefore false.

Perhaps the moral significance of mindedness has prevented dualists from defending themselves by denying a fact of the matter to the question of when embodiment occurs. In any case, Waismann's argument against the thesis that predictions can 'become true' constitutes a close gappy counterpart to Campbell's argument. In order for a prediction to become true, it must shift in status from being neither true nor false to being true. Waismann then asks,

> But how are we to figure the change from 'undecided' to 'true'? Is it sudden or gradual? At what moment does the statement 'it will rain tomorrow' begin to be true? When the first drop falls to the ground? And supposing that it will not rain, when will the statement begin to be false? Just at the end of the day. 12 p.m. sharp? . . . We wouldn't know how to answer these questions; this is due not to any particular ignorance or stupidity on our part but to the fact that something has gone wrong with the way the words 'true' and 'false' are applied here.[30]

As is typical of philosophers following the later Wittgenstein, Waismann takes our inability to answer a question as grounds for concluding that the question has no answer. Since asserting that the answers to such questions are unknowable often leaves the

and the Argument from Continuity', *Philosophical Studies*, 37/1 (Jan. 1980), 55–9. Emmet L. Holman replies in 'Continuity and the Metaphysics of Dualism', *Philosophical Studies*, 45/2 (Mar. 1984), 197–204.

[30] F. Waismann, 'How I See Philosophy', in H. D. Lewis (ed.), *Contemporary British Philosophy*, (New York: MacMillan Company, 1956), 456–7.

audience still assuming there is a fact of the matter, Waismann may have been unhappy with saying that 'It is impossible to know exactly when predictions become true.' Perhaps he would have preferred to say that the question of knowability fails to arise. Nevertheless the form of his objection remains a modal argument from ignorance.

Some philosophers are suspicious of the arguments advanced by Campbell and Waismann because of their resemblance to the sorites paradox.

1. Base step: One minute past noon is noonish.
2. Induction step: If n minutes past noon is noonish, then $n + 1$ minutes past noon is noonish.
3. Midnight is noonish.

Since 'noonish' means 'near noon' and midnight is far from noon, we must accept the base step and reject the conclusion. Classical logic then forces us to deny the induction step. But the negation of the induction step is equivalent to the assertion 'There is a number n such that n minutes past noon is noonish and $n + 1$ minutes past noon is not noonish.' A sceptic who wishes to show the incoherence of our ordinary concepts, such as 'noonish', can defend the induction step by pointing out our difficulty in specifying the number. He has us consider the class composed of propositions of the form 'Number i is the threshold' where i runs from 1 to 720. We can easily rule out most of the high values for i since we know that the last noonish time falls well before, say, 4 p.m. But that still leaves an irreducible number of candidates. Neither empirical nor conceptual investigation will enable us to decide which is the correct answer. The sceptic then infers, in the fashion of Benacerraf, that there is no true proposition in the set. Like Benacerraf's argument, the sceptic's alternatives are mutually exclusive. Like the class of animal belief attributions, the sceptic's alternatives vary in plausibility. But unlike both, the sceptic's alternatives are finite.

Indeed, there are instances of this argument involving only two alternatives. Suppose that my brain is treated so that it can be transplanted into two bodies, Lefty and Righty. After the transplant, Lefty and Righty bear a strong psychological resemblance to me. The resemblance is so strong that had only Lefty received part of my brain and the remaining part had been destroyed, we would be inclined to say that I was identical to Lefty. But since Righty has also survived, we have two competitors for the identity claim. Am I Lefty or am I Righty? Since there can be no more reason for thinking I am one rather than the other, it is concluded that I am neither.

Other examples of unbreakable tie arguments are controversial. For there can be disagreement over the truth of the premiss which asserts that there is necessary ignorance. Consider the ship of Theseus. Gradually all the ship's parts are replaced. The old parts are then reassembled into a distinct ship. Which is the real ship of Theseus? Some commentators argue that spatio-temporal continuity takes precedence over compositionality. Others claim the reverse. The remainder deny that we can know one criterion takes precedence over the other. They then apply the unbreakable tie argument to either conclude that there is no truth of the matter or (more rarely) that neither ship is identical to the ship of Theseus.

V. LOGICAL ANALOGIES

Although there is rarely any formal way to prove invalidity, one can dislodge *justified belief* in the validity of an argument by presenting analogous arguments that the audience regards as invalid. To perform its dissuasive task, the analogue must exhibit the form that the audience took to validate the original argument. Once one concedes that there is no relevant difference between the two arguments, belief in the invalidity of the analogue forces a change of mind about the validity of the original. In order for the method of logical analogy to work against an entire class of arguments, the audience must be persuaded that every member of the class has a defeating analogue. The goal of this section is to produce such a general belief with respect to unbreakable tie arguments.

A. *Hypertasks and Symmetrical Blindspots*

Since the simple gappy form of the argument from ignorance is a special case of the unbreakable tie argument, an objection to the former is also an objection to the latter. In particular, the existence of symmetrical blindspots shows that these forms do not have full generality. A proposition is a symmetrical blindspot if and only if both it and its negation are inaccessible. Reason to believe that there are such propositions was provided by critics of logical positivism. The positivists quickly discovered that a requirement of full verifiability could not be satisfied by any universal generalization having an unrestricted domain of discourse. The suggestion that they switch to a requirement of full falsifiability only served to make existential generalizations the problem case. Indeed, J. W. N. Watkin's 'all and some' propositions will be neither verifiable nor falsifiable.[31] Since propositions of the form $(x)(\exists y)Rxy$ have both universal and existential quantification, unlimited domains of discourse for x and y ensure joint failure of full verifiability and falsifiability. Watkin's examples include:

(3) Every event has a cause.
(4) For all metals there exists some acid that will dissolve them.
(5) For every social misfortune there will be an overcompensating boon.

Of course, some propositions of the form $(x)(\exists y)Rxy$ can be verified or falsified. For example, 'Every human being has a mother' would be falsified by a test-tube baby created from inanimate matter. Here our search space is limited because motherhood requires biological contribution. Unfalsifiability obtains only when the relation always entitles us to say 'Maybe we have not looked far enough.'

Symmetrical blindspots of a more generalizable nature can be summoned from measurement problems. For example, our inability to measure the lengths of objects with complete precision makes the following a symmetrical blindspot:

(6) The bottom left-hand edges of this page are commensurable.

If the result of dividing the length of the longer edge by the shorter is a rational number, (6) is true. If the result is an irrational number, (6) is false. But since an arbitrarily small difference in the length of either

[31] Watkins discusses 'all and some' propositions in 'Confirmable and Influential Metaphysics', *Mind*, 67/267 (July 1958), 344–65.

Knowledge Blindspots

can make the crucial difference between whether (6) is true or false, we can only know the truth value of (6) if we know their lengths with complete precision. Since their precise lengths are unknowable, it follows that we can neither know (6) nor its negation. Notice that our necessary ignorance does not depend on uncertainty about what is and what is not an edge of the object. Even if the edges were perfectly distinct, their commensurability would be absolutely undetectable. Should the vagueness of 'edge of the object' intrude, we could always supply a precisifying definition that permits the investigation to continue. The arbitrariness of these precisifications is irrelevant since they are only made with a view to isolating one source of our irremediable ignorance about the commensurability of the object's edges. Clearly, *one* of the reasons that I cannot know (6) is that the measurement problem is a hypertask. Completing the task would require infinitely many steps.

Contrary to what is suggested by the simple gappy form and the unbreakable tie arguments from ignorance, we cannot infer that (6) is not true simply because neither it nor its negation is knowable. And contrary to the falsity form of the argument from ignorance, we cannot infer that (6) is false because it is unknowable. As long as it is conceded that the edges have specific lengths, it must be conceded that they are either commensurable or incommensurable. The only hope of escaping the problem is to deny that they have specific lengths. Actually, one would have to deny that any two objects have specific lengths in order to avoid having the problem resurface with another example. Thus one would have to develop a general theory of indeterminate lengths, weights, and so forth. The theory would have to enable us to rule out determinate lengths a priori. It would have to make nonsense of the claim that the longest edge of this page is exactly 200 millimetres. But given that this is nonsense, how are we to make sense of the upper and lower bounds of 'The longest edge is between 199 and 201 millimetres'? For talk of millimetres has to be analysed in terms of comparisons with the lengths of the standard metre. The boundaries themselves cannot be intervals.

Since this example only involves two alternatives, a proposition and its negation, it might be hoped that the unbreakable tie argument would fare better when the number of alternatives is large. However, it is possible to show that the unbreakable tie argument can fail regardless of how the range of alternatives is structured. For the key feature of the commensurability example can be generalized.

The hypertask problem was behind Brouwer's comment that

although finite inspection might reveal that there are three consecutive sevens in the decimal expansion of pi, the method cannot demonstrate the non-existence of three consecutive sevens. For the three might be found further down the expansion.

Can we conclude that Brouwer's question, 'Are there three consecutive sevens in the decimal expansion of pi?', cannot be known to have a negative answer? No, because for all we know, a clever mathematician might come along and discover a property of pi that permits him to prove that the maximal string of sevens is less than three. Of course, the fact that nothing we now know excludes the possibility of an answer by a clever mathematician does not imply that the possibility is genuine. But it does vitiate the claim that a negative answer to Brouwer's question is unknowable.

The hitch is that the person answering the question knows the generating function of the sequence. Knowledge of the function sometimes provides knowledge of the sequence that could not be derived from finite inspections. For example, consider the sequence formed by having each instance of the digit 1 preceded by n zeros and succeeded by $n + 1$ zeros: .1010010001. . . . Like pi. this sequence is irrational. Nevertheless, it can be demonstrated that it does not contain three consecutive sevens.

We can salvage the thesis that some questions cannot be knowingly answered in the negative by supposing that the questionee is faced with an opaque equivalent of Brouwer's question. This equivalent question will have the same answer as Brouwer's. However, the opacity of the question ensures that there is no alternative to the 'brute force' method of finite inspections. For example, suppose we are asked to determine the size of a particular enclosure relative to a smaller enclosure. Unbeknownst to us, the area of larger enclosure is pi times as large as the area of the smaller enclosure. We are asked whether the decimal expansion of the area has three consecutive sevens in it. The measurement process will only feed us new parts of the sequence in a piecemeal fashion, restricting us to the method of finite inspection.

B. *Mystery Numbers*

Counterparts to the measurement version of Brouwer's question can be used to derive 'mystery numbers'. These numbers possess unknowable identities but are still knowable enough to allow probability judgements about their identities. Since each mathematical question asked in the derivation of the mystery numbers has a corresponding measurement question, we can avoid the clever mathematician objection. Since it would be cumbersome to ask about measurements, I will ask about their non-opaque counterparts. The fact that there is an opaque version of each of the questions legitimizes the restriction that the respondent not exploit his knowledge of the generating function in answering the question. For the mathematical questions are to be taken as ersatz measurement questions. Only brute force is allowed.

Instead of pi, we will make use of infinite sequences of irrational numbers. The first sequence is composed of the square roots of the prime numbers 2, 3, 5, . . . Call the first member of this sequence index-1, the second member index-2, and so on. Since the nth root of any prime is irrational, it should be noted that in addition to our 'horizontal' reference numbers obtained from successive primes along the number line, we can if need be, derive 'vertical' reference numbers from the infinitely many roots of each prime. We let $p_1, p_2, p_3, \ldots, p_n$ stand for the primes and abbreviate the nth root of a number m as $m^{1/n}$. Thus the first row of Table 4.1 lists the horizontal reference numbers, and the columns below that row represent the vertical reference numbers.

TABLE 4.1

$$p_1^{1/2}, p_2^{1/2}, p_3^{1/2}, \ldots, p_n^{1/2}$$

$$p_1^{1/3}, p_2^{1/3}, p_3^{1/3}, \ldots, p_n^{1/3}$$

$$p_1^{1/4}, p_2^{1/4}, p_3^{1/4}, \ldots, p_n^{1/4}$$

$$p_1^{1/5}, p_2^{1/5}, p_3^{1/5}, \ldots, p_n^{1/5}$$

.
.
.

$$p_1^{1/n}, p_2^{1/n}, p_3^{1/n}, \ldots, p_n^{1/n}$$

Consider the decimal expansions of our horizontal reference numbers.

1.1 The decimal expansion of index−1 contains 1 consecutive 7.
1.2 The decimal expansion of index−1 contains 2 consecutive 7s.
.
.
.
1.n The decimal expansion of index−1 contains n consecutive 7s.

At first blush one might feel certain that there is a false proposition in the index −1 sequence. If there is a false proposition, it is impossible to know that the proposition is false. However, the strings of sevens may be finite but of arbitrarily large size making all of the propositions true. For example, ever expanding strings of sevens might be sandwiched between strings of eights as in 878 . . . 8778 . . . 87778 . . . Those impressed by the notion that all possibilities are realized in the infinite might believe that such ever expanding strings of sevens surely exist in the decimal expansion of the square root of two, $2^{1/2}$. This worry rests on the principle of plentitude. I know of no coherent formulation of the principle that has application to the present case, so it is tempting to dismiss the reservation as incoherent. But even if there is a coherent formulation, it should be observed that we can appeal to 'higher levels of plentitude'. That is, in addition to expecting ever expanding strings of sevens in the square root of two, proponents of plentitude should also expect expanding strings of sevens in the cube root of two, $2^{1/3}$. However, they cannot reasonably have this expectation for all decimal expansions of numbers of the form $2^{1/n}$ collectively. Since there are infinitely many expansions of this form, the belief that all possibilities are realized in the infinite should lead one to the conclusion that some of these 'vertical' expansions have a largest string of consecutive sevens. Of course, this argument does not guarantee that there are expansions having maximal strings. The argument is only intended to lower the probability to insignificance.

Nevertheless, to cover the possibility that there are no maximal strings, we shall define 'mystery–1' as equal to 1 if and only if there are no largest strings of sevens in expansions of the form $2^{1/n}$. Otherwise 'mystery–1' equals $x + 1$ where x equals the position of the first false proposition in the index–1 sequence (or the nearest sequence with reference number $2^{1/n}$ that has a false member). In a like manner, we can define 'mystery–2' in terms of the index–2 sequence which consists of propositions of the form 'The decimal expansion of index–2 contains m consecutive sevens'. So if all of the expansions of $3^{1/n}$ lack maximal strings of sevens, 'mystery–2 equals 1. Otherwise 'mystery–2' equals $x + 1$ where x equals the position of the first false proposition in the index–2 sequence (or of the nearest sequence with reference number $3^{1/n}$). An infinite stock of other unknown numbers can be obtained with the index–3 sequence, the index–4 sequence, and so on.

C. *Applications to the Modal Appeals to Ignorance*

We now have the resources to draw logical analogies with any unbreakable tie argument. Let us begin with Benacerraf's argument. The following is an infinite list of equiprobable and mutually exclusive propositions of which at most one is true:

1. Mystery–1 is the uniquely highest mystery number.
2. Mystery–2 is the uniquely highest mystery number.
   .
   .
   .
n. Mystery–n is the uniquely highest mystery number.

If there are two or more highest numbers, all of the members of the list are false. Otherwise, exactly one is true. Since we cannot tell which of two conditions is satisfied, there is an unbreakable tie between the alternatives. But despite this resemblance to the situation Benacerraf describes, we cannot use our irremediable ignorance to conclude that none of the alternatives is true. So whatever force there is to Benacerraf's argument must emanate from a source other than the existence of an unbreakable tie between infinitely many equiprobable and mutually exclusive alternatives.

The many private worlds argument differs from Benacerraf's in that it only contains finitely many alternatives (since there are only finitely many species). So an analogue for this argument can be constructed by restricting ourselves to a sublist of the one above. By letting n equal the number of species of interest to the promoter of the private worlds argument, we obtain a structurally similar argument that we would reject as fallacious. By letting n equal two, we obtain a fallacious counterpart to the personal identity argument for why I can be neither Lefty nor Righty. Some might find a disanalogy in the fact that they assign a much higher absolute probability to the alternatives 'I am Lefty' and 'I am Righty'. But this difference can be smoothed away by changing to more probable claims about mystery−1 and mystery−2. For example,

1. Mystery−1 is at least twice as large as mystery−2.
2. Mystery−2 is at least twice as large as mystery−1.

Should this example not reflect the same absolute probability, other examples will.

Campbell's continuity argument against dualism differs from the preceding examples in that the dualist is certain that one of the alternatives is true and he does not assign them equal probabilities. The dualist can exclude the possibility that minds enter the evolutionary scene prior to the development of multi-cellular life forms. As the life forms exhibit behaviour of growing complexity, the dualist becomes more inclined to say they have minds. Although the candidates for the 'First Minded Organism' title becomes more promising, the rise in probability is too smooth to adjudicate between neighbouring candidates. A similar probability distribution arises from the following list of claims.

0. Exactly 0 of the first hundred mystery numbers are even.
1. Exactly 1 of the first hundred mystery numbers is even.
2. Exactly 2 of the first hundred mystery numbers are even.
.
.
.
100. Exactly 100 of the first hundred mystery numbers are even.

Exactly one of these propositions is true and it is probably located in the middle of the list. For the propositions in the middle are much more probable than those at the extremes. Nevertheless, the highest probability of any particular proposition is too low to merit belief in it. As in the case of the dualist trying to locate the first minded organism, we are confident about the very general location of the true proposition but cannot pinpoint it precisely.

Since the sorites and Waismann's objection to 'become true' have the same structure as Campbell's continuity argument, the above analogue is equally effective against those unbreakable tie arguments. However, Armstrong's argument about animal belief differs from these three in that it involves infinitely many nonexclusve alternatives. Although we may not be completely confident in saying 'Fido believes there is a bone buried where he is digging', we have much more confidence in that attribution than in 'Fido believes that a bone from a three-year old cow is buried where he is digging'. We can also play favourites with the following:

1. Mystery−1 is divisible by 2.
2. Mystery−2 is divisible by 3.
   .
   .
   .
n. Mystery−n is divisible by $n + 1$.

Some may see a disanalogy in the absence of high probability propositions. This can be remedied by enlarging the set of divisors. For example, each member of the list could take the form 'Mystery−i is divisible by $i + 1$ or $i + 2$.'

What I hope to convey by these examples is that the epistemic structure of every unbreakable tie argument is shared by some unacceptable argument based on the mystery numbers. So the epistemic structure cannot be a source of validation for these arguments. This does not eliminate the possibility that the arguments have another source of validation. They may be good arguments in disguise. But until we are given some reason to suspect that things are not as they appear, we should stick to appearances.

5
Blindspot Predicates

SOME predicates generate blindspots systematically.[1] Call them 'blindspot predicates'. For example, 'modest' is a blindspot predicate for the subjects of the predication: Einstein cannot know 'Einstein is modest', Moore cannot know 'Moore is modest', and so on. These are personal blindspots; others can know that Einstein and Moore are modest. We can also find examples of predicates that yield patterns of impersonal blindspots. Apply 'immortal' to any particular individual and one obtains a sentence expressing a proposition that cannot be known to be true. Applying other predicates to individuals yields a mixture of blindspots and non-blindspots. But since the blindspots tend to cluster together, the predicates qualify as systematic producers of blindspots. In view of their interesting epistemic properties, it is natural to expect that instances of these three types of blindspot predicates have been put to use in philosophical arguments. In the first section I concentrate on the way that impersonal blindspots have been used to argue for local scepticism about miracles, parapsychology, alternative conceptual schemes, safety, and other items of interest. These arguments are criticized for their tendency to assume that ignorance is compositional. Criticism of arguments turning on personal blindspots is given in the second section. In the final section, I argue that all vague predicates comprise a subset of blindspot predicates, which I call 'blurry predicates'. Thus my study of blindspot predicates is intended to provide a theory of vagueness.

I. UNLIMITED BLINDSPOT PREDICATES

Some predicates always yield propositions that are blindspots for everyone at every time. Thus they are doubly universal. Establishing that a predicate F has this feature generates a type of

[1] Portions of this chapter are taken from 'Uncaused Decisions and Pre-decisional Blindspots', *Philosophical Studies*, 45/1 (May 1984), 51–6.

epistemological scepticism about Fs. Since the distinction between epistemological scepticism and ontological or semantic scepticism tends to go undrawn, we will frequently have to read in the distinction to pull out the example. For the most part, I will refrain from endorsing claims to the effect that F is an unlimited blindspot predicate. I only intend to make it plausible that there are such predicates by exhibiting types of arguments that can be used to make their existence probable. At the most general level, the pattern of reasoning is always the same. First, establish a necessary condition for knowledge. Second, show how this condition fails for claims of the form 'x is an F'. Variety arises from the plurality of exploitable requirements. Since there are many such requirements, our tour is only intended to be suggestive, not comprehensive.

A. *Best-explanation Blindspots*

1. *A Compositional Fallacy*

Before considering examples, it will be useful to consider a fallacy that tends to follow the discovery of blindspot predicates.

Compositionality of Ignorance:
$$\frac{(p)\ \Box-Kp}{\Box-K(\exists p)p}$$
(where p ranges over some designated class of propositions)

Notice that the argument has the same premiss as the unbreakable tie argument but has a different conclusion. In essence, the argument form embodies a belief in the compositionality of necessary ignorance. If no member of a group can be known to be an F, then the whole cannot be known to contain an F. One might suggest that the root of the fallacy is a confusion between more basic types of inference. From $(\Box-Kp\ \&\ \Box-Kq)$ we may infer $\Box-K(p\ \&\ q)$. Necessary ignorance does collect over conjunction. However, $(\Box-Kp\ \&\ \Box-Kq)$ does not imply $\Box-K(p\ \text{v}\ q)$. Another explanation of the error traces the problem to the assumption that existential generalizations can only be inferred by the rule of existential generalization. The falsity of the assumption is illustrated by Kyburg's lottery paradox and Mackinson's preface paradox. I cannot know that a particular belief I now hold is a mistake but I do know that at least one of my current beliefs is a mistake. The basis for the existential generalization 'I now have at least one false belief' is analogy with my past beliefs and analogy with my contemporaries, not a particular current error.

The fallacy can also be viewed as a confusion between a strong and weak form of epistemological scepticism. The premiss describes case-by-case scepticism; a type of scepticism compatible with knowledge of an existential generalization. The conclusion describes EG scepticism; a type that is incompatible. The English language invites the confusion through the ambiguity of 'It is impossible to know that something is an F'. Showing that F is a blindspot predicate only yields case-by-case scepticism about Fs. But since we have a healthy appetite for strong results, we tend to jump to the conclusion that EG scepticism has been established. This systematic overestimation of the philosophical pay-off may be responsible for motivating a portion of the interesting work that has been done with blindspot predicates. If so, we have an example of a fallacy that has benefited philosophy.

2. *Hume, 'Miracle', and Explanatory Rivalry*

Hume's analysis of miracles illustrates the tendency to assume the compositionality of necessary ignorance. In 'On Miracles', he attacks the argument from miracles:

1. If there are miracles, then God exists.
2. <u>There are miracles.</u>
3. God exists.

The first premiss can be made analytically true by defining 'miracle' as divine intervention contrary to accepted scientific laws. The price of this move lies in the epistemological problem it poses for the second premiss. As Hume pointed out in his critique of the argument from design, one cannot infer an infinite cause from a finite effect. Regardless of how stupendous the event, witnesses will only have grounds to infer that *either* God, or a very powerful finite, or a collectively powerful *group* of beings is the cause of the event. So even if a miracle occurs, they will not be able to know that it is a miracle.

Although the above supports scepticism about miracles with

Humean premisses, Hume used a different objection. Instead of exploiting the fact that our evidence for an infinite cause is always incomplete, he appealed to the inevitable improbability of miracle reports. Contemporaries of Hume supported the existence of miracles by appealing to the many reports of miracles people have made (especially those in the Bible). Hume objected that such reports cannot be known to be true on the grounds that it is always more likely that the report is false than it is likely that the miracle took place. The improbability of miracles is analytic. By definition, miracles run counter to well-established scientific laws. Since rational probability judgments are formed on the basis of observed regularities, and scientific laws rest on a great accumulation of such observations, violations of these laws are always improbable. So when a wise man is confronted with a report of a miracle, he will consider it more likely that the report is false than it is likely that our reporter has witnessed a counter-example to our best science.

This appeal to relative likelihood is a methodological criticism. Hume is claiming that the desiderata of explanation are structured in such a way as to condemn all miracle hypotheses as explanatorily inferior to their rivals. Since we can only know h is true if h is the best available explanation, the inevitable availability of superior rival hypotheses makes h unknowable. So by showing that a given type of hypothesis will always be overshadowed by a rival type, one establishes an a priori limit on what can be known. One thus achieves a classic sort of epistemological result. Such powerful results are highly prized and so epistemologists are motivated to make claims about what types of hypotheses are always preferable to others. For example, prior to certain developments in microphysics, there seemed to be support for the view that determinist theories are always preferable to statistical ones. Nowadays one can find similar support for always preferring mechanical explanations over teleological ones, nurture explanations over nature, and individualistic explanations over (irreducible) group explanations. Once one combines these overriding explanatory preferences with the view that theories of the preferred sort are never exhausted by incoming evidence, one obtains case by case epistemological scepticism about phenomena of the dispreferred sort. Often this seems to be what 'methodological' determinists, mechanists, individualists, and nurture theorists have in mind. Unlike the parallel metaphysical positions, the epistemological ones do not treat the vocabulary of the dispreferred theories as having empty extensions. Rather they prevent us from knowing that the vocabulary applies. Perhaps there are innate beliefs, objectively random phenomena, and so forth, but we can never know so, therefore there is no point in searching for them. The metaphysical issues are avoided, easing the burden of proof.

The sort of local scepticism generated by appeals to explanatory domination can be achieved with weaker premises. For one only needs a tie between rival hypotheses to produce ignorance. That is, one could argue as follows:

1. One can know that 'Fx' only if 'Fx' can provide a better explanation than any rival hypothesis.
2. Hypotheses predicating F can never be better than those predicating G.
3. F-predications and G-predications are always rival hypothesis.
4. One can never know that a given thing is an F.

If we only wish to deny that anyone can know that a given event is a miracle, we need not claim that naturalistic explanations must always be better. It suffices to claim that naturalistic explanations can never be worse. Indeed, we can further weaken the premises by substituting for (2) the claim that the F-hypothesis can never be better than some rival hypothesis or other. Of course, this would only leave you with negative methodological imperatives. 'Do not describe things teleologically'. 'Do not describe things theologically', and so on. One's hunger for positive guidance would persist. But one would have produced a bonanza of unlimited blindspot predicates.

Sometimes the evidence for explanatory domination accumulates gradually. For example, history reveals a slow but steady retreat of mentalistic hypotheses to make way for mechanistic ones. 'Every step forward in the neuroscientific analysis of brain mechanisms will shrink the area of operation within which *mind* and *thought, mental* and *rational* categories, have any application. Like the God of the Natural Theologians, the Human Reason will find itself on a diminishing bank, with the tide of Science rising around it.'[2] Perhaps connected with this trend is the retreat of ethics in response to the broadening of our notion of illness by medicine, psychiatry, and sociology. Appeals to explanatory domination are sometimes made by extrapolating from these trends. Thus ambitious meta-scientific criticisms will grow from the first level scientific erosion. 'Religion is still parasitic on the interstices of our knowledge which have not yet been filled. Like bed-bugs in the cracks of walls and furniture, miracles lurk in the lacunae of science. The scientist plasters up these cracks in knowledge; the more militant Rationalist swats the bugs in the open. Both have their proper sphere and they should realise that they are allies.'[3] Although we may now be unable to provide sufficient details, in the future we will. So our continued use of the soon to be outdated categories can only be justified on instrumental grounds. In deference to the authority of future science, we no longer can claim to know that a particular thing is an F.

Justifiying a claim to explanatory domination requires appeal to explanatory desiderata. Although these desiderata have yet to be tightly formulated, there is agreement on a large number of virtues and vices. Theories receive credit for simplicity, completeness, conservativeness, and fruitfulness. Demerits are earned for inconsistency, circularity, and untestability. From these criteria, more specific maxims can be derived. Maximize common causes. Minimize mentality. (Arab physicist of the twelfth century: 'We know that the magnet loves the lodestone, but we do not know whether the lodestone also loves the magnet or is attracted to it against its will.') Explain the obscure in terms of the familiar. Don't appeal to *ad hoc* hypotheses. From these maxims we can move on to evaluating the virtues and vices of types of explanations. Invisible-hand explanations are prized because they explain what appears to be the product of an intentional design in terms of a filtering or equilibrium process free of the apparent intentional design. Contrast the merits of this type of explanation with hidden-hand explanations: 'A hidden-hand explanation explains what looks to be merely a disconnected set of facts that

---

[2] Quoted by Stephen Toulmin in 'Reasons and Causes', Robert Borger and Frank Coffi (eds.) *Explanation in the Behavioral Sciences* (Cambridge: Cambridge University Press, 1970), 1–2.
[3] John Haldane, *Science and Life: Essays of a Rationalist* (London: Pemberton and Barrie & Rockliff, 1968).

(certainly) is not the product of intentional design, as the product of an individual's or group's intentional design(s).'[4]

Conspiracy theories, theological explanations of fortunate events, and demonical explanations of misfortunes are species of this genus. Homunculus theories are widely (though not universally) rejected as a matter of course. Critics complain that their circularity invites infinite regress, that they explain the obscure in terms of the more obscure, and that they unparsimoniously multiply agents and mentality.

Hume is sometimes interpreted as maintaining the metaphysical thesis that miracles are impossible. Indeed there are passages that suggest Hume flirted with the argument 'No one can know that an event is a miracle, therefore, miracles are impossible.' But this extreme metaphysical scepticism about miracles is incompatible with his central tenet that whatever is conceivable is possible. Since Hume found it conceivable that objects vanish when unobserved, billiard-balls remain stationary when violently struck, and flames be found cold when touched, he should have found no difficulty in conceiving of men walking on water, rods turning into serpents, and manna falling from heaven. So the most charitable interpetation of Hume classifies his occasional assertions that miracles are impossible as slips and overstatements. Indeed, the received view is that Hume's scepticism about miracles is only epistemological. His attack on the argument from miracles is not devoted to a demonstration of the necessary falsehood of the premiss 'There are miracles'. Hume was instead concerned to establish the necessary *implausibility* of this premiss. In effect, Hume argues that propositions of the form '*e* is a miracle' are consistent but unknowable propositions. 'Miracle' is an unlimited blindspot predicate; no one can justifiably apply it.

Although Hume's liberal criterion of possibility discourages the attribution of the modal argument from ignorance to Hume, there is room to charge him with the fallacy of reasoning in accordance with the compositionality of ignorance principle. For Hume is content to show that no particular report of a miracle can be justifiably believed. He does not show why these reports cannot be collectively considered evidence for the indefinite claim 'There are miracles.' Since his goal is to show our necessary ignorance of this

---

[4] Robert Nozick, *Anarchy, State and Utopia* (Cambridge: Harvard University Press, 1974). 19.

existential premiss, and he has at most shown that particular reports of miracles cannot be known, there is a gap in his argument. This is not to say that the gap cannot be filled. But the absence of any obvious way of filling the gap coupled with the fact that Hume makes no gesture toward filling it, is evidence that he did not notice any gap. And the best explanation of this oversight is an inference in accordance with the compositionality principle.

The search for further instances of the compositionality fallacy is aided by an appreciation of the generality of Hume's argument. It should first be observed that conflicts with *natural science* are inessential to the basic sort of argument Hume employs. A passage from Hume's 'On Liberty' provides an illustration:

> Should a traveller, returning from a far country bring us an account of men, wholly different from any with whom we were ever acquainted; men, who were entirely divested of avarice, ambition, or revenge; who knew no pleasure but friendship, generousity, and public spirit; we should immediately, from these circumstances, detect the falsehood, and prove him a liar, with the same certainty as if he had stuffed his narration with stories of centaurs and dragons, miracles and prodigies.[5]

The existence of such virtuous people is not ruled out by the natural sciences. Rather their existence is precluded by common sense (tutored by history). People are quite predictable as far as the general outlines of their behaviour is concerned. Deviations from these basic patterns are less likely than error or fraud made in reports of deviations. This is not to deny that gullible people can be persuaded by tales of strange people. Stories of UFOs, the Bermuda Triangle, and ancient astronauts are a staple of book stores. Nor is it even to deny that intellectuals can be persuaded. After quoting the above passage from Hume, Derek Freeman points out that Margaret Mead's violation of Hume's principle in her *Coming of Age in Samoa* did not stimulate objections.

> And yet when Mead depicted the Samoans as a people without jealousy, for whom free lovemaking was a pastime *par excellence*, and who, having developed their emotional lives free from any warping factors, were so amiable as to never hate enough to want to kill anybody, no anthropological or other critic, in the fervid intellectual climate of the 1920's seriously questioned these extravagant assertions.[6]

---

[5] David Hume, *An Inquiry Concerning Human Understanding* (London, 1809, orig. 1748), II, 86.
[6] Derek Freeman, *Margaret Mead and Samoa: The Making and Unmaking of an Anthropological Myth* (Cambridge, Mass.: Harvard University Press, 1983), 95–6.

Amongst the acceptors of Mead's story was Bertrand Russell, so the acceptance cannot be explained in terms of the philosophical *naïveté* of anthropologists and social commentators. Since both the uneducated and educated contemporaries of Hume accepted reports of miracles, Hume would not be greatly surprised to find the uneducated and educated natives of the twentieth century accepting reports of anthropological 'miracles'. Hume only means to exclude the possibility of being justifiably persuaded by such reports.

3. *Inter-field Competition*

G. E. Moore also attached considerable weight to common sense. In fact, his 'principle of weighted certainties' formed the cornerstone of his general philosophical position. In response to philosophers who seem to have denied the knowability and even the truth of such judgements of perception as 'That is an inkstand' and 'This is a finger', Moore avers:

> It seems to me a sufficient refutation of such views as these, simply to point to cases in which we do know such things. This, after all, you know, really is a finger: there is no doubt about it: I know it and you all know it. And I think we may safely challenge any philosopher to bring forward any argument in favour either of the proposition that we do not know it, or of the proposition that it is not true, which does not at some point, rest upon some premise which is, beyond comparison, less certain than is the proposition which it is designed to attack.[7]

Moore's principle requires us to decide in favour of common sense whenever philosophical claims conflict with it. One reason why this principle is appealing is that the long history of error and disagreement in philosophy puts each philosophical assertion in a reference class of statements containing a high proportion of errors. Common-sense beliefs are in a reference class with a much lower proportion of errors. So in the absence of narrower reference classes, conflicts between common-sense propositions and philosophical ones are to be resolved in favour of the former. Thus Moore denies that philosophy has the power to diminish our confidence in common sense. Moore did concede that common sense can lose out to the natural sciences. For example, astronomy has shown the error of the old common-sense view 'That the

---

[7] G. E. Moore, *Philosophical Studies* (London: Kegan Paul, 1922), 228.

heavenly bodies were small compared to the earth, and at comparatively short distances from the earth'.[8] Although Moore here concedes that one's confidence in common-sense beliefs can be shaken in a focused fashion, he did not consider the possibility that common-sense beliefs could be weakened collectively. Each philosophical belief might be overridden in a case-by-case fashion without the exclusion of the possibility that some of the philosophical beliefs were nevertheless true. Since we are speaking of those philosophical beliefs which conflict with common sense, the concession that some of them are true would imply that some common-sense beliefs are false. So Moore's principle of weighted certainties fails to show that philosophy cannot compromise common sense.

Since the claims of natural science have higher reliability than common sense, showing that a proposition conflicts with the natural sciences (especially physics) is a more effective criticism than showing that it conflicts with common sense. For example, one of the most powerful objections to interactionist dualism, such as that promoted by Descartes, is that it is in conflict with the law of conservation. If my mind is a non-physical thing that causes the movement of physical things, such as parts of my body, then it is transferring or redirecting energy. However a transfer of energy would change the level of energy in a closed physical system— contradicting the law of conservation. Since the law also conserves linear momentum, interaction cannot be explained as a matter of redirecting energy. The only plausible response to this objection is to maintain that, despite appearances, there really is no conflict.

Nevertheless, some people would have us respond differently by deciding against physics. Indeed, some say they can supply empirical evidence against materialism and in favour of dualism. The evidence is supposed to issue from parapsychology. Parapsychology is the study of paranormal actions, that is, psychological events that run contrary to accepted scientific laws. Psychokinesis, clairvoyance, telepathy, and so on, are defined negatively, in terms of scientific principles to which they would constitute counter-examples. This systematic conflict recalls the systematic conflict Hume pointed out in the case of miracles. In his controversial article 'Science and the Supernatural', George R.

---

[8] Moore makes this concession in *Some Main Problems of Philosophy* (London: Allen & Unwin, 1953), 156.

Price asserts that this resemblance led him to abandon his belief in ESP. Price maintains that scepticism about miracles and scepticism about parapsychology are a package deal.[9] For the fact that paranormal events must violate fundamental expectations generates a presumption of experimental error or fraud. Since any given report of paranormal phenomena is more likely to be false than true, parapsychology is an epistemologically bankrupt field. If the subject matter of the field exists, it is unknowable. I think Price's appeal to Hume succeeds in showing that 'psychokinesis', 'telepathy', 'clairvoyance', and the more general term 'paranormal event' are blindspot predicates. But like Hume, Price does not address the issue of why individually implausible parapsychological reports cannot collectively provide knowledge of the existential generalization 'There are paranormal events'. This existential generalization is at the crux of the anti-materialism issue. For only this weak claim appears as a premiss in the anti-materialistic argument:

1. If there are paranormal events, then materialism is false.
2. There are paranormal events.
3. Materialism is false.

Those who find these examples of blindspot predicates persuasive may also consider 'time-travel' a blindspot predicate. Although time-travel is incompatible with accepted physics, attempts to show that it is logically impossible have failed. If it is indeed a coherent notion, time-travel's conflict with accepted physics and common sense may leave it an unknowable phenomenon. Reports and demonstrations of time-travel would bear a striking resemblance to reports and demonstrations of miracles and paranormal phenomena. Rather than resort to the hypothesis that time-travel has really taken place, we would opt for more conservative explanations. Thus the criteria for good explanation

---

[9] Price's article appeared in *Science*, 122/3165 (1955), 359–67. It provoked a sequence of replies, some rather nasty. Price's article, along with commentary from critics has been reprinted in Jan Ludwig (ed.), *Philosophy and Parapsychology* (Buffalo: Prometheus Books, 1978). Anthony Flew credits Price with being the first to extend Hume's scepticism about miracles to parapsychology in 'Parapsychology: Science of Pseudo-Science', *Pacific Philosophical Quarterly*, 61/1–2 (Jan–Apr. 1980), 100–14. Price, however, is not consistently Humean. For he also describes experimental results that would lead him to accept parapsychological hypotheses.

may close off the possibility of recognizing an instance of time-travel.

The value we attach to conservativeness may conspire with the looseness of psychological explanations to leave other exotic predicates overshadowed. Evidence for applying 'reincarnated', 'resurrected', and 'changed personal identity' can be at least equally well accommodated by appeals to fraud, error, and dramatic psychological changes. The richness of our stock of redescriptions is proportional to the radicalness of the original description. A further problem for radical descriptions is that they compete with one another. Simultaneous admission of miracles, psychokinesis, clairvoyance, telepathy, time-travel, reincarnation, and so on, gives rise to a plethora of rival radical hypotheses for each purported instance of a radical phenomenon. The result is internecine epistemological scepticism. For example, those that think 'reincarnated' applies to Bridey Murphy build their case by citing the reincarnation hypothesis as the best explanation of Ruth Simmons's knowledge and behaviour. But we can equally well accommodate the evidence by the hypothesis that Ruth Simmons is a time-traveller, or has a telepathic connection with past people, or that her performance is a miracle, or by some combination of these hypotheses. There can be no unequivocal exemplification in this arena of hyper-speculation.

4. *First-person Authority*

In addition to appealing to conflicts with present science, philosophers also appeal to conflicts with *future* science. For example, one objection to the view that some of our beliefs are incorrigible is that future science may develop a 'cerebrescope' that will be more reliable than the beliefs in question. By adopting the view that some beliefs are incorrigible, we are ruling out a priori the invention of such devices. Since this a priori exclusion is dogmatic, we should deny that any beliefs are incorrigible.

Notice that this argument does not establish 'No belief is incorrigible.' At most it shows 'No one can know that he has incorrigible beliefs.' For all I know, Fermat's last theorem might be disproved in the future. So it is *epistemically* possible that it is false. From this, it does not follow that it is possibly false. If it did, I could now conclude that Fermat's last theorem is necessarily false. For any possibly false mathematical statement is necessarily false because all mathematical statements are either necessarily true or necessarily false. So from the epistemic possibility that a cerebrescope would refute an 'incorrigible' belief, we cannot infer that it is non-epistemically possible. But given that I cannot exclude the possibility of my beliefs being shown wrong, I cannot know them to be incorrigible. Thus the appeal to (epistemically possible) future science can at most succeed in showing that 'incorrigible' is a blindspot predicate. Of course this result would suffice for most philosophical purposes since the point is to criticize those views which require us to *recognize* some incorrigible beliefs.

Incorrigibility is immunity from refutation. Other types of privileged access can be described in terms of their immunities: immunity from ignorance (omniscience), from error (infallibility), and from doubtfulness (indubitability). William Alston has suggested that immunity from lack of justification is a neglected form of privileged access. According to Alston, beliefs about the intrinsic nature of one's conscious states are *self-warranted*. They are justified just by being beliefs of that sort. These beliefs (called Bs) qualify as self-warranted because they meet the reliability condition along with a second condition; no specific sorts of B are significantly more reliable than Bs in general. The role of this second condition is to avoid the need to check for further features of Bs in order to assign the proper level of justification. This condition disqualifies perceptual beliefs because we are able to specify further features of perceptual beliefs that materially increase the proportion of correct beliefs in the more specific class (such as normal lighting). Alston explains the reliability of Bs in terms of their resistance to falsification. He thinks he can afford to allow for the possibility that Bs are sometimes falsified by independent tests as long as those falsifications are rare. However, he is inclined to deny that they are ever really falsified. But as Douglas Odegard has pointed out, it is doubtful that Alston can afford to allow for even rare falsifications.[10] For the tests which successfully falsify a B will be generalizable. A subclass of Bs will then be easier to falsify than the remaining Bs and so have significantly lower reliability. This lower reliability violates Alston's second condition for self-warrant. Given that Alston cannot afford to rest his analysis on the weak thesis of rare-

---

[10] Douglas Odegard makes this point in 'Alston and Self-Warrant', *Analysis*, 39/1 (Jan. 1979), 42–4.

falsification, his argument for the strong thesis of no-falsification is of heightened importance.

Are B's always, or almost always, correct? Of course, if they are infallible, logically or nomologically, they are guaranteed to be correct. Even if they are indubitable or incorrigible, no contrary evidence can ever prevail against the subject's sincere belief, and so we will be debarred from having any reason for ever thinking any of them incorrect. But since we are assuming these strong immunities to be inapplicable, how can we justify the claim?

At this point I would simply allude to the extreme difficulty of finding *actual* cases in which a B is shown wrong. This difficulty is partly due to the absence of independent checks on the accuracy of B's; to a large extent we have no alternative to taking the believer's word for it . . . [When we do employ independent checks,] we rarely find them at variance with the subject's report; where they are, the rarity of this will justify us in either opting for the self-report, or putting its falsity down to insincerity rather than mistake. Thus insofar as we have independent empirical evidence, we have no reason to think that B's are ever mistaken.[11]

Once we consider the independent tests to be reports which conflict with the more authoritative reports of the subject, the Humean character of Alston's argument becomes clearer. For it is argued that since independent reports are always less likely to be true than the first-person report, it is likely that no first-person report is mistaken.

5. *Charitable Interpretation*

Quine has used the principle of charity to support the universality of classical logic.[12] We should credit foreign people with the same logical principles we ourselves hold because translators should follow the principle of charity. Translations which attribute well-supported beliefs to others should be preferred over those that attribute unreasonable ones. We can credit people with reasonable beliefs only if their beliefs are in accordance with our logical principles. Therefore, our attribution of a deviant logic to others is ruled out. Thus Quine uses the impropriety of conflicts with the principle of charity to derive scepticism about belief and deviant logics. This explanation of the universality of logic accounts for the circumstances that seemed to drive us toward the view that logical truths are based on the conventions of language.

[11] William Alston, 'Self-Warrant: A Neglected Form of Privileged Access', *American Philosophical Quarterly*, 13/4 (Oct. 1976), 257–72.

[12] See Quine's section on translating logical connectives in his *Word and Object* (Cambridge, Mass.: MIT Press, 1960), 57–61.

One was the circumstance that alternative logics are inseparable practically from mere change in usage of logical words. Another was that illogical cultures are indistinguishable from ill-translated ones. But both of these circumstances are adequately accounted for by mere obviousness of logical principles, without help of a linguistic doctrine of logical truth. For, there can be no stronger evidence of a change in usage than the repudiation of what had been obvious, and no stronger evidence of bad translation than that it translates earnest affirmations into obvious falsehoods.[13]

In *Word and Object* Quine cites an extremely strong principle of charity (maximize the number of truths of one's interpretee) to support the view that 'one's interlocutor's silliness, beyond a certain point, is less likely than bad translation'.[14] Passages such as these lead Michael Levin to observe:

> This recalls Hume's argument against miracles: because a miracle is by hypothesis extremely unlikely, it is always more probable that testimony supporting a miracle is mistaken than that the miracle really occurred. For Quine, S's denying a logical law would be a miracle. But the catch is that Hume's argument does not show that miracles are impossible: it shows only that it is impossible rationally to believe in miracles.[15]

According to Levin, the conclusion that interpretees *probably* are not denying logical truths is too weak to be compatible with other claims that Quine makes about deviant logic. So he suggests that Quine be read as permitting the possibility of *alogical* interpretees but not *illogical* interpretees. Interpretees could have alternative conceptual schemes. Although this reading of Quine succeeds in distinguishing his account from ones which view logical laws as highly-confirmed empirical generalizations, other objections remain. The comparison with Hume's argument still leaves the question of why particular interpretees cannot be illogical (even if they might be alogical). Indeed, the translation argument only yields the conclusion that any particular report of non-assent to a logical truth is improbable. It does not show why we cannot aggregate the reports to conclude 'Genuine dissent from logical truths sometimes occurs.' Furthermore, the appeal to alternative

---

[13] W. V. Quine, 'Carnap and Logical Truth', in *The Ways of Paradox* (Cambridge: Harvard University Press, 1976), 112–13.

[14] W. V. Quine, *Word and Object*, 59.

[15] Michael Levin, 'Quine's View(s) of Logical Truth', in Robert W. Shahan and Chris Swoyer (eds.), *Essays on the Philosophy of W. V. Quine* (Norman: University of Oklahoma Press, 1979), 52.

conceptual schemes to buttress the translation argument is objectionable in light of Donald Davidson's use of translation arguments to generate scepticism about alternative conceptual schemes.

Davidson's argument against alternative conceptual schemes begins by associating these schemes with language.[16] Specifically, an individual can have a different conceptual scheme from me only if it is impossible to translate his language into mine. This premiss reflects the connection between concepts and language as well as our belief that people with different conceptual schemes are cut off from each other to some extent. Secondly, Davidson maintains that translatability is a necessary condition for counting something as a language. Failure of translatability can be total or partial. In response to the question of total failure,

> It is tempting to take a very short line indeed: nothing, it may be said, could count as evidence that some form of activity could not be interpreted in our language that was not at the same time evidence that that form of activity was not speech behavior. If this were right, we probably ought to hold that a form of activity that cannot be interpreted as language in our language is not speech behavior. Putting matters this way is unsatisfactory, however, for it comes to little more than making translatability into a familiar tongue a criterion of languagehood. As fiat, the thesis lacks the appeal of self-evidence; if it is a truth, as I think it is, it should emerge as the conclusion of an argument.[17]

Davidson's basic argument for the conclusion appeals to the relationship between the attribution of propositional attitudes and language. In order to view someone as speaking, one must credit him with a multitude of finely discriminated beliefs and intentions. For speakers must intend to represent themselves as believing what they are saying. But we cannot attribute such complex propositional attitudes to him unless we can translate his words into ours. The 'cannot' must be construed as logical impossibility to keep the premiss plausible. Otherwise, we face counter-examples in the form of difficult ciphers and historical cases of untranslated languages such as Egyptian hieroglyphics and Babylonian cuneiforms. Once Davidson's premiss is construed as claiming that alternative conceptual schemes make the languages

[16] See his 'On the Very Idea of a Conceptual Scheme', *Proceedings and Addresses of the American Philosophical Association*, 47 (1973–4) 5–20.
[17] Ibid., 8.

logically impossible to translate, the 'counter-examples' can be dismissed as examples of untranslated but not untranslatable languages. Given the difficulties with recognizing a total failure of translatability, one might turn to the thesis that alternative conceptual schemes could be detected because the failure of translatability need only be partial. This suggestion runs afoul of Davidson's version of the principle of charity which requires interpreters to maximize agreement. The point of the maximization is not to eliminate disagreement but to make disagreement meaningful since disagreements always require a background of agreement. So we can only portray the deep disagreement that is supposed to hold between us and holders of an alternative conceptual scheme by enlarging the portion of translatable language. This enlargement leaves us free to describe our differences as differences in opinion rather than scheme.

If we choose to translate some alien sentence rejected by its speakers by a sentence to which we are strongly attached on a community basis, we may be tempted to call this a difference in schemes; if we decide to accommodate the evidence in other ways, it may be more natural to speak of a difference of opinion. But when others think differently from us, no general principle, or appeal to evidence can force us to decide that the differences lie in our beliefs rather than in our concepts.

We must conclude, I think, that the attempt to give a solid meaning to the idea of conceptual relativism, and hence to the idea of a conceptual scheme, fares no better when based on partial failure of translation than when based on total failure. Given the underlying methodology of interpretation, we could not be in a position to judge that others had concepts or beliefs radically different from our own.[18]

Davidson's translation argument shares the Humean features Levin attributes to Quine's translation argument. The resemblance ensures that Quine's translation argument succeeds only if Davidson's also succeeds. Given Levin's suggestion that the Humean difficulties should be resolved through an appeal to alternative conceptual schemes, Quine's argument would succeed only if Davidson's failed. Levin could criticize Davidson's argument in the light of its own Humean difficulties. From Davidson's premises, it does follow that one cannot know that a particular individual has an alternative conceptual scheme. However, this still leaves us with the aggregation problem. Although I might be

[18] Ibid., 19–20.

sceptical about whether particular people had alternative conceptual schemes, I need not be sceptical about whether any people had alternative conceptual schemes. The case-by-case scepticism would be sufficient to refute the anthropologists, philosophers, and historians of science who report discovering examples of alternative conceptual schemes. But Davidson's additional target of removing justification for belief in the existential generalization and indeed proving the impossibility of alternative conceptual schemes, could only be reached through a questionable appeal to the compositionality of necessary ignorance (followed by a modal appeal to ignorance). But this criticism of Davidson would validate parallel criticism of Quine's argument.

In any case, the arguments advanced by Quine and Davidson do illustrate how the principle of charity can be used like the principle of conservativeness to support the contention that certain interesting predicates are blindspot predicates. In addition to 'illogical culture' and 'alternative conceptual scheme', a strong principle of charity can be used to make the case that 'fallacy', 'intransitive preferences', and 'psychotic' are blindspot predicates. For both predicates require attribution of the sort of irrationality that the principle of charity counsels us to minimize. Given the general looseness of psychological statements, it is seldom difficult to think of a way to explain peculiar behaviour without an invocation of irrationality. Indeed we do find the principle of charity contributing to the scepticism about fallacies expressed by some critics of textbooks on the subject. And R. D. Laing is well-known for showing how even behaviour that appears to constitute paradigmatic irrationality amongst mental patients is capable of charitable interpretation.

B. *Incompleteness Blindspots*

In addition to the blindspots induced by the criteria of good explanation, there are blindspots induced by the inevitability of incomplete evidence. Some universal generalizations are often claimed to be unknowable for this reason. Absolutely conclusive verification of a universal generalization requires an exhaustive examination of every item in the domain of discourse. Sometimes this is possible as with 'All the coins in my pocket are dimes'. But most of the interesting generalizations have large domains of discourse encompassing items inaccessibly distant from us in space and time. For example, the law of gravitation extends to regions of the universe outside our light cone making it physically impossible for us to observe them. Since almost all of the universe lies outside the portion we can study, the law of gravitation along with the remaining laws of physics rest on a surprisingly small sample of their domains of discourse. Overlapping cases involving spatially and temporally distant items are generalizations referring to things that are inaccessibly minute, or fleeting, or that lead a problematic existence in another 'possible world'. Yet other generalizations have infinite domains of discourse which can only be studied by means of (non-accelerated) finite sampling. For example, some big bang theorists believe that the universe will expand infinitely. Since the speed of light limits our travel speed, our survey of the size of the universe will only reveal that the universe has so far achieved a certain finite size.

An enumeration of absolute terms would constitute a promising list of blindspot predicates in this category.[19] An absolute term marks an absolute limit. If F is an absolute term, then things which are merely close to being absolutely F are not really F. In order for something to qualify as being F it must be such that nothing could be 'more F' than it. For example, a surface is flat only if it is without bumps, curves, or irregularities. This ensures that nothing can be flatter than a flat object. After all, we are defining the predicate in terms of a total absence of something. If our domain of discourse contains portions of the surface of arbitrarily small size, then few if any objects are flat. For microscopic bumps, curves, and irregularities are almost always revealed by close inspection. Closer scrutiny may reveal that the survivors of past minute inspections actually harbour bumps. Since we cannot conduct an exhaustively minute inspection, we cannot know that a surface is *perfectly* flat. Thus 'flat' qualifies as a blindspot predicate as long as its hidden quantifiers are understood as being 'wide open'. Some philosophers, dubbed 'invariantists' by Peter Unger, maintain that the quantifiers must always be understood this way.[20] Thus they would be unqualified epistemological sceptics

---

[19] For a discussion of absolute terms see Peter Unger: *Ignorance* (Oxford: Clarendon Press, 1975), ch. 2.

[20] Unger contrasts invariantism with contextualism at length in *Philosophical Relativity* (Minneapolis: University of Minnesota Press, 1984).

about flatness. 'Contextualists' allow the domain of discourse to vary with interests, precedents, and stipulations. So they are only qualified sceptics about flatness. Since my sympathies lie with the contextualists, my assertions that certain absolute terms are blindspot predicates must be understood as qualified. For example, my claim that 'cube' is a blindspot predicate means that it is a blindspot predicate when its implicit quantifiers are wide open. This could be signalled by instead saying '(perfect) cube' is a blindspot predicate.

The sceptical fertility of absolute terms is due to the asymmetry of confirmation and disconfirmation. Applying an absolute term commits you to a universal generalization. Universal generalizations are conclusively disconfirmed by counter-examples but are not conclusively confirmed by positive examples. So unless it is possible to run an exhaustive census, there will be room for doubt. Such a census is possible for generalizations implied by application of 'naked', 'broke', 'expired', 'toothless', 'submerged', and 'extinguished'. So they are absolute terms that are not blindspot predicates. Since life forms, diseases, and wiggles are sometimes undetectable, 'sterile', 'healthy', and 'straight' are blindspot predicates. Another example is 'immortal'. To say that I am immortal is to say that I am alive at all future times. Those checking on my immortality can only hope to resolve the issue with the benefit of bad news. In the optimistic scenario, they only learn that I have yet to die. Their evidence for my immortality is never sufficient. Hope of resolving the issue through the discovery that I have an immortality gene is vain. For establishing that it is a gene that makes its possessor immortal raises the same problem as one it was intended to solve. Since 'immortal' behaves this way for 'x is immortal' in general, it is a blindspot predicate.

Although Peter Unger introduced absolute terms to establish global scepticism (through the absoluteness of 'knows'), they are more frequently used to establish local scepticism. For example, the psychologist and statistician, Richard Runyon, advances his scepticism about safety by taking 'safe' to exclude all possibility of harm and then pointing to the enormity of the possibilities:

> There is no way that anything — not even water — can be proved safe. All we can say is that given the sample of subjects and the measures that we chose to study, we did not find any evidence of undesirable effects. That's as far as we're entitled to go. This is not saying that there is

anything wrong with science. And this is not saying that there is anything wrong with medicine or with the pharmaceutical houses. I am simply stating that it would be an impossibility to study all conceivable reactions to any given drug, or food additive, or pesticide, or chemical agent of any kind.[21]

Epistemological scepticism about safety illustrates how scepticism can have practical import. The public has a tendency to demand absolute proof of safety when the possible harms are profound. For example, people often insist that the probability of AIDS infection from casual contact must be proven to be zero in order for them to permit any contact with AIDS victims. Since health officials cannot provide the proof, they have to resort to conceptual arguments. Only by emphasizing the general problem of scientific uncertainty can they shift the issue to a question of acceptable risk. If officials can show that the probability of casually contracting AIDS is not higher than, say, the probability of being struck dead by lightning, they can conclude that the risk of the first is acceptable because we accept the risk of the second.

Sometimes local scepticism can serve a non-sceptical thesis. Consider the way that Warnock wards off the libertarian's attempt to empirically demonstrate the falsity of determinism. Warnock takes the determinist's thesis to be the claim that 'for every event E, there is some set of antecedent conditions such that, whenever these conditions obtain, an event of kind E occurs' which he calls S. He points out that the thesis never specifies which conditions are sufficient. Thus determinism never delimits the area of search in a way that will open him to refutation. Warnock concludes, 'there could never occur any event which it would be necessary, or even natural, to describe as an uncaused event. It could never be said that among its complex and indefinitely numerous antecedents none could be said to be sufficient for its occurrence. And this is to say that nothing could occur which would require us to hold that S is false.'[22] Since Warnock denies that 'uncaused event' is a contradiction in terms, he takes its predications to be consistent yet unknowable. So under his analysis, 'uncaused event' is a blindspot predicate.

---

[21] Richard Runyon, *How Numbers Lie* (Lexington, Mass.: Lewis Publishing Company, 1981), 180.

[22] G. J. Warnock, 'Every Event Has a Cause', in Anthony Flew (ed.), *Logic and Language*, 2nd ser. (Oxford: Basil Blackwell, 1959), 106–7.

Sometimes the local scepticism is restricted; if we are restricted to using method m, we cannot know that a given thing is an F. For example, in the 'Fallacy behind Fallacies' Gerald Massey argues for epistemological scepticism about invalidity. He concedes that you can know that a particular argument is invalid by 'the trivial logic-indifferent method' of showing that the premisses are true and the conclusion false. However, if we are to know that an argument is invalid by means of logic, its invalidity must be detectable by *form*. Massey first argues that 'invalid' must be defined as 'instantiates no valid argument form'. This makes 'invalid' an absolute term. He then points out that one can prove validity by providing a translation of the argument which instantiates a valid argument form. But one cannot prove invalidity by showing that the argument instantiates an invalid argument form.

Suppose further that every translation you can come up with in every formal language you know and respect yields an invalid argument form. What may you then infer about the invalidity of the original argument? Nothing! Why? *First*, someone more clever than you might have been able to come up with an ingenious translation that yields a valid argument form. *Second*, even if it were somehow impossible to get a valid argument form by translating the argument into any of the formal languages you know and respect, or even into any of the extant formal languages you would respect if you knew them, there might be hitherto undreamt of formal languages congenial to you such that translation into them would yield a valid argument form.[23]

With a minor amendment, Massey's conditional scepticism about invalidity is correct. If the premisses of an argument are all logical truths, and its conclusion is logically false, form alone suffices to establish invalidity. So the scepticism must be modified to exempt this special case. For the remaining cases, we can conclude that there is an asymmetry between validity and invalidity emanating from the asymmetry between confirmation and disconfirmation.

The pattern of the sceptical argument is clear. First, one argues that the target predicate is an absolute term. For example, one might insist that 'masterpiece' has to be defined absolutely as 'an artwork upon which no improvement is possible'. Second, one stresses the impossibility of conclusively confirming the implied

---

[23] Gerald Massey, 'The Fallacy Behind Fallacies', in Peter A. French, Theodore E. Uehling, and Howard K. Wettstein (eds.) *Midwest Studies in Philosophy*, 4 (Minneapolis: University of Minnesota Press, 1981), 494.

generalization. So in the masterpiece example, it might be claimed that there is no exhaustive list of candidate improvements that can be checked off. Third, one appeals to the general premiss that universal generalizations can be known only if all their instances are known. The argument ends with the conclusion that it is impossible to know that a given thing is an F, in this case, a masterpiece.

In addition to containing many asymmetrical blindspot predicates, our stock of absolute terms also contains some symmetrical blindspot predicates. Consider probabilistic predicates like 'fair die', 'unbiased coin', and 'well-shuffled deck of cards'. Members of the extension of these predicates are required to behave randomly. However, any finite stretch of behaviour is compatible with the hypothesis that they are random and the hypothesis that they are not behaving randomly. According to the frequentist, we could conclusively determine which hypothesis is true with an experiment composed of infinitely many trials. But since we cannot perform such an experiment, this suggestion does not relieve our ignorance. On the bright side, finite experiments can affect the probability of the hypotheses, so we can reach any level of confidence short of complete certainty. So unlike the symmetrical blindspot predicate 'irrational length', these predicates are sensitive to evidence.

Predicates such as 'fair die' are coined to simplify our theorizing. With their help we can concentrate on the relationship between a small number of variables. They entitle us to treat other variables as irrelevant. Thus all fields have 'ideal types'. They are populated with ideal gases, perfect (terrestrial) vacuums, frictionless planes, pure water, perfect monopolies, pure rational bureaucracies, and ideal observers. This lends an air of unreality to much theorizing. Since we believe that there are few if any instances of ideal predicates, one naturally wonders why we talk about them, how we confirm the laws they help to express, and how we apply theories laden with these predicates. However, our metaphysical scepticism about ideal types is only rarely on purely logical grounds. We instead base the scepticism on the enormous improbability that the extraneous variables will be completely irrelevant in an actual case. When we deny that there are actual examples, we are making empirical claims about the universe. We might be wrong. Perhaps a long voyage out into distant portions of the universe will bring us face to face with a purely rational bureaucracy. We will know that 'purely rational bureaucracy' only applies to organizations that are maximally efficient at achieving their goals. And we can know that this distant organization is very close to being maximally efficient. But our evidence will not distinguish between the possibility that it is merely very close to maximum efficiency and the possibility that it is indeed maximally efficient.

Since most ideal types give rise to consistent but unknowable predications, they generate blindspots. Since the probability of these blindspots is almost always very low, most of the blindspots are false. Nevertheless, ideal types do provide a large stock of interesting incompleteness blindspot predicates.

C. *Incomprehensibility Blindspots*

Given that understanding 'Fx' is a precondition of knowing that 'Fx', F can be shown to be a knowledge blindspot predicate by showing that 'Fx' is an understanding blindspot. One subclass of incomprehensibility blindspots are based on our finitude. For example, some epistemologists object to infinite justified belief on the grounds that no one could understand the proposition expressing the justificatory chain. Our restriction to propositions of finite length also becomes relevant in the context of iterative predicates. If 'p' is true, then ' "p" is true' is true, as is ' " "p" is true" is true', and so on. Once we slip in the assumption that one understands p only if one understands all of its logical consequences, understanding any truth becomes an infinitely complex affair.

Another class of incomprehensibility blindspots turns on the claim that I can understand Fs in terms of Gs only if I can directly compare Fs and Gs. For example, I can only understand hearts in terms of pumps if I can directly compare a heart with a pump. The rationale is that understanding one thing in terms of another is a matter of drawing an analogy between the two.

Theologians have appealed to this point to support the incomprehensibility of 'God'. Since God is infinite and we are only familiar with finite things, our understanding of God can only be of the negative sort. We can know that he is not weak, not stupid, and not evil, but we cannot know how strong, knowledgeable, or good he is. The predicates 'omnipotent', 'omniscient', 'omnibenevolent', only allude to absences of limits. We have no positive understanding of God and so no positive knowledge of Him.

One version of the problem of the external world issues from similar considerations. According to representative realism, I am only directly aware of my representations of external things. So although I can compare a representation of a water-melon with another representation of a water-melon, I cannot compare a representation of a water-melon with an actual water-melon. So if I persist in thinking that 'water-melon' refers to an external object independent of my representations of it, I am forced into the conclusion that I cannot understand 'That is a water-melon.' And given that I cannot understand it, I cannot know it to be true. The most I can know to be true are facts about my inner world. Dissatisfaction with this cramped perspective motivates the semantic thesis that 'water-melon' does not refer to an external object unmediated by my representation of it. By analysing 'water-melon' as referring to facts about my representations of it, direct comparability is preserved. The external world drops out of the picture.

Some forms of scepticism about interpersonal comparisons provide a last example. These rest on a type of epistemological solipsism. Given that predicates describing private experiences are learned ostensively, it seems to follow that I can only understand my own usage of predicates such as 'pain'. For my only direct samples of pain are my own. I cannot directly feel the pain of another person. So when he uses 'pain', I cannot understand him. Since I cannot understand descriptions of his experiences, I can never know that his claims about his own inner states are correct. Since only I can know what 'pain', 'sweet', and 'yellow' mean in my mouth, these are blindspot predicates for everyone except me. So they fall just shy of being unlimited blindspot predicates. However, predicates requiring interpersonal comparisons go all the way. In order to apply 'is in greater pain than', 'tastes sweeter to', and 'looks more yellowish to', a comparison between private experiences is necessary. Since no one can ever have access to the private experiences of two people, no one can understand these predicates. Hence they are unlimited blindspot predicates.

D. Causality Blindspots

A plausible necessary condition for knowledge is that the knower be causally connected with what he knows. Whether or not one adopts a full fledged causal theory of knowledge, it seems that naturalism demands that we at least accept this requirement. Although the causal connection requirement seems satisfied in the case of concrete entities (those having either a spatial or temporal position), abstract entities appear to violate it. Since universals, numbers, and sets have neither spatial nor temporal positions, they cannot be causally connected with us. Mark Steiner formulates the problem from the vantage point of the philosopher of mathematics:

> The objection is that, if mathematical entities really exist, they are unknowable—hence mathematical truths are unknowable. There cannot be a science treating of objects that make no causal impression on daily affairs. All our knowledge about the earth and the fullness thereof arises from the causal interaction of earthly bodies with our bodies. Since numbers, *et al.*, are outside all causal chains, outside time and space, they are inscrutable. Thus the mathematician faces a dilemma: either his axioms are not true (supposing mathematical entities not to exist), or they are unknowable.[24]

One response to the problem is to reject the causal connection requirement. Kurt Godel, for example, speculated that mathematical intuition is akin to perception. Rather than postulating a non-causal mode of access to abstract entities, conceptualists cast abstract entities as mental phenomena. Others appeal to convention and practices. Still others argue that treating mathematical entities as fictions does not lead to scepticism about mathematics. Parallel moves are made to avoid the conclusion that our ethical and aesthetic vocabularies are composed of blindspot predicates. For goodness, beauty, and so on, are not natural properties.

The indispensability of mathematics for the natural sciences precludes unqualified scepticism about mathematical entities from being a serious option. However, the great utility of possible worlds in the analysis of a variety of important forms of discourse has not saved it from sceptical dismissals. Brian Ellis objects:

---

[24] Mark Steiner, 'The Causal Theory of Knowledge and Platonism', *Journal of Philosophy*, 70/3 (8 Feb. 1973), 58.

If a counterfactual conditional is a claim about the existence of some world more like our own than any other of a certain kind, then it is hard to see how we could ever be justified in thinking it to be true. Since different possible worlds cannot causally interact, we cannot learn about their existence, or investigate them, in any of the usual ways. Therefore, we have to suppose that we can know about them just by taking thought. But other possible worlds are not supposed to be abstract entities, like numbers, about which we might be said to have acquired knowledge just by taking thought, but physical realms like ours, in which physical beings of various kinds exist. How then can we know anything at all about them?[25]

Ellis is not alone in his scepticism about possible worlds. Indeed, few philosophers are realists about possible worlds as Ellis characterizes them, David Lewis being the best known member of this minority. Most modal realists characterize possible worlds as non-physical things, say as maximally consistent sets of sentences or as alternative combinations of actual things. The spirit of this approach is nicely captured by the title of one of Lewis's lectures: 'Ersatz Modal Realism: Paradise on the Cheap'.

II. LIMITED BLINDSPOT PREDICATES

Whereas unlimited blindspot predicates generate blindspots for everyone at every time, other predicates only generate more limited blindspots. They hold only for some times or for some people.

A. *Temporally Limited Blindspots*

I once had a friend who objected to assigning chores by lot on the grounds that random selection was biased in favour of lucky people. He claimed to be serious and went on to compare unlucky people with blacks, homosexuals, and other groups he took to be victims of discrimination. Sincere or not, wherein lies the absurdity of my friend's objection?

The short answer can be cast in Goodman's terminology. Unlike 'black', 'homosexual', or 'poor', 'unlucky' is not a projectible predicate. The fact that Greg has been unlucky in the past five selections does not entitle us to infer that he will be unlucky in the

---

[25] Brian Ellis, *Rational Belief Systems* (Totowa, N.J.: Rowman and Littlefield, 1979), 48–9.

sixth. Nor does the premiss support the conclusion that Greg will be lucky. This second argument would be an instance of the gambler's fallacy, that is, the fallacy of supposing that the law of averages works by compensation rather than swamping. In so far as the following generalization is true, it is not a law.

> (U) All who are assigned extra burdens by chance are unlucky people.

For to interpret (U) as true we must take their poor luck to concern the fact that they received those extra chance burdens. Interpretations of (U) that do not make it a tautology, leave it empirically false. For past bad luck is not associated with future bad luck.

To say that someone is lucky is to say that chance has worked in his favour. By describing an event as a matter of chance we are disavowing knowledge of whether it will occur. Of course, nothing prevents us from knowing existential generalizations involving 'lucky'. Casino operators are certainly in a position to predict that some customer or other will be lucky. Their ignorance is confined to the future luck of particular patrons. Suppose, for instance, that they rig slot machine A so that its next user will win. As they observe uninformed Louis depositing a coin in the machine, the casino operators will know that Louis was lucky in that he chose to play machine A. But does their knowledge that he will win give them knowledge that Louis will be lucky when he pulls the lever? No, after the choice, nothing remains a matter of chance. Whenever we are in a position to predict a chain of events, the chance event becomes the earliest unpredictable event. Appeals to luck circumscribe our explanations. When I answer the question 'Why did p come to pass?' with 'p was due to luck', I signal that I am leaving p unexplained.

What makes random selections fair is that they distribute risks and opportunities fairly. Ignorance of the outcome of the decision procedure divides the *expected* value of the otherwise indivisible burden or benefit. Our ignorance of who will be lucky and who will be unlucky justifies our consent to the decision procedure.

Although we cannot foresee luckiness, we can recognize it when it comes to pass. Luck judgements are implicitly conditional: 'Given g, s was lucky that p.' Given that I am driving a normal car, it is bad luck to have a flat. Given that I am driving a normal car to catch a flight doomed to crash, it is good luck to have a flat. Luck is essentially a comparative notion. Roughly, I am lucky when and only when things turn out better than I had a right to expect. What I have a right to expect is based on g. The lucky event described by p is additional information that improves my prospects. Thus to say that 'It will be lucky that I bet on red' is to say that things will turn out better than I now have a right to expect. Although this is possible, I cannot justifiably believe that I am now underestimating how nice the future will be. This explains the oddity of sentences of the form 'It will be lucky that p.' The problem is not sheer improbability. If I play Russian roulette, there is a ⅚ chance that the chamber of the gun will be empty. Nevertheless, if I pull the trigger and survive, I was lucky. The magnitude of the potential harm makes up for the low probability. Prior to pulling the trigger, my prospects are poor. After the chamber is found empty, my prospects are better. Good luck is good news, but not necessarily a big surprise.

B. *Agent-limited Blindspots*

'Luck' induces temporary but impersonal blindspots. Other predicates induce blindspots limited to particular individuals or groups. 'Jerry Brown is an anonymous writer for *Playboy*' is true only if it is not known by readers of the magazine. The proposition can be known by the people who hired Brown given that they are not among those who are intended to be ignorant. Whereas 'anonymous' generally requires a group to be ignorant, 'secret' is at home with both groups and individuals. 'Modest', 'dreaming', and 'insentient' only induce blindspots for the subject of predication. Other examples are 'self-deceived', 'dead', 'mistakenly believes that', 'unaware that', 'never thinks of', and 'famous solipsist'. Aristotle's view of happiness introduces another possibility. He held that I cannot now know that I am happy because that requires a global judgement about my entire life. My ignorance of the future makes such judgments hasty. Only once all the evidence is in can we make the judgement. But by then I am no longer alive to make the judgement. So I cannot know that I am happy, although future people and contemporaries who survive me can know. Since the remainder are as shut off from the evidence as I am, there is a large class of people who share my ignorance; all those who die at or before the time I die. Other predicates only induce 'hiatus' blindspots: 'will forget that', 'will discover that', 'will decide that'. In order for 'I forgot that my car's model number is 2TC' to be true, there must be a period in which I do not know it. I can know the proposition beforehand and know it afterward but I cannot know it continuously. My epistemic state has to be interrupted. Likewise, 'surprised', 'disappointed', 'learned', 'unforeseen' and 'unanticipated' yield true predications only when there is a preceding period of unbelief or ignorance. There must be an epistemological discontinuity.

C. *Three Misadventures with Personal Blindspot Predicates*

Personal blindspot predicates have played a crucial role in some anti-materialistic and anti-deterministic arguments. For example, Arthur Collins has used 'error' to argue for the thesis that beliefs cannot be representations in the brain.[26] The gist of the argument can be formulated as follows:

(C1) If beliefs were representations in the brain, it would be possible for you to have specific knowledge of an omissive error.

(C2) It is impossible to have specific knowledge of an omissive error.

(C3) Beliefs cannot be representations in the brain.

Since Collins's argument is valid, those who wish to defend the possibility of beliefs being representations in the brain must reject a premiss. There is a good argument supporting (C2):

1. $Ka(p \& -Bap)$	Assume
2. $Kap \& Ka-Bap$	1, Knowledge distributes over conjunction
3. $-Bap$	2, Knowledge implies truth
4. Bap	2, Knowledge implies belief
5. $-Ka(p \& -Bap)$	3,4, Reductio
6. $\Box-Ka(p \& -Bap)$	1,5 Necessitation

---

[26] Collins advances his argument in 'Could Our Beliefs Be Representations in Our Brains?', *Journal of Philosophy*, 74/5 (May 1979), 225–43.

Some epistemologists deny that knowledge implies belief, so they may reject the fourth step of the argument.[27] However, only a few of this minority would maintain that this is the kind of context in which the connection between knowledge and belief breaks down. Most of those with doubts about whether knowledge implies belief base those doubts on cases involving a lack of awareness of the reliableness of one's judgements. In Collins' situation the knower does not have this problem. So despite scepticism as to whether the thesis that knowledge implies belief holds in full generality, it may be admitted that the connection holds in this restricted content.

In any case, Michael Levin has chosen to challenge (C1) rather than (C2).[28] After raising suspicions about Collins' argument by pointing out that similar arguments can be constructed to rule out any correlation involving belief, Levin suggests a diagnosis. Levin first notes that Collins assumes that if an observer can discover something about an individual, then the individual can himself discover the same fact in the same way. Levin conveys his misgivings about this symmetry principle by appealing to the fact that you can note how I behave when I am completely absorbed in a chess problem, but I cannot. Levin explains how this asymmetry arises by pointing out that I can sincerely assert p only if I can also assert 'I believe p' whereas others can assert p while being neutral as to my belief in p. This asymmetry in assertion conditions explains how the questions 'p?' and 'Do I believe p?' are pragmatically equivalent despite their divergence in truth conditions. The asymmetry thereby also explains the oddity of reporting both belief that p and neutrality about the truth of p.

In a footnote, Levin claims that the symmetry principle has also been abused in the problem of whether decisions are predictable. However, he chose not to pursue the point since the problem is another topic. I think Levin is basically on track here and it will be worth our while to pick up where he left off.

The problem of the predictability of decisions received much commentary in the early sixties and was couched in a variety of

---

[27] The most persuasive argument against the thesis that knowledge implies belief is based on Colin Radford's 'counter-example' of the unconfident examinee. I object to Radford's argument on the grounds that guessers can be non-accidentally right in 'Knowing, Believing, and Guessing', *Analysis*, 42/4 (June 1983), 212–13.

[28] Levin's criticism of Collins appears in 'Yes, Our Beliefs Could Be . . .', *Journal of Philosophy*, 77/4 (Apr. 1980) 233–7.

ways. One of the clearest formulations is Carl Ginet's.[29] Ginet argues that one can soundly conclude that the will cannot be caused from the following two premises:

(G1) It is conceptually impossible for a person to know what a decision of his is going to be before he makes it.
(G2) If it were conceptually possible for a decision to be caused, then it would be conceptually possible for a person to know what a decision of his was going to be before making it.

Both premises have been challenged. My reservations concerning (G1) can be allayed by substituting the weaker

(G1′) It is conceptually impossible for a person to know what a decision of his is going to be immediately before he makes it.

Unlike (G1), (G1′) is compatible with someone predicting his own decision as long as there is a period of ignorance immediately preceding the decision. Unlike 'omissive error about the fact that', 'will decide that' only induces hiatus blindspots. The substitution preserves the spirit of the argument because (G2) can be replaced by

(G2′) If it were conceptually possible for a decision to be caused, then it would be conceptually possible for a person to know what a decision of his was going to be immediately before making it.

Ginet's argument for the uncausability of decisions resembles Collins's argument for the unrepresentability of beliefs. Both arguments turn on implications about the knowability of blindspots. Under Levin's analysis, both arguments rest on abuses of the symmetry principle:

(S) Whatever others can know about you, can also be known by you in exactly the same way.

[29] Ginet presents his argument in 'Can the Will be Caused?', *Philosophical Review*, 71/1 (Jan. 1962), 49–55.

By 'abuse' of the symmetry principle, I take Levin to mean that the symmetry principle is false. Levin attributes to Collins and Ginet the fallacy of supporting their conclusions with this false principle. However, the appeal to (S) is not essential to their arguments. There are alternative principles of access. Richard Taylor's 'Deliberation and Foreknowledge', for example, employs a weakened version of (S): the interpersonal access principle.

>(IA) Whatever others can know about you, can also be known by you.

The interpersonal access principle is weaker than the symmetry principle because it does not imply that the proposition in question be knowable in the same way.

> If someone knew what another was going to do as a result of forthcoming deliberation, then he would know on the basis of some kind of evidence; that is, on the basis of knowledge of certain conditions that were sufficient for the agent's doing the thing in question, and from which it could be inferred that he would do that. But if there were such conditions they could also be known by, or made known to, the agent himself, such that he too could infer what he was going to do. Indeed, the agent cannot even believe that any such conditions, known or unknown, exist, and at the same time believe that it is within his power both to do, and to forgo doing, the thing in question. This, we have seen, appears to be a necessary condition for deliberation.[30]

Taylor goes on to deny that even God can have foreknowledge about decisions. 'If God had foreknowledge of the deliberate act of some man, then that knowledge could be shared with that man himself. At least, there is no reason why it could not. But that is impossible, for no man can continue to deliberate about whether to do something, if he already knows or can know what he is going to do.'[31] Taylor's tacit appeal to the interpersonal access principle provides grounds for supposing that Levin is pretty much right in diagnosing the issue of the predictability of decisions as resting on the symmetry principle. However, it should be noted that when Ginet formulated the problem, he was well aware of the fact that the symmetry principle does not hold in full generality.

[30] Richard Taylor, 'Deliberation and Foreknowledge', *American Philosophical Quarterly*, 1/1 (Jan. 1964), 78.
[31] Ibid., 79.

One can, of course, describe a set of circumstances that it would be logically impossible for the decider to know in advance of his decision. (One need only include in the set of circumstances that the decider remains ignorant of certain other circumstances in the set at least until the time of the decision. It might be imagined, for example, that an agent's having a certain set of desires, beliefs, perceptions, and attitudes was always sufficient to produce a certain decision provided also that the agent was not aware at the time of some of those attitudes.) And a set of circumstances would not be a less plausible candidate for the cause of a decision merely because it has this feature. But neither could a set of circumstances be ruled out as a candidate for the cause merely because it lacked this feature.[32]

Although Ginet is willing to concede that decisions sometimes rest on ignorance, he does not see how we can claim that decisions always rest on ignorance. But at this point, we can provide an explanation of why some ignorance is always required. We need not turn to ignorance of external circumstances in order to explain how a person can be systematically ignorant. For Ginet's own commitment to (G1), the claim that one cannot know what one will decide beforehand, is the key to the account. In effect, (G1) states that all decisions are knowledge blindspots for their deciders preceding the time of the decision. These pre-decisional blindspots are systematic cases of ignorance. Since blindspots are unknowable, we have a perfectly good reason for ruling out any set of circumstances which enables the decider to predict his own decision. Accepting such a set would conflict with (G1). Given this simple alternative explanation of our ignorance, we are not forced to explain the unpredictability of our own decisions by the hypothesis that they lack causes. So Ginet's argument fails to show that our decisions are not caused. The blindspots associated with deciding are no more grounds for indeterminism than are the blindspots associated with ignorance, surprise, and error.

Given that omissive errors are knowledge blindspots, we can extend the above objection to Collins' argument. Collins' argument presupposes that indicators of our beliefs would be *credible* indicators. But since these indicators could be pointing to our current errors, the indicators could be evidence for unoccupiable positions. The indicators could be correct without us being able to

[32] Carl Ginet, 'Can the Will be Caused?', 53–4.

know that they are correct. Only extreme epistemological optimism would preclude this possibility.

Note that neither Collins nor Ginet are optimists. Essential to their arguments is the fact that certain kinds of propositions are unknowable. Thus Collins and Ginet reject the absolute access principle: all consistent propositions are knowable. Furthermore Collins and Ginet are also committed to the rejection of another access principle, the intertemporal access principle.

(IT) Whatever can be known at one time, can be known at any other.

A person can know what some of his past decisions and errors were. So applying (IT) results in the conclusion that a person can know what his decisions will be and can know which of his current beliefs are errors. Since this conclusion is false, Ginet and Collins would be correct in their rejection of the principle. But the intertemporal access principle is a close analogue of the interpersonal access principle. Indeed, the intertemporal principle can be stated in an interpersonalistic fashion: whatever can be known by one temporal stage of a person can be known by any other temporal stage of that person. Given this close affinity between the principles, it is difficult to see how (IA) can be accepted and (IT) rejected.

Metaphysical determinism is the thesis that each state of the world is determined by its prior states. Given a complete description of the initial conditions holding in the world at one time, there is a set of true laws which can be conjoined with this description to yield any future state of the world as a deductive consequence. In other words, metaphysical determinism states that there is a *complete* deductive-nomological explanation of every state of the world. Predictive determinism states that it is possible to know the premises of this grand argument and thereby know the conclusion. Thus the predictive determinist says that everything can be predicted in principle.

Although predictive determinism implies metaphysical determinism, metaphysical determinism does not imply predictive determinism. But given our natural tendency toward epistemological optimism, we tend to equate the two theses. This conflation leads many philosophers to attack predictive determinism when

Blindspot Predicates

they should be attacking metaphysical determinism. For the principal motivation for anti-determinists has been the resolution of the problem of free will and determinism. This problem can be formulated in terms of a set of propositions that are individually plausible but jointly inconsistent:

(D1) All acts are determined.
(D2) If an act is determined, then one could not have done otherwise.
(D3) If one cannot have done otherwise, then one is not responsible.
(D4) Some of us are responsible for some of our acts.

Hard determinists accept (D1)–(D3), and deny (D4). Soft determinists accept (D1), (D2), and (D4), while rejecting (D3). Soft determinists point out that the broad scope of 'determined' ensures that our actions are being determined by such things as our beliefs, desires, and uncoerced choices. So determinism permits us to act as we please. And since they regard freedom as a matter of doing as one chooses (more or less) they fail to see any incompatability between free will and determinism. Although the point about compatibility is agreed upon by most contemporary philosophers, fewer of them affirm determinism. So nowadays the popular position is that *if* determinism is true, some of us are nevertheless responsible for some of our acts. However, there remain able defenders of incompatibilism. Since most incompatibilists find (D4) more plausible than (D1), they reject determinism. This position is called libertarianism. Since the libertarians have the greatest motive to refute determinism, the fallacy of confusing predictive determinism with metaphysical determinism is frequently (although not invariably) committed by members of this group.

D. M. MacKay's 'On the Logical Indeterminacy of Free Choice' is a prize specimen. An examination of his arguments provides vivid illustrations of what can happen when blindspots are mixed with epistemological optimism.

MacKay first argues that predicting someone's decision requires that the predictor keep his prediction secret from the decider. If the decider were to learn what the prediction is, his decision might be affected, and a new prediction would have to be made incorporating the decider's exposure to the first prediction. Without secrecy, the predictors fall into an infinite regress.

MacKay's next step is to argue that if there is such secrecy, a kind of perspectivalism arises. In the situation where a group of predictors keep their prediction about A's decision a secret, the predictors are right in believing that the decider's decision is determined and the decider is right in believing that his decision is not determined.

> There is no dispute that *they* are right to believe what they do about A's brain-processes. [MacKay is interested in brain-process determinism.] But even they would insist that A would not be right to believe the same, since a precondition of [the prediction's] validity is that A must not be influenced by it. Clearly then the onlookers' view represents a true description of the state of affairs only *for the onlookers*, since if it were universally true, A would be wrong *not* to believe it. . . . Thus on the one hand, the idea that either party can give a universally-valid description of the 'true state of affairs' in this case is false; on the other hand, any idea that this proves that there is no 'true state of affairs' is invalidated on the assumption that the two descriptions stand in a rigid relationship. We might call them two different but related 'linguistic projections' of one and the same state of affairs. It is perhaps not surprising, if tantalising, that no single standpoint, whether of onlooker or agent, appears to allow us to put into words the whole truth about ourselves.[33]

Notice how McKay's perspectivalism arises as a compromise between the demands of the interpersonal access principle and the apparent inability of the predictor to publicly predict the decision of the chooser. MacKay compromises by saying that both predictor and decider are right despite their conflicting ways of describing how things stand. One route of compromise is to claim that there is a 'pluriverse'—two realities. The slightly more conservative route, the one adopted by MacKay, is to invoke different ways of correctly describing a single universe. MacKay uses this predictor/decider perspectivalism to attack the inference from 'A does not know what B knows' to 'A is ignorant of a fact known to B.'

> The interesting point which emerges is that what we are tempted to call A's 'ignorance' *would not be remedied by supplying him with the proposition P describing the state of affairs to which we are trying to say he*

[33] D. M. MacKay, 'On the Logical Indeterminacy of Free Choice', *Mind* 69/1 (Jan. 1960), 35–6.

is ignorant, since P would lose its factual status if A were to entertain it. In short, the onlookers *have no predictive information to give* A, even if they would. A may not realise this, and may even 'wish he knew' what they know; but in respect of predictive information his wish is based on a fallacy—the fallacy of supposing that what he wants to know is a universal fact. The truth would seem to be that at this point there is no gap in his knowledge; the place of the onlookers' knowledge is already preoccupied for him by the knowledge that the choice awaits his decision. To make room for it, he would have to resign from his role as agent: but then the choice would not be made.[34]

According to MacKay, one can only be ignorant of that which is logically determinate. In the case of logical indeterminacy, the question of ignorance does not arise. For MacKay, all ignorance is remedial. Since we cannot relieve the decider of his ignorance, he is not really ignorant after all.

According to MacKay, a proposition is logically indeterminate just in case its being believed is one of the factors determining its truth-value. Our subjective conviction of freedom does not rest on our own unpredictability but rather on the fact that

For us as agents, any purported prediction of our normal choices as 'certain' is strictly *incredible*, and the key evidence for it is *unformulable*. It is not that the evidence is unknown to us; in the nature of the case, no evidence-for-us at that point exists. To us, our choice is logically indeterminate, until we make it. For us, choosing is not something to be observed or predicted, but to be done.[35]

MacKay disagrees with those who maintain that 'One cannot predict one's own decision because one must overlook at least one relevant bit of information about one's decision (due to the infinite regress)'. This disagreement does not mean that he believes one can predict one's own decision. MacKay disagrees because the situation is logically indeterminate; there is nothing to overlook because one can only overlook something one is ignorant of.

MacKay explicitly rejects what he calls the presupposition of *transferability*:

if A agrees that B is right in believing P, A logically commits himself to P and to all consequences deducible from it. Despite its obvious validity in most contexts, we have seen that it can break down where P is an assertion

---
[34] Ibid., 36.
[35] Ibid., 37.

about an agent viewed by an observer.... This denial of simple transferability constitutes a kind of philosophical Principle of Relativity, very different from that exaltation of the arbitrary which goes by the name of 'moral relativism'. It resembles rather Einstein's physical principle in its insistence (i) that only one rigorously prescribable belief is valid for A if B's belief is also valid, but (ii) that the validity and meaningfulness of a belief may depend in a definite and rigorous way upon who entertains it. It differs, however, in giving no guarantee that A can even formulate from his standpoint the belief that would be valid for B (until it is out of date) and in making no assumption that their situations must be symmetrical.[36]

MacKay denies that he is committed to two kinds of truth. However, he adds that the Principle of Relativity 'does suggest that—and why—the traditional method of *comparing notes* in order to "arrive at the truth" must break down in certain special cases, leaving the truth in such cases incapable of unique and universally valid expression.[37] Thus MacKay endorses a form of ineffabilism.

MacKay's resulting position is bizarre. But it is not bizarre because of dreamy inferential leaps. He follows his assumptions to their logical conclusion. The lessons he wishes to draw are to be drawn from these assumptions. Given the unlimited access principle, 'Everything is knowable', and 'Knowledge implies truth', it follows that

(M1) If A is ignorant of the fact that p, then it is logically possible that A knows that p.

MacKay's case of the predictor and the decider is a case where it is impossible for B to know the prediction. MacKay's commitment to (M1) thus forces him to deny that 'A does not know what B knows' implies 'A is ignorant of a fact known to B.' MacKay's attack on the presupposition of transferability springs from his acceptance of

(M2) If B believes A wrong to hold a certain position, then B believes A can adopt B's position.

Since A, the predictee, cannot adopt the position of B, the predictor, then by (M2), B should find nothing wrong with A

[36] Ibid., 38–9.
[37] Ibid., 39.

holding a different position. MacKay's 'philosophical Principle of Relativity' is the negation of the interpersonal access principle with a dash of perspectivalism and ineffabilism.

Although I agree with MacKay's rejection of the interpersonal access principle, I think he should also reject the unlimited access principle and thus (M1). This would undermine his ineffabilism since it undermines

> (M3) If there is a universally correct description of a situation, then it is possible for anyone to know this description is accurate.

I think MacKay's rejection of transferability is due to the ambiguity of 'B is right to believe P.' This can mean 'B has a true belief that P' and it can mean 'B has a justified belief that P.' Philosophers who hold the presupposition of transferability read the principle in the first sense, not the second. MacKay attacks the second reading of the principle. His point is that people can reasonably disagree by virtue of their roles (predictor vs. decider).

III. BLURRY PREDICATES

Intermediate between predicates that always induce blindspots and those that only induce some in a haphazard way is a group that yields a pattern of symmetrical blindspots; vague predicates. Everyone agrees that a predicate is vague if and only if it has a borderline case. Disagreement begins when we ask 'What is a borderline case?' Since I will be defining 'borderline case' in terms of symmetrical blindspots, I need to bring some of their special features into the foreground.

Recall that a proposition is a symmetrical blindspot just in case both it and its negation are inaccessible. If, as in previous examples, p is a synthetic proposition, it counts as a symmetrical blindspot if and only if both it and its negation are blindspots. If p is analytically true, however, its negation cannot be a blindspot because the negation is inconsistent and all blindspots are consistent propositions. Nevertheless, the analytic truth will count as a symmetric (knowledge) blindspot if it is a blindspot. For if p is analytic and a blindspot, then neither it nor its negation is knowable (since knowledge implies truth and the negation must be false). Some may balk at the idea of an analytic truth being a blindspot. Evidence for the claim will be presented later. For now, I shall only invoke Kripke's admonition about the importance of distinguishing between analyticity and aprioricity. A statement's being true by virtue of its meaning does not entail its knowability. Having made the assumption that some analytic truths are blindspots, it follows that some symmetrical blindspots are not blindspots (just as some conditional blindspots are not blindspots). However, some universal generalizations remain. All *synthetic* symmetrical blindspots are blindspots. All *analytic* symmetrical (knowledge) blindspots are symmetrical blindspots. And the negation of any symmetrical blindspot is itself a symmetrical blindspot.

If z is a borderline F, then 'Fz' is a symmetrical (knowledge) blindspot. However, the converse does not hold. 'This table has an irrational length' is a symmetrical blindspot but the table is not a borderline case of 'has an irrational length'. In addition to yielding the symmetrical blindspot 'Fz', a borderline case of an F must be a member of a certain type of sequence. First, the sequence must be such that it can be known that any predecessor of F is itself an F. Second, it must be impossible to know whether a member is the last F in the sequence. Although there are sequences in which individuals have irrational lengths if their predecessors do, we can only pick out these sequences by making knowable the last member having an irrational length. Hence 'has an irrational length' is not vague. However, paradigm cases of vague predicates, 'short', 'bald', 'heap', and so on, do have sequences satisfying all the requirements. That is, they have borderline cases as defined as follows (where the blindspots are knowledge blindspots and the domain of the quantifiers is composed of the members of S):

> z is a borderline F if and only if z is a member of a sequence S such that
> (a) it can be known that (x)('Fx_{k+1}' ⊃ 'Fx_k'), and
> (b) $(\exists y)$('y is the last F' is a symmetrical blindspot), and
> (c) 'Fz' is a symmetrical blindspot.

Most predicates count as vague under this definition. 'Tall' qualifies as vague because I qualify as a borderline case of 'a tall man'. I qualify as a borderline case of 'a tall man' because I am a member of a suitable sequence. The members of such a sequence could be recruited from the next meeting of the American Philosophical Association. First we line up the male conventioneers from tallest to shortest. Condition (a) is satisfied because we would know that any predecessor of a tall man was a tall man. Condition (b) is satisfied because the last tall man cannot be known to be the last tall man. And condition (c) is satisfied because 'I am tall' is a symmetrical blindspot.

A predicate is precise just in case it is not vague, that is, a precise predicate has no borderline cases. Thus, 'precise' is an absolute term like 'flat', 'clean', and 'empty'. Absolute terms are normally used with restricted domains of discourse; not all bumps, dirt, and contents are relevant. Likewise, some borderline cases are ruled out by the context in which 'precise' is deployed. But as with other absolute terms, one might wonder whether any term is *absolutely* precise, that is, is precise given an absolutely unrestricted domain of discourse. To see that it is impossible to know that 'Every expression is vague', note the incompatibility between knowing a term to be completely general and knowing it to be vague. Were I to know that all of language is vague, I would know that 'vague' lacks borderline cases. But then 'vague' itself would be a counter-example to 'All language is vague.'

One might be puzzled as to why I restrict the incompatibility to *known* generality and vagueness rather than just generality. The reason is that I wish to allow for the possibility of vague analytic predicates. I must allow for this possibility because the vagueness of entailment provides good reason to expect that some vague predicates are devoid of clear positive cases, others are devoid of clear negative cases, while yet others have neither clear positives nor clear negatives.

It is difficult to show that a *particular* predicate has only borderline and negative cases. Fortunately, I need only convince the reader that some predicate or other has this property. My first list of candidates features predicates of the form 'somewhat later than noon but more than n minutes after noon'. As n increases, the clear positive cases decrease until finally one reaches clearly contradictory predicates. But in between must lie predicates having only borderline cases and clear negative cases. Familiarity with philosophical controversies will convince most readers that some members of this second list qualify: 'synthetic a priori', 'telepathy', 'moral expert', 'saint', 'time-travel', 'causal loop', 'uncaused event', 'self-evident', 'alternative conceptual scheme', 'disembodied mind', 'incorrigible', 'reincarnation', 'miracle', 'soul', 'basic moral disagreement', 'unfelt pain', 'ineffable', 'innate belief'. More hum-drum candidates can be drawn from lists of oxymorons: 'wooden can', 'four-wheeled motor cycle', 'synonymous homonyms', 'female snail', 'neckless bottle', 'castrated spinster', 'moral murder', 'tiny vat', 'rectangular barrel', 'one-footed skipping', 'gently hurled', 'threaded nail', 'three-person love seat', 'non-refundable deposit'. The reader can obtain more candidates by listing borderline counter-examples to dictionary definitions.

Theoretical reason to expect that there are vague predicates lacking clear positive cases is provided by the vagueness of 'entails'. Consider the following sequence of entailment theses:

1. 'n is less than 2' entails 'n is a small number'.
2. 'n is less than 3' entails 'n is a small number'.
3. 'n is less than 4' entails 'n is a small number'.
   .
   .
   .
1,000,000. 'n is less than 1,000,001' entails 'n is a small number'.

The first member of this sequence is clearly true while the ones toward the end are clearly false. But it is impossible to determine the last true statement. Since the only term used in the sentences is 'entails', it follows that 'entails' has borderline cases and hence, is vague. The generality of the phenomenon is evidenced by the general impossibility of determining which vague predication is the strongest statement entailed by another statement. For example, it is impossible to specify the maximal n for which 'It is now 12.01' entails 'n minutes from now is noonish'.

Further reason for thinking that 'entails' is vague is suggested by debates centring on opposed entailment theses. Most epistemologists claim 'Knowledge entails belief', while a few claim

'Knowledge implies lack of belief.' Incompatibilists claim 'Free will entails indeterminism', while some soft determinists claim 'Free will entails determinism.' Volitionists maintain that 'Acting entails trying', while some of their opponents assert 'Acting entails not trying', on the grounds that attempt implies failure to act. A diplomatic observer might suggest that neither side is clearly right or wrong. His explanation could be that the opposed entailment theses reflect the vagaries surrounding the criteria for applying 'entails'. Such a diagnosis is supported by difficulties surrounding attempts to detect whether the opposition between certain pairs is semantic or pragmatic. Consider the pairs (human, animal), (love, like), (mouse, object), (knowable, doubtable), (whole, part), (deductively valid, inductively cogent), (many, few), (certain, probable). For each of these pairs, some speakers maintain the first member entails the second, while others maintain the members are contraries. Advocates of entailment claim that advocates of contrariness have been misled by conversational maxims such as 'Make the strongest claim' and 'Don't state the obvious.' Advocates of contrariness will complain that the complicated pragmatic theories supporting the entailment thesis rest on a failure to recognize the intimate connection between use and meaning. Still others will claim that the dispute is verbal, resting on a failure to recognize systematic ambiguities. The debaters will field apparent counter-examples with a host of fuzzy distinctions: implication/ implicature, ambiguity/generality, connotation/association, emotive meaning/cognitive meaning, technical use/ordinary use, central meaning/peripheral meaning, figurative/literal, elliptical/ explicit, required component/optional component, pragmatic/ semantic. In addition to the alleged counter-examples that can be handled neatly with these distinctions, there will often be those lying in various borderline areas. In these cases, the issue becomes irresolvable. Thus the entailment relation can be infected with the vagaries of theories of meaning. Hence we should expect some irresolvable questions about entailment.

Once borderline entailments are granted, the existence of singly anchored predicates readily follows. When 'Fx' clearly entails 'Gx', the description 'an x that is F but not G' is contradictory and so has an empty extension. This explains the emptiness of 'round square', 'married bachelor' and 'live dead man'. When ' "Fx" entails "Gx" ' is a borderline case of a true statement, we should expect the description 'an x that is F but not G' to lack clear positive cases. For clear positive cases of non-G Fs would ensure that the entailment statement is clearly false. After all, they would be clear counter-examples to the entailment thesis. On the other hand, if 'an x that is F but not G' only had clear negative cases, the entailment thesis would be clearly true. In order for the thesis to be neither clearly true nor clearly false, there must be borderline non-G Fs without any clear positive cases.

If a vague predicate lacks clear positive cases, then its complement must lack clear negative cases. In addition to listing the complements of members of the previous lists as candidates, we can add some of our metaphysical vocabulary: 'determined', 'mechanistic', 'composite', 'extended', 'changeable', 'particular', 'explainable', 'mortal'. Since metaphysicians hope to give a general description of all that exists, they are naturally drawn to predicates whose claim to universal application cannot be clearly refuted.

A vague predicate lacking clear positives and clear negatives would have only borderline cases. Every thing would constitute a borderline case of the predicate. Some students of the debate between materialists and idealists might be willing to accept 'material thing' as a purely vague predicate. However, it is best to continue our policy of strength through numbers and adapt our old lists to this new purpose. Certain relations are general enough to inflate indeterminacies to a grand scale. Here is one example that should work for those who believe that (a) every thing is in time and (b) 'uncaused event' is a vague predicate without clear positive cases: 'temporally related to an uncaused event'. Others may be taken with 'part of a causal loop', 'has no fewer thoughts than the first saint or time-traveller', and 'falls under a predicate having as many instances as "wooden can" and "unfelt pain" combined'. Let us say that predicates F and G share alethic status just in case either $[-\Diamond(\exists x)Fx \ \& \ -\Diamond(\exists x)Gx]$ or $[\Diamond(\exists x)Fx \ \& \ \Diamond(\exists x)Gx]$. For example, 'round square' and 'married bachelor' share alethic status as do 'spoon' and 'tree'. However, 'round square' and 'spoon' do not share alethic status. Given that 'tiny vat' is a vague predicate devoid of clear positive cases, it is unclear whether 'Something is a tiny vat' is possible. So knowing whether a predicate is possible will not enable us to know whether it shares the alethic status of 'tiny vat'. Now consider the expression 'x falls under a predicate that shares the alethic status of "tiny vat" ' and abbreviate it to 'alethic tiny vat'. Is my pinky an alethic tiny vat? It falls under the predicate 'finger' and I know that 'finger' shares the alethic status of 'table', but I cannot know whether 'finger' shares the alethic status of 'tiny vat'. My pinky is a borderline case of 'alethic tiny vat'. Since every thing is an instance of some predicate, and parallel reasoning applies, every thing is a borderline case of 'alethic tiny vat'. A similar case can be made for 'alethic saint', 'alethic unfelt pain', 'alethic wooden can', and so on. Thus our list of ostensible examples of vague predicates without clear positive cases can be used to generate a similar list to show that there are purely vague predicates.

My definition of a 'borderline F' does not require that F have clear cases because '(y) $(Fy_{k+1} \supset Fy_k)$' can be known without knowledge that anything is an F. For example, I know that the kth prime number is far below the largest twin primes if the successor of the kth prime is far below the largest twin primes. But since no one knows whether the largest twin primes exist, I do not know whether 'far below the largest twin primes' applies to anything. Of course, this does not show that 'far below the largest twin primes' is vague. If we learn that there are finitely many twin primes, we will learn that the predicate is vague. If we learn that there are infinitely many, we will learn that the predicate is not vague. For the contradictoriness of the predicate will have been demonstrated to be knowable. A contradictory predicate can only be vague if it is impossible to know that it is contradictory. This explains why 'round square', 'bladeless axe missing a handle', and 'married bachelor' are not vague. Likewise, a tautologous predicate can only be vague if it is impossible to know that it is tautologous. Hence 'self-identical' and 'bald or non-bald' are not vague.

In defining borderline cases in terms of symmetrical blindspots, I become a gung-ho semantic realist. All borderline predications have truth values. We just can't know which are true and which are false. Conceptual inquiry can settle the question of whether 1 is a prime (look up 'prime number' in a mathematics dictionary). Empirical inquiry can settle the question of whether there is a ten thousand foot mountain on the far side of the moon. But neither conceptual nor empirical inquiry can settle the question of whether I am a tall man given that I am a borderline case of 'tall man'.

Most philosophers disagree. Most maintain that saying 'He is tall' of a borderline tall man results in a claim that is neither fully true nor false. Some are willing to assign a 'degree of truth' to the claim while others flatly deny it a truth value. So my claim that vague predicates are a species of blindspot predicates is a controversial one.

A. *Defining Blurry Counterparts to Vague Predicates*

In order to make my account of vagueness more persuasive, I shall advance a no-relevant-difference argument. For the sake of neutrality, call the predicates I have defined as vague 'blurry' predicates. In a nutshell, the argument is that since there is no relevant difference between vagueness and blurriness, vagueness is identical to blurriness; hence my account of vagueness is correct. My first step will be the construction of artificial predicates that are clearly blurry. I will then show that every vague predicate has a functionally equivalent blurry predicate. They behave the same. So those who wish to say that vague predicates are not identical to blurry predicates will be forced to claim that the difference is unobservable. As a semantic realist, I am willing to countenance undetectable differences. However, those opposing my view cannot be as sanguine because their opposition emanates from anti-realist scruples. These scruples prevent them from denying the identity thesis on the grounds that there is an unverifiable difference between vague predicates and their blurry mimics. So I am hoping to put the anti-realist in a position where he can only object to the identity thesis on realist grounds. For if I can do that, the anti-realist is left without an objection to a thesis he must deny. The refuted anti-realist will be free to point out that given realism, I cannot *prove* that vague predicates are blurry predicates by merely showing their behavioural indistinguishability. Realist commitments will require more than that. But before specifying how the case for the identity thesis is to be completed, I had better get to the business of beginning it.

Consider the set containing the following propositions.

1. Mystery−1 is an even number.
2. Mystery−2 is an even number.
   .
   .
   .
100. Mystery−100 is an even number.

The probability of each of these symmetrical blindspots is 0.5 since we have no more reason to believe that a particular mystery number is even than we do to believe that it is odd.[38] Further, the probabilities are independent. Call the number of true propositions in this set 'murk'. Call a number 'miny' just in case it is less than or equal to murk. 0 is a miny number because the minimum number of true propositions in the set is 0. 101 is not miny because the maximum number of true propositions in the set is 100. Is 1 miny? Well, the probability of 1 not being miny is 0.5^{100} since all of the propositions in the set would have to be false. Thus the probability of 1 being miny is very close to unity. (By selecting a larger set, the probability can be made arbitrarily close to unity.) The probability of 2 being miny is also extremely high. Likewise for 3, 4 and 5. But gradually the probability diminishes so that once we reach 100 we are virtually certain it is not miny.

A blurry predicate always raises an unanswerable question about where to draw the line. Sometimes, part of our ignorance about where to draw the line is remedial. For one can make better or worse probability judgments as to where the dividing line is. However, even the best judgement will leave a residue of ignorance. Blurriness imposes a graduated limit on knowledge. A blurry predicate spawns gradations even when it has an empty extension. For example, let us define 'hi-halfer' as an integer greater than 50 but less than murk. Define 'lo-halfer' as an integer less than 50 but greater than murk. At least one of these predicates has an empty extension but it is impossible to detect its emptiness. The probability that 'hi-halfer' is empty is slightly greater than 0.5. We know that 51 is a hi-halfer if 52 is, and 52 is if 53 is, and so on. If 'hi-halfer' is empty, no integer is the last hi-halfer. But since we do not know whether the predicate is empty, we cannot know '51 is the last hi-halfer' is false and we cannot know that it is true. Thus 51 gives rise to a symmetrical blindspot. As with 'tiny vat', 'hi-halfer' has no clear positive cases but still manages to evoke gradations of uncertainty.

Is 'miny' a vague predicate? It has the characteristic binomial

---

[38] Those who suspect that this probability assignment constitutes a fallacious appeal to the principle of indifference should bear in mind that the assignment does not have any of the features exploited by the standard objections to the principle. Specifically, it is not a geometrical probability (Bertrand's paradox), does not involve attributes which vary continuously (von Kries's problem), and the probability does not equal an irrational number (Kyburg's problem).

probability distribution of many vague predicates. It has an unknowable division point. Should it be introduced into ordinary English, it would behave like a vague predicate. My neighbour permits me to pick miny apples from his tree. If I pick none, I am within the bounds of his permission. Likewise, I can be sure that picking four apples is permitted. Should my neighbour discover that I picked eighty apples we might quarrel over whether I took more than a miny number of apples. Neither of us can be certain, but it is possible to have better grounds. Controversy can be the result of honest mistakes due to the various difficulties and fallacies associated with calculating probability distributions and varying rules of acceptance. Of course, the debate can be a sham where one party abuses the inherent uncertainty of the situation. To prevent abuse and quarrels, and to promote clarity, precisifying definitions could be introduced to reduce the blurriness. My neighbour could stipulate that 'miny' is to be understood as twenty. Perhaps the stipulation would catch on and the original definition abandoned. But it is more likely that 'miny' would survive many *ad hoc* redefinitions. Notice that such precisifying definitions would not be purely stipulative. There are acceptable and unacceptable precisifying definitions. There would be arbitrariness in drawing the line but it would be false to say that anything goes.

Blurriness and vagueness carry the same linguistic advantages and disadvantages. In speaking of their advantages and disadvantages, we should bear in mind that they are relative to interests. The fact that vagueness can create uncertainty and irresolvable disagreement can be counted as a virtue of vagueness if one's purposes are served by it. For example, a diplomat who warns of a 'strong response' to the contemplated invasion of one of its allies may thereby deter the aggressor without committing his country to a predictable reaction. So the first advantage of blurriness and vagueness is that it can saddle others with disadvantages. A second, less paradoxical advantage is that assertion conditions are easier to satisfy. Casual observation is usually sufficient for the application of 'small number' or 'miny'. From a glance I know that there are miny ice-cubes in my freezer but more than miny flakes of Wheaties in my cabinet. A rudimentary grasp of 'miny' can be quickly acquired by children through a few examples and tips. Trial and error will refine their usage. Even if they never learn the formal definition of 'miny', they can teach it to others. 'Miny' can survive even if I take its definition to the grave. However, as the probability distribution associated with 'miny' is slowly but surely distorted, the authority of my definition is eroded, and the meaning changes.

A third advantage is that we can communicate whole probability distributions. Casual observation of a speckled hen does not enable one to know how many speckles the hen has. One could estimate by means of a range specification; you might say that there are between ten and a hundred speckles on the hen. However, this description fails to convey characteristics of your probability distribution. There is a loss of information. If I tell you that I will arrive between 8.20 a.m. and 11.40 a.m., you have no more reason to expect that I will show up within the 9.45 to 10.15 interval than to expect that I will show up within the 9.10 to 9.40 interval. But if I tell you that I will show up within miny minutes of 10 a.m., you would consider it more likely that I will arrive within the 9.45 to 10.15 interval than within the 9.10 to 9.40 interval. Blurriness increases predictive power by allowing us to efficiently express and evoke confidence distributions.

Although 'miny' bears an interesting resemblance to vague predicates, one might still have doubts as to whether it is vague. For if 'miny' is vague, it is a counter-example to the compositionality of precision. The definiendum would be vague even though its definientia are precise. And despite the unknowability of the division point, we can nevertheless be sure that it exists. Consequently, the predicate has unlimited sensitivity.

In light of these peculiarities, one might deny that 'miny' is vague. If so, the possibility of eliminating vagueness from ordinary language arises. For example, one might define 'noonish' as 'any time that is within a miny number of minutes from noon'. Here one would be attempting to mirror the probability distribution people have for propositions of the form 'Time x is noonish'. Psychological research might disclose that our probability distribution for these propositions could be better reflected with a predicate other than 'miny'. If so, a superior redefinition could be offered by constructing another predicate from the mystery numbers. No matter what our ordinary probability distribution is, an identical one can be constructed with a predicate based on the mystery numbers.

Most of our ordinary language words could not be defined simply in terms of mystery integers; mystery rationals would have to be employed. For example, 'succotash' is a mixture containing an appropriate ratio of corn kernels and lima beans. If I mix 100 corn kernels with 100 lima beans, I have created succotash. But if I mix 100 corn kernels with 1,000,000,000 lima beans, I do not have succotash. A 1:1 ratio is permitted but a 1:10,000,000 ratio is not. But what is the minimum ratio? We do not know and I think we cannot know. However, this does not prevent the construction of blurry counterparts to succotash. For example, one proposal is that the actual ratio be between (murk+1):(murk+10) and (murk+10):(murk+1). This proposal yields a confidence distribution similar to that given by ' "Succotash" is roughly a 1:1 mixture of corn kernels and lima beans.' However, to completely eliminate the vagueness one would have to define 'mixture'. In the ordinary sense of the word, mixtures must have their parts close to each other. They need not touch for I can spill my succotash on the floor and still have succotash to clean up. However, there are limits to how far I can scatter my succotash. If I enclose each kernel and bean in separate envelopes, and send the envelopes to friends and admirers all over the world, that is the end of my succotash. Further, the kernels and beans have to be integrated. If I pour half a barrel of lima beans into half a barrel of corn, I don't yet have a barrel of succotash. I still need to mix them up. As I begin to mix them, I wonder whether I have succotash yet. After ten minutes of mixing, I am certain that I have succotash. But I do not know exactly when I first had succotash. This ignorance is a symptom of the vagueness of the integration requirement. The integration of a collection of objects is a function of homogenous distance and heterogenous distance. The homogenous distance between the kernels is the average distance from one kernel to another kernel; likewise the homogenous distance between the beans is the average bean-to-bean distance. The heterogenous distance between kernels and beans is the average distance from a kernel to a bean. A collection is integrated to the extent that the result of dividing the homogenous distance by the heterogenous distance is small. The blurry version of the integration requirement might read 'The degree of integration must be a miny number.' The question of how scattered the parts of the succotash can be might then be answered by determining the average distance between the kernels and beans. It could be proposed that this average distance be miny millimetres.

Regardless of the success of our definitions for 'appropriate ratio' and 'mixture', there still remains the problem of defining the vague words 'corn kernel' and 'lima bean'. These definitions would in turn appeal to parts of the kernels and beans. New definitions will be required for these parts and their subparts. Perhaps, eventually, we reach the atomic level. If there is no vagueness at this level, the replacement reduction is complete. But must there be an ultimate non-vague level? Could the vagueness continue infinitely? There is a sense in which an infinity of levels would threaten the completeness of the reduction and a sense in which it would not. The reduction would be incomplete in the sense that there would always be an unreduced element. However, it would be complete in the sense that no particular element is unreducible. The important type of completeness is the latter. I need only claim that any vague predicate is reducible to a blurry one; I do not need to claim that, if need be, infinitely many replacements could be supplied in practice. Compare my reduction claim to the claim that any Spanish sentence has a French translation. If there is an infinite stretch of Spanish discourse or if the Spanish sentences are produced faster than their French translations, there will always be some untranslated Spanish sentences. But these sentences will not show that Spanish enables one to express facts that cannot be expressed in French.

As previously mentioned, there are many different ways to obtain the desired probability distributions. Each is equally successful in explaining our linguistic behaviour. However, most will be undetectably inadequate from the point of view of truth. For example, by considering the second hundred mystery numbers, we can come up with a number resembling murk; call it 'nurk'. Nurk is the number of true propositions in the set of propositions of the form 'Mystery$-(100 + n)$ is an even number' (for n between 1 and 100). Just as we defined 'miny' as less than or equal to murk, 'niny' can be defined as less than or equal to nurk. The predicates 'miny' and 'niny' give rise to the same probability distribution over propositions of the form 'n is miny' and 'n is niny'. However, it is unlikely that the predicates have the same extensions because it is unlikely that murk = nurk. If there really is a number n such that 'noonish' means 'within n minutes of noon' spawning the same probability distribution as murk and nurk, it is likely that the number is neither murk nor nurk. However, the number will be identical to one of the cousins of murk and nurk. The good news is that blurry counterparts to vague expressions can have the same probability distributions and extensions. Indeed, since identical numbers are necessarily identical, the blurry counterparts will have the same intensions as well. The definitions will hold across all possible worlds. The bad news is that we cannot know which of the definitions are correct. We can narrow down the field of candidates. But we cannot determine the winners.

The underdetermination of our blurry definitions of vague predicates is reminiscent of the underdetermination found within the reduction of numbers to sets. There are two ways in which the resemblance between the two reductions is instructive. First, the reduction of numbers to sets forewarns us of the importance of uniform translation. Just as trouble looms for those who mix Zermello's definitions with von Neumann's, disaster awaits those who mix definitions based on different mystery numbers. Equally warranted translations of 'I will arrive noonish' are achieved with 'I will arrive miny minutes from noon' and 'I will arrive niny minutes from noon'. However, we cannot translate 'Either I will arrive noonish or I will not arrive noonish' as 'Either I will arrive miny minutes from noon or I will not arrive niny minutes from noon.' For the former is a tautology and the latter is (probably) contingent. As in the case of the reduction of numbers to sets, we must abide by a uniformity requirement, i.e. use 'miny' or 'niny' for 'near' but not sometimes one and sometimes the other.

Other hazards await us in 'Although John is not old, his dog is old.' This statement is true if John and his dog are both fifteen years old. An adequate translation will reflect the difference between being old for a dog and old for a man. Old dogs are located near the tail end of the distribution of dog ages. Old men are located near the tail end of the distribution of man ages. Sometimes claims are controversial because of their context relativity rather than because of pure vagueness. Suppose an employer tells his secretary that 'If I do not reach you by tenish, I will ask you to type no more than tenish pages.' At noon he reaches her and asks her to type twelve pages. She complains that he has broken his promise. For the antecedant of the conditional was made true by his late arrival (he concedes noon is not tenish) and the consequent was made false by his twelve-page typing request. The secretary reasons that if twelve is not a tenish time, twelve is not a tenish number of pages. Her boss invokes a double standard in which twelve is a tenish number of pages although not a tenish time. Since they both agree that tenish means 'near ten', their disagreement turns on the difference between being near in time and being near in number of pages.

The second way in which a comparison between the reductions is illuminating lies in the parallel between possible reactions to them. Recall that Paul Benacerraf has used the fact that we cannot know which definition of three is correct as grounds for concluding that all of the definitions are false. Others take the underdetermination to be another example of the general phenomenon of indeterminacy of translation and conclude that there is no fact of the matter. Yet others view the underdetermination as showing that we can dispense with numbers in favour of sets.

Since the reduction of vague predicates to blurry ones also features an unbreakable tie between rival definitions, one's position on this reduction may well parallel the one taken in response to reduction of numbers to sets. As a realist, I deny that underdetermination (lack of possible knowledge) implies indeterminacy (lack of truth value) or falsehood. And as emphasized in the previous chapter, we should be as suspicious of modal arguments from ignorance as other appeals to absence of evidence. Such arguments are only acceptable as enthymemes having as their missing premiss a conditional of the form 'If p is true, then p is known/knowable.' Benacerraf and the indeterminists draw whatever support they have for the missing conditionals from theories of meaning that my reduction is designed to subvert. So it would be question begging to object à la Benacerraf that unknowability falsifies all the blurry definitions or to object that my reduction reintroduces a type of vagueness in the form of translational indeterminacy.

B. *Dispensability or Identity?*

Those who view the reduction of numbers to sets as showing that we can dispense with numbers in favour of sets, might well suggest that the blurry reduction shows that we can dispense with vague predicates in favour of blurry ones. Talk of dispensability can be clarified with a distinction between positive, neutral, and negative ontology. One's positive ontology consists of what one affirms to exist, one's negative ontology consists of what one denies to exist, while what one neither affirms nor denies to exist constitutes one's neutral ontology. Thus God is in the positive ontology of the theist, the negative ontology of the atheist, and the neutral ontology of the agnostic. Our ability to paraphrase number talk in terms of set talk allows us to eject numbers from our positive ontology. Since few have denied the existence of numbers, weak ejection into one's neutral ontology is more popular than strong ejection into one's negative ontology. Since a strong ejection of vague predicates entails metaphysical scepticism about ordinary things, most will have a parallel preference for placing vague predicates in their neutral ontology. This would enable one to avoid denying the existence of heaps, flowers, and chairs, while affirming the existence of blurry-heaps, blurry-flowers, and blurry-chairs. Since the 'blurry-' prefix would be pervasive, speakers would abbreviate it away, yielding a language homophonic with the original. But when speaking without abbreviation, they will not affirm bridge conditionals of the form 'If there are blurry-Fs, then there are Fs.' For assent to these conditionals will force the return of vague predicates into one's positive ontology by *modus ponens*. Since these conditionals are more persuasive than the corresponding conditionals bridging sets and numbers, some may argue that this constitutes an important disanalogy between the set-theoretic and the blurry reduction. It may be insisted that conditionals bridging blurry predicates and vague ones are important enough to force the proponent of the blurry reduction to make an identity claim between the two. Under this account, 'heap' is identical to some blurry predicate that cannot be pinpointed.

I favour the identity thesis. Its alternative is too coy. Can I really be neutral on the question of whether I have a nose? Philosophy should be believable. Common-sense ontological beliefs are compulsive beliefs; partisanship is forced on the questions of whether there are flowers, chairs, and people. A view that requires us to be impartial in the face of the obvious is as unacceptable as one which requires us to be partisan where there is no evidence. Furthermore, the identity thesis has the not inconsiderable virtue of simplicity. Simplicity is a crucial principle amongst realists because they must appeal to it in order to ward off the sceptical hypothesis anti-realists standardly handle with verification requirements. Why suppose that the telephone on my desk is the same one I saw yesterday rather than an exact replica? Indeed, why suppose that I am the same person who saw the telephone yesterday rather than an exact replica? Since the hypotheses are designed to be unverifiable, the realist must appeal to simplicity in order to defend his strong preference. Given the weight he attaches to it in other contexts, it is not arbitrary of him to wield it with vigour when asked whether there might be two distinct types of predicates, vague and blurry.

Aside from its simplicity, the thesis that vague predicates are identical to blurry predicates is also supported by a line of reasoning inspired by the sorites paradox. Given that we are committed to an unadulterated common sense ontology, our unqualified assent to 'There are heaps' commits us to viewing 'heap' and all other vague predicates as blurry predicates. For corresponding to each vague predicate is a sorites argument that forces the issue.

1. A collection of one million grains of sand is a heap.
2. If a collection of n grains of sand is a heap, then a collection of $n-1$ grains of sand is a heap.
3. A collection of 1 grain of sand is a heap.

Anyone who straightforwardly holds a common sense ontology believes that a (suitably arranged) collection of one million grains of sand is a heap and that no single grain of sand is a heap. Given this acceptance of the first premiss and the rejection of the conclusion, the validity of the argument forces rejection of the second premiss. But the second premiss can only be false if there is a counter-example to it, that is, a number n such that n grains of sand is a heap and $n-1$ is not a heap. This requires 'heap' to be sensitive to very slight changes. Indeed, it must be sensitive to units of arbitrarily small size in order to be immune to all sorites paradoxes. Any predicate that has this sort of unlimited sensitivity while inducing graduated irremediable ignorance is a blurry predicate. Thus common sense ontology plus standard logic implies the identity of vague predicates and blurry predicates.

Although I think that this is a good argument for the identity thesis, most philosophers will find it unpersuasive. For they are under the sway of background theories of meaning which preclude the possibility of vague predicates having unlimited sensitivity. This allegiance will incline them to the view that the sorites will yield to a different sort of resolution. So in order for my argument to be convincing, I must promote pessimism about the feasibility of an alternate resolution. This will require a general survey and critique of rival responses to the sorites.

6
Rival Responses to the Sorites

MY thesis is that the sorites paradox can be resolved by viewing vagueness as a type of irremediable ignorance.[1] I begin by showing that the paradox cannot be solved through restrictions, revisions, or rejection of either classical logic or common sense. I take the key issue raised by the sorites to be 'limited sensitivity'; are there changes too small ever to affect the applicability of a vague predicate? I argue that the only consistent answer is negative and blame our tendency to think otherwise on a fallacious proportionality principle and a background of anti-realist theories of meaning. These theories of meaning encourage the view that perceptual, pedagogical, and memory limits would preclude unlimited sensitivity.

The sorites appears to have originated with Eubulides. The heap version takes the form of a mathematical induction. The base step of the argument claims that a collection of sand containing one million grains of sand is a heap. The induction step claims that any heap remains a heap if only one grain of sand is removed from it. Classical logic allows us to validly infer from these two propositions that a collection of sand containing one grain of sand is a heap. One has resolved the paradox of the heap if and only if one has shown how Eubulides' argument (and its variations) is defective.

I. REVERSIBILITY AND NON-STANDARD SORITES ARGUMENTS

There are two reasons why everyone agrees that at least a large portion of sorites arguments are unsound. The most obvious is the absurdity of the conclusions. A close second is that sorites arguments are vulnerable to refutation by logical analogy. Call an argument a 'positive' sorites if its base step uses a positive case of the inductive predicate. For example,

[1] Portions of this chapter are taken from my 'Vagueness, Blurriness, and Measurement', *Synthese*, forthcoming.

(A) 1. One minute after noon is noonish.
2. If n minutes after noon is noonish, then $n+1$ minutes after noon is noonish.
3. Six hundred minutes after noon is noonish.

Sorites arguments using a negative case of the predicate will be called 'negative sorites'. For example,

(B) 1. Six hundred minutes after noon is not noonish.
2. If n minutes after noon is not noonish, then $n-1$ minutes after noon is not noonish.
3. One minute after noon is not noonish.

As (A) and (B) illustrate, it is sometimes possible to construct a positive and a negative sorites with the same predicate. Since the conclusion of each negates the base step of the other, it is impossible for both arguments to be sound. Hence, everyone agrees that at least some sorites arguments are unsound. Those that wish to accept one of the arguments must reveal either a difference in argument form or a difference in the plausibility of the premises. Since (A) and (B) are so analogous in form and premiss plausibility, most people reject both arguments.

All standardly discussed sorites arguments are reversible in the manner of (A) and (B). However, sorites concocted from predicates devoid of clear positive cases or clear negative cases are not reversible.

(C) 1. A one million litre container is not a tiny vat.
2. If an n millilitre container is not a tiny vat, then an $n-1$ millilitre container is not a tiny vat.
3. A one millilitre container is not a tiny vat.

The absence of a clear positive case of 'tiny vat' ensures the attempt to reverse (C) will yield a counterpart with an implausible base step. It is a 'one-way' argument. Once we acknowledge the existence of purely vague predicates that have neither clear positives nor clear negatives, we must give up the belief that the vagueness of a predicate is a sufficient condition for sorites-embeddability. If 'tiny vat' is a vague but contradictory predicate,

(C) is a sound argument. Since there are thousands of vague predicates lacking clear positive cases, it is nearly certain that some of those predicates are contradictory and so form sound negative sorites arguments. Therefore, I affirm that some (non-standard) sorites arguments are sound. However, I also maintain that they are bad arguments on the grounds that their induction steps are not plausible. My position on standard sorites arguments (those using predicates having clear positive cases and clear negatives) is that they all have false induction steps and so are unsound.

Since non-standard sorites arguments have not been considered by other commentators, they have assumed that all sorites are reversible. Thus the problem has been construed as a matter of explaining how soundness fails to obtain for either half or for all sorites arguments. Since all commentators reject the claim that some positive sorites arguments are sound, positions on the puzzle can be classified in accordance with the way that they constitute objections to the soundness of Eubulides' (standard) sorites argument to the effect that one grain of sand is a heap. There are two basic kinds of objections to the soundness of an argument: a challenge to the truth of the premises and a challenge to its validity.

II. REJECTING THE ARGUMENT'S VALIDITY

One can reject the validity of an argument in two ways. First, one can claim that the argument is not valid in the same way that, say, affirming the consequent is not valid. Here, one concedes that the concept of validity applies. So were Eubulides' argument to be rejected along these lines, one would be claiming that the sorites embodies a formal fallacy. The second approach is to claim that the argument is neither valid nor invalid. The most straightforward way of motivating 'validity gaps' is to maintain that validity verdicts rest on a *presupposition*. When this presupposition fails to be true, the question of validity fails to arise.

A. *The Invalidity Approach*

Joseph Wayne Smith argues that paradoxes such as the sorites illustrate the complete invalidity of mathematical induction.[2] In response to the objection that the sorites can be formulated without mathematical induction, as a giant chain argument, Smith replies that this only shows there are two types of paradoxes. Sorites arguments not requiring mathematical induction are not genuine sorites arguments. They demand separate treatment. This total rejection of mathematical induction is unacceptable because of its costs to mathematics and its incompleteness as a resolution of the problem. Giving up an important portion of mathematics for the sake of a solution to only some of the initial puzzles is a bad deal.

Paul Ziff's position is more moderate. Rather than rejecting mathematical induction, we should simply put restrictions on it.

> A man with only one penny is poor. That's true. And giving a poor man a penny leaves him poor: if he was poor before I gave him the penny he's poor after I gave him the penny. That's true too. Both of those statements are obviously true. Nonetheless if you keep doing this if you repeat this argument over and over again you'll get into trouble. You must stop before it's too late or you'll end up with a false conclusion. The moral of the fallacy is plain: it's a perfectly good inference to make if you don't make it too often. (How often can in fact be worked out in precise detail for it obviously depends on the size and character of the increment in question. Thus if one were concerned with increments of the form: 1 penny then ½ penny then ¼ penny and so on one could go on *ad infinitum*.)[3]

Some may be attracted to this proposal because the 'not too far' restriction guarantees that we will never draw a false conclusion from true premisses. But notice that the same can be said of a 'not too near' restriction. By substituting for 'poor' the predicate 'is either poor or rich', we are guaranteed to draw a true conclusion as long as the argument goes far enough. Despite this guarantee, the 'not too near' requirement is suspicious because it seems to countenance an inference through a false lemma. For the corresponding chain argument would require us to draw inter-

---

[2] Smith's scepticism about mathematical induction is advanced in 'The Surprise Examination on the Paradox of the Heap', *Philosophical Papers*, 13 (May 1984), 43–56.
[3] Paul Ziff, 'The Number of English Sentences', *Foundations of Language*, 11/4 (1974), 530. Ziff also presents this position in his *Epistemic Analysis* (Dordrecht: D. Reidel, 1984), 141–2.

mediate conclusions to the effect that middle-income people are either poor or rich.

In addition to its resemblance to the problematic 'not too near' requirement, the 'not too far' restriction appears trivial. In order to know whether I have gone too far, I must already know the truth value of the conclusion. Ziff's claim that the question 'How far is too far?' can be worked out in detail is based on an unrepresentative sample. This question cannot be given an exact answer for standard sorites arguments. For an exact answer would require us to locate the last F in circumstances in which we are unable to draw the line between Fs and non-Fs.

Stephen Weiss has also proposed that mathematical induction be restricted.[4] Weiss is aware of the triviality problem and tries to avoid it with an analysis that is far more detailed and technical than Ziff's. Essentially, Weiss requires that the induction predicate be no less precise than the relation by which the objects in the induction class are ordered. Like Ziff, he regards the following argument as invalid.

(D) 1. A 500 pound man is fat.
2. If an n pound man is fat, then an $n-1$ pound man is fat.
3. A 50 pound man is fat.

Both 'heavier than' and 'is fat' are partitions of the weight parameter. That is, both can divide, according to height, *some* sets of people into mutually exclusive and exhaustive subsets. The present group of individuals vary in weight from 50 pounds to 500 pounds by one pound increments. The 'heavier than' relation can partition this set but 'is fat' cannot. Thus the ordering relation is more precise than the inductive predicate which invalidates the argument.

The most serious problem with Weiss's proposal centres on how he hopes to use his criterion to solve the paradox. He formulates the criterion as follows:

---

[4] Weiss' restrictions on mathematical induction are specified in 'The Sorites Fallacy: What Difference does a Peanut Make?' *Synthese*, 33 (1976), 253–72. Jay Rosenberg also appears to adopt the invalidity approach judging from his discussion of the ship of Theseus problem in his introductory text *The Practice of Philosophy* (Englewood Cliffs, N.J.: Prentice Hall, 1978) 2nd edn., 42–3.

An instance of mathematical induction applied to any subject is an acceptable argument (sound) if it satisfies the conditions for induction within mathematics but does not satisfy the condition that with respect to the induction set, the ordering relation partitions more precisely one of the parameters that the inductive predicate partitions.[5]

Notice that this criterion is formulated as a sufficient condition for soundness; not a necessary condition. As such it has no power to show that an argument is invalid. Yet Weiss repeatedly treats the criterion as if its satisfaction were necessary for soundness. For instance, immediately after stating the above criterion he says that the criterion 'has banned all mathematical inductions involving imprecise terms'.[6] Since Weiss grants that the premisses of standard sorites arguments are true, his criterion can only ban them as unsound if its violation is a sufficient condition for invalidity.

In light of this difficulty, one might suggest that Weiss meant by 'if' the stronger 'if and only if'. This interpretation has the advantage of bringing Weiss' criterion into harmony with the rest of his discussion. For the stronger interpretation does portray violation of the criterion as a sufficient condition for invalidity. The disadvantage is that it exposes Weiss to a fatal objection. First note that it would invalidate the following argument:

(D′) 1. A 500 pound man is fat.
　　　2. If an n pound man is fat, then an $n-1$ pound man is fat.
　　　3. A 50 pound man is fat or squares are squares.

But since the conclusion is a tautology, (D′) is valid regardless of whether it is also valid by mathematical induction. Since Weiss also accepts the truth of the premisses he must also admit the argument is sound even though the argument would count as unsound according to the strong interpretation of his restriction. Other counter-examples can be formed by taking any Weiss-invalid argument and adding a premiss that implies the conclusion,

---

[5] Ibid., 266. The above is actually Weiss' penultimate criterion. His final criterion is designed to handle a technical problem. Since the solution of the problem considerably complicates the criterion's formulation and nevertheless shares the same flaw with its predecessor, I have used the simpler one.
[6] Ibid.

or taking as a new conclusion the disjunction of the old conclusion and any implication of the premises.

The above difficulties are symptoms of the fact that the approach is vulnerable to Massey's scepticism about invalidity. With one irrelevant exception, invalidity can only be proved by 'the trivial logic-indifferent method' of showing that the premises can be true while the conclusion is false. Since this method can only be applied on a case-by-case basis, it cannot show the general invalidity of sorites arguments. Weiss appears to think that invalidity can also be proved by formal criteria. He appears to be among those who believe that just as we can formally prove an argument valid by showing that it instantiates a valid argument form, we can also formally prove an argument invalid by showing that it instantiates an invalid argument form. Logic textbooks promulgate this error through their lists of 'formal fallacies'. For example, it is said that valid categorical syllogisms must distribute their middle terms. But as critics of logic textbooks point out, the fact that an argument instantiates an invalid argument form does not establish its invalidity:

All bachelors are rich.
All unmarried adult males are rich.
All unmarried adult males are bachelors.

Although this argument violates the criterion, it is none the less valid. As Gerald Massey has stressed, there is an asymmetry between formally proving validity and formally proving invalidity. The former only requires us to find one valid argument form that the argument in question instantiates. But since an argument is invalid if and only if it instantiates *no* valid argument form, formal proof of invalidity requires proof of a universal generalization. The absence of an exhaustive list of valid argument forms and scruples about argument translation normally blocks the possibility of a *principled* proof of invalidity.[7] The only invalid arguments that can be *formally* proved invalid are those having premises

---

[7] J. Willard Oliver was the first to stress the asymmetry of proving validity and proving invalidity in his 'Formal Fallacies and other Invalid Arguments', *Mind*, 76/304 (Oct. 1967), 463–78. The implications of the asymmetry have been the topic of a sequence of articles by Gerald Massey starting with 'Are there any Good Arguments that Bad Arguments are Bad?', *Philosophy in Context*, 4 (1975), 61–7.

which are logical truths and logical falsehoods as their conclusions. Call these 'abnormal arguments'. Although Weiss might claim that some sorites are abnormal arguments, sorites having contingent propositions as their base steps are not abnormal:

(E) 1. Pete du Pont is rich.
    2. <u>If a rich man loses a penny, he will still be rich.</u>
    3. If Pete du Pont loses all of his money, he will still be rich.

Thus the one exception to Massey's asymmetry thesis is irrelevant to the sorites problem. No amount of tinkering with the fallacy of undistributed middle will make instantiation of its form a sufficient condition for invalidity. Likewise, no amount of tinkering with Weiss's criterion will make its satisfaction a (non-trivial) sufficient condition for invalidity. The same holds for Ziff's suggestion that the sorites is invalidated by the fact that it goes too far. The whole project of devising formal criteria for invalid mathematic inductions is fundamentally misconceived.

B. *Validity Gaps*

Given that we cannot formally demonstrate that the sorites is invalid, we could adopt the position that it is neither valid nor invalid. For instance, Bertrand Russell held that logic does not apply to the ordinary world, it only applies to the Platonic heavens.[8] The immediate objection to this view is that it makes the scope of logic intolerably narrow. Since most of our reasoning employs vague predicates, logic would be useless in the evaluation of most of our reasoning.

This objection divides the validity-gappers into two subschools. Philosophers such as Carnap and Susan Haack claim that the restriction of logic to non-vague predicates is not as drastic as it appears at first blush.[9] They maintain that our vague predicates

[8] Russell adopts this position in 'Vagueness', *Australasian Journal of Philosophy*, 1 (1923), 297–314.

[9] In *Logical Foundations of Probability*, ch. 1, Carnap proposes that prior to formalization, qualitative expressions should be replaced by comparative ones, or better yet quantitative ones. Susan Haack supports Carnap in *Deviant Logic*, (London: Cambridge University Press, 1974), ch. 6.

could be replaced by precise counterparts without serious loss. For example, the predicate 'swizzle-stick' is vulnerable to the sorites because it seems that the removal of one atom from a swizzle-stick never turns it into something that is not a swizzle-stick. However, 'swizzle-stick' could be replaced by 'one billion atom swizzle-stick'. Since this new predicate is defined as a swizzle-stick containing at least one billion atoms, it is sensitive to one atom differences. Thus it escapes the heartbreak of sorites.

The other subschool of validity-gappers denies the feasibility of the replacement project. For instance, Russell objects on the grounds that since our whole language is vague, there are no precise predicates to use as replacements.[10] A more recent objection to the replacement project has been raised by Patrick Grim.[11] As defined, something is a one billion atom swizzle-stick only if it is also a swizzle-stick (in the ordinary sense of the term). The precisified predicates will have logical relations with the vague predicates by which they are defined. So applying logic to precisified predicates will require the extension of logic to vague predicates. Thus the sorites will regain a foothold.

One might suggest that this consequence could be avoided through more sophisticated definitions employing no vague predicates. Perhaps this could be done with the help of a mathematical definition of a perfect swizzloid. A 'gizzle-gick' might then be defined as an object varying within a precisely specified range of being a perfect swizzloid. This ensures that the precisifying definition will not explicitly license inferences involving vague predicates. One might then be able to avoid accepting 'If there are gizzle-gicks, then there are swizzle-sticks.' Notice that it is also important not to reject the conditional because its negation carries commitment to applying logic to vague predicates. Perhaps the persuasiveness of these bridge conditionals can be explained away. But in the absence of an explanation, the validity-gappers' inability to preserve them will count against their proposal.

---

[10] Russell argues this way in 'Vagueness', as does Max Black in 'Vagueness', *Philosophy of Science*, 4/3 (1937), 427–55. M. Kohl criticizes Russell's argument for the universality of vagueness in 'Bertrand Russell on Vagueness', *Australasian Journal of Philosophy*, 4/1 (Jan. 1969), 31–41.

[11] Grim discusses this difficulty in 'What Won't Escape Sorites Arguments', *Analysis*, 42/1 (Jan. 1982), 38–43.

III. REJECTING A PREMISS

Since Eubulides' mathematical induction has only two premisses, there are only two ways to solve the paradox by rejecting a premiss. Both are problematic.

A. *Rejecting the Base Step*

The most radical response is to reject the base step of the induction. According to Peter Unger and Samuel Wheeler, the negative sorites argument shows that there really are no heaps.[12] 'Heap', along with all other vague concepts, is incoherent. Since most, if not all, of our observational vocabulary is vague, it follows that there are no ordinary things such as chairs, trees, and people.

Note that only the base steps of *positive* sorites arguments are being rejected as false. Negative sorites arguments are accepted as veridical paradoxes. One can soundly argue to the conclusion that a million grain collection of sand is not a heap but one cannot soundly argue to the conclusion that one grain of sand is a heap. Only half of the sorites arguments are deemed bad; the others are judged good arguments. Thus negative sorites arguments are pictured as insightful demonstrations of the impoverished extensions of vague predicates.

However, non-standard predicates show that the incoherence theorists have overestimated the extent to which sorites arguments cause grief to vague predicates. Vague predicates lacking clear negative cases are immune to negative sorites arguments. Vague predicates having only borderline cases are invulnerable to both positive and negative sorites arguments. So unless the incoherence theorist uses another method of establishing incoherency, some vague predicates will emerge unconvicted of incoherency.

But not many. The surviving predicates will only be scattered and unrepresentative reminders of how things were prior to the final solution. The prospect of carnage to our common sense ontology stimulates second thoughts about the incoherentist's argument.

---

[12] Unger and Wheeler have defended this position in a number of articles. Representative are Unger, 'There are no Ordinary Things', *Synthese*, 41 (1979), 117–54, and Wheeler, 'On That Which is Not', ibid., 253–72. Sympathy to the incoherence thesis can be found in the writings of W. V. Quine, Michael Dummett, and Bertil Rolf.

1. There are ordinary things only if the predicates used to describe them have extensions.
2. These ordinary predicates are vague.
3. All vague predicates lack extensions (for they are incoherent as shown by the sorites).
4. Therefore, there are no ordinary things.

Given that 'vague' is vague, the argument has inconsistent premises. For if 'vague' is in the extension of 'vague', then 'vague predicate' lacks an extension by (3), which is inconsistent with (2). Hence, the Unger–Wheeler argument can be shown to be necessarily unsound if the vagueness of 'vague' can be established.

Since most predicates are vague, there is a statistical syllogism supporting the widespread view that 'vague' is vague.[13] Reason to suspect that there is a deductive argument issues from the consensus that sorites arguments require a vague inductive predicate. For this suggests that the vagueness of a predicate can be established by embedding it in a sorites argument. For example, the vagueness of 'small integer' is established by:

(F) 1. 0 is a small integer.
2. If n is a small integer, then $n+1$ is a small integer.
3. One billion is a small integer.

If a corresponding sorites argument can be constructed for 'vague', we will have sufficient grounds for concluding that 'vague' is vague.

The desired argument can be constructed with the help of a sequence of numerical predicates: '1-small', '2-small', '3-small' etc. The nth predicate on the list is defined as applying to only those integers that are either small or less than n. These predicates can be used to construct a sorites paradox for the predicate 'vague'.

(G) 1. '1-small' is vague.

[13] I have only seen the autologicality of 'vague' defined once (in print), and that was fifty years ago in a discussion note by Virgil Aldrich. He denies it in 'Some Meanings of "Vague" ', *Analysis*, 4/6 (Aug. 1937), 94. The ensuing argument in favour of its autologicality was first presented in 'An Argument for the Vagueness of "Vague" ', *Analysis*, 27/3 (June 1985), 134–7.

2. If 'n-small' is vague, then '$n+1$ small' is vague.
3. 'One-billion-small' is vague.

The vagueness of '1-small' equals the vagueness of 'small' because both predicates clearly apply to 0 and apply exactly in the same way to all the other integers. The same holds for '2-small' and '3-small'. Slowly but surely we reach predicates in which the 'less than n' disjunct eliminates some borderline cases. Once we reach a predicate in which all borderline cases are eliminated, we have reached a non-vague predicate. But it is unclear where the predicates with borderline cases end and the ones without borderline cases begin. In short, 'vague' is vague.

The vagueness of 'vague' also creates difficulties for validity-gappers. The restriction 'Logic does not apply to vague predicates' will only be useful to validity-gappers if they can draw inferences from it that exclude applications to vague predicates. But since the restriction contains the vague predicate 'vague', it forbids us from applying logic to itself, rendering it inferentially impotent. This self-referential problem cannot be avoided by substituting a synonym for 'vague' or reformulating it negatively as 'Logic only applies to non-vague predicates.' For synonyms and complements of vague predicates are themselves vague. Matters are not helped by switching to 'Logic only applies to clearly non-vague predicates'. For in addition to there being predicates that are clear cases of 'clearly non-vague predicate', there are borderline cases of 'clearly non-vague predicate'. Higher order vagueness ensures that 'clearly non-vague' is vague.

In addition to the self-referential problem, it should be noted that the restriction runs into difficulties with counter-examples to the compositionality of vagueness. As can be seen from his argument that all language is vague, Russell assumed that any term that is defined with vague terms must itself be vague. However, there are at least two ways to define precise predicates in terms of vague ones. First, one can superimpose vague predicates in such a way that everywhere one of them is indefinite the other is definite. For example, the indefinite range of 'is an integer somewhat greater than 104' is within the definite range of 'is an integer somewhat less than 106', and vice versa. Thus the conjunctive predicate 'is an integer somewhat greater than 104 and somewhat less than 106' is perfectly precise. Second, one can follow a method of exhaustion. The cases which are indefinite for 'small integer' and 'medium integer' are definite positive cases for 'is either a small or medium integer' because the disjunctive predicate exhausts the possibilities for these cases. Since the same holds for 'medium integer' and 'large integer', the disjunctive predicate 'is either a small, medium, or large integer' is precise. These counter-examples to the compositionality of vagueness show that vague predicates are not always infectious and can even 'cure' prior vagueness. An expression such as 'is an integer somewhat greater than 104 and somewhat less than 106' creates an embarassment for the view that logic applies to all and only precise predicates. For its precision places the whole expression within the scope of logic while the vagueness of its defining terms places the parts of the expression outside the scope of logic. Yet the parts are related to the whole by the logical operation of conjunction.

Counter-examples to the compositionality of vagueness also create trouble for incoherence theorists. Those who believe that vague predicates are inconsistent can tolerate some failures of compositionality.[14] They can happily concede that the vagueness of 'heap' fails to make 'is either self-identical or is a heap' vague. For disjoining a consistent predicate with an inconsistent one yields a consistent predicate, as is illustrated by 'is a triangle or is a round square'. They can also concede that 'large' fails to make 'is large and is a round square' vague. For conjoining an inconsistent predicate with any other predicate yields an inconsistent predicate. However, they cannot tolerate the possibility that two vague predicates can be conjoined to form a precise predicate with a non-empty extension. If vague predicates are inconsistent, 'is an integer somewhat greater than 104 and somewhat less than 106' would be inconsistent. Yet it has the non-empty extension {105}. Notice that this example also poses a problem for anyone who might read 'incoherent' as 'meaningless'. For conjunctions (as opposed to concatenations) of meaningless expressions yield meaningless expressions.

[14] Indeed, an incoherence theorist, Bertil Rolf, was the first to point out that examples involving empty extensions refute the compositionality principle. See his 'A Theory of Vagueness', *Journal of Philosophical Logic*, 9/3 (1980), 315–25.

B. Rejecting the Induction Step

The more popular approach has been to reject the induction step of the argument. The initial appeal of this move is dampened by the recognition that rejecting the induction step is tantamount to asserting its negation. For the negation of the induction step is equivalent to the proposition that there is a precise minimum number of grains of sand necessary for being a heap. In other words, there must be a sharp division point between heaps and non-heaps. Philosophers usually try to avoid this counter-intuitive commitment by altering the interpretation of the negation of the induction step through departures from classical logic.

1. *Intuitionism*

Perhaps the most direct evasion of this consequence is Putnam's.[15] Putnam points out that the offensive negation does not follow in intuitionist logic. So by abandoning classical logic in favor of intuitionism, we can comfortably reject the induction step. However, as Cargile has point out, the paradox can be formulated in another way by appealing to the intuitionist's least number theorem.[16] Indeed, Stephen Reed and Crispin Wright have shown that the sorites can be couched in even low level intuitionist logic.[17] The paradoxical nature of the sorites persists even when deprived of the devices disallowed by the intuitionist.

2. *Denying that the Induction Step has a Truth Value*

Max Black has suggested that classical logic be viewed in the same way as geometry — only applicable in a tentative, rough-and-ready way to our terrestrial surroundings.[18] Just as geometry *presupposes* rigid boundaries, logic presupposes sharp boundaries for predicates. We can confidently apply geometrical principles to physical objects to the extent that we are confident those objects approximate perfect rigidity. Likewise, logical principles such as

---

[15] Putnam makes this point in 'Vagueness and Alternative Logic', *Erkenntnis*, 19 (1983), 297–314.

[16] Cargile commented on the futility of the move to intuitionism in 'The Sorites Paradox', *British Journal for the Philosophy of Science*, 20/3 (Oct. 1969), 193–202.

[17] They present a low level version in 'Hairier than Putnam Thought', *Analysis*, 25 (1985), 56–8.

[18] Black advances this position in 'Reasoning with Loose Concepts', *Dialogue*, 2 (1963), 1–12.

the law of excluded middle apply just to the extent that our concepts are sharp.

'Presupposes' was a harmless enough term before Strawson's use of it in his critique of Russell's theory of descriptions. It helpfully distinguishes between what a statement entitles us to assume and what it entails. However, we could get along without 'presupposes' because we have a number of alternative expressions that will also do the job: 'suggests', 'leads us to assume', 'invites the inference that', and so on. Use of these alternatives is preferable nowadays because philosophers tend to equivocate between pragmatic presupposition and Strawson's *semantic* presupposition. S_1 semantically presupposes S_2 if and only if the truth of S_2 is a necessary condition of S_1 having a truth value. For example, Strawson claims that the falsity of 'The present King of France exists' ensures that 'The present King of France is bald' is neither true nor false. Those sceptical of semantic presupposition complain that its advocates take its logical consequences too lightly and maintain that the linguistic phenomena the notion is intended to explain are largely pragmatic rather than semantic.[19] We should bear this complaint in mind as the details of Black's proposal unfold.

After making his general observation about logic presupposing that predicates have sharp boundaries, Black goes on to concede that the sorites is valid and also grants that the base step is true and the conclusion is false. He then claims that the induction step lacks a truth value. Thus informal talk about logic presupposing sharp boundaries evolves into an endorsement of *semantic* presupposition. The logical price begins with commitment to a non-standard concept of validity that permits an argument to be valid even if it has a false conclusion but no false premises. This deviation requires Black to also use deviant logical connectives. For instance, Black must reject double negation in order to escape sorites arguments such as the one resulting from prefacing the induction step of (A) with 'It is not true that it is not true that'. Black explains the induction step's lack of truth value by appealing to the fact that it quantifies over borderline cases. The premiss

---

[19] Stephen Boer and William Lycan provide a detailed defence of the sceptical position in *The Myth of Semantic Presupposition* (Bloomington, Ind.: Indiana University Linguistics Club Publications, 1976). Lycan updates the scepticism in *Logical Form in Natural Language* (Cambridge: MIT Press, 1984), ch. 4.

'bundles together proper and improper instances' of the vague concept in question.

J. L. King has objected that the requirement that borderline cases be excluded from the domain of discourse would render many of Black's own statements neither true nor false. For instance, consider the statement 'If a man is tall, then he is not a borderline case (for "tall"), but some men are borderline cases (for "tall")':

$$(x)(Mx \supset (Tx \supset -B_t x)) \& (\exists x)(Mx \& B_t x)$$

This statement is plainly true. Indeed, it is just the sort of statement Black could make in his analysis of the sorites. Yet it cannot come out true under Black's requirement. If the quantifiers range over borderline cases for 'tall', the first conjunct is illegitimate since it will have substitution instances in which the predicate 'tall' applies to borderline cases. On the other hand, if the quantifiers do not range over borderline cases, the second conjunct is false. King points out that there are analogous difficulties for other seemingly true statements about the relationship between clear cases and borderline cases. He diagnoses the general problem as follows.

> The obvious source of the difficulty is the fact that, in general, the clear cases for the concept of a borderline case of a given concept are (necessarily) the borderline cases for the given concept. If we wish to apply both a concept C and the concept of borderline case for C, we will have to forego any general restriction on quantification over borderline cases. On the other hand, if we treat the general premise of the sorites argument as an inductive statement and do not impose any restriction on such quantification, the sorites paradox will be reinstated.[20]

King concludes that Black's rule against quantifying over borderline cases is too strong.

Problems with the logical status of Black's own analysis are made more vivid with the realization that his key concept of 'failed presupposition' is itself vague. To see this, consider the following sorites:

---

[20] John L. King, 'Bivalence and the Sorites Paradox', *American Philosophical Quarterly*, 16/1, (Jan. 1979), 20.

(H) 1. Any induction step using '1−small' has a failed presupposition.
2. If induction steps using 'n−small' have failed presuppositions, then so do those using '$n+1$ small'.
3. Induction steps using 'one billion small' have failed presuppositions.

Since 'one billion small' is not vague, the conclusion of (H) is false. To solve this sorites, Black must say that the induction step has a failed presupposition due to the vagueness of its inductive predicate. The consequent vagueness of 'has a failed presupposition' places it outside the scope of logic. Since the restriction 'Logic presupposes sharp boundaries' uses a concept without sharp boundaries, inferential impotence haunts Black's restriction in the way it haunts the restriction of the validity-gappers.

3. Many-valued Logic

Perhaps the most popular way to reject the induction step is through an attempt to reflect the intuition that vague predicates have degrees of applicability by introducing intermediate truth values. It can then be maintained that a one-grain difference cannot be the crucial difference between whether a collection of sand is a heap. For one can claim that the grain only makes a difference to the degree of truth or accuracy there is in the claim that the body of sand is a heap. The plausibility of the induction step is then explained in terms of the high degree of truth possessed by each conditional of the form 'If an n grain collection of sand is not a heap, then an $n+1$ grain collection of sand is not a heap.' Although each conditional of this form has a high degree of truth, the degree of some of them is slightly less than full truth. These small differences can accumulate into a big difference. Thus the induction step of Eubulides' argument should be rejected because it implicitly states that 'If it is true to degree x that "An n grain collection of sand is not heap", then it is also true to degree x that "An $n+1$ grain collection of sand is not a heap." '

One cost of this solution is the revision to logic. Intuitively, 'This collection of sand is either a heap or not a heap' is a tautology and so should have a degree of truth equal to 1. But given that the collection of sand is a borderline heap, 'This is a heap' and 'This is not a heap' will have degrees of truth equal to less than 1. The standard many-valued rule for determining the truth value of a disjunction is to assign the disjunction the higher of the truth values assigned to its disjuncts. Accordingly, the truth value of 'This is a heap or not a heap' will be less than 1. So unless the standard rule is replaced, many-valued theorists must either follow Sanford and deny the truth functionality of the logical connectives (to preserve classical theorems) or follow Machina and deny the classical theorems (to preserve truth functionality).[21]

Although Machina's approach seems more radical, it may be the only way the many-valued theorist can go. Consider the following sequence of sentences.

1. An integer is small if and only if it is 1–small.
2. An integer is small if and only if it is 2–small.
3. An integer is small if and only if it is 3–small.
   .
   .
   .

1,000,000,000. An integer is small if and only if it is 1,000,000,000–small.

The early propositions in the sequence are analytically true. The last is not. Which is the last analytically true proposition? Since there is no way to tell, we conclude that 'analytic' is vague. Now consider the following two claims.

(i) If a proposition is analytic, it has a truth value (of 1 or 0).
(ii) If 'p' is analytic, then 'p is analytic' is analytic.

Given (i), it is impossible for 'analytic' to apply to any proposition that the many-valued theorist is willing to call vague. Yet the above list of sentences shows that some propositions are vaguely analytic. Given (i) and (ii), it is impossible for a many-valued theorist to resort to a higher order paraphrase; ' "(10) is analytic" is true to degree 0.9.' In light of these difficulties, many-valued

---

[21] David Sanford's approach is presented in 'Borderline Logic', *American Philosophical Quarterly*, 12 (1975), 29–39. Kenton Machina's approach appears in 'Truth, Belief, and Vagueness', *Journal of Philosophical Logic*, 5/1 (1976), 47–78.

Rival Responses to the Sorites

theorists should reject (i). But once one grants that an analytic proposition can have a truth value of less than 1, it is pointless to follow Sanford and sacrifice truth functionality in order to preserve the 1 value for classical tautologies.

Since analyticity implies necessity, the above sequence can be used to show that 'necessary' is vague. Since we cannot know where the analytic truths end, we cannot know where the necessary truths end. The vagueness of 'necessary' points to the vagueness of 'valid'. Under the semantic definition of 'valid', an argument is valid if and only if it is possible for its premises to be true and its conclusion false. Since impossibility is necessary falsehood, the vagueness of 'necessary' infects 'valid'. And indeed the above sequence provides an example of the vagueness of 'valid'. Consider the sequence of deductive arguments of the form 'n therefore $n+1$'. As long as '$n+1$' refers to an analytic proposition, the argument is classically valid. But if we cannot know where the analytically true propositions end, then we cannot know where the valid arguments end.

None of this is bad news to Machina. Indeed, he has explicitly invoked the notion of degrees of validity in order to explain the persuasiveness of the sorites. Although Machina's denial of classical theorems is radical, it should be remembered that he assents to the theorems in the special case where the propositions involved have the extreme values of either 1 or 0. Thus he views classical logic as acceptable under the simplifying idealization of full truth and full falsehood. But to have a logic whose scope includes both the ideal and the less than ideal cases, we have to deny the full generality of classical theorems.

Those reluctant to view classical theorems as only correct in limiting cases may wonder whether an acceptable many-valued theory could be obtained by altering the standard rules for assigning truth values to disjunctions. But is there a reasonable replacement? To answer this question, we need to get a firmer idea of what goes wrong with the standard rule. It should first be observed that grounds for rejecting the standard rule for disjunction are grounds for rejecting the standard rules for the remaining binary connectives. For example, the conjunction rule assigns conjunctions the minimum value of its conjuncts. So 'This is a heap and this is not a heap' receives a truth value of greater than 0 even though it is a contradiction. Since the rule guarantees that conjunctions will have truth values no lower than their lowest conjunct, the rule also has difficulty in explaining our growing clarity as predicates are added after the most doubtful one. For example, suppose a speaker begins by describing Ted as short and then adds that he is also fat, bald, smart, athletic, and rich. We assign a degree of truth of 0.5 to 'Ted is short' and 0.6 to each of the remaining attributions. But contrary to the conjunction rule, we do not believe that 'Ted is short, fat, bald, smart, athletic, and rich' equals the degree of truth of 'Ted is short.' Our uncertainties compound making us assign a much lower degree of truth to the claim that Ted exemplifies the conjunctive predicate. Also notice that 'Ted is fat, or bald, or smart' is less of a borderline attribution than 'Ted is fat.' Contrary to the disjunction rule, disjuncts of equally borderline predications can add up to produce a disjunctive statement 'closer to the truth' than any of its disjuncts. Acceptance of both the disjunction rule and the conjunction rule requires one to assign the same degree of truth to disjunctions of propositions with equal degrees of truth as to the conjunctions of the same propositions. The error is akin to the card-player who assigns equal probabilities to 'My first hand will contain an ace and my second hand will contain an ace' and 'My first hand will contain an ace or my second hand will contain an ace.' Indeed, the obvious solution to the problems with accumulation and compounding effects now appears to be that of replacing the standard rules with those given in the probability calculus. However, this would trivialize many-valued logic. For what would be the difference between degrees of truth and degrees of probability?

4. *Super-valuationism*

The dilemma of choosing between classical theorems and truth functionality is softened by super-valuationists such as Kit Fine.[22] Instead of appealing to intermediate truth values, super-valuationists only appeal to truth-value gaps. According to them, vague predicates have a gap extension in addition to their positive and negative extensions. The gap can be filled in as the language develops. The ways in which these reserve areas can be completely filled are precisifications of the predicate. Some precisifications can be ruled out a priori. For example, it would be perverse to

[22] Fine's supervaluational treatment of vagueness appears in 'Vagueness, Truth and Logic', *Synthese* 30/3 (1975), 265–300.

claim that fifteen minutes after noon is not noonish but sixteen minutes after noon is noonish. This precisification violates the rule that new Fs be preceded by old Fs and new non-Fs be followed by old non-Fs. Once equipped with such rules, the notion of an 'admissible precisification' is well-defined. The super-valuationist can then maintain that all classical theorems hold for vague predicates because the theorems come out true under all admissible precisifications of the predicates. Given a borderline case of a heap, 'This is a heap or this is not a heap' is true even though 'This is a heap' and 'This is not a heap' both lack truth values. Of crucial interest is the fact that the induction steps of sorites arguments are ruled false by this procedure. Under every admissible precisification of 'noonish', for instance, the second premiss of (A) and (B) turns out false. Since we know that every possible resolution of our uncertainty about 'noonish' will make the statement false, super-valuationists urge that we are entitled to claim 'There is an n such that n minutes after noon is noonish and $n+1$ minutes is not noonish.'

Before turning to the more serious objections to super-valuationism, we should first note some technical problems with the rules determining 'admissible precisification'. These problems arise with vague predicates lacking clear positive cases or clear negative cases. Predicates having only clear negative cases show we cannot require that new Fs always be preceded by old Fs. For the absence of old Fs would only permit a single precisification; the one making all borderline cases non-Fs. Thus the predicate will have the same status as contradictory predicates. Parallel reasoning ensures that vague predicates having only clear positives and borderline cases would acquire the status of tautologous predicates. Worse, predicates having only borderline cases would resist precisification altogether.

A revised set of rules for admissible precisifications must allow new clear cases to be created *ex nihilo*, that is, without the precedent of old clear cases. However, it must still retain the precisification in which all borderline cases are transmuted into clear Fs (or non-Fs as the case may be). For example, given that 'tiny vat' has no clear positives, it will have one 'contradictory' precisification where it acquires the status of a contradictory predicate. Now suppose 'tiny vat' is embedded in a negative sorites:

(C) 1. A one million litre container is not a tiny vat.
2. If an n millilitre container is not a tiny vat, then an $n-1$ millilitre container is not a tiny vat.
3. A one millilitre container is not a tiny vat.

Under 'consistent' precisifications where we allow some borderline cases of 'tiny vat' to be resolved as clear positive cases, the second premiss is false. But under the 'contradictory' precisification the premiss is true. We thus have an example of a sorites whose induction step does not come out false under all precisifications. Hence the super-valuationist cannot diagnose all sorites as unsound because of a false induction step.

The super-valuationist may be able to handle the problems posed by non-standard vague predicates through technical adjustments. However, technical changes will not pacify critics who complain that hypothetical precisifications are irrelevant. Sanford points out that the super-valuational approach distorts the existential quantifier and disjunction.[23] For the super-valuationists are claiming that there are true disjunctions that lack true disjuncts. To deny the induction step, they must say that there is a minimum number of grains necessary for a heap. Yet they say that no number is actually the minimum number.

Further doubts about the super-valuationist's ontological honesty arise from more general discourse about sorites arguments. Consider a set of 101 sorites arguments, each reaching its absurd conclusion in 100 steps. Just as the pigeon-hole principle tells us that two New Yorkers must have the same number of hairs because the maximum number of hairs is smaller than the number of New Yorkers, it also tells us that two of the sorites arguments must fail at the same step. So in addition to saying 'Each sorites has a threshold number but no particular number is its threshold number', the super-valuationist must also say 'Two of the threshold numbers are equal but the equality does not hold between any two particular numbers.' There is no entity for the identity. Other scenarios involving sets of sorites arguments will produce more mathematical mumbo-jumbo.

In addition to saddling us with double-talk, Kenton Machina further objects that the super-valuational approach requires us to abandon classical rules of inference even though the classical

[23] Sanford makes this point in 'Competing Semantics of Vagueness: Many Values versus Super-truth', *Synthese*, 33/2, 3 and 4 (1976), 195–210.

tautologies which mirror those rules remain.[24] In general, critics of the super-valuationists have maintained that the conservativeness of the theory is illusory.

It should also be noted that the super-valuationists share Sanford's problem with the vagueness of validity. On the one hand, they purport to have developed a logic that permits validity judgments even when parts of the arguments lack truth-values. On the other hand, they say that borderline cases engender truth-value gaps. So a borderline case of 'valid argument' seems to require the super-valuationist to concede that some arguments are neither valid nor invalid, after all.

5. *The Epistemological Approach*

According to the epistemological approach, the induction step is false and there is no need to alter standard logic. There are precise division points. However, it does not follow that we are in a position to know where those division points are. Thus the existence of sharp division points is reconciled with our inability to specify them. According to Cargile, this ignorance is due to our imperfect understanding of vague words. Campbell describes our ignorance as 'semantic uncertainty'. Both urge the acceptance of the epistemological thesis on the grounds that it is far more plausible than any departure from classical logic.

Viewed from the epistemological perspective, there is a resemblance between the sorites and the lottery paradox. This resemblance can be highlighted by expressing a sorites as a chain of alternations. We begin with the observation that a 2000 millimetre man is not a short man but a 1000 millimetre man is a short man. We then consider the following alternations:

1. A 2000 and a 1999 millimetre man are either both short or both not short.
2. A 1999 and a 1998 millimetre man are either both short or both not short.

.
.
.

1000. A 1001 and a 1000 millimetre man are either both short or both not short.

---

[24] Machina makes this criticism in 'Truth, Belief, and Vagueness'.

According to the epistemic proposal, exactly one of the above propositions is false but we do not know which. At least one of the propositions must be false because the conjunction of (1)–(1000) implies the false proposition that either the two metre man and the one metre man are both short or are both not short. At most one of the propositions is false because otherwise there would be a short man who was taller than a non-short man. Thus classical logic plus common sense knowledge of short men ensures that each of these propositions has a high probability; high enough to merit the belief of a man who had the acceptance rule: believe a proposition if and only if its probability exceeds 0.99. However, the probability of the conjunction of these propositions is lower than 0.01. Therefore, the follower of the acceptance rule would believe each member of the conjunction of (1)–(1000) and yet believe the negation of the conjunction. So he would have inconsistent beliefs. Given a lottery of 1000 tickets with only one prize, the same sort of inconsistent beliefs would be formed concerning propositions of the form 'Ticket number i is a losing ticket.' The lottery situation is paradoxical since it appears to show that one can have rational inconsistent beliefs. The proponent of the epistemological approach can maintain that the same holds for the above 1000 propositions. This resemblance is useful to the proponent of the epistemic view because he can use it to explain our willingness to assent to each step of the chain argument and our reluctance to accept the argument's conclusion. He can admit that vagueness engenders inconsistent beliefs without concluding that we are irrational or that vague language is incoherent. The lottery situation serves as a precedent for the rationality of believing an existential generalization ('There is a winning ticket') while disbelieving of each instance that it confirms the generalization.[25] Thus the 'incoherency' is restricted to the doxastic level.

The epistemological approach provides a ready explanation of the many-valued theorist's troubles with his standard rules for evaluating disjunctions and conjunctions of vague predications: vagueness uncertainty, like all other types of uncertainty, falls

---

[25] Those who doubt this point because of misgivings about probabilistic rules of acceptance are urged to consider the preface paradox. Here belief that one of the beliefs expressed in the book is false need not be interpreted as the product of an acceptance rule and yet it nevertheless provides an example of rational inconsistent belief.

under the scope of probability theory. Thus the non-compositionality of vagueness is no surprise. In addition to predicting that compounds of vague statements will tend to behave as applications of probability theory would lead us to expect, the epistemological approach predicts that these compounds will appear to behave counter-probabilistically just where we would expect probabilistic fallacies. For example, research in the psychology of reasoning documents our tendency to overestimate the probability of conjunctions and underestimate the probability of disjunctions. Hence people trained in statistics will tend to assign vague conjunctive predicates smaller positive extensions than those ignorant of statistics. The statistically sophisticated will also assign larger positive extensions to vague disjunctive predicates. Joining this pair of predictions enables us to picture the prediction in terms of a shift in the borderline area of the predicate. Suppose that C is a conjunctive predicate equivalent to F_1 & F_2. Its positive extension is conjunctive and hence overestimated by the probabilistically naïve. Its negative extension is equivalent to the disjunction $-F_1$ v $-F_2$ and so is underestimated. Probabilistic sophistication corrects these errors yielding a rightward shift in the perceived borderline area as illustrated in Figure 6.1.

FIGURE 6.1

Naïve extension of conjunctive predicate C		
Perceived negative extension of C	Perceived borderline extension of C	Perceived positive extension of C

Sophisticated extension of conjunctive predicate C

In addition to predicting that probabilistic sophistication will produce a right shift for conjunctive predicates, the approach predicts a left shift for disjunctive predicates. Furthermore the magnitude of the shift should be expected to increase with increases in the predicate's 'degree of conjunctiveness' (number of conjuncts) or disjunctiveness. Since degrees of probabilistic sophistication vary, we can also test for a direct correlation between sophistication and shift magnitude. Expertise in psycholinguistics, experimental design, and the psychology of reasoning should put one in a position to check these predictions and generate new ones. Specifically, one could design a questionnaire to be answered by groups of students ranging from the statistically naïve to the statistically sophisticated. Since the gradations correspond to course levels in statistics, the cooperation of a statistics department would make the experiment affordable.

Three general objections to the epistemic approach can be raised. The first is that, like its brethren, the epistemic approach cannot handle higher order vagueness. In particular, it cannot make sense of the possibility of there being a borderline clear case of an F. Given the epistemic conception of vagueness, x is a clear F only if it is possible to know that x is F. Something is a borderline case of an F only if it is impossible to know it is an F. Now suppose that x is an F but that it is a borderline case of a clear F. That means that that x can be known to be an F, and yet x cannot be known to be a knowable F. But, the objection continues, it is possible to know that x is an F only if it is possible to know that x can be known to be F.

To escape this argument, proponents of the epistemological approach must reject the tacit appeal to the KK principle: if one knows that p, then one knows that one knows that p. Since KK is out of favour nowadays, his rejection should find a sympathetic audience. However, the objector may insist that he only needs a weak version of KK:

> If it is possible to know that p, then it is possible to know that one knows that p.

This weak version of KK avoids many of the standard counter-examples to the KK principle. As it stands, however, it is still vulnerable to examples involving conceptual poverty. For instance, it might be said that although it is possible that a child know that his milk is in the refrigerator, it is not possible that he knows that it is possible for him to know that his milk is in the refrigerator. For his insufficient grasp of 'possible' and 'know' prevents him from understanding the claim. But unless the defender of the epistemological approach wishes to maintain that we display similar conceptual immaturity, he is vulnerable to an appeal to a still weaker version of the KK principle restricted to conceptually mature individuals. The better reply is to explain the failure of KK in terms of the vagueness of 'know'. For if 'know' is vague, it is possible to know that x is F without it being clear that one can know that x is F. Since most of our vocabulary is vague, and since the vagueness of 'know' is conceded by epistemologists, there should be little resistance to the thesis that 'know' is vague. The fact that a sorites argument can be constructed from 'know' just about clinches the issue.

(I) 1. I know that there will be living people one second from now.
2. If I know that there will be living people n seconds from now then I know that there will be living people $n+1$ seconds from now.
3. I know that there will be living people one billion years from now.

So unlike most of the previous theories, the epistemological approach can accommodate higher order vagueness.

The second general objection is that loyalty to classical logic in the face of the sorites is pointless since classical logic must be deserted anyway in the face of other difficulties. Classical logic has been criticized for its inability to cope with logical fatalism, fiction, quantum mechanics, presupposition, and the liar paradox. That is just the beginning of a long list. Unless the proponent of the epistemological approach maintains that none of the members of this list warrants deviant logic, he cannot claim that his solution to the sorites has the virtue of conservativeness. Given that he will depart from classical logic in the face of another problem, he cannot condemn sorites-inspired departures in the strong way Cargile and Campbell do. Cargile and Campbell maintain that the counter-intuitiveness of their position is a peccadillo compared to any position that runs contrary to classical logic. They could not condemn logical deviancy in this fashion if they themselves treated it as a venial rather than mortal sin elsewhere. If one deviant is permitted, there goes the neighbourhood.

To my knowledge, neither Cargile nor Campbell have deviated elsewhere. They have not taken positions that make them vulnerable to the fallacy of special pleading. However, it might be replied that they have only managed to do this because they have not addressed all of the problematic issues. Undercutting this reply is the fact that almost all proposed deviations are controversial. Few contemporary philosophers believe that logical fatalism is best handled by denying truth values to future contingent propositions. Advocates of quantum logics are greeted with scepticism as to whether quantum logic is really logic. Proponents of semantic theories of presupposition face competing pragmatic theories in which apparent truth-value gaps are explained away as confusions between what is misleading and what is false. Fictional discourse remains equally puzzling once we depart from classical logic. And the liar has proved no less recalcitrant to deviant approaches than to conservative ones. Historically, rivals to classical logics (as opposed to supplements) have never solved a philosophical problem without creating another of equal severity. Thus the assumption that deviancy will be required elsewhere is open to challenge. Best of course, would be a vindication of this challenge through a complete collection of classical solutions to the problems. But this can hardly be made an adequacy condition for a solution to the sorites.

The third and most influential objection is that the epistemological approach makes an unrealistic assumption about the sensitivity of vague concepts. As J. L. King emphasizes, proponents of the epistemic approach must say that a millimetre difference can make the difference between a runner starting from New York being far from San Francisco and his not being far from San Francisco.[26] According to King, there can only be division points if there are determinants. The determinant for 'far' cannot be conventional, for ordinary usage is indecisive. The determinant cannot be natural, because there are no natural boundaries between far and non-far points from San Francisco. Since the determinant must be either conventional or natural, there is no determinant and thus no sharp division point.

What are determinants? They are the things that *make* a proposition true. But what things make a proposition true? King alleges that clear propositions have these things but borderline propositions lack them. But we have only been told that that there are two sorts of truth-making things; the conventional ones and the natural ones. If these things are creatures of the correspondence theory of truth, then the reply to King's objection is that the

[26] This objection appears in King, 'Bivalence and the Sorites Paradox', *American Philosophical Quarterly*, 16/1 (Jan. 1979), 17–25.

correspondents (facts, states of affairs, situations, and so on) are pliable enough to make borderline propositions true. What *makes* it true that 'The runner is just now far from New York'? Well, the *fact* that the runner is just now far from New York. Those who object that this is a queer fact must go on to adumbrate how the queerness is objectionable. After all, facts have a reputation for queerness. General facts, existence facts, negative facts, belief facts, moral facts, aesthetic facts, and mathematical facts form a zoo of ontological exotica. Some may balk at the suggestion that the correspondence theory commits us to ontological determinants. They suggest that the theory merely requires that the truth predicate be a disquotational device. But note that this view does not preclude the possibility that borderline propositions have (albeit unknowable) truth values.

King takes his argument against the epistemic approach to be 'a semantical point, not an epistemological one. There could be a boundary which we were unable to discover, but there could not be a boundary without a determinant.'[27] The crux of the issue for King is the absence of a theory explaining how there could be imperceptible boundaries for our vague vocabulary. But as he would concede, the absence of the theory does not preclude the existence of the boundaries. Indeed, once it is agreed that true semantical premisses partake in a classically valid argument for the existence of imperceptible boundaries, then we have a jolly good reason to believe that the boundaries exist. To quote Quine, 'If sheer logic is not conclusive, what is?' Given that King happily harbours unknowable truths, then he should harness them in his moment of need. The paradox of sharp boundaries should be greeted as veridical rather than falsidical, as an ontic revelation rather than a chimera.

Recall Russell's objection to nominalism. Nominalists are committed to at least one universal, resemblance; therefore, they have no motive to pay dearly for the exclusion of other universals. By committing himself to unknowable truths, King is left without a motive to exclude them in the face of the sorites.

Resistance to the epistemic theory of vagueness can only be motivated by a prior resolve to allow no unknowable truths. The standard basis for this resolve is the requirement that every truth make a difference to what can be experienced. This requirement

[27] Ibid., 18.

has its attractions and often our aversion to the thesis is that borderline statements have hidden truth values emanates from lingering sympathy to anti-realist theories of truth such as the coherence and pragmatic theories. Once we take blindspots seriously, the aversion diminishes. It becomes clear that as long as we distinguish between the questions 'What makes p true?' and 'What makes us sure that p is true?', we will have no grounds to suppose that there is a *special* problem about what makes borderline propositions true. The special problem only arises for those who abrogate the distinction thereby embracing semantic anti-realism.

Thus the proper response to the objection that the epistemological approach makes an unrealistic assumption about the sensitivity of vague predicates proceeds in three steps. First, point out that the objection can only find a home amongst semantic anti-realists. Second, argue against semantic anti-realism (as I did in Chapter 4). Third, argue specifically for the incoherency of the thesis that vague predicates have limited sensitivity (which I shall do forthwith).

IV. THE UNTENABILITY OF THE LIMITED SENSITIVITY THESIS

Although the sensitivity objection is rightly recognized as a persuasive point against the epistemic approach, it is not widely recognized that it is equally applicable to super-valuationism, the many-valued approach, and some incoherence theories.

Its impact on the super-valuationists and many-valued theorists was first emphasized by Unger.[28] Unger points out that the many-valued theorists are committed to saying that a one atom difference can affect the degree to which a predicate like 'stone' applies to an object. Yet it seems absurd to suppose that the degree of truth or accuracy of 'This is a stone' can be decreased from say 0.7399995 to 0.7399994 by removing an atom. Likewise, the super-valuationists are committed to saying that the removal can make the difference between a proposition having a truth value and having no truth value. For they treat the set of admissible sharpenings as a sharply delineated set. The ultimate

[28] Unger makes this criticism in 'There are no Ordinary Things'.

source of the commitment to varieties of unlimited sensitivity is the use of a classical meta-language. One can find super-valuationists and many-valued theorists who express awareness of this commitment. The super-valuationist, Hans Kamp, observes:

> This predicament is of course inescapable: any semantic account of a vague predicate P according to which at least some objects are definitely P and some others are definitely not P or belonging to the truth value gap of P, will produce ... a sharp distinction if the language in which this account is given contains only sharply defined predicates and the apparatus of classical logic and set theory. For whatever the condition may be which separates the objects that are definitely P from the others, it is bound to make a sharp division — such is the classical theory of sets.[29]

Kamp's observation also extends to many-valued logic since it too has a classical meta-language. After all, fuzzy logic is a product of standard set theory. The many-valued theorist, J. Goguen, remarks:

> Our models are typical purely exact constructions, and we use ordinary exact logic and set theory freely in their development. This amounts to assuming we can have at least certain kinds of exact knowledge of inexact concepts. (When we say something, others may know exactly what we say, but not know exactly what we mean.) It is hard to see how we can study our subject at all rigorously without such assumptions.[30]

What makes the assumptions appear indispensible is the non-existence of non-standard meta-languages. This leaves the alternative logics without an alternative. This is bad news because all approaches having a classical meta-language fall prey to the sensitivity objection. So advocates of alternative logics that use the sensitivity objection against the epistemic approach are guilty of special pleading. Given that the super-valuationists and many-valued theorists cannot use the sensitivity issue to claim an advantage over classical logic, what is left to recommend their positions? The central motive for appealing to these alternative logics was to avoid the commitment to unlimited sensitivity. Once it is conceded that this appeal cannot succeed, there is no longer any point in departing from classical logic.

Does the limited sensitivity thesis deserve the credence we are

[29] Hans Kamp, 'The Paradox of the Heap', in Uwe Monnich, *Aspects of Philosophical Logic* (Dordrecht: D. Reidel, 1981), 254–5.

[30] J. Goguen, 'The Logic of Inexact Concepts', *Synthese*, 19/3–4 (1969), 327.

inclined to lend it? The answer emerges as we draw out the details of the doctrine. A predicate is sensitive to unit u if and only if there is a possible positive instance and a possible negative instance which only differ by one u. Thus, 'short man' is sensitive to metres but apparently not millimetres. For a one metre man is short and a two metre man is not short, while two men differing only by one millimetre in height apparently must be either both short or both non-short. Now consider the predicate 'is sensitive to unit u'. Is this a vague predicate? Here's an argument that should persuade the proponent of limited sensitivity. Consider the following sequence of propositions:

1. Two men differing by 1 millimetre can differ in that only one is short.
2. Two men differing by 2 millimetres can differ in that only one is short.
   .
   .
   .
1000. Two men differing by 1000 millimetres can differ in that only one is short.

Our proponent of limited sensitivity maintains that 'short man' is not sensitive to millimetres but is sensitive to metres. Thus he denies (1) and affirms (1000). We now ask him which of the members of the sequence is the first true proposition. Perhaps he will be confident that (999) is true and also affirm (998), (997), and (996). But eventually his confidence diminishes. He does not know which is the first true member of the sequence and there appears to be no way he could find out. So he concludes that there is no first true member of the sequence even though he believes that there are some true members. This is hard saying because it violates the least number theorem which asserts that if there is a number that has a property, then there is a least number possessing that property. But the proponent of limited sensitivity cannot very well maintain that there is an unknowable first true proposition since he would then be left without an objection to the view that there is an unknowable first short man in a sequence of 1001 men descending in height from two metres to one metre by one millimetre decrements. The proponent of the limited sensitivity thesis will argue for a restriction, revision, or rejection of the least number theorem. He will maintain that vague predicates show that such modification is necessary. The proponent of the limited sensitivity thesis draws the moral that 'sensitivity' is vague; that 'limited sensitivity' has limited sensitivity.

Another way of looking at the autologicality of 'limited sensitivity' is from the point of view of someone trying to construct a sorites argument. Given that his inductive predicate is 'short man', he cannot use increments of one metre in his induction step to 'prove' that all men are short. Nor can he use 0.9999 metre increments. What is the largest increment he can use and still have a true induction step? The question is made more vivid by considering a 'meta-sorites':

1. A sorites argument concerning 'short man' has a false induction step if the step's increment equals or exceeds ten thousand millimetres.
2. If a sorites argument concerning 'short man' has a false induction step if the step's increment is n millimetres, it also has a false induction step if the step's increment is $n-1$.
3. All sorites arguments concerning 'short man' having induction steps with increments convertible to millimetres have false induction steps.

The proponent of the epistemological approach should view this argument as sound. He should accept the induction step because the unlimited sensitivity of 'short' guarantees that all sorites concerning 'short' have false induction steps.

The proponent of limited sensitivity is forced to agree with the classical logician but on different grounds. His commitment to (2) springs from his commitment to the limited sensitivity of 'short'. To reject (2) as false is to affirm the unlimited sensitivity of 'limited sensitivity'. To refuse to accept (2) on the grounds that it is neither true nor false is doubly lamentable. First of all, to believe the limited sensitivity thesis is to believe that it is true. Since (2) is just a special instance of the thesis, it should be believed true. What are we to make of the claim that someone believes what he considers to be neither true nor false? Second, the position that (2) is neither true nor false is susceptible to the objections to which

Black fell victim. The same goes for the position that (1) is neither true nor false. Since the proponent of the limited sensitivity thesis cannot reject (1), he can only escape the conclusion by denying the validity of the argument. And he must try to escape the conclusion because his talk of limited sensitivity was designed to deny the falsity of the sorites's induction steps. Thus, these considerations constitute a third objection to Unger's position. For Unger claims that the sorites is valid and his commitment to limited sensitivity saddles him with acceptance of (1) and (2). So Unger's attempt to shore up the truth of the sorites's induction steps through appeal to limited sensitivity ultimately backfires.

The meta-sorites show that the limited sensitivity thesis can only be consistent if the meta-sorites is not valid. For the limited sensitivity thesis commits its proponent to both of the premisses of the argument and to the negation of the conclusion. However, the position that such arguments are not valid has already been shown to be untenable. Therefore, the limited sensitivity thesis is inconsistent.

Given its inconsistency, why is the thesis so compelling? One can often win assent to the limited sensitivity thesis by appealing to the proportionality of cause and effect. According to this principle, little causes cannot have big effects. So we infer that a tiny change cannot produce a substantial change. This leads us to deny that the subtraction of one grain of sand could cause an object to undergo the substantial change from heap to non-heap. The appeal to proportionality can even be persuasive in contexts which we are inclined to view as determinate. For example, we are inclined to think that there is a fact of the matter as to whether the person undergoing an operation is you or another person. Derek Parfit weakens this conviction by supposing that you are gradually changed into a person that has Greta Garbo's psychology and physiology. Although you clearly are not the person emerging from the final stage of the operation, it is not clear exactly which stage was your last. As Parfit puts the matter, it is hard to believe that there was a pair of stages such that at one you exist and at the next you do not exist. It is hard to believe that

> the difference between life and death could just consist in any of the very small differences described above. We are inclined to believe that there is *always* a difference between some future person's being me, and his being someone else. And we are inclined to believe that this is a *deep* difference.

But between neighbouring cases in this Spectrum the differences are trivial. It is therefore quite hard to believe that, in one of these cases, the resulting person would quite straightforwardly be me, and that, in the next case, he would quite straightforwardly be someone else.[31]

If a small cause cannot have a large effect, changing a person in a tiny way cannot have the huge effect of making him pass out of existence. Graeme Forbes also argues this way when addressing modal versions of the sorites. 'The distinction between what is possible and what is impossible for an object is as large a distinction as that between the tall and the short, one primary colour and another, or persons and non-persons, and therefore cannot turn upon a small degree of change in the respect relevant to making the difference.'[32] Both Parfit and Forbes appear to assume that the magnitude of a modification must be proportional to its effect. Although this proportionality principle has considerable intuitive appeal, it is plagued by counter-examples. An extremely tiny change in the velocity of an object can make the crucial difference as to whether it achieves escape velocity and travels far out into space, or fails to escape and crashes to earth. Of course, it is enormously improbable that the impact of a particular rain drop on a rocket will make the crucial difference. Likewise it is enormously unlikely that changing a brain cell will make the crucial difference between life and death. The proportionality principle virtually always provides the correct answer when applied to any particular miniscule change. But its distributive reliability does not entail its collective reliability. There is no empirical evidence of limited sensitivity. If science has anything to say about the limited sensitivity thesis, it is negative. For it multiplies counter-examples to the proportionality principle. A difference of one proton, one neutron, and one electron is responsible for the dramatic difference in the chemical properties of fluorine and neon. The question of whether the universe will expand endlessly or contract in on itself turns on the issue of whether the neutrino has appreciable mass. A considerable portion of interesting scientific results owe their interest to their violation of the proportionality principle. Counter-examples can

---

[31] Derek Parfit, *Reasons and Persons* (New York: Oxford University Press, 1984), 239.
[32] Graeme Forbes, *The Metaphysics of Modality* (Oxford: Clarendon Press, 1985), 168.

also be drawn from everyday life. A banana peel can elicit spectacular acrobatics from a lumbering pedestrian, a pebble in the fuel line of a truck can bring it to a halt, and one vote amongst millions can determine the result of a presidential election.

Psychological research has provided support for John Stuart Mill's remark that 'The most deeply rooted fallacy . . . is that the conditions of a phenomenon must, or at least probably will, resemble the phenomenon itself.'[33] Mill illustrated this fallacy with examples drawn from early stages of Western medicine. Because foxes have remarkable respiratory power, their lungs must hold a remedy for asthma. The brilliant yellow colour of turmeric indicates that it has the power of curing jaundice. Richard Nisbett and Lee Ross have supported Mill's view with examples from psychoanalysis, the beliefs of the Azande, popular diagnoses of social problems, and experimental research indicating that

> People have strong a priori notions of the types of causes that ought to be linked to particular types of effects, and the simple 'resemblance criterion' often figures heavily in such notions. Thus, people believe that great events ought to have great causes, complex events ought to have complex causes, and emotionally relevant events ought to have emotionally relevant causes.[34]

This resemblance criterion also explains some of the attractiveness of the proportionality principle that small changes have small effects. Unless defenders of the view that vague predicates have limited sensitivity propose a decent theoretical defence, it threatens to explain all of it. When an intuition conflicts with good theory and its attractiveness is vulnerable to psychological diagnosis, it acquires the status of fallacy. For the theory tells us that the intuition is an error while the diagnosis reveals a common tendency to succumb to it.

I have no more direct evidence for the thesis that the sorites can be solved through an appeal to blindspots. Further support will be of an indirect nature. That is, I will be trying to establish greater confidence in my thesis by showing how similar appeals are successful when applied to similar problems. Indeed, I will ultimately show how the study of blindspots places the sorites on a continuum of slippery slope fallacies.

---

[33] John Stuart Mill, *A System of Logic* (Toronto: University of Toronto Press, 1974, orig. 1843), 765.

[34] Richard Nisbett and Lee Ross, *Human Inference* (Englewood Cliffs, N.J.: Prentice-Hall, 1980), 115–16.

7
History of the Prediction Paradox

THE origin of the prediction paradox is uncertain. However, a letter written in response to Martin Gardner's *Scientific American* article on the puzzle provides some evidence. The letter was sent by a Swedish mathematician, Lennart Ekbom. He reported that sometime during 1943–4, the Swedish broadcasting system announced that a civil defence exercise would take place the following week. The exercise only concerned a number of Swedish industries. To test the efficiency of the relevant civil defence units, the announcer did not disclose the day of the exercise and stated that no one should be able to predict it. Ekbom detected a paradox and discussed it with some mathematics and philosophy students at Stockholm University. One of those students visited Princeton in 1947 and heard Kurt Godel present the paradox.

Ekbom's first impression was that the paradox was a variant of an older problem. But learning from Gardner that the puzzle only began to circulate in the early 1940s led Ekbom to suspect elsewhere. This prompted research into the files of the Swedish Civil Defence and Swedish broadcasting system in an unsuccessful attempt to find the original manuscript. So for the sake of exposition, I shall use Bryan Bunch's paraphrase of the announcement:[1] 'A civil-defense exercise will be held this week. In order to make sure that the civil-defense units are properly prepared, no one will know in advance on what day this exercise will take place.' The paradox begins with the observation that the exercise could not take place on the last day of the week. For if the exercise occurred then, all concerned would be in a position to predict the drill on the previous evening. Having ruled out the last day, the audience would also be in a position to rule out the next to last

[1] My source for these historical points is Ekbom's correspondence with Martin Gardner. Attributing the discovery of the paradox to Ekbom is consistent with what I have learned about its dissemination from early commentators on the problem (although none of them had heard of Ekbom). Bryan Bunch's confidence in the evidence is reflected in his attribution of the puzzle to Ekbom in *Mathematical Fallacies and Paradoxes* (New York: Van Nostrand, 1982), 34, which also contains the paraphrase of the announcement. Although my confidence falls short of Bunch's, I am fairly sure no one anticipated Ekbom.

day. For on the evening preceding the penultimate day, the audience would know that the exercise must take place on either the next to last or the last day — and the first step of the argument has ruled out the possibility of a last day exercise. By applying the same sort of reasoning to the remaining alternatives, the audience concludes that the exercise cannot take place.

The clever elimination argument can be formulated as a 'backwards' mathematical induction:

  i. Base step: The audience can know that the exercise will not occur on the last day.
  ii. Induction step: If the audience can know that the exercise will not occur on day n, then they can also know that the exercise will not occur on day $n-1$.
  iii. The audience can know that there is no day on which the exercise will occur.

This formulation has the advantage of brevity but might be criticized on several counts. First, the conclusion of the argument does not cleanly contradict the announcement. The announcement was expressed in terms of what the civil defence units *will* know. The conclusion is stated in terms of what they *can* know. Since officials of the Swedish broadcasting system were well aware of the fact that their compatriots were not ideal thinkers, they might accept the conclusion and yet insist that their announcement's truth was safeguarded by the limited acuity of the civil defence units. Although appeal to the epistemic imperfections of the audience might establish the truth of the particular announcement that spawned the prediction paradox, the appeal to imperfections cannot provide a general solution to the problem. For the paradox can be reformulated in terms of what *can* be known. Talk of what can be known can be made precise by idealizing the audience. The abilities of these thinkers can be explicitly stated. Thus members of the audience are standardly assumed to be perfect logicians who never forget and who do not overlook important facts. A second objection is that the above formulation is somewhat misleading since it invites the assumption that mathematical induction is essential to the puzzle. Since the argument only requires the elimination of a finite number of alternatives, the same conclusion could have been reached through a long chain argument.

Although there are some variations of the prediction paradox which do require mathematical induction, it is correct that the standardly discussed variations do not require it. Conceding this should allay concern that the formulation misleads the reader into believing that mathematical induction is essential to the paradox. I shall persist in formulating the argument this way because of the gains in brevity and generality. Lastly, it may be objected that the formulation is too crude. It may be felt that the two premises mask a host of background assumptions that should be brought into the foreground. However, the gain in precision accruing from the fine grained approach to argument formulation has to be balanced against the cost of cumbersomeness. Our policy should be 'if it doesn't itch, don't scratch.' Nevertheless, ensuing discussion will disclose a number of areas which call for scratching. Thus there is some point in viewing the two premises of the mathematical induction as subconclusions supported by premises of more direct interest.

I. EARLY COMMENTARY ON THE PREDICTION PARADOX

The fact that Ekbom was never cited in forty years of philosophical literature on the puzzle is some evidence that the entry of the prediction paradox into philosophical circles was an informal one. Perhaps a contributing cause of Ekbom's obscurity was the early reputation of the prediction paradox as a mere curiosity. This early lack of status can be explained in terms of its perceived irrelevance to important theories. Problems gain respect in two ways. The first and most common source of respect is through their threats to respected theories and firm intuitions. Should the threat be fulfilled we would be compelled to make deep revisions of our beliefs. Since expected degree of revision is a measure of informativeness, apparent counter-examples to central beliefs are interesting in so far as they threaten to be genuine counter-examples. Thus most paradoxes gain respect parasitically by being trouble-makers. Goodman's new riddle of induction and the raven paradox are great mischief-makers in confirmation theory. The lottery paradox is a rusty nail in the knee of the acceptance theorist. Newcomb's problem entered as a counter-example to standard decision theory. The problem of incontinence undermines the prospects for belief-desire explanations of actions. The problem of negative existentials challenges fundamental intuitions about reference. The sorites and the empty universe problem shake our faith in the very laws of logic.

The second way in which a problem can gain respect is through its recalcitrance. Repeated failures to solve a problem generate interest in it. Of course, subsequent investigation may further upgrade the problem's status by disconfirming its apparent irrelevance. Mathematics has many nice examples of problems which began as curiosities. The Koenigsberg puzzle was first debated by the townsfolk of Koenigsberg before it was solved by Euler. The four-colour problem began as a curiosity about map-making. The question of whether there are infinitely many twin primes principally owes its charm to its unsolved status. Assessing the significance of a problem is a notoriously risky business. Contemporary philosophy has its share of curiosities. Can a man imagine himself witnessing his own funeral? May an effect precede its cause? Why do mirrors reverse left and right but not up and down? One might explain the growth of interest in such isolated problems as a sort of one-upmanship. Solving what others cannot is evidence of intellectual prowess. A second explanation is that a problem's recalcitrance is evidence that we have underestimated the relevance of the problem to our cherished beliefs. Often we learn that the apparent irrelevance was an illusion generated by misplaced loyalties or a gap in our understanding. Such was the case with the prediction paradox.

A. *Assimilation to the Pragmatic Paradoxes*

The prediction paradox made its first appearance in philosophical literature in D. J. O'Connor's 'Pragmatic Paradoxes' in a 1948 issue of *Mind*. O'Connor first heard of the paradox while in Chicago in 1946, in a discussion with Arthur Pap, Frank Ebersole, and E. H. Hutten.[2] O'Connor's version of the puzzle runs as follows:

> The military commander of a certain camp announces on a Saturday evening that during the following week there will be a 'Class A blackout'. The date and time of the exercise are prescribed because a 'Class A

[2] This assertion is based on personal correspondence with Professor O'Connor (1985).

blackout' is defined in the announcement as an exercise which the participants cannot know is going to take place prior to 6.00 p.m. on the evening in which it occurs. It is easy to see that it follows from the announcement of this definition that the exercise cannot take place at all. It cannot take place on Saturday because if it has not occurred on one of the first six days of the week it must occur on the last. And the fact that the participants can know this violates the condition which defines it. Similarly, because it cannot take place on Saturday, it cannot take place on Friday either, because when Saturday is eliminated Friday is the last available day and is, therefore, invalidated for the same reason as Saturday. And by similar arguments, Thursday, Wednesday, etc. back to Sunday are eliminated in turn, so that the exercise cannot take place at all.[3]

O'Connor considered the argument cogent. He took its interest to lie in the fact that the definition of a 'Class A blackout' is consistent and yet it is pragmatically self-refuting. It is thus akin to the following sentences:

(1) I remember nothing at all.
(2) I am not speaking now.
(3) I believe there are tigers in Mexico but there aren't any there at all.

Although (1)–(3) are consistent, they 'could not conceivably be true in any circumstances'.[4] In his commentary on O'Connor's article, L. Jonathan Cohen also accepted the soundness of the argument. In addition, he agreed that the announcement should be classified as a pragmatic paradox which Cohen defined as a consistent proposition falsified by its own utterance.[5]

The first doubts about whether the announcement is contradictory were voiced by Peter Alexander. In effect, Alexander rejects the base step of the argument. According to Alexander, any announcement of an intention is implicitly conditional on the possibility of fulfilling the intention. So if I say that I will go to the cinema tomorrow, I am really saying that I will go if I am not in any way prevented. The omnipresence of this implication explains why announcements of intentions rarely explicitly contain an 'if I

---

[3] D. J. O'Connor, 'Pragmatic Paradoxes', *Mind*, 57/227 (July 1948), 358.
[4] Ibid., 358.
[5] L. Jonathan Cohen, 'Mr O'Connor's "Pragmatic Paradoxes" ', *Mind*, 59/233 (Jan. 1950), 86–7.

can' qualification. The base step owes its persuasiveness to the fact that we overlook this qualification. Once we explicitly insert it we find that the announcement of the exercise is no more puzzling than any conditional whose condition is unrealizable. 'If the conditions for a surprise drill can be realized, then there will be a surprise drill' is no more paradoxical than 'If I can live without air, I will not breathe all day.'

B. *Surprise as Unprovability*

The first publication devoted exclusively to the prediction paradox was Michael Scriven's 'Paradoxical Announcements' in 1951. Whereas O'Connor regarded the paradox as rather frivolous and Alexander considered it interesting but of no great concern, Scriven was deeply impressed by the paradox. Scriven compares the announcement of the exercise to statements like

(4) You are going to have a surprise at lunch-time tomorrow. You are going to have steak and eggs.
(5) I'll wager you can't find the roots of the equation $x^2 + 5x + 24 = 0$ within thirty seconds. The roots are 3 and -8.

Although the person who says (4) or says (5) does not contradict himself in the usual sense, his saying (4) or (5) is pointless since he has undermined part of what he says. Scriven goes on to insist that the unexpectedness of the exercise be given a logical rather than a psychological interpretation. The drill is unexpected by the participants in the sense that they cannot produce a proof that it will occur on a given day. Scriven argues that a solution to the paradox requires that one distinguish between publicly uttered statements and ordainments. Ordainments are guarantees, as when the dates of performances and meetings are announced. As a private prediction,

(6) There will be a Class A blackout next Saturday,

is proper, but it cannot be used as an ordainment for the drill participants. Construed as an ordainment, (6) guarantees a blackout which will, on the one hand, have an unspecified date, and on the other hand, will have a specified date. This incompatibility forces one to conclude that either the blackout will occur on Saturday and not be Class A, or it will not occur on Saturday and will be Class A. Neither conclusion is proper. We would only be led to these conclusions if we inferred from the self-refuting character of the announcement that there was a mistake. Since no proper conclusion can be drawn from (6) as an ordainment, a Saturday blackout will be a Class A blackout, making (6) correct. Scriven next considers

(7) There will be a Class A blackout next week.

He claims that this announcement is also self-refuting since if the blackout does not occur before Saturday, it will be equivalent to (6) on Saturday morning.

> Saturday is therefore not a real possibility or else [(7)] is self-refuting. In general, a Class-A blackout cannot occur on the last day of any sequence of nights during which it is ordained or else the governing announcement will be self-refuting. The first five nights of the week now forms such a sequence at the next stage, the next four. And thus the nights of the reversed week fall one by one: falling with the last is the point of ordainment.
> Now if the governing announcement is [(7)] which is self-refuting, and a blackout occurs on any night of the week, the statement [(7)] will be verified. And if publicly stated, it would still be correct.
> Conclusion. At first we thought that the reductive proof showed a Class-A blackout to be impossible while in fact any blackout that took place was a Class-A blackout. Now we have come to see that the suicide of the announcement as an ordainment is accompanied by its salvation as a statement.[6]

Scriven's proposal deviates sharply from the proposals of his predecessors. Whereas O'Connor and Cohen held that the paradox was veridical, Scriven classifies it as falsidical. In the next issue of *Mind*, O'Connor reported that he had converted to Alexander's view. Since Alexander believed that the alleged paradox is dissolved by his paraphrase, O'Connor's conversion deepens his disagreement with Scriven. Scriven believes that there is a significant paradox.

---

[6] Michael Scriven, 'Paradoxical Announcements', *Mind*, 60/239 (July 1951), 406–7.

C. *Assimilation to Logical Fatalism*

Apparently in the hope of undermining Alexander's proposed dissolution, Paul Weiss reformulated O'Connor's paradox.

> A headmaster says, 'it is an unbreakable rule in this school that there be an examination on an unexpected day.' The students argue that the examination cannot be given on the last day of the school year, for it if had not been given until then, it could be given only on that day and would then no longer be unexpected. Nor, say they, can it be given on the next to the last day, for with the last day eliminated, the next to the last day will be the last, so that the previous argument holds, and so on and so on. Either the headmaster gives the examination on an expected day or he does not give it at all. In either case he will break an unbreakable rule; in either case he must fail to give an examination on an unexpected day.[7]

Weiss explains that O'Connor's formulation makes it possible for the announcement to be rescinded, so that the non-occurrence of the blackout can be predicted. Weiss's stipulation that the rule is unbreakable corrects this flaw. In addition, Weiss believes that it is more appropriate to call the paradox 'the prediction paradox'. A plurality of commentators (me included) have adopted this name to *generically* refer to all variations of the puzzle. Nowadays, Weiss's particular puzzle is simply referred to as the 'unexpected examination' or 'the surprise test'.

Weiss attempts to solve the paradox by assimilating it to the problem of logical fatalism. By the law of excluded middle, each proposition about the future is either now true or now false. But then there is nothing one can do to change the truth values of these propositions. Thus the law of excluded middle seems to imply that we are not free. For example, tomorrow I will either eat squid or not. But given that 'I will eat squid' is true now or false now, there is nothing I can do to avoid eating squid if it is true now that I will. And there is nothing I can do which will bring it about that I eat squid tomorrow if it is now false. According to Weiss and many others, Aristotle tried to avoid logical fatalism by denying that (8) implies (9).

(8) It is true that p or not-p.
(9) Either it is true that p or it is true that not-p.

---

[7] Paul Weiss, 'The Prediction Paradox', *Mind*, 61/242 (April 1952), 265.

According to this interpretation, the statement 'Either I will eat squid or I will not eat squid' is true given the collective reading, represented by (8), but is not true given the distributive reading, represented by (9). This view holds that contingent propositions about the future lack truth values. So although the non-contingent disjunction about the future is true, neither of its disjuncts is true. After tomorrow, one of the disjuncts will have become true but neither is true *yet*. Thus it is proposed that logical fatalism can be escaped by distinguishing between the collective and the distributive senses of 'or'. Weiss argues that the same distinction solves the prediction paradox.

> When we predict we refer to a range of possibilities which are as yet undistinguished one from the other. They are connected by means of a collective 'or', prohibiting the separation of any one of them from the other, without the introduction of some power or factor not included in the concept of the range. Since predictions always refer to a range and never to the specific determinations of it produced in fact, the predictions must be supplemented by history or the imagination if we are to select and eliminate first one and then the other alternative. What is selected and eliminated in history or in the imagination will be something distinct, focused on, actualized, connected with others by means of a distributive 'or'. If we avoid confusing these two meanings of 'or', our paradox, I think, will disappear.[8]

When we are asked to consider whether the examination could be given on the last day, we imagine ourselves in the future and thus shift from the realm of the possible to the realm of the actual. The disjunction of examination dates is distributive in the realm of the actual but is collective in the realm of the possible. The shuttling back and forth in time invites confusion between realms and thus confusion between kinds of disjunctions.

This distinction between types of disjunction requires a departure from standard logic. Lukasiewicz dealt with this type of disjunction in the context of fatalism by introducing many-valued logic. However, Weiss does not provide a positive account of how logic should be revised. Indeed, with the exception of B. Meltzer, logicians have displayed little interest in applying many-valued logic to the prediction paradox.[9]

---

[8] Ibid., 265–6.
[9] Meltzer suggests a many-valued approach in 'The Third Possibility', *Mind*, 73 (1953), 65–7. In 'Two Forms of the Prediction Paradox', *British Journal for the*

J. T. Fraser agrees with Weiss in viewing time as playing a crucial role in the paradox. Fraser illustrates his view with the surprise egg version of the prediction paradox. Here we are confronted with ten closed boxes labelled one to ten which will be opened in that order. We are informed that a surprise egg has been placed in one of the boxes. It is a surprise in the sense that we will not be able to foresee which box it is in on the basis of already opened boxes. The familiar regress begins with a consideration of whether the egg can be in the last box. According to Fraser, the ensuing paradox

is produced when arguments involving temporal order are mixed with arguments disregarding time. A world where the logical test holds must be one of 'being', for it must accommodate temporal and reversed temporal orders on equal footing. In that world time is unreal, and the unexpected cannot happen. Contrariwise, a world where the unexpected does happen, is one of 'becoming' and time by this test at least is not an illusion. Philosophically, therefore, the paradox harks back to the antinomical views of Heraclitus and Parmenides.[10]

Thus Fraser argues that a proper solution to the prediction paradox requires an insight into the nature of time.

D. *Quine's Accusation of* Argumentum ad Ignorantiam

Another popular version of the prediction paradox is the Hangman. A man, K, is sentenced to hang on one of the following seven noons but must be kept in ignorance until the morning before the execution. K argues that he cannot be hung on the last day since he would know after the penultimate noon. Having eliminated the last day, the rest are eliminated in the familiar way.

Amongst the philosophers who have commented on the paradox in print, Quine has the earliest recollections of its beginnings. The paradox was circulating amongst cryptanalysts in Washington where Quine was a naval officer around the end of 1943. His impression is that the puzzle was passed along from Tarski in

Philosophy of Science, 16/61 (May 1965), 50–1, co-authored with I. J. Good, Meltzer expresses doubt as to whether the many-valued approach applies to the original paradox.

[10] J. T. Fraser, 'Note Relating to a Paradox of Temporal Order', appearing in his *Voices of Time* (New York: George Braziller, Inc. 1966), 525.

Berkeley. Although Quine seems to remember Tarski telling him that he thought the puzzle a genuine antinomy, Quine thought that it was a soluble paradox.[11]

> I wrote up my solution and circulated it among my friends, to their apparent satisfaction. In the fall of 1952 I was surprised to find that the paradox was going strong, sometimes in the form I had known and sometimes as a paradox about a surprise examination, and that it had called forth a flurry of papers in *Mind* of varying degrees of absurdity. I published my solution in *Mind*. It is clear to me that I solved the puzzle, but is still perhaps not clear to all concerned.[12]

Quine's analysis aims to derail the elimination process at its first step. Recall that the argument begins with the supposition that the hanging has not occurred on the first six days. At this point, the puzzle is equivalent to the one day case in which the judge says:

(10) You will be hanged tomorrow at noon and will not know the date in advance.

Although there is something queer in saying (10), Quine fails to see a contradiction. According to Quine, K should reason as follows:

> We must distinguish four cases: first, that I shall be hanged tomorrow noon and I know it now (but I do not); second, that I shall be unhanged tomorrow noon and I know it now (but I do not); third, that I shall be unhanged tomorrow noon and do not know it now; and fourth, that I shall be hanged tomorrow noon and do not know it now. The latter two alternatives are the open possibilities, and the last of all would fulfill the decree. Rather than charging the judge with self-contradiction, therefore, let me suspend judgement and hope for the best.[13]

Quine points out that the *reductio ad absurdum* is of the supposition that *K knows the announcement*; the *reductio* is not of the announcement itself. To conclude that the announcement cannot be true because K cannot know it to be true is to commit a modal version of *argumentum ad ignorantiam*. Once we realize that the 'paradoxical' argument only shows that you cannot know

---

[11] The claims about Tarski are drawn from personal correspondence with Professor Quine (1985).
[12] W. V. Quine, *The Time of My Life* (Cambridge: MIT Press, 1985), 234.
[13] W. V. Quine, 'On a so-called Paradox', *Mind*, 62/245 (Jan. 1953), 66–7.

the announcement, we can simply agree and accept the ignorance. What we have accepted, in Quine's eyes, is an unremarkable proposition, so there really is no paradox at all.

II. EMERGENCE OF THE SENTENTIAL SELF-REFERENCE APPROACH

Quine's analysis was influential. Thirty years later we can still find philosophers referring to it as the correct resolution of the paradox.[14] The immediate effect of Quine's article was dissatisfaction with Quine's use of 'know'. It was suspected that Quine had only succeeded in evading the paradox through an exploitation of the vagaries of our ordinary talk of knowledge. In contrast, Scriven's interpretation of the announcement made the key term 'prove', a technical term that avoids the difficulties of ordinary language. Thus the Scriven interpretation offered a way of reformulating the paradox in a way that would avoid Quine's anticlimactic conclusion. Careful study of this reformulation revealed a new twist to the paradox; self-reference. For now the announcement seemed to say, in the case of the surprise test version, 'There will be a test whose date you will be unable to deduce from the conjunction of this announcement and any background information you may acquire.'

A. *Shaw's Seminal Contribution*

The first attempt to assimilate the prediction paradox to the self-referential paradoxes appeared in R. Shaw's 'The Paradox of the Unexpected Examination'. Shaw insists that ' "knowing" that the examination will take place on the morrow' must be 'knowing' in the sense of 'being able to predict, *provided* the rules of the school are not broken'.[15] Shaw complains that 'If instead one adopted a vague common-sense notion of "knowing", then one could perhaps agree with Professor Quine that an unexpected examination could take place even in a one-day term; but to my mind, this

---

[14] For example, Donald Regan's acceptance of Quine's proposal appears in *Utilitarianism and Cooperation* (Oxford: Clarendon Press, 1980), 74. Russell Hardin's acceptance is evident from *Collective Action* (Baltimore: Johns Hopkins University Press, 1982), 148.

[15] R. Shaw, 'The Paradox of the Unexpected Examination', *Mind*, 67/267 (July 1958), 386.

would be evading the paradox rather than resolving it.'[16] Given that 'unexpected' means 'not deducible from certain specified rules of the school', Shaw believes he can formulate two rules for the school described in Weiss's prediction paradox.

> Rule 1: An examination will take place on one day of next term.
> Rule 2: The examination will be unexpected, in the sense that it will take place on such a day that on the previous evening it will not be possible for the pupils to deduce *from Rule 1* that the examination will take place on the morrow.[17]

Although a last day examination can be eliminated since it would violate Rule 2, an examination on any other day would satisfy Rules 1 and 2. By adding a third rule, the possibility of an examination on the last two days can be eliminated.

> Rule 3: The examination will take place on such a day that on the previous evening it will not be possible for the pupils to deduce *from Rules 1 and 2* that the examination will take place on the morrow.[18]

If only two days remain in the term, the pupils can deduce by Rule 1 that the examination is on one of the two remaining days. By Rule 2, they can eliminate the last day, leaving the next to the last day as the only possibility. Since this deduction would violate Rule 3, the last two days are not possible examination days. However, an examination on any other day of the terms would satisfy Rules 1, 2, and 3. In general, the last n days of the term are eliminated by appealing to Rule 1 and n additional rules of the form:

> Rule $n+1$: The examination will take place on such a day that on the previous evening it will not be possible for the pupils to deduce from the conjunction of rules 1, 2, ..., n, that the examination will take place on the morrow.

[16] Ibid.
[17] Ibid., 383.
[18] Ibid.

The $n+1$ rules are incompatible with an n day term.

Shaw concludes that the original paradox arose by taking in addition to Rule 1,

> Rule 2*: The examination will take place on such a day that on the previous evening the pupils will not be able to deduce from *Rules 1 and 2** that the examination will take place on the morrow.

By applying rules 1 and 2*, one can eliminate every day of the term. Once we realize that 2* is self-referential, the paradox is resolved.

B. *Lyon's Charge of Equivocation*

In a subsequent article, Ardon Lyon complained that Shaw's choice of the rules for the school is an evasion rather than a solution of the paradox. Lyon points out that mere self-referentiality is not sufficient for paradox. For example, 'This sentence is written in black ink' is perfectly unproblematic. Lyon also rejected Quine's analysis on the grounds that Quine's criterion for knowing implies that we cannot know anything about the future. According to Lyon, the paradox rests on an equivocation. Shaw's Rule 2* can mean either S1 or S2, but not both.

> S1: The examination will be unexpected in the sense that ... it will not be possible for the pupils to deduce from Rules 1 and S1 that the examination will take place on the morrow, unless it takes place on the last day.
>
> S2: The examination will be unexpected in the sense that ... it will not be possible for the pupils to deduce from Rules 1 and S2 that the examination will take place on the last day.[19]

Lyon argues that if one reads Rule 2* as S1, like a sensible person should, then the clever student's argument is fallacious. And even if one reads it as S2

> it can have no possible application, must always remain false, for nothing,

---

[19] Ardon Lyon, 'The Prediction Paradox', *Mind*, 67/272 (Oct. 1959), 512–13.

including setting the examination earlier, would make it true that the boys would be unable to deduce on the eve of the last day that it would occur on the morrow, *if* the master were to wait that long. For R1 and S2 applied together on the eve of the last day give us:

(1) The examination must take place tomorrow.
(2) (The examination will be unexpected in the sense that) it is not possible to deduce from (1) and (2) that it will take place on the morrow.

which clearly contradict each other, as opposed to Quine's solution.[20]

C. *The Kaplan–Montague Analysis*

In 1960, David Kaplan and Richard Montague published 'A Paradox Regained' in the *Notre Dame Journal of Formal Logic*. Kaplan and Montague rigorously develop Shaw's self-referential approach as applied to the Hangman version. After setting up their formal apparatus, Montague and Kaplan are able to replicate Quine's analysis. Like Shaw, they reject Quine's analysis on the grounds that it fails to capture the self-referential aspect of the decree. Once we interpret the judge's decree as saying that the man to be hung, K, cannot deduce the day of the hanging from the conjunction of accumulated information about past non-hanging days and the decree *itself*, the strange argument is revived. Whereas Shaw argued, in effect, that the judge's decree is genuinely paradoxical, Kaplan and Montague argue that the decree is merely incapable of fulfillment. For the supposition that the decree can be fulfilled leads to absurdity. Suppose that the man is hanged on Tuesday noon. In order for this to happen, the hangman must show that the decree does not imply that the hanging will take place on Tuesday. According to Kaplan and Montague, however, the Tuesday hanging is implied by the decree given the general epistemological principles they think we should accept. So they think we can just accept the argument without paradox much like we accept the 'paradoxes' of material implication.

Kaplan and Montague maintain that we can obtain a genuinely paradoxical decree by having a judge try to make the decree capable of fulfillment through the addition of a stipulation: '*Unless*

[20] Ibid., 513.

K knows on Sunday afternoon that the present decree is false, one of the following conditions will be fulfilled: '(1) 'K is hanged on Monday noon' is true, or (2) K is hanged on Tuesday noon but not on Monday noon, and on Monday afternoon K does not know on the basis of the present decree that 'K is hanged on Tuesday noon' is true.'[21] Kaplan and Montague argue that this version is a complicated variation of the liar paradox leading to the conclusion that the decree can and cannot be fulfilled. They go on to consider a one-day version of this variation: 'Unless K knows on Sunday afternoon that the present decree is false, the following condition will be fulfilled: K will be hanged on Monday noon, but on Sunday afternoon he will not know on the basis of the present decree that he will be hanged on Monday afternoon.'[22] Finally, they consider a version in which 'the number of possible dates of execution can be reduced to zero'. Here the judge asserts:

> K knows on Sunday afternoon that the present decree is false.[23]

Although most logicians would be inclined to view such a decree as a fancy liar sentence, it is possible to maintain that it is a distinct puzzle. The mixture of self-reference with a propositional attitude is the hallmark of a type of puzzle Jean Buridan discussed in his fourteenth-century work *Sophismata*, recently revived by Tyler Burge.[24] Consider the following 'Buridanean' sentence:

> (13) I do not believe (13).

If I believe (13), it is false and so I should not believe it. If I do not believe (13), it is true and so I should believe it. So my cogitations upon the truth value of (13) will inevitably be in vain. For I will be either omissively or commissively mistaken. (13) is anti-incorrigible, making me an anti-expert about its truth value. However, others can know its truth value. Outsiders need only wait for me to tire of

---

[21] David Kaplan and Richard Montague, 'A Paradox Regained', *Notre Dame Journal of Formal Logic*, 1/3 (July 1960), 84.
[22] Ibid., 87.
[23] Ibid.
[24] Burge discusses these sentences in 'Buridan and Epistemic Paradox', *Philosophical Studies*, 39/1 (Jan. 1978), 21–35, and in 'Epistemic Paradox', *Journal of Philosophy*, 81/1 (Jan. 1984), 21–35.

thinking about (13) and then check whether (13) is on the list of things I believe. Unlike the liar, (13) only threatens internal incoherence. Others can consistently assign a truth value to it; I cannot. A related difficulty arises with

(14) I do not know that (14) is true.

If I know that (14) is true, it follows that (14) is false. So it is obvious to me that I do not know that (14) is true. But if that is obvious, I must know that (14) is true after all. Sentence (14) seems to drive a wedge between proof and knowledge. The wedge can be an impersonal one:

(15) No one knows that (15) is true.

Likewise, the 'commissive' versions of (14) and (15),

(14') I know that (14') is false.
(15') Everyone knows that (15') is false.

appear to be provably false and yet unknowable.

Although the analogy between Buridanean sentences and liar sentences is striking, the analogy does not constitute a reduction. In the absence of a reduction, the Kaplan-Montague proposal does not qualify as a reduction of the prediction paradox to the liar.

D. *Assimilation to Godel's Sentence*

Another branch of the self-referential approach was introduced by G. C. Nerlich in his 'Unexpected Examinations and Unprovable Statements'. After expressing his view that the prediction paradox is neither trivial nor easy to solve, Nerlich suggests that

it is a quite unique kind of ordinary language problem, having some connection with the situation posed by Godel's famous sentence, to the effect that the sentence itself cannot be proved. It will be clear, when I have dealt with the paradox, why I think it is of some importance to logic—of more importance than the comparatively simple Grelling paradox, for example.[25]

[25] G. C. Nerlich, 'Unexpected Examinations and Unprovable Statements', *Mind*, 70/280, 503.

Nerlich reviews Shaw's treatment of the paradox. Shaw provided a non-self-referential formulation of the school rules and a self-referential formulation. Shaw then argued that the first formulation is not paradoxical since no unexpected examination can be given during the term and that the second formulation is paradoxical. Nerlich insists that both formulations are paradoxical. After all, if an examination is given on Wednesday, it would not be expected. Thus Shaw's first formulation shows that self-reference is not an essential feature of the prediction paradox.

Nerlich next considers Lyon's claim that the paradox rests on an equivocation. Lyon argued that the sensible interpretation of the announcement is (a) rather than (b):

(a) it will not be possible to deduce from the statement when the examination will occur at any time prior to its occurrence, *unless it occurs on the last day*.
(b) it will not . . . *whether or not it occurs on the last day*.

Nerlich objects that the announcement cannot mean (a) since there is a perfectly proper and strict sense of 'unexpected' in which (a) is equivalent to the disjunctive paraphrase: 'the examination will occur unexpectedly, unless it occurs expectedly on the last day'. Since the announcer can plainly mean strictly what he said, that the examination will be unexpected, the equivalence of (a) and the disjunctive paraphrase ensures that the announcer's original announcement does not mean (a). On the other hand, denying that the announcement means (a) is not tantamount to asserting that it means (b). One is only denying that the examination will occur on any day such that on a previous day, the examination day could be deduced. Nerlich further argues that (a) is not equivalent to the announcement because

> there are tests which actually *require* the rejection of the 'unless' clause and such tests occur daily. The trial emergency stop in every driving test is a case in point. The trial is improper if the order does not take the candidate unawares, so it cannot be allowed to occur expectedly even at the end of the test. Yet proposing such a trial is not proposing anything contradictory.[26]

Nerlich's example of the trial emergency stop may be ill-chosen

[26] Ibid., 506–7.

The Prediction Paradox

since the driver does not know when the last opportunity for the surprise will occur. Better illustrations can be drawn from safety codes that require schools and dormitories to have at least one surprise fire drill a year.

Nerlich admits that his own solution is 'rather bizarre'. He first points out that at each stage of the student's argument a negation of a statement of the form 'Examination on -day' is derived. But after deriving a negation for each of the alternatives, the students have no basis for thinking one day rather than another is the examination date. So if the examination is given on one of the days, it will be unexpected. To falsify the announcement, the students must derive a statement that excludes 'a day such that it is not possible to deduce from the head's statement, at any time prior to the day, that the examination *has* been arranged for that day'.[27] Since only negations are derived, Nerlich concludes that the announcement is not falsified. The possibility of deriving an examination date from a contradiction should be ignored since it would be of no use to the pupils.

> So *due to the fact* that it entails not, e.g., Examination on Wednesday, but something else (a contradiction), the statement is self-consistent.
> This is hard saying. However, let us look again at the curious logical features of this everyday remark. The statement is partly about an examination and partly about its own logical consequences, *viz.* that the examination date is not among them. . . . The only way in which this metalogical statement can be falsified is by proving that the examination *has* been arranged for a certain day. It is this that the students attempt to do but fail to do, producing only days on which it seems *not* possible to hold it. And that is because in the attempt, they are forced to use the very premise (or set of premises) which they hope to falsify.[28]

Thus the students can only complain 'Ah, this Godel is killing me!'. Nerlich admits that the fact the students must work with a premiss they hope to falsify is not enough to account for the odd state of affairs. After all, *reductio ad absurdum* arguments also begin with premisses the arguer hopes to falsify. According to Nerlich, the relevant difference between the cases is that the key premiss in the student's argument describes *itself* as one that cannot be used to derive truths, for it says that only false statements can be deduced.

---
[27] Ibid., 507.
[28] Ibid., 508.

Nerlich goes on to further claim that in so far as it is about provability, the prediction paradox resembles Godel's incompleteness proof. Central to the proof is a sentence, G, that is true only if G is not provable. If the logical system is consistent, then G must be undecidable. For if G is proved, then G is also unproved, and if the negation of G is proved, then G is proved. So here consistency is incompatible with completeness. Nerlich claims that the same holds true for the announcement of the prediction paradox. By implying that there is a true but unprovable alternative, the announcement is, as it were, describing itself as incomplete. 'But just that remark about incompleteness seems to make the system now complete, and therefore contradictory. Yet, as we have seen, it is really neither complete nor inconsistent.'[29] Nerlich concludes that when one's sole source of information seems to impeach himself, one does not know what to make of it. This is just what the teacher wants. He manages to say nothing by contradicting himself.

E. *Assimilation to the Langford Visiting Card Paradox*

In *The British Journal for the Philosophy of Science*, Martin Gardner compared the prediction paradox to Langford's Visiting Card Paradox. Langford's paradox consists of a visiting card on the front of which is written 'The assertion on the other side of this card is true' while on the back is written 'The assertion written on the other side of this card is false.' To show the analogy between the prediction paradox and the Langford paradox, Gardner constructs a 'New Prediction Paradox'. Here, one puts a card in an envelope and instructs the receiver to send it to a mutual friend only after writing on its (as yet blank) back 'Yes' or 'No' according to whether the receiver feels justified in predicting that the mutual friend will find that 'No' has been written on its back. In 'A Comment on the New Prediction Paradox', Karl Popper agrees that Gardner has established a close analogy between the two paradoxes. As a friendly amendment, however, Popper argues that Gardner's paradox can be formulated in such a way that it is free of the idea of negation (common to the liar and Langford paradoxes). Here, one instructs the receiver to write 'Yes' in a blank rectangle to the left of one's signature if, and only if, the

[29] Ibid., 509.

receiver feels justified in predicting that when it is sent back, the rectangle will still be blank.

F. *Further Refinements and Criticisms of the Approach*

In the first issue of the *American Philosophical Quarterly*, Brian Medlin begins by expressing disappointment with all of the previous contributions to the problem except Shaw's. Nerlich is first criticized for offering a solution that merely reformulates the paradox. Medlin then moves on to formalize the paradox. The chief difference between Medlin's account and that of Montague and Kaplan is that he defends the thesis that the prediction paradox is a variation of the liar rather than an offshoot of a Buridan puzzle. I will return to Medlin shortly when I recount Jonathan Bennett's criticism of the self-referential approach.

In the next issue of the *American Philosophical Quarterly*, Frederic Fitch's 'A Godelized Formulation of the Prediction Paradox' appeared. Fitch first argues that the announcement is merely self-contradictory. He then modifies the prediction paradox by weakening the notion of surprise so that an expected last day examination counts as a surprise examination. Fitch shows that this prediction is consistent and considers it a resolution of the paradox. Third, Fitch develops Nerlich's suggestion by modifying the prediction in the prediction paradox so that it is an undecidable proposition equivalent to Godel's.

The earliest general criticism of the self-referential approach appeared in Jonathan Bennett's review of the articles written by Shaw, Lyon, Nerlich, Medlin, and Fitch. Bennett's first criticism of the attempt to solve the prediction paradox by showing that it has an element of self-referentiality is that Nerlich's objections have not been satisfactorily answered. Nerlich first argued that Shaw illegitimately assumed that all self-reference is improper. Medlin conceded that some cases of self-reference may be permissible, citing R. M. Smullyan's 'Languages in which Self-Reference is Possible',[30] but denies that self-reference is proper in the case in question. Medlin formulates the announcement as:

(M) The information concerning d_x [the day on which the

---

[30] Smullyan's article appeared in *The Journal of Symbolic Logic*, 22/1 (1957), 55–67.

examination occurs] is not sufficient to allow determination of x at any stage before the examination is actually given.[31]

The impropriety of (M) is then argued for on the grounds that

> The proposition (M) says something about the propositions in a non-empty set S; namely, that the conjunction of all these propositions does not constitute a premiss of sufficient power to permit the determination of x at any stage before the examination is given. . . . But if (M) is in S, then what (M) says is (roughly) that (M) does not permit us to determine x. This kind of self-reference is circular. It invites the question, '*What* does not permit us to determine x?' We do not understand (M) until we know what (M) is about, which set S happens to be. If (M) is itself in S, then we shall never know this and never understand (M).[32]

Bennett objects to this argument since if it is valid, one could prove that 'No universal proposition entails that all men are mortal' is unintelligible. Nerlich's second objection was that self-reference is not essential to the paradox. Medlin formulates Nerlich's objection with the help of the following (letting p_i be the proposition 'The examination occurs on the i-th day').

(I) $(p_1 \lor p_2 \lor p_3) \,\&\, -(p_i \,\&\, p_j)$ $(i \neq j;\ i \leq j, j \leq 3)$

(M1) From (I) it is not possible to determine x, even given as additional information one of $-p_1$, $-(p_1 \lor p_2)$.

(M2) From (I) & (M1) it is not possible to determine x, even given as additional information $-p_1$.

(M3) From (I) & (M1) & (M2) it is not possible to determine x.

(C)   (M1) & (M2) & (M3).

Nerlich argues that self-reference is not essential to the prediction paradox because (I) & (C) imply a contradiction by steps parallel to the self-referential cases. In reply, Medlin argues that Nerlich's own proposed solution keeps the paradox alive with the help of self-reference. Medlin explains that Nerlich argues in favour of the compatibility between (I) & (C) and p_2 on the grounds that there is no sound deduction from the former to $-P_2$.

---

[31] Brian Medlin, 'The Unexpected Examination', *American Philosophical Quarterly*, 1/1 (Jan. 1964), 67.
[32] Ibid., 68.

But if this is to be taken as providing a model for (I) & (C), then we must interpret (C) as saying of *itself* that it does not, with (I), constitute sufficient information for the determination of x. The statement for which p_2 does provide a model is

> (M4) The conjunction of (I) & (C) does not constitute sufficient information for the determination of x.

Unlike (C), the statement (M4) is true. It is true because (C) is false. Nerlich confuses (M4) with (C). He is then led to say that (C) is true because it is false. We should note in passing that the case p_1 provides a model for (M4). So does the case p_3: that is why Nerlich finds that even an examination on d3 is unexpected.[33]

Despite Medlin's report that Nerlich agrees with all of Medlin's comments about Nerlich's analysis, Bennett dismisses Medlin's attempt to meet Nerlich's objection that self-reference is inessential as *ad hominem*. Even if the above criticism of Nerlich's constructive analysis succeeds, it does not show that Nerlich's destructive analysis fails. After noting the common diagnosis that the Lyon ambiguity in the announcement is the source of our puzzlement, Bennett concludes:

> Perhaps there is that ambiguity and perhaps it might puzzle someone; but it has nothing to do with the fact which makes the announcement teasing to everyone, namely the fact — noted by Fitch on page 161 — that 'in practice the event may nevertheless occur on some one of the specified set of days, and when it does occur it does constitute a sort of surprise'. But *that* puzzle cannot be handled by someone who thinks that 'the Prediction Paradox can be formulated in a . . . way that makes no use of epistemological or pragmatic concepts' (p. 161).[34]

Bennett's review is followed by James Cargile's review of Kaplan and Montague, Gardner, and Popper. Cargile dismisses Gardner's 'new prediction paradox' as not being a genuine paradox. Cargile also claims that although Langford presents some similar paradoxes, the visiting card paradox is due to Jourdain. Cargile concludes that the alleged paradoxes of Gardner and Popper have already been treated in Lewis's and Langford's chapter on logical paradoxes in their *Symbolic Logic*.

---

[33] Ibid., 69.
[34] Jonathan Bennett in a review appearing in *The Journal of Symbolic Logic*, 30/2 (June 1965), 102.

Cargile summarizes 'A Paradox Regained' as variations on the theme:

A: 'K knows that A is false.'

He points out that this is an old theme appearing in Buridan's *Sophismata*. In Cargile's opinion,

These 'knower'-type paradoxes are just Liar-family paradoxes in which knowing is involved only in that it entails truth. 'K knows that p is false' is logically equivalent to 'p is false and K knows it.' So A is fundamentally the same as

B: 'B is false and K knows it.'

B is just a case of the Conjunct-Liar. 'This conjunction is false and q', which makes possible a semblance of proving the falsity of any q you please. Similarly with

C: 'K does not know that C is true,'

which appears to be true but unknowable but unknowable by K. It is fundamentally the same as:

D: 'Either D is false, or D is true but K does not know it,'

which is a case of the Disjunct-Liar.[35]

So unlike Bennett's, Cargile's review is quite sympathetic to the self-referential approach.

J. M. Chapman and R. J. Butler in 'On Quine's "So-called Paradox" ', propose a 'perverse solution' taking Quine's rejection of the base step of the induction as their inspiration. Like others, they argue that if the examination has not been given by Thursday, the students can deduce that the examination has not been given by Thursday. The students can then deduce that the examination is on Friday. But they can also deduce that the examination is not on Friday.

---

[35] James Cargile in a review appearing in *The Journal of Symbolic Logic*, 30/2 (June 1965), 103. In his *Paradoxes: A Study in Form and Predication* (New York: Cambridge University Press, 1979), 288–9, Cargile retracts his claim that the Knower paradoxes are just a branch of the Liar family.

The conclusion that the examination must be held on the last day is just as warranted as the conclusion that it cannot be held. Therefore the boys cannot predict, by a valid process of logical argument and without laying themselves open to contradiction, that the examination will be held on the last day. Therefore the examination, even if it is held on the last day, will be unexpected in the required sense.[36]

Another proposal put forth by commentators professing sympathy with Quine appears in 'The Prediction Paradox Again'. Here, James Kiefer and James Ellison first insist that the problem can only be made interesting and precise if 'surprise' is defined in terms of deducibility.

Let us use 'deduce1' to mean 'deduce, using as premises the nonoccurrence of the examination up to the moment of deduction, plus the truth of this announcement'. Let us use 'deduce2' to mean 'deduce, using as the premise the nonoccurrence of the examination up to the moment of deduction'. Let us define 'surprise1' and 'surprise 2' in terms of 'deduce1' and 'deduce2' respectively.[37]

Kiefer and Ellison interpret the prediction paradox as showing that the announcement is contradictory, given the 'surprise1' reading. However, if the announcement is given the 'surprise2' reading, the announcement will be true if the examination is given on any day of the week. Once this ambiguity is noted, the authors claim the paradox is resolved. They claim that if they have correctly understood Quine, he has largely anticipated their solution.

Quine's suspicions about the base step of the induction are shared in Judith Schoenberg's 'A Note on the Logical Fallacy in the Paradox of the Unexpected Examination'. The elimination argument begins with the last day: if the examination has not been given by the penultimate day, then . . . Schoenberg claims that the antecedent of this conditional illegitimately assumes that conditions laid down by the teacher have already been violated. The rest of the student's argument is 'merely a verbal play'. So although Schoenberg agrees with the student that the examination cannot be given on the last day, she believes that the student is arguing fallaciously when he begins his argument with the conditional 'If

---

[36] J. M. Chapman and R. J. Butler, 'On Quine's "So-called Paradox" ', *Mind*, 74/295 (July 1965), 424–5.

[37] James Kiefer and James Ellison, 'The Prediction Paradox Again', *Mind*, 74/295 (July 1965), 426–7.

the examination has not been given by the penultimate day, then it must be given on the last'. '. . . the premise entertains a condition under which the event cannot occur as defined, and thus cannot serve as the point of departure for a line of reasoning about the event's possibility. All it can lead to deductively is a clarification of the conditions under which the event cannot occur by definition.'[38]

Later in 1967, M. J. O'Carroll published 'Improper Self-Reference in Classical Logic and the Prediction Paradox' in *Logique et Analyse*. O'Carroll claims that although the prediction paradox has received much attention, it has not been correctly formulated. He argues that the teacher is really claiming that the students cannot deduce the day of the examination without there also being a counterdeduction that it is not that day. O'Carroll also claims that the conclusion to be drawn is 'either it is not true that there is an exam on one and only one afternoon "next week" *or* the teacher's statement . . . falls outside the field of valid application of two-valued, non-levelled logic'.[39]

After a few years of silence, the self-referentialists surfaced again with A. K. Austin's 'On the Unexpected Examination' in 1969. Apparently in the hope of refuting the objection that the elimination argument fails to show that the students are expecting anything since they have an argument for eliminating every day of the week, Austin argues that the students can 'expect' the examination every day of the week by a series of incomplete proofs. The students should first construct a proof which follows the elimination argument only to the elimination of every day except Monday. Thus on Sunday, the students will be expecting a test on Monday. If a test is not given on Monday, the students should construct a similar proof which eliminates Wednesday, Thursday, and Friday. Thus on Monday evening, the students will be expecting a test on Tuesday. In a like manner, an expectation is formed for every day of the week. However, Austin concedes, in a later article, that if the announcement means that a single date cannot be deduced, the paradox returns.[40]

---

[38] Judith Schoenberg, 'A Note on the Logical Fallacy in the Paradox of the Unexpected Examination', *Mind*, 75/297 (Jan. 1966), 125–7.

[39] M. J. O'Carroll, 'Improper Self-Reference in Classical Logic and the Prediction Paradox', *Logique et Analyse*, 10/38 (June 1967), 171.

[40] Austin's first article was 'On the Unexpected Examination', *Mind*, 78/309 (Jan. 1969), 137. His second article was 'The Unexpected Examination', *Analysis*, 1979, 63–4.

Further self-referentialist contributions were made by Peter Windt, in his 'The Liar in the Prediction Paradox', and by Martin Edman, in his 'The Prediction Paradox' Edman's approach resembles Fitch's. The teacher tells his class that (a) during the coming week there will be an examination, and (b) the day of the examination will be a surprise. According to Edman, when we are tempted to view (a) and (b) as incompatible, we are interpreting (b) as self-referentially saying that the date of the examination cannot be deduced from (a) and (b). When we view (a) and (b) as compatible, we are interpreting (b) as either saying that the only relevant known fact about the examination date is (a) or as saying that the examination date cannot be deduced *two* days in advance. On the latter interpretation, the examination is a surprise because 'If the warning time is shorter than the necessary reaction time we tend to say that the event came as a surprise.' Thus Edman's proposal differs from Fitch's only in the kind of alternative sense of the announcement which can be confused with the self-referential one.

A late, but distinguished newcomer to the debate was A. J. Ayer in 1973 with his 'On a Supposed Antinomy'. Ayer argues that the puzzle turns on the ambiguity 'between being unable to predict *before the sequence is run through* when the event in question will occur and being unable to make this prediction *in the course of the run, however long it continues*. In the first case, there is uncertainty, but in the second there may not be'.[41] To see how Ayer intends this distinction to work, consider the two-day version of the surprise test variation. If the announcement means that the students do not know which day has been selected at the time of announcement, then the announcement can be fulfilled. If the announcement means that there could not be a time when the students knew which day the examination will take place, then the announcement is false. We fall into puzzlement when we project the second case on the first and argue that because there could be circumstances in which all uncertainty has been removed, there is no uncertainty at the start.

In 'The Surprise Exam: Prediction on the Last Day Uncertain', J. A. Wright launches another attack on the base step of the induction. He suggests that the usual interpretation of the announcement is to the effect that:

[41] A. J. Ayer, 'On a Supposed Antinomy', *Mind*, 82/325 (Jan. 1973), 125–6.

(1) A test will be held, and any one day of a given finite set of days is possible for it.
(2) It will not be possible to predict the test, with logical necessity, on the morning of that day.

Wright then suggests that the paradox can be avoided by reading the announcement as saying

(A) Any one of a finite set of days is a possible day for the test to be *planned*.
(B) It will be cancelled if it is *actually* predicted on the morning of that day.[42]

The change from 'the test will be held on' to 'the test is planned for' allows (A) to be cancelled rather than contradicted by (B). The change from possibility of prediction to actual prediction undermines the base step of the induction according to Wright. The teacher will only refuse to consider a Friday examination if he is certain that a student will come to him with a prediction. Although it is highly probable that a student will do this, it is not certain. Thus the students cannot eliminate a Friday examination with certainty.

III. GAME-THEORETIC SELF-REFERENCE

According to R. A. Sharpe, the prediction paradox arises if both parties know and apply the rules set by the teacher's announcement. For then, *all* the days are eliminated. If the rules excluded all but one day, no paradox would arise.

Since the rule here excludes all days in the week as possible days for the examination, to choose a day at all will be a surprise in the sense of displaying ignorance of or a deliberate breaking of the rule. An element of self-reference arises from the fact that on the terms by which the paradox can occur, the master must take into account the boy's own prediction before choosing a day. Since he cannot choose days which they have predicted, they negatively affect the choice and if they played a part in making the choice it is difficult to see how it can surprise them.[43]

---

[42] J. A. Wright, 'The Surprise Exam: Prediction on the Last Day Uncertain', *Mind*, 76/301 (Jan. 1967), 115.
[43] R. A. Sharpe, 'The Unexpected Examination', *Mind*, 74/294 (Apr. 1965), 255.

Sharpe points out that an announcement that only excluded one day would still be self-referential but no paradox would arise. He therefore concludes that self-reference is not a sufficient condition for the paradox. It is interesting to note that the 'element of self-reference' to which Sharpe alludes, is not the kind of self-reference Bennett and Cargile considered. Sharpe's conception of self-reference seems to be game-theoretic. The teacher's choice is self-referential in that it depends on his beliefs about the boy's prediction which in turn depends on the boy's beliefs about the teacher's choice.

Two years after his sympathetic review of the self-referential approach to the prediction paradox, James Cargile suggested that the puzzle can also be interpreted game-theoretically. Cargile conceives the problem as involving rational agents, one of which is trying to make a choice that cannot be predicted by others even though all the rational agents have the same relevant information. Cargile stipulates that the teacher has no means of randomizing his choice and that this is common knowledge. Besides knowing that the teacher prefers to give a surprise test, the students know that it is common knowledge that both teacher and students are ideally rational agents. Since Cargile is interested in the two-day version of the prediction paradox, it is also common knowledge that the test must take place on either Thursday or Friday. Cargile believes this situation leads to a puzzle because

the following would appear to be an essential truth about ideal rationality: If two ideally rational agents are asking independently whether a given proposition is true and if both have exactly the same relevant data and exactly the same knowledge about what is relevant, then they will both reach the same conclusion. The conclusion may be 'Yes' or 'No' or 'insufficient data to determine' or 'the question is unclear', etc., but it must be the same for both. For suppose that the two agents arrive at different answers, X and Y. The X cannot be a better answer than Y on the information given, since that would contradict the assumption that both agents are ideally rational — that is, think as well as possible in every case. But then the answer 'X' is no better than answer 'Y' determinable on the information given and is clearly a better answer than Y, which contradicts the assumption that both agents will give the best possible answer on the information available to them.[44]

[44] James Cargile, 'The Surprise Test Paradox', *Journal of Philosophy*, 64/18 (Sept. 1967), 557–8.

The teacher will think that the students might be surprised by a Thursday test just in case the students will. If the teacher thinks that there is no chance that a Thursday test will be surprising, then the students will know this as well, because they will have arrived at the same conclusion. If the teacher concludes that he cannot know whether there is a chance, then the students will know this. Cargile's point is that someone can surprise someone else only if the surpriser and the surprisee (that is, those who are intended to be surprised) disagree about something at some time. Since the teacher and the students are ideally rational agents with the same relevant information, such a disagreement is impossible.

Nevertheless, a surprise test can be given. Cargile discusses three responses to the paradox. First, we can conclude that the assumptions made about the players in this game are indeed contradictory. Second, we can reject the principle that similarly informed ideal thinkers will reach the same conclusion 'on the grounds that the *situation* the agent is in matters in determining what he is justified in concluding.'[45] And third, we could limit the application of the assumptions standard to game theory. We could deny these assumptions apply in games in which the goal is the acquisition of knowledge (as opposed to getting a job, winning a race, and so on). The rationale for the limitation may be that the notion of knowledge is too abstract and unrelated to practical courses of action.

Cargile tries to solve the problem by introducing a third ideally rational agent: a judge to adjudicate the students' claim. Cargile argues that the students know that the test will be given on Thursday only if the judge would agree that they know. The students cannot know that the test will be given on Thursday because the teacher will only give the test on Thursday if he knows that the students do not know that the test will be given on Thursday. If the judge ruled in favour of the students, he would be ruling against the judgement made by an ideally rational agent, the teacher. Since the students cannot satisfy this criterion of knowledge, they do not know. Cargile concedes, however, that the students can have justified confidence in the test being held on Thursday. Indeed, since the standards for certainty fluctuate from context to context, Cargile is willing to allow that the students are certain that the test will be on Thursday in other, less stringent

[45] Ibid., 561–2.

contexts. But since the relevant context is an extremely strict one, Cargile maintains that the students can be surprised by a Thursday test.

IV. EMERGENCE OF THE EPISTEMIC APPROACH

Whereas self-referentialists viewed Quine's analysis of the prediction paradox as a deflationary one, other commentators came to view it as basically correct but incomplete. For Quine did not supply a positive explanation of K's ignorance. It was furthermore felt that Quine had been insensitive to the impropriety of the announcement corresponding to the one-day case. These perceived gaps stimulated a sequence of articles that is still growing.

A. *Misgivings about the Propriety of the Announcement*

In 'The Examiner Examined', B. H. Slater claims that the teacher is doing something reprehensible when he makes the announcement although the teacher does not thereby contradict himself. In the single day version

> He says 'There will be an exam on Tuesday', but he also denies that the pupils can know this by saying in addition 'The exam will be unexpected'. While not making the contradictory remarks, by *making* the first remark in his position of authority he influences the truth of the second. It is not so much that the truth of the first opposes the truth of the second, but that his asserting the first makes the second untrue.[46]

Slater compares the teacher's announcement with someone saying 'My name is Tom; but you don't know what my name is.' According to Slater, although the conjuncts are compatible, the person's

> performance in telling us his name ... makes impossible our remaining in ignorance of it. 'We don't know what your name is' is an inference from what has been said. 'We have been told your name is Tom' is a description of what has been said. It is these two which are at odds: one can't both not know, and at the same time have learnt, what his name is. But 'We learn, from what you say, that your name is Tom' is not *deduced* from what is

[46] B. H. Slater, 'The Examiner Examined', *Analysis*, 15/4 (Dec. 1974), 50.

said. It is something we say on the basis of observation, not inference. We learn by listening, not by arguing.[47]

In 1976, further dissatisfaction with the propriety of uttering the announcement corresponding to the single day version was expressed in T. S. Champlin's 'Quine's Judge' in *Philosophical Studies*:

> The function of the notorious regress argument, *bête noire* of most commentators on the paradox, is to show: (i) that the judge who utters the words of the traditional version . . . is committed to uttering the words of the shortened version . . . should the execution occur on the last day (a thesis to which we have seen that Quine subscribes): and (ii) that a sincere judge who uttered the traditional words in normal circumstances would have to agree that for him to utter the words of the shortened version . . . would indeed be self-contradictory and thus he would detect a hidden contradiction in his original seemingly harmless pronouncement. Far from being incompatible with (ii), the possibility of Quine's querulous K and of the judge telling him the date whilst predicting his remaining ignorant is actually required by it. By shifting from the [many day version] to the [one day] version Quine sidesteps the key question posed by (ii) viz. 'Could a sincere and sober judge deliver his sentence as in [the longer version] to a reasonable K without self-contradiction?'[48]

B. *Assimilation to Moore's Problem*

Six months after publishing Cargile's article, the *Journal of Philosophy* published Robert Binkley's 'The Surprise Examination in Modal Logic'. Binkley's main achievement was to provide a rationale for Quine's claim that K cannot eliminate the last day because he does not know that the announcement is true. Binkley points out that the announcement corresponding to the single day version,

> (10) You will be hanged tomorrow noon and will not know the date in advance,

resembles the sentences G. E. Moore was puzzled by:

> (11) It is raining but I believe it is not raining.

---

[47] Ibid.
[48] T. S. Champlin, 'Quine's Judge', *Philosophical Studies*, 29/5 (May 1976), 351.

(12) It is raining but it is not the case that I believe it is raining.

In *Knowledge and Belief*, Jaakko Hintikka argued that these sentences cannot be believed by perfect logicians even though (11) and (12) are consistent. Since the prediction paradox is a paradox for perfect logicians, Binkley points out that Hintikka's explanation of the incredibility of (11) and (12) can be extended to the question of why the prisoner cannot know (10). The prisoner cannot believe, and therefore, cannot know (10) because (10) is logically incredible to K. Binkley demonstrates that the announcement corresponding to the $n+1$ day case is also incredible given the following principle: if a perfect logician believes p, then he believes that he will believe p thereafter. Since Binkley thinks we should accept this principle, he concludes that the prediction paradox is in the same family as Moore's problem.

In 'Believing and Disbelieving', Kathleen Johnson Wu arrives at much the same conclusion as Binkley, differing only in that she sees no need to restrict the analysis to perfect logicians. Igal Kvart's analysis is also quite similar to Binkley's, chiefly differing in the greater weight it assigns to formalization.

Later in 1972, another self-referentialist appeared in order to attack the 'Quine–Binkley interpretation' and to exhibit the merits of conceiving the problem in terms of "formal prediction". Jorge Bosch provides five reasons for rejecting the Quine–Binkley interpretation:

(a) Before considering from the beginning as a possibility that the announcement will not be fulfilled, it is necessary to clarify the sense of 'to know in advance'.
(b) In Quine's version from 'K persuaded himself that the sentence could not be executed' and 'the arrival of the hangman took place at 11:55 the following Thursday morning', the conclusion 'K's argument was erroneous' does not follow.
(c) If we give the announcement the more precise form [that is, the self-referential form], the paradox remains in exactly the same terms, but the Quine–Binkley interpretation does not apply.
(d) If we accept the Quine–Binkley interpretation, which leads to the form $[p \ \& \ -Kap]$, the paradox does not remain in the same terms but we are faced with *another* problem. [It does not fulfill the following condition:] 'To explain' or 'to solve' the paradox

signifies to give the announcement an interpretation such that the informal proof be still relevant, and to decide — within the framework of this interpretation — whether the informal proof is correct or not and where does 'the cause' of the paradoxical effect lie.

(e) In the usual form of the paradox, the announcement seems normal and the conclusion seems paradoxical, while in the Quine–Binkley interpretation the announcement seems paradoxical and the conclusion seems normal.[49]

Bosch then goes on to argue that although Bennett's review of Shaw shows that self-reference is not essential to the paradox, there is a kind of circularity involved due to 'the unusual fact that *the formal unpredictability of a proposition is referred to a system which includes the formal unpredictability of the same proposition*'.[50] Despite the new terminology, Bosch's conclusion resembles Fitch's. The announcement is self-contradictory and is only psychologically puzzling because we tend to fall into the confusion Lyon dwelt on.

C. *Rejection of the Temporal Retention Principle*

In 1977 'The Paradox of the Unexpected Examination' was published by Crispin Wright and Aidan Sudbury in the *Australasian Journal of Philosophy*. After stating the paradox, Wright and Sudbury list six conditions which they claim to be jointly sufficient for an intuitively satisfying solution.

(A) The account given of the content of the announcement should make it clear that it *is* satisfiable, since a surprise examination is palpably, a logical possibility.

(B) The account should make it clear that the headmaster can carry out the announcement *after* he has announced it since, palpably, he can. The two conditions require that the paradox not be construed as straightforwardly one of impredicativity or 'pragmatic self-refutation'.

(C) The account must do justice to the intuitive meaning of the announcement. An extraordinary proportion of commentators have chosen to discuss quite unnatural interpretations of it.

(D) The account must do justice to the intuitive plausibility of the pupil's reasoning.

---

[49] Jorge Bosch, 'The Examination Paradox and Formal Prediction', *Logique et Analyse*, 59–60 (Sept.–Dec. 1972), 510–11.
[50] Ibid., 524.

(E) The account should make it possible for the pupils to be *informed* by the announcement: we want the reaction of someone who notices no peculiarity but just gets on with his revision to be logically unobjectionable.

(F) The account must explain the role, in the generation of the puzzle, of the announcement's being made to the pupils; there is, intuitively, no difficulty if, e.g., the headmaster tells only the second master or keeps his intentions to himself. Most of the interpretations in the literature which identify the problem as one of impredicativity fail to meet this condition.[51]

The proposal which Wright and Sudbury believe can satisfy all of these conditions can be stated simply: reject the temporal retention principle. This principle states that the students do not lose any of the knowledge they acquire over time. Following Binkley, Wright and Sudbury note the resemblance between the announcement corresponding to the single day case and Moore's problem. They agree with Binkley and Quine that the students cannot reasonably believe the announcement corresponding to the one-day case. According to Wright and Sudbury, the students *can* reasonably believe the $n+1$ day announcement as long as there are n days left. After all, there is nothing wrong with believing on Sunday that on one of the next five days it will be the case that 'Today is the examination day but it is not the case that I believed so the night before.' However, if the test is not given by Thursday, there is something wrong in believing that on Friday it will be true that 'Today is the examination day but it is not the case that I believed so the night before.' The problem is Moore's problem since one would in effect be believing that it is both the case that there will be an examination tomorrow and that one does not now believe it. Thus the teacher's announcement makes a hiatus in reasonable belief possible. People who are not surprisees are not vulnerable to this hiatus since Moorean sentences implied by the fact that the examination will be a surprise, are not about them. Conditions (A), (B), (E), and (F) are met since the teacher can give an informative announcement which will surprise the students even if he gives it on the last day. Yet such a last day examination will not surprise non-students.

---

[51] Crispin Wright and Aiden Sudbury, 'The Paradox of the Unexpected Examination', *Australasian Journal of Philosophy*, 55/1 (May 1977), 42.

D. *Assimilation to the Lottery Paradox*

The basic epistemological approach of revealing the role of Moorean propositions in the prediction paradox underwent a refinement in Doris Olin's 'The Prediction Paradox Resolved'.[52] Recall that in the lottery paradox, the agent has strong evidential support for each member of a set of propositions which jointly imply a *contradiction*. If we suppose that the lottery has 1000 tickets, then the set is {'Ticket 1 is a loser', 'Ticket 2 is a loser', ... 'Ticket 1000 is a loser', 'One of tickets 1 to 1000 is not a loser'}. According to Olin, a similar situation obtains at each step of the prediction paradox. At each step the agent has strong evidential support for each member of a set of propositions which jointly imply a *contingency* that cannot be justifiably believed. Each set is composed of propositions of the following form:

(A) There will be an examination on exactly one of the days Monday–Friday.
(B) If an examination is held on the afternoon of day D then you will not be justified in believing this before that day.

When day D is Friday the relevant set of propositions jointly implies

(C) There will be an examination on Friday afternoon and you are not now justified in believing that there will be an examination on Friday afternoon.

Although (C) is consistent, it cannot be justifiably believed by the students. Olin explains this in terms of epistemic blameworthiness. If a person is justified in believing p, then he is not (epistemically) blameworthy for believing it. But if he is justified in believing that he is not justified in believing p, then he is at fault for believing p. So if a person is justified in believing that he is not justified, he is not justified.

According to Olin, the prediction paradox shows us that we must reject the principle that good evidence for p is sufficient for a justified belief in p. 'Even though on Thursday night the student would have good evidence for (A), etc., he would not be justified

[52] Doris Olin, 'The Prediction Paradox Resolved', *Philosophical Studies*, 44/2 (Sept. 1983), 225–33.

in believing (A). For he cannot be warranted in believing (A) without also being justified in accepting a proposition of the form "p and I am not now justified in believing p".[53] Since Olin believes that the lottery paradox also shows that strong support by the total available evidence is insufficient for justified belief, she concludes that the prediction paradox is a close cousin of the lottery paradox.

V. THE KK-REJECTORS

When most people learn about the prediction paradox, they are inclined to accept the base step of the induction more readily than the induction step. The first commentator to plausibly follow this inclination was Craig Harrison in 'The Unanticipated Examination in View of Kripke's Semantics for Modal Logic'. Harrison considered the paradox as it arises in the following form. Student a is told by his instructor that there will be a test on either the second or the fourth of the month. The test will be unforeseen in the sense that if the test is given on the fourth of the month, the a will not know so on the third, and if the test is given on the second, a will not know so on the first. Although Harrison provides a formalization of prediction paradox as it arises in this variation, I prefer a slightly different formalization for reasons which will become apparent in the next chapter. Let '$Ka_i p_k$' read 'a knows at day i that the test occurs on day k'. Where $i < j$, let 'S' be the conjunction:

$((p_2 \supset -Ka_1 p_2) \& p_4 \supset (-Ka_3 p_4 \& Ka_3 - p_2)) \&$
$((p_2 \vee p_4) \& (Ka_i p \supset Ka_j p)).$

S represents the situation a is in. The second small conjunct of S states that if the test should be given on the fourth, a will not know it on the third but will realize that no test has been given on the second. The fourth conjunct is the temporal retention principle: anything a knows, he knows thereafter. In addition to the standard rules of inference (TF), I shall appeal to the following rules:

KD: $\dfrac{K(A \& B)}{KA \& KB}$ $\dfrac{K(A \supset B)}{KA \supset KB}$ KI: $\dfrac{\vdash A}{KA}$ KE: $\dfrac{KA}{A}$

[53] Ibid., 229.

KEI: $\dfrac{KA \quad \text{Where } (A \,\&\, B) \supset C \text{ is a truth}}{KC}$ KK: $\dfrac{KA}{KKA}$
of sentential logic

KD entitles distribution of the knowledge operator over conjunctions and material conditionals. KI makes all logical truths known and KE represents 'Knowledge implies truth'. KEI ensures that the knower knows all of the consequences of what he knows, and can be derived from the preceding rules. KK guarantees that if one knows, then one knows that one knows.

{1}	1.	$Ka_3 S$	Assumption
{2}	2.	p_4	Assumption
{1}	3.	$Ka_3(p_2 \vee p_4)$	1, KD, TF
{1}	4.	S	1, KE
{1, 2}	5.	$-Ka_3 p_4 \,\&\, Ka_3 - p_2,$	4 TF
{1, 2}	6.	$Ka_3 p_4$	3, 5, TF, KEI
{1, 2}	7.	$-Ka_3 p_4$	5, TF
{1}	8.	$-p_4$	2, 6, 7, Reductio
{ }	9.	$Ka_1 S \supset -p_4$	1, 8, Conditionalization
{10}	10.	$Ka_1 S$	Assumption
{10}	11.	$Ka_3 S$	10, KE, TF (Temporal Retention)
{10}	12.	$-p_4$	9, 11, TF
{ }	13.	$Ka_1 S \supset -p_4$	10, 12, Conditionalization
{ }	14.	$Ka_1(Ka_1 S \supset -p_4)$	13, KI
{ }	15.	$Ka_1 Ka_1 S \supset Ka 1 - p_4$	14, KD
{10}	16.	$Ka_1 S \supset Ka_1 Ka_s$	10, KK
{10}	17.	$Ka_1 S \supset Ka_1 - p_4$	15, 16, TF
{10}	18.	$Ka_1 - p_4$	10, 17, TF
{10}	19.	$Ka_1(p_2 \vee p_4)$	10, KD
{10}	20.	$Ka_1 p_2$	18, 19, KEI
{10}	21.	$p_2 \supset -Ka_1 p_2$	10, KE
{10}	22.	p_2	20, KE
{10}	23.	$Ka_1 p_2 \,\&\, -Ka_1 p_2$	21, 22, 23, TF

Whereas Binkley suggests that we reject lines 1 and 10, Harrison suggests that we reject KK. KK is the most philosophically controversial principle in the set of rules and so is a prime suspect. Further, we can follow our inclination to accept the base step of the induction and yet reject the induction step since appeal to KK is only necessary at step 16, leaving lines 1 to 9 intact. In other words, the teacher can give the test on any day except the last. One might then conclude that the philosophical significance of the prediction paradox is that it is further evidence against KK.

A couple of years later, J. McLelland published a paper that was largely anticipated by Harrison's.[54] In 1975, McLelland published another paper co-authored with Charles Chihara in the *Journal of Philosophical Logic*. Although rejection of KK is still the theme, the authors maintain that more than a flat denial of the principle is necessary for a solution. They note that even those ill disposed to accept the KK principle are still puzzled by the paradox. Moreover, they concede that the paradox can be generated with a principle weaker than KK:

(K5) $K_i p \supset K_i K_j p$ ($i < j$)

This principle says that whatever is known at time i is also known at i to be known at a later time j. It sounds like the temporal retention principle which says that whatever is known will continue to be known. Indeed, one application of KK allows us to infer (K5) from the temporal retention principle. Since (K5) and the temporal retention principle sound alike and only differ by one application of KK, McLelland and Chihara suggest that some people may be puzzled because they do not notice the difference between temporal retention and (K5). They also suggest that some puzzlement might result from the confounding of (a) and (b):

(a) deducing q from the proposition that p is known by N
(b) deducing q from the proposition that p is true, when it has been given that p is known by N

Nevertheless, McLelland and Chihara think that these two confusions are too simple to be the major source of the paradox.

Their diagnosis of the central error is an 'inner-outer' fallacy that results from shifting back and forth from the perspective of a theorizer and the viewpoint of the participants in the theorizer's thought experiment. Suppose we were to list what these two parties know on two sheets of paper.

[54] McLelland's first paper was 'Epistemic Logic and the Paradox of the Surprise Examination', *International Logic Review*, 3/1 (1971), 69–85.

Unless some such axiom as KK is accepted, the two lists will not be identical. For we can put on our list K*p* when and only when they can put on their list *p*. Thus, our list will be longer than theirs. It follows that in general we cannot assume that they can infer *p* from their list from the fact that we can infer *p* from our list. According to this analysis, the paradox is generated by slipping back and forth between what we, as 'postulational theorizers', can deduce about the situation and what the subjects can deduce. By assuming that they will know what we can deduce from our list of defining axioms, we in effect gain the power of the weakened version of the KK rule.[55]

Notice that all three of their diagnoses centre on the KK principle. McLelland and Chihara have modified Harrison's analysis by showing ways in which ersatz KK reasoning can sneak into our thinking about the prediction paradox.

VI. ASSIMILATION TO THE SORITES

The sorites paradox, like the prediction paradox, is most compactly formulated as a mathematical induction. When formulated as a long chain argument, both puzzles violate intuitions in a gradualized fashion. Our assent to the early steps of the sorites is hearty, and very slowly dissipates. By the time we reach the end, we are entirely sceptical of the argument but are at a loss to pinpoint our error. With the prediction paradox, our assent is strongest for the argument which rules out a Friday test. Next strongest is the intuition that a test cannot be given on a Thursday. As we proceed backwards we reach borderline days and finally days that we are sure are adequate test times. But once we get on the slippery slope, we lack a graceful exit. In light of the similarities between the two paradoxes, it is surprising that few commentators have tried to exploit the resemblance. Indeed, no one has simply asserted that the following is just another instance of the sorites.

    i. Base step: The audience can know that the exercise will not occur on the last day.

---

[55] J. McLelland and Charles Chihara, 'The Surprise Examination Paradox', *Journal of Philosophical Logic*, 4/1 (Jan. 1975), 87.

ii. Induction step: If the audience can know that the exercise will not occur on day n, then they can also know that the exercise will not occur on day $n-1$.
iii. The audience can know that there is no day on which the exercise will occur.

Why not blame the whole puzzle on the vagueness of 'can know'? Placing the blame there would reconcile loyalty to the base step with antipathy toward the conclusion by relieving us of the burden of specifying the counter-example to the induction step. Despite its attractiveness, I have not found any clear examples of this strategy. However, there are a couple of writers who seem to have been influenced by the resemblance to the sorites.

The first is Paul Dietl, whose 'The Surprise Examination' appeared in a 1972 issue of *Educational Theory*. After criticizing Quine for failing to realize that a last day surprise examination is logically impossible, Dietl sets out to show that there are progressively weaker empirical grounds for ruling out the preceding days. The teacher will not give an examination on the penultimate day because he would have to assume that his students are stupid enough not to expect it since it is the last possible day. The third to last day is a highly improbable examination day but not as improbable as a penultimate day examination since we must assume that the teacher has gone through the preceding reasoning in order to rule out Friday and Thursday. The fourth to last day is a genuine possibility since another assumption about the teacher's reasoning must be made. According to Dietl, once we reach say, the twenty-third to last day, it is plain that the students have no grounds to expect it then. So like the KK rejectors, Dietl accepts the base step of the induction but rejects the induction step. However, unlike the KK rejecters, Dietl provides a rough probabilistic ranking of the examination dates.

The second and more explicit example is Joseph Wayne Smith's 'The Surprise Examination on the Paradox of the Heap'. Smith's grounds for grouping the prediction paradox together with the sorites rest on his scepticism about mathematical induction. According to Smith, the two paradoxes are counter-examples to this well accepted argument form. Smith argues that the principle of mathematical induction is an unjustified mathematical principle on a par with the principle of empirical induction. Thus standard proofs involving mathematical induction are unsatisfactory, and both elementary and advanced mathematics are in a crisis until either (1) the problem of mathematical induction is solved or (2) proof theory is reformulated so that classical theorems are provable without resort to this principle.[56]

One objection to the view that the sorites and the prediction paradox are evidence that mathematical induction should be rejected is the familiar point that mathematics is free of vagueness and epistemic terms. At worst, we would only be forced to *restrict* rather than reject mathematical induction when it comes to mathematical contexts. Smith counters that vague terms are essential to approximation theory citing Stirling's Formula as an example:

For a large n, $n! \sim \sqrt{2\pi n}.n^n.e^{-n}$.

A second objection to Smith's proposal is that mathematical induction is inessential to the sorites and the prediction paradox. For these paradoxes can be expressed as long (but finite) chain arguments. Consider the example of the sorites Dummett calls 'Wang's Paradox':

1. The number 0 is small.
2. If the natural number n is small, then the natural number $n+1$ is small.
3. Every natural number is small.

Dummett has suggested that rejection of mathematical induction would prevent us from deducing (3) but would not prevent us from deducing each particular instance of (3). For each particular instance can be deduced by means of (1) and a finite sequence of premisses of the following form:

(a) If 0 is small, then 1 is small.
(b) If 1 is small, then 2 is small.

---

[56] Joseph Wayne Smith, 'The Surprise Examination on the Paradox of the Heap', *Philosophical Papers*, 13 (May 1984), 43–56.

(m) If m is small, then $m+1$ is small.

Repeated application of the *modus ponens* will establish the smallness of any number. But Smith objects:

> Now this counter-argument seems to me to skate completely over the problem of mathematical induction: how do we know that the finite number of instances of the conclusion of this inductive argument are established? Indeed we know that the conclusion of this argument is not established, a datum with which we began our inquiries. But if Dummett's methodology was accepted we could establish that an intuitively large number such as $100!^{100!}$ is both small (by the above argument) and large (*ex hypothesi*), and this is contradictory. It is concluded that Dummett has not shown that the sorites paradox survives the rejection of the principle of mathematical induction. Indeed, the principle of mathematical induction is essential to the formulation of the sorites and surprise examination paradoxes, so that any paradox derived from any alleged reformulation of either paradox is best classified as an entirely new paradox.[57]

Thus Smith ends up dividing the paradoxes into two groups. Genuine versions of the prediction paradox essentially appeal to mathematical induction. The remainder require separate treatment.

VII. THE RISE OF THE PREDICTION PARADOX

As suggested in the introductory portion of this chapter, I view the prediction paradox as an example of a curiosity which evolved into a significant problem. Early discussion was largely spawned by the fact that others had failed to solve it. During this early phase, philosophers promised solutions at a cheap price. O'Connor maintained that we need only attend to the pragmatic/semantic distinction. Others maintained that a solution could be purchased by merely accepting the existence of certain ambiguities. The apparent low price of some of the ambiguity proposals was a false economy. Quine emphasized that buying Weiss's distinction between distributive and collective 'or' would cost us the law of excluded middle. Quine's analysis of the problem was largely prompted by a desire to end the inflation of the prediction paradox. As a leading denigrator of the puzzle, he refused to even

[57] Ibid., 52–3.

dignify it by describing it as a paradox. According to Quine, we had merely been taken in by an *argumentum ad ignorantiam*. Yet Quine's proposal also displayed false economy. The hidden cost was epistemological rather than logical: scepticism about either authority or the future. Interest in the prediction paradox rose sharply with Shaw's suggestion that the puzzle involved an element of self-reference. For the suggestion linked the prediction paradox to a whole family of problems of intense interest to logicians. The possibility that the paradox was related to the liar or Godel's theorem did for the prediction paradox what rumours of a rich relative do for an orphan. With investigations and refinements of the self-referential theme came divisions and subdivisions of this school of thought. With the introduction of Binkley's thesis that the prediction paradox was in the same family as Moore's problem came a second source of respectability. Although Moore's problem lacked the pre-eminence of the self-referential family, the problem was current, having been given a recent well-received analysis from Hintikka. Hintikka had created a surge of interest in doxastic and epistemic logic which spilled over into discussions of the prediction paradox. Thus the prediction paradox now had two important family ties. This produced a rivalry between the two assimilation strategies that created a sub-issue. The connection with Moore's problem also prompted interest in the prediction paradox's relevance to other epistemological problems such as the lottery paradox and the KK principle. Thus the prediction paradox's early status as a mere curiosity has been upgraded over the years through its association with other significant problems.

8
Appraisal of Past Proposals

So far I have tried to maintain a historian's neutrality in discussing past attempts to solve the prediction paradox.[1] In this chapter I will be a partisan to the debate. In the first section, I remind the reader of several good objections to the sentential self-referential approach that were mentioned in my historical account. After embellishing upon one of them, I set out to explain away the attractiveness of this approach. For the self-referential approach has enjoyed popularity out of proportion to the seriousness of the objections that have been levelled against it. I argue that it owes its popularity to the fact that the self-referentialists' twisted interpretation of the teacher's announcement generates a complicated version of an obscure medieval paradox. This denizen of the Dark Ages is reducible to the liar. Furthermore, it has sufficient logical interest to motivate the attempt to mould the prediction paradox after its likeness — especially to those worried by Quine's trivialization of the paradox. The self-referentialists overlap with a group I dub the clarifiers. The clarifier's claim that the puzzle rests on an equivocation or misconstrual of the teacher's announcement is criticized in the second section. Third, I list the main problems with the epistemological approach. My main complaint is that they have understated their conflicts with common-sense and consensus positions amongst epistemologists. Consequently, they have failed to answer questions raised by their proposals. Fourth, I criticize the view that the prediction paradox should be resolved by rejecting the KK principle. I object that the usual grounds for scepticism about KK are inapplicable to the context in which the paradox is studied, and that in any case, there are variations of the paradox that do not require appeal to KK. Further recalcitrant variations are advanced in the following section to discourage adherents of the game-theoretic approach. Lastly, I promote pessimism about the prospects of an unqualified assimilation of the prediction paradox to the sorites.

[1] Portions of this chapter are taken from 'Recalcitrant Variations of the Prediction Paradox, *Australasian Journal of Philosophy*, 60/4 (Dec. 1982), 355–62.

I. CRITICISMS OF THE SELF-REFERENTIALISTS

A plurality of commentators are self-referentialists: people who believe that an element of self-reference is responsible for the prediction paradox. The popularity of this position has made it the most tempting target for critics. Early on, Nerlich raised two important objections. First, if there is any self-reference, why is it vicious self-reference? The second and more serious objection is that self-reference is inessential to the paradox. Wright and Sudbury cover the additional objections that have been raised after Nerlich in their list of adequacy conditions. The self-referential approach has difficulties in accommodating the intuition that the teacher can give the test after his announcement and difficulties in explaining why the announcement is unproblematic if it is not announced to the students. The final objection is that the self-referential approach distorts the intuitive meaning of the announcement. This last point deserves elaboration.

A. *Knowability, Deducibility, and Gratuitous Self-reference*

If there was an element of self-reference in the prediction paradox announcement, then any statement addressed to you describing your ignorance would be self-referential. However, (1) does not imply (2):

(1) You do not know the capital of Texas.
(2) You do not know the capital of Texas even if you know (1).

It may be perverse of me to say to you

(3) Austin is the capital of Texas but you do not know it,

but (3) is certainly not a contradiction. In fact, (3) would be true if my utterance of (3) left you in ignorance of Texas's state capital. But if we follow the self-referentialists in equating knowability with deducibility, (3) would be a contradiction. For (3) would imply

(3') Austin is the capital of Texas but this fact cannot be deduced from this sentence.

The statement '*a* deduces that *p*' neither entails nor is entailed by '*a* knows that *p*'. Likewise '*a* soundly deduces that *p*' and '*a* knows that *p*' are mutually independent. Lastly, it should be noted that those who try to show that the prediction paradox is liar-paradoxical, cannot be said to have *solved* the paradox even if they achieve their goal. There is a difference between problem reduction and problem solution. If one reduces the prediction paradox to the liar paradox and one does not have a solution to the liar paradox, one has only reduced two mysteries to one mystery. Although there is much to be said for mystery reduction, it is always preferable to have a solution.

B. *Pseudo-Scotus and the Self-referentialists*

Despite my objection that the self-referentialists have been unfaithful to the original puzzle, it must be conceded that they have at least had the good fortune to slip into another interesting puzzle. Although this offshoot paradox is reducible to the liar paradox, as suspected by most of the self-referentialists, the self-referentialists have not followed the proper path of reduction. This is not surprising in view of the fact that the path from Ekbom's prediction paradox to Eubulides' liar passes through a paradox discovered by an obscure medieval logician fated to be called 'Pseudo-Scotus'.

Under the classical, semantic definition of validity, an argument is valid if and only if it is impossible for its premisses to be true and its conclusion false. In his commentary on Aristotle's *Prior Analytics*, Pseudo-Scotus presents examples which appear to show that this definition is incoherent. The most forceful examples all involve reference to the argument's own validity. The first kind of example we shall consider works by taking any necessary truth as a premiss and a denial of the argument's validity as a conclusion.

(A) 1. Squares are squares.
    2. This argument is invalid.

If the argument is invalid, then it is possible for the premiss to be true and the conclusion false. But since the premiss is necessarily true, the argument is invalid only if the conclusion is false. So if the argument is invalid, then it is valid. On the other hand, if the argument is valid, then its conclusion must be true. So (A) is valid if and only if it is invalid.

Paradox also results if a contingent premiss is used.

(B) 1. Mexico will be a communist state in 2027.
    2. This argument is invalid.

If argument (B) is valid, then it is impossible for (1) to be true and (2) false. The validity of (B) would ensure the falsity of (2) without ensuring the falsity of (1), so (B) cannot be valid. On the other hand, if (B) is invalid, it is possible for (1) to be true and (2) false. But the invalidity of (B) would ensure the truth of (2). So (B) cannot be invalid.

We can also take the argument's own validity as a premiss.

(C) 1. This argument is valid.
    2. This argument is invalid.

If (C) is valid, it has a true premiss, and so it is also sound. Sound arguments have true conclusions. So if (C) is valid, then it is invalid. But this is just to demonstrate that (2) follows from (1), so (C) cannot be invalid.

Pseudo-Scotus suggested that our puzzlement about argument (A) could be resolved by adding an extra requirement for validity: the conclusion must not explicitly deny its own validity. But as Stephen Read points out, the added condition does not handle what might be loosely termed the contrapositive of (A).[2]

(D) 1. This argument is valid.
    2. Squares are not squares.

This type of argument was discussed by fifteenth- and sixteenth-century logicians. Despite the fact that its conclusion does not

---

[2] Stephen Read, 'Self-Reference and Validity', *Synthese*, 42/2 (October 1979), 269.

Appraisal of Past Proposals

deny the validity of the argument, (D) puts us in much the same quandary as (B). Since (2) is necessarily false, the argument is valid only if (1) is false. So (D) is valid only if invalid. But it is invalid only if it is possible for (1) to be true. So it is invalid if and only if valid.

C. Reduction to the Liar

If pessimistic about the possibility of a solution to the paradoxes based on a revised definition of validity, one may be content to reduce the paradoxes to another unsolved paradox.[3] A strong case can be made for the thesis that the paradoxes of validity are just complex variations of the liar. We might support this intuition through intermediate cases. For example, we can first enrich the liar with a modal concept:

(P) Sentence (P) is possibly false.

Clearly, (P) is true only if it is possible for it to be false. But the supposition that it is false is equivalent to the supposition that (P) is necessarily true. Since (P) cannot be both necessarily true and possibly false, the supposition must be rejected. But once we conclude that it is impossible for (P) to be false, we are committed to saying that (P) is necessarily true. But this contradicts (P).

Second, we can note the existence of conjunct-liars such as 'This sentence is not true and cows fly.' This conjunct-liar is unparadoxical because the second conjunct is false. If we were to replace 'Cows fly' with

(E1) Squares are squares,

paradox would result. We can now blend the possible liar with the conjunct liar to get:

---

[3] In 'Self-Reference and Validity' Stephen Read takes the position that 'whatever solution one takes to the paradoxes of self-reference will undercut' the Pseudo-Scotus puzzles. In analysing one of the cousins of Pseudo-Scotus's puzzle, G. B. Keene takes a similar stand. Indeed, his optimism about the efficacy of a Ryle-like solution to the liar leads him to extend it to the puzzling argument and so claim a solution rather than a mere reduction of the paradox. Keene presents his analysis in 'Self-referent Inference and the Liar Paradox', *Mind*, 92/367 (July 1983), 430–3.

(E2) It is possible for (E1) to be true and (E2) to be false.

Since (E1) is a necessary truth, (E2) is true only if (E2) is possibly false. But the previous reasoning about the possible liar, (P), has shown us that this condition leads to paradox. We can turn the conjunct-possible-liar into a paradox of validity by viewing (E1) and (E2) as the premiss and conclusion of an argument. Conclusion (E2) would then be equivalent to 'This argument is invalid.' At this point, the argument is the same as (A). To reduce (B) to the liar simply substitute (B1) for (E1).

The remaining two arguments require a negated form of (E2) in order to simulate 'This argument is valid':

(E3) It is impossible for (E3) to be true and (E4) to be false,

where (E4) refers to the conclusion of the argument. If the conclusion is a contradiction, we have a (D)-type argument. If the conclusion affirms the argument's invalidity, we have a (C)-type.

The fact that Pseudo-Scotus's arguments are reducible to the liar provides reason to expect that lessons about the liar can be extended to the puzzles about validity. The first lesson to be drawn is that just as explicit self-reference is not needed for the paradox, it is not needed for Pseudo-Scotus's puzzles. This point can be illustrated with the arguments appearing in Figure 8.1.

FIGURE 8.1

1. Squares are squares.
2. Some of the arguments in this box are invalid.

1. Squares are squares.
2. Squares are squares.

Since the second argument is valid, the first argument is valid only if it is invalid. But if the first argument is invalid, it is possible for the premise to be true and the conclusion false. But if the conclusion is false, all of the arguments in the box are valid and thus the first argument would be valid. So the first argument is valid if and only if invalid.

Appraisal of Past Proposals

The second lesson worth noting is that self-reference can be contingent as well as indirect. For example, suppose Chris is presented with the following argument:

1. <u>Squares are squares.</u>
2. The next thing Chris says is true.

If the next thing Chris says is 'That argument is invalid', paradox arises. But if he says 'Cigars burn' or just about anything else, there are no difficulties. The conclusion makes the argument 'risky'.

D. *Pseudo-Scotus and the Prediction Paradox*

By insisting that the prediction paradox be understood in terms of a mixture of self-reference and deducibility, the self-referentialists have concocted a complex version of Pseudo-Scotus's puzzle. Recall that the self-referentialists maintain that the teacher's announcement should be interpreted as:

(i) A test will be given next week but you will not be able to deduce which day it occurs from the conjunction of this announcement and the fact that the test has not been given on any prior day.

The clever student begins his argument by envisioning the possibility that the students learn that a test has not been given on the previous four days. The students would then be able to advance the following argument:

(P5) 1. A test will be given next week but you will not be able to deduce which day it occurs from the conjunction of this announcement and the fact that the test has not been given on any prior day.
2. <u>No test has been given up till the last day of the week.</u>
3. The test will be given on Friday.

The student then points out that this argument is valid. So if the test is put off until the last day of the week, argument (P5) will become available to the students. So they will be able to deduce the day of the test. But this contradicts the first premiss which is just the teacher's announcement. So if the test is given on Friday, the announcement is false. Therefore, the teacher's announcement is true only if the test is given on a day earlier than Friday. The students are thus entitled to use this fact as a premiss in evaluating the possibility of a Thursday examination. The clever student then points out that if no test has been given by Wednesday, the following valid argument becomes available to the students:

(P4) 1. A test will be given next week but you will not be able to deduce which day it occurs from the conjunction of this announcement and fact that the test has not been given on a prior day.
2. No test has been given up till the second to last day.
3. <u>The test will not be given on Friday.</u>
4. The test will be given on Thursday.

Since the third premiss can be deduced from the first premiss (as established by consideration of (P5)), the validity of (P4) would falsify the first premiss. So if the test is given on Thursday, the teacher's announcement is false. This fact can now be used as a premiss in evaluating the possibility of a Wednesday test. This enables the clever student to construct another argument like (P4), (P3), which eliminates Wednesday. In turn, (P3) leads to (P2), eliminating Tuesday, and to (P1) which eliminates Monday. Since all the alternatives are eliminated by this point, the announcement is revealed as contradictory.

Of course, this argument only works if we interpret 'deduce' as 'validly infer'. If we were to interpret 'deduce' as 'soundly infer', the argument would fail at the base step.

The general pattern of reasoning amongst the philosophers in this self-referentialist tradition is fairly uniform. After arguing that the announcement must be interpreted in terms of deducibility, they proceed to derive a contradiction from the announcement. They then must cope with the counter-intuitiveness of this result. For obviously the teacher can give a surprise test. Most explain the counter-intuitiveness in terms of an ambiguity. Thus our puzzlement is blamed on an equivocation. A minority maintain that the announcement is somehow consistent just because each deduction has a corresponding counterdeduction.

I now wish to show how Pseudo-Scotus's puzzles about validity undermine the consensus position that a contradiction can be derived from the self-referential version of the teacher's announcement.

The self-referential interpretation of the teacher's announcement can be expressed more precisely in terms of validity: 'There will be a test but there will be no valid argument available to you which concludes with a correct test day.' Given that we take S to be the sequence of available arguments and 'p1' to be 'There is a test on Monday', 'p2' to be 'There will be a test on Tuesday', and so on, the announcement can be formalized as:

(T) $(\exists n)pn$ & $(n)(pn \supset Pn$ is invalid$)$.

The sequence of available arguments runs as follows:

(P1) 1. $\underline{T}$
 2. p1

(P2) 1. $\underline{-p1\ \&\ T}$
 2. p2

(P3) 1. $\underline{-(p1 \vee p2)\ \&\ T}$
 2. p3

(P4) 1. $\underline{-(p1 \vee p2 \vee p3)\ \&\ T}$
 2. p4

(P5) 1. $\underline{-(p1 \vee p2 \vee p3 \vee p4)\ \&\ T}$
 2. p5

The clever student's argument can be recast as follows.

For the sake of a *reductio*, assume that the announcement, (T), is true. Clearly argument (P5) is valid since it is just a disjunctive syllogism. So from (T) it follows that (p5 $\supset$ P5 is invalid). But since P5 is valid, we can deduce $-$p5. So the announcement (T) implies $-p5$. This result permits us to demonstrate the validity of argument (P4). For it too is just a disjunctive syllogism once the hidden implication of (T) is added. Therefore, (T) can be true only if p4 is false. Thus we discover that (T) also implies $-p4$. This in turn enables us to discover the validity of (P3). In a like manner, we discover that (T) is false for each value of n. Therefore, the negation of (T) follows by reductio revealing the contradictory nature of (T).

The point of this laborious reconstruction of the student's reductio is to show that he is using arguments whose premises indirectly refer to their own invalidity.[4] This can be seen more clearly by considering the one-day version of the prediction paradox. Here the teacher announces 'The test is on Monday but you cannot deduce this fact from this announcement.' The set of available arguments is now composed solely of (P1) with n equal to 1. The argument is thus equivalent to:

(P1′) 1. There is a test on Monday but this argument is invalid.
   ────────────────────
2. There is a test on Monday.

This argument is strongly reminiscent of Pseudo-Scotus's paradoxes of validity by virtue of the 'This argument is invalid' conjunct. The one day version of the prediction paradox has the advantage of making the self-reference direct. In $n+1$ day versions of the paradox, the self-reference is indirect. Although the indirectness of the self-reference mutes its presence, it does not diminish its potential for paradox. Given the semantic irrelevance of the direct/indirect distinction, one can disarm the $n+1$ day version of the paradox by disarming the one-day version.

Is argument (P1′) really valid? The answer *appears* to be affirmative because the argument seems like an instance of the valid argument form of simplification (just as the more compli-

---

[4] Some may be suspicious of my reconstruction of the student's argument because it does not prominently represent the temporal aspect of the original story. However, this element will be shown to be inessential in the third and fourth sections of this chapter.

cated arguments appear to be instances of disjunctive syllogism). Unlike the Pseudo-Scotus puzzles, argument (P1′) does not drive us directly into contradiction by a consideration of its validity. For we can say that the validity of the argument only serves to make the 'This argument is invalid' conjunct unparadoxically false.

The first point I wish to make against the validity of the argument is that there are other arguments that apparently instantiate valid argument forms which we nevertheless have qualms about calling valid. For example,

(Q) 1. There is a test on Monday but this argument is unsound.
2. There is a test on Monday.

This argument cannot be sound because the truth of the second conjunct would make the argument unsound. If the argument is unsound, it is either invalid or has a false premiss. But given that it is valid by simplification, it follows that the first conjunct is false. Yet the content of the first conjunct played no special role in our reasoning, so any proposition can be 'proved' false by having it be the first conjunct. So if we accept the validity of argument (Q), everything is provable.

But note that the premiss of (Q) is a weakened version of the premiss of (P1′). For the premiss of (Q) is equivalent to:

(ii) There is a test on Monday but either this argument is invalid or it has a false premiss.

One of the reasons we find the validity of (P1′) plausible is that we feel entitled to ignore the second conjunct. We can appeal to the principle that the addition of a premiss never turns a valid argument into an invalid argument. And we need only add 'This argument is invalid' to the valid argument.

(M) 1. There is a test on Monday.
2. There is a test on Monday.

in order to obtain (P1′). So we conclude that (P1′) must be valid by the added premiss principle. However, if we accept this application of the added premiss principle, we should also be willing to apply the principle to derive (Q) from (M) by adding (ii). Since we are unwilling to do so, we cannot use the added premiss principle to establish the validity of (P1'). Indeed, unless we adopt a restriction as to what counts as adding a premiss to a valid argument, we are forced to reject the added premiss principle altogether.

The fact that the premiss of the problematic argument (Q) is weaker than (P1') suggests an alternative formulation of my objection to the validity of (P1'). If (P1') is valid by simplification, it is a 'redundant' argument; it has a premiss that is not needed to validly infer its conclusion. The validity of a redundant argument is not affected by weakening its superfluous premisses. So the validity of the redundant argument (P1') would entitle us to weaken its superfluous premiss 'This argument is invalid' to 'This argument is either invalid or has a false premiss.' But this weakened version of (P1') is equivalent to the non-valid argument (Q). Therefore, (P1') is not valid.

Further grounds for denying that (P1') is a valid argument spring from our unclarity as to what '(P1') is valid' means. The classical definition of validity is that an argument is valid if and only if it is impossible for the premisses to be true and the conclusion false. Applying this definition to (P1') yields:

(a) It is impossible for (p1 & This argument is invalid) to be true and p1 to be false.

This in turn means:

(b) It is impossible for [p1 & It is possible for (p1 & This argument is invalid) to be true and p1 to be false] to be true and p1 to be false.

In turn (b) leads to a more complicated claim which in turn leads to ever more complicated sentences. But no matter how far we go, we never eliminate the 'This argument is invalid' clause. For some philosophers, such as Gilbert Ryle, the impossibility of ever fully unpacking what the sentence means is a sufficient condition for the sentence being neither true nor false.[5] For these philosophers use

[5] Ryle presents this view in 'Heterologicality', *Analysis*, 11/3 (Jan. 1951), 61–4.

this condition in their attempt to resolve the liar paradox. Consider the early unpackings of 'This statement is false':

(c) This statement, namely 'This statement is false', is false.
(d) This statement, namely 'This statement, namely "This statement is false" is false' is false.

Since the statement never gets around to saying what it is saying, it does not say anything. The same applies to 'This statement is true.'

The claim that finite unpackability is a necessary condition for meaningfulness is dubious. For many important mathematical and logical principles would also be ruled meaningless. For example, the self-referential nature of 'No statement is both true and false' ensures that it is not finitely unpackable. Nevertheless, Ryle's observation does highlight the unclarity of the thesis that (P1') is valid. For in addition to not being finitely unpackable, the thesis also has infinitely iterated modalities. As Quine emphasizes, we have a poor understanding of possibility, and a poorer understanding of iterated possibility. And once we toss in the elements of infinity and self-reference, we have quite a brew.

The foregoing is not intended as a solution to the Pseudo-Scotus interpretation of the prediction paradox. It is only intended to clarify the problem that stimulates the self-referentialists and to reveal the haste of their validity verdicts. As I have previously argued, we have little reason to suppose that the Pseudo-Scotus prediction paradox is what the original framers of the prediction paradox had in mind. For sentential self-reference has been read into the problem. Similar projections of our fascination with self-reference can be found in the literature on Descartes's *cogito*, the preface paradox, and omniscience.[6] Injecting self-referentiality into old problems does create legitimate new problems. However, it does not impose a new adequacy condition for the solution of the old problem. The solution need not extend to the new problem because the introduction of self-reference puts the hybrid into

[6] For the *cogito* see William Boos, 'A Self-Referential "*Cogito*" ', *Philosophical Studies*, 44/2 (Sept. 1983), 269–90; and Peter Slezak, 'Descartes' Diagonal Deduction', *British Journal for the Philosophy of Science*, 34/1 (Mar. 1983), 13–36. For the self-referential version of the preface paradox, see Arthur Prior, *Objects of Thought* (Oxford: Oxford University Press, 1971), 85–6. For self-referential problems with omniscience see Patrick Grim, 'Some Neglected Problems of Omniscience', *American Philosophical Quarterly*, 20 (July 1983), 265–76.

another family of puzzles. There is a conceptual discontinuity. If we were to demand that the self-referential variants also be solved, a great many problems would gain a formidable new adequacy condition. For we can give a self-referential twist to almost any problem involving propositional attitudes. Since there are no grounds for according self-reference special status, we would also be bound to allow other conceptual injections to breed new adequacy conditions. We would then find ourselves sitting with Hegel at the bottom of the slippery slope, agreeing that the solution of one problem requires the solution of all problems.

II. CRITICISMS OF THE CLARIFIERS

Overlapping the self-referentialists are the clarifiers. Clarifiers believe that people who are puzzled by the prediction paradox are puzzled because they do not fully understand the announcement. For example, Alexander argues that we overlook the fact that every declaration of an intention has an implicit 'if possible' clause. Most clarifiers think that there is an ambiguity involved whose exposure solves the paradox. The most influential commentator amongst these equivocationalists is Ardon Lyon. In an unusual display of confidence in his fellow philosophers, Lyon began his proposal with the prediction that anyone who read it would accept it. Lyon's over-confidence is symptomatic of a difficulty common to all instances of this approach. If the paradox is really due to any of the equivocations that have been proposed, why do the vast majority of people who understand the proposal continue to be puzzled?

III. CRITICISMS OF THE EPISTEMOLOGICAL APPROACH

The basic problem with Quine's analysis is that it commits us to an unacceptable sort of scepticism. In the case of the Hangman version, Quine maintains that the elimination argument simply shows that the judge's declaration is insufficient evidence for K to know that he will be hung on an unforeseen day. But why is the evidence insufficient? Remember that K confronts an epistemologically ideal judge in epistemologically ideal circumstances. So the reason cannot be that K needs to know more about the judge's record or sincerity. Nor can the ignorance of K be due to the unpredictability of free human beings. A passage from Hume's 'Of Liberty' is particularly germane:

> A prisoner, who has neither money nor interest, discovers the impossibility of his escape, as well from the obstinacy of the goaler, as from the walls and bars with which he is surrounded; and in all attempts for his freedom chuses rather to work upon the stone and iron of the one, than upon the inflexible nature of the other. The same prisoner, when conducted to the scaffold, foresees his death as certainly from the constancy and fidelity of his guards as from the operation of the ax or wheel.[7]

Judges, jailors, and executioners are a dependable lot. Why can't K be as sure of his hanging as ordinary people are of death and taxes? Those who persist in thinking free-will relevant are encouraged to consider other variations of the paradox. Suppose someone announces that he has placed the ace of spades in a position in the deck such that as the cards are turned over one by one, the audience will not be able to predict when the ace of spades will be revealed. The audience is permitted to verify the normality of the deck and knows that the dealer has no talent as a magician. Here doubts akin to the one about a last minute change of heart or the fidelity of the judge and jailors do not create uncertainties. Only a broad scepticism seems to suffice to prevent the audience from knowing there is an ace of spades if fifty-one of the remaining cards have been removed from the deck.

The significance of Binkley's paper is that it seems to save Quine from the scepticism objection. Ideal thinkers cannot know a Moorean proposition about themselves. Unfortunately, Binkley's doxastic principles are so strong as to make the original announcement uninformative to the announcees. The announcement 'There will be a surprise test next week' is not a Moorean sentence. The fact that Binkley's doxastic logic makes it Moorean is an excellent reason to reject his logic of belief.

Wright and Sudbury save Binkley's insight that Moore's problem is relevant to the prediction paradox by adopting weaker principles. The weaker system allows the announcement to be

---

[7] David Hume, *A Treatise of Human Nature*, ed. L. A. Selby-Bigge (Oxford: Clarendon Press), 406.

temporarily, or better yet, *contingently* informative. When the students first hear the announcement, they know it. They will continue to know it unless all of the alternative exam days are eliminated except one. At that point they lose their knowledge because the conjunction of the announcement and their new information implies the Moorean sentence 'The test is on the last day but the students do not believe it.' The ability of the Wright–Sudbury analysis to preserve the informativeness of the announcement is its most satisfying feature. For distrust of such a humdrum claim would force us to go too far. If you cannot trust your teachers, who can you trust?

However, the Wright–Sudbury analysis leaves a number of loose ends. First, nothing they say excludes the possibility that non-surprisees, say the parents of the students, are able to predict the last day of exam. For the conjunction of the announcement and the information that remaining alternatives have been eliminated does not imply a proposition that is Moorean *for the parents*. So why couldn't the parents simply tell the students that the exam is on Friday? Can't they share their knowledge? To deny that the knowledge can be shared is to affirm that the students have a sort of underprivileged access. It implies that ideal thinkers can disagree given the same information. Indeed, it suggests that the two parties must reason differently. Second, we want to know more about how one manages to lose knowledge without forgetting it. Third, as Charles Chihara has objected, why can't the paradox be reformulated by having the teacher guarantee his students that they will not lose knowledge? Doesn't this suffice to save the temporal retention principle? Fourth, why even suppose that the temporal retention principle is essential to all variations of the paradox? Indeed, it will be shown in the next section that there are variations of the prediction paradox in which this principle plays no role.

IV. CRITICISMS OF THE KK-REJECTORS

The KK-rejectors have both formal elegance and our inclinations about the base step on their side. I have two basic criticisms of this proposal.

A. Relevance of the Alleged Counter-examples to KK

Formally, all the KK-rejector can do is show that a set of assumptions and principles lead to a contradiction. Doing so casts suspicion on the members of that set. The substantive task is to isolate a prime suspect and show why it should be rejected. The mere fact that it is a member of a set of assumptions and principles that leads to a contradiction does not in itself make a particular member more suspicious than any other.

Arguing that KK should be rejected because it does not hold for ordinary knowers in everyday circumstances attracts the charge of special pleading. Neither the temporal retention principle nor principles guaranteeing that all logical truths are known would survive this test. Most of the members of the problematic set would be eliminated if they were judged by the criteria of psychological adequacy. The principles are only taken to be descriptive of an idealized situation. Of course, the idealized situation is relevant to ordinary situations in so far as they reflect prescriptive ideals. The purpose of idealizing is to answer questions about what *can* be known, not questions about what *would* be known.

In order for the standard sort of counter-examples to be relevant, they must apply to ideal thinkers in ideal environments. Further, they must apply to the sort of situation that the participants of prediction paradoxes are in. This is a tall order.

In the prediction paradox, the knowers are free from the sort of epistemic shortcomings which the standard 'counter-examples' to KK exploit. The ideal knowers in the prediction paradox are conceptually mature, unforgetful, and free from deep error. However, most of the persuasive counter-examples to KK involve knowers with epistemic shortcomings. For example, we are presented with examples of young children who appear to know certain facts about their surroundings but because of their conceptual immaturity, do not appear to know that they know these facts. KK can be made to fail for adults as well. For example, John may know that he has a broken finger without John knowing that *John* knows that he has broken finger. For John may not know he is John. Here, the shortcoming is lack of self-knowledge.

Defenders of KK usually avoid this counter-example by restricting KK to people with self-knowledge. Lemmon maintains that

KK fails in the case of momentary forgetters. Since the forgetter soon recalls the answer, he knew even when he did not know that he knew. Apparent counter-examples involving inexplicable knowledge, such as the boy who is able to spontaneously pick winning horses, involve an absence of justification. The same goes for Colin Radford's example of the unconfident examinee whose excellent record of correct answers prompts us to credit him with knowledge of the answers even though he sincerely claims to be merely guessing as he gives each answer. Later the unconfident examinee remembers that he once studied the topic on which he was quizzed, thus explaining his excellent peformance. So in addition to the shortcomings of a lack of justification and confidence, there is the element of forgetting. Danto has presented two alleged counter-examples to KK. The first is the case of the sceptic who sincerely says that he does not know he has two hands. We want to say that the sceptic's philosophical beliefs do not prevent him from knowing that he has two hands. However, we are less sure about whether he knows that he knows he has two hands. For given the sceptic's consistency, and the fact that knowledge implies belief, the sceptic cannot know that he knows if he believes that he does not know. Those persuaded by this example must attribute the defect of deep epistemological error to the sceptic.

Danto's second objection to KK is that knowledge implies understanding and since there are many knowers who do not understand what knowledge is, there are many cases in which someone knows without knowing that he knows. By 'understanding', Danto has in mind the Socratic requirement of an ability to define. In light of the Gettier literature, it is fairly clear that no one has a philosophically adequate definition of 'know', so no one understands knowledge according to the Socratic standard. Since knowing requires understanding, according to Danto, it follows that no one knows that he knows! A peculiar feature of this 'counter-example' is that it only constitutes an objection to KK, not to KKK (if one knows that one knows, then one knows that one knows that one knows). Of course, most epistemologists reject this second example of Danto's because of its extravagant conception of what is required for understanding. But even if we accepted Danto's high standards, there is no reason to suppose that they could not be met by ideal knowers.

McLelland and Chihara first criticize KK by maintaining that it sets a high standard of knowledge. Following Hintikka, they take it to imply that $Kp \supset Kq$ can be inferred from $Kp \supset q$. The reasoning is that the knower must be able to rule out all possible counter-evidence. McLelland and Chihara observe that ordinary people rarely if ever satisfy this high standard, and so conclude that KK should be rejected in order to avoid scepticism. One might object that ideal thinkers could know in this strong sense. McLelland and Chihara answer that casting the prediction paradox in terms of this strong sense of knowledge removes the paradoxical air of the conclusion that the students cannot know the announcement to be true. For we are rarely, if ever, in a position to rule out all possible counter-evidence. Thus McLelland and Chihara would fall back on Quine's solution if we were to insist on using 'know' in the strong sense.

My first misgiving about this objection is that however effective it may be against the claim that we actually have knowledge in the strong sense, it does not establish that we *cannot* have knowledge in the strong sense. But let us suppose that one accepts modal scepticism about knowledge in the strong sense. Does this make the puzzle unparadoxical? If one were sceptical as to whether anyone *could* know in the strong sense, then 'The students cannot know the announcement' should not be counter-intuitive. However, it would still be surprising that this statement could be established by the reductio associated with the prediction paradox. For the reductio does not appeal to the possibility of counter-evidence. So casting the puzzle in the strong sense of 'know' would not remove all paradox. Lastly, Hintikka's argument that KK requires one to know in a way that entitles one to ignore future evidence is vulnerable. For the argument turns on the same reasoning that is responsible for Harman's paradox of dogmatism: ' "If I know that *h* is true, I know that any evidence against *h* is evidence against something that is true; so I know that such evidence is misleading. But I should disregard evidence that I know is misleading. So, once I know that *h* is true, I am in a position to disregard any future evidence that seems to tell against *h*." '[8] As Harman points out, the argument overlooks the fact that gaining further evidence can change what I know, so that I may no longer know that the evidence is misleading.

[8] Gilbert Harman, *Thought* (Princeton: Princeton University Press, 1973), 148.

The second objection McLelland and Chihara make against KK begins with the observation that many epistemologists are sympathetic to the view that knowledge is undefeated justified true belief. Given that something like this view is correct,

> it should be evident that much more is required to know that one knows that p than is required to know that p. Thus, Al may be said to know that Carol is in the next room: Carol is in the next room. Al believes it, and he has grounds for his belief that are rationally compelling and non-defective. But must Al know that he knows Carol is in the next room? Must he have non-defective evidence that the grounds for his belief that Carol is in the next room are both rationally compelling and non-defective? We cannot see why.[9]

McLelland and Chihara are correct in taking the undefeated justified true belief definition of knowledge as a definition hostile to the KK thesis. But that still leaves the problem of translating the hostility into scepticism about KK as applied in the prediction paradox. How can the problem of checking whether one's evidence is non-defective arise for the sort of ideal situations described in presentations of the prediction paradox? The requirement that one's evidence be non-defective was formulated to exclude the Gettier counter-examples. If our ideal thinkers are prevented from knowing that they know because of worries about being Gettiered, then how can they ever know that they know? If Gettier worries cannot be overcome here (by ideal thinkers in ideal environments), how can they be overcome anywhere? The scepticism about KK threatens to become too strong, like Danto's. Critics of KK need to preserve the intuition that we commonly know that we know. But once this is conceded, it is difficult to show how iterated knowledge could be impossible to achieve in the prediction paradox. Showing that iterated knowledge is not *necessarily* achieved in ordinary circumstances is irrelevant.

The last standard objection to KK with which I am familiar is that it requires infinite knowledge. If I know that p, then KK entitles us to infer that I know that I know that p. But we need not stop there. We can also then derive KKKp, KKKKp, KKKKKp, and so on indefinitely. But my finitude makes the attribution of a billionfold iteration of knowledge operators to me quite implausible. As long as our ideal thinkers are finite beings, the same

---

[9] J. McLelland and Charles Chihara, 'The Surprise Examination Paradox', *Journal of Philosophical Logic*, 4 (1975), 81.

Appraisal of Past Proposals

objection extends to them as well. So unlike the previous cases, the complexity objection is extendable to ideal thinkers.

However, the amount of iteration necessary for the prediction paradox is modest. Given that there are n alternatives to eliminate, one only needs $n-1$ iterations. So although the KK principle may not hold for the ideal thinkers in its full, infinite glory, it may hold for the situation in question. To put the matter differently, the prediction paradox only requires a limited version of the KK principle. For example, we could formulate a capped KK principle, KK-sub-5: if you know, then you know that you know as long as the iterations are below 5.

B. *The Dispensability of the KK principle*

My second criticism of the KK-rejectors also applies to the temporal retention rejectors, Wright and Sudbury; neither the KK principle nor the temporal retention principle is essential to all variations of the prediction paradox. Consider the designated student paradox. Robinson Crusoe discovers four people on his island in addition to Friday and names the rest of them for each day of the working week. Crusoe decides to teach them English history. Since his resources are limited, he can only give one student a test. Since he wants the test to be a surprise, he first lines the students up in accordance with the order of the days in the week so that Friday can see the back of Thursday and the backs of all those in front of Thursday, and Thursday can see the backs of Wednesday, Tuesday, and Monday (but not Friday's since Friday is behind him), and so on. Robinson Crusoe then shows the students four silver stars and a gold star. He announces that he will put a gold star on the back of the student who has to take the test and silver stars on all the rest. Further, the test will be a surprise in the sense that the designated student (the one with the gold star) will not know he is the designated student until after the students break formation (although others can know). One of the students objects that such a test is impossible. He says, 'We all know that Friday cannot be the designated student since, if he were, he would see the four silver stars in front of him and deduce that he must have the gold star on his back. But then he would know that he was the designated student. The designated student cannot know that he is the designated student; contradiction. We all know that Thursday cannot be the designated student since, if he were, he would see silver stars in front of him, and since he knows by the previous deduction that Friday is not the designated student, he would be able to deduce that he is the designated student. In a similar manner, Wednesday, Tuesday, and Monday can be eliminated. Therefore, the test is impossible.' Robinson Crusoe smiles, has them break formation, and Wednesday is surprised to learn that he has the gold star, and so is the designated student, and so must take the test.

In this variation, knowledge is accumulated perceptually rather than by memory. So no appeal to the temporal retention principle is needed. Thus, the designated student paradox undermines the Wright–Sudbury proposal. Indeed, all analyses which assign time a crucial role in the paradox are undercut. In particular, we should reject both the Weiss analysis and the Fraser analysis.

The designated student paradox also undermines the proposal that KK be rejected since it does not require KK. For the sake of simplicity and to stress the resemblance between the designated student variation and the traditional variations, consider a two-person version of the designated student paradox. Here, Alvin the first and Alvin the third are the students. Let '$Ka_i p_k$' read 'Alvin i knows that Alvin $k-1$ is the designated student'. Let 'S' be the conjunction

$$((p_2 \supset -Ka_1 p_2) \& (p_4 \supset (-Ka_3 p_4 \& Ka_3 - p_2)))$$
$$\& (p_2 \vee p_4)).$$

In order to meet the requirements of informativeness, one is tempted to prefix S with $(x)Kx$ where x ranges over the students. However, $(x)KxS$ corresponds to a variation in which the teacher makes a private announcement to each student (so that none know the others know the announcement). Since we are concerned with a variation in which the announcement is public, where everyone knows that everyone knows the announcement, it appears that a faithful representation demands $(x)Kx(y)KyS$. However, it can be demonstrated that $(x)Kx(y)KyS$ leads to a contradiction in an epistemic version of the modal system KT. KT is the system one obtains if one deletes the rule KK from the set of rules used in the proof appearing in the last chapter. Any normal modal analysis of epistemic logic must contain KT, so acceptance of any representation of the situation described by the designated student paradox which implies Ka_1Ka_3S requires rejection of the normal modal analysis of epistemic logic. By reinterpreting lines 1 through 9 in the previous proof in accordance with the interpretation above, the first nine lines of that proof can double as the first nine lines of the proof that Ka_1Ka_3S is inconsistent in KT.

{ }	10.	$Ka_1(Ka_3S \supset -p_4)$	9, KI
{ }	11.	$Ka_1Ka_3S \supset Ka_1-p_4$	10, KD
{12}	12.	Ka_1Ka_3S	Assumption
{12}	13.	Ka_1-p_4	11, 12, TF
{ }	14.	$Ka_3S \supset S$	1, 4, Conditionalization
{ }	15.	$Ka_3(KaS \supset S)$	14 KI
{ }	16.	$Ka_1Ka_3S \supset Ka_1S$	15, KD
{12}	17.	Ka_1S	12, 16, TF
{12}	18.	$Ka_1(p_2 \vee p_4)$	17, KD, TF
{12}	19.	Ka_1p_2	13, 18, KEI
{12}	20.	$p_2 \supset -Ka_1p_2$	17, KE, TF
{12}	21.	p_2	19, KE
{12}	22.	$Ka_1p_2 \& -Ka_1p_2$	19, 20, 21, TF

Since Ka_1Ka_3S is inconsistent in KT, anything implying it is likewise inconsistent. Thus the unquantified $Ka_1Ka_3S \& Ka_3Ka_1S$ cannot be a faithful representation of a public, informative announcement to the pair, Alvin I and Alvin III. One can infer Ka_1Ka_3S from $(x)Kx(y)KyS$ in a quantified KT, so it is inconsistent as well.

Like the traditional variations of the prediction paradox, the designated student paradox can be generalized to the 'n-day' case. These variations can be generalized in a second way as well. Consider the $1 \leq m \leq n$ case where n is the number of days and m is the number of surprises. It is easy enough for the students to argue that the mth test cannot be a surprise, since after the $m-1$ surprise they can perform the standard elimination for the single surprise case. The students can then argue that the $m-1$ test cannot be a surprise since after the $m-2$ surprise, there would be only one surprise test forthcoming (since the mth test has been shown to be unsurprising), thus enabling them to employ the standard elimination argument once more. Having tamed the last two tests, the students can run the test through the routine. The

320   *Appraisal of Past Proposals*

upshot seems to be that it is impossible to inform someone that he will be surprised m times within a period of n occasions. A parallel argument for the designated student variation seems to show that it is impossible to publicly inform a group of n students that they are going to receive m tests Crusoe-style.

V. A FURTHER PUZZLE FOR THE TEMPORALISTS

Although the designated student variation of the prediction paradox is sufficient to refute the view that the prediction paradox is essentially a puzzle about time, it is worthwhile to consider a further puzzle which may serve to further discourage temporalism. Part of the attraction of temporalism lies in the fact that the familiar versions of the prediction paradox involve a rigid order of elimination. We picture the alternatives as floating toward us down the river of time. We suspect that our puzzlement might be due to a failure to note that the asymmetry of time imposes restrictions on the order in which we are permitted to examine future alternatives. Since we are shuttling back and forth from what we will (hypothetically) know to what we now know, the 'backwards induction' comes to resemble time-travel. We are tempted to conclude that just as we cannot travel into the future physically we cannot travel into the future epistemically. The paradox of the undiscoverable position is intended to undermine this picture of our puzzlement by demonstrating that the order of elimination can be flexible.

Consider the game played in Figure 8.2.

The object of the game is to discover where you have been initially placed. The seeker may only move Up, Down, Left, or Right, one box at a time. The outer edges are called walls. If the seeker bumps into a wall, say by moving left from 1, his move is recorded as L* and his position is unchanged. Bumps help the seeker discover his initial position. For instance, if he is at 7 and moves U, U, L*, the seeker can deduce that he must have started from 7. The seeker has discovered where he started from if he obtains a completely disambiguating sequence of moves, i.e. a sequence which determines the seeker's initial position.

If the seeker is given only two moves, it is possible to put him in an undiscoverable position. For instance, if he is put in position 4,

FIGURE 8.2

1	2	3
4	5	6
7	8	9

every possible two move sequence is compatible with him having started from some other position. Now suppose the seeker is told 'You have been put in an undiscoverable position'. He disagrees and offers the following *reductio ad absurdum*: 'Suppose I am in an undiscoverable position. It follows that I cannot be in any of the corners since each has a completely disambiguating sequence. For instance, if I am in 3, I might move U*, R*, and thereby deduce my position. Having eliminated the corners, I can also eliminate 2, 4, 6, and 8, since any bumps resulting from a first move completely disambiguates. For instance, U* is sufficient to show that I am in 2. Since only 5 remains, I have discovered my position. The absurdity of the supposition is made further manifest by the existence of eight other arguments with eight distinct conclusions as to my initial position. For example, I could conclude that I am in 6 by first eliminating the corners, then 2, 4, 8, and then 5 (by sequence L, L*, leaving only 6 remaining). If one individuates arguments by distinct orders of elimination, there are indeed more than eight arguments. I could also conclude that I am in 6 by eliminating in this order: 7, 4 (by U, L*), 8, 1, 2, 5, 9, and 3. Thus I cannot be put in an undiscoverable position.' Since the undiscoverable position paradox does not have a rigid order of elimination, it discourages the view that the prediction paradox is guilty of some sort of time-travel fallacy.

VI. CRITICISMS OF THE GAME-THEORETIC APPROACH

According to Sharpe, the fact that the students' expectations negatively influence the teacher's choice of an examination day introduces an element of self-reference. For given that both are ideal thinkers, the teacher's beliefs about the best exam day are evidence against themselves because the teacher realizes that the students must be having similar thoughts. Cargile agrees with Sharpe in portraying the teacher's difficulty as arising from the fact that the students can replicate the reasoning of the teacher. The standard game-theoretical resolution of such quandaries is to randomize, but Cargile rules this out. We are then thrown back on establishing whether the students can be *certain* as to when the test will be given. And although Cargile's point about the context dependency of certainty is novel to the prediction paradox literature, the essential puzzle has only been repackaged in the language of game theory.

Although Sharpe and Cargile may be criticized for not offering much in the way of a *solution* to the prediction paradox, I will eventually show how their observations accurately track a connection between the surprise test paradox and some game-theoretical paradoxes. But in the meantime, it will be useful to concentrate on a small point concerning replication. For the participants in a prediction paradox situation need not *replicate* each other's reasoning. They may instead merely *repeat* an argument type. This lesson can be drawn from the 'sacrificial virgin' paradox. As a bonus, this variation of the prediction paradox shows that the participants need not know how many alternatives must be eliminated.

Every fifty years the inhabitants of a tropical paradise sacrifice a virgin to the local volcano in an elaborate ceremony. Virgins from all around are blindfolded and brought before the volcano. They all hold hands in a line and can only communicate one sentence: 'No one to your right is the sacrificial virgin.' This sentence can only be signalled by squeezing the hand of the virgin to one's left. The virgins are reliable and duty-bound to signal if and only if the sentence is known to be true. Besides all this, the virgins also know that a necessary condition for being the sacrificial virgin is that one remain ignorant of the honour until one is tossed in. The chief must take the leftmost virgin up to the mouth of the volcano, and if the offering is acceptable, toss her in and tell the rest of the virgins to go home. If the offering is unacceptable, he sends that virgin home and repeats the procedure with the new leftmost virgin. This procedure continues until one virgin is sacrificed, so it is known that one will be sacrificed. After hearing the announcement that one virgin will be sacrificed, someone objects that the ceremony cannot take place. The rightmost virgin knows she is rightmost since her right hand is free. She knows that if she is offered, then none of the virgins to her left have been sacrificed. So if she is the sacrificial virgin, then she will have to be offered knowing that she is the only alternative remaining, and thus would know she is the sacrificial virgin. Since the sacrificial virgin must not know, the rightmost virgin knows that she is not the sacrificial virgin. This knowledge obliges her to squeeze the hand of the virgin to her immediate left signalling the sentence 'None of the virgins to your right is the sacrificial virgin.' This virgin is either the leftmost virgin or a middle virgin (a middle virgin is any virgin between the leftmost and rightmost virgins). If she is a middle virgin, she will reason that if she is offered she will know that none of the virgins to her left have been sacrificed. By the signal she knows that none to her right are sacrificial virgins, and thus she will be able to deduce that she will be sacrificed. But since the sacrificial virgin cannot know that she will be sacrificed, this middle virgin knows she will not be sacrificed. Therefore, she will squeeze the hand of the virgin to her left, triggering the same deduction if this third virgin is a middle virgin. Once the leftmost virgin is reached, she will know that none of the virgins to her right is the sacrificial virgin since she is the only alternative left. However, she would then both know and not know she is the sacrificial virgin. Therefore, the ceremony is impossible.

The rightmost and leftmost virgins only know that there are at least two virgins in line. Middle virgins know that there are at least three virgins in line. In the versions previously considered it is essential that the subjects know what the alternatives are. In the surprise examination version, the students need to know that the test is on one of the five working days. In the sacrificial virgin variation, the subjects do not even have a rough estimate as to how many alternatives there are. Middle virgins only know that they are somewhere in the middle of an arbitrarily long line. So it is not essential that the subjects know the order in which members of the series are arranged. Unlike the designated student paradox, the middle virgins *repeat* the same deduction but do not *replicate* each other's deductions. No middle virgin knows more than any other middle virgin. Unlike the other versions, there is no characteristic deduction for each subject. In the designated student paradox, Mr Thursday can only eliminate himself by replicating Mr Friday's reasoning; Mr Wednesday can only eliminate himself by replicating Mr Thursday's replication of Mr Friday's reasoning, and so on. As in the surprise examination paradox, each virgin replicates the reasoning of her 'future self', but not the reasoning of others.

Jointly, the sacrificial virgin, the designated student, and the undiscoverable position paradoxes show that the temporal retention principle, the KK principle, the order of elimination, and knowledge of the number of alternatives to be eliminated, are each inessential to the prediction paradox.

VII. CRITICISMS OF THE SORITES ASSIMILATORS

One immediate qualm about assimilating the prediction paradox to the sorites is that the prediction paradox would be a very 'fast' sorites. When commentators emphasize that the surprise test can be given, they often assert that if the test were given on Wednesday the test would clearly be surprising. If a Wednesday test is a clear case, then Thursday would be the only borderline case. Yet standard sorites arguments involve a great many borderline cases.

Defenders of the assimilation could parry this objection by denying that a Wednesday test would be clearly surprising. Yet it is doubtful that they could significantly enlarge the range of borderline cases. For the standard surprise test version only contains a total of five cases. A more promising reply would be to simply concede that the prediction paradox only contains one borderline case and then deny that a sorites paradox must have more than one borderline case. After all, some might insist that a single borderline case is sufficient to produce the familiar sorites pattern of clear cases being buffered by unclear cases.

A more serious objection emanates from the epistemological approach to the prediction paradox. Those who assimilate the prediction paradox to the sorites paradox accept the base step of both paradoxes. In the surprise test version, they agree with the

Appraisal of Past Proposals

clever student's claim that the test cannot be a surprise if given on the last day. This accords well with most people's initial reaction to the puzzle. But as proponents of the epistemic approach have shown, there are grounds for doubt about this premiss. Neither Deitl nor Smith provides any replies to these objections. Yet it is clear that the analogy with the sorites is considerably weakened if the base step of the prediction paradox is uncompelling. This point can be made with the following 'sorites':

1. It is unlikely that a random group of 23 people will contain two people who share a birthday.
2. If it is unlikely that a random group of n people will contain two people who share a birthday, then it is also unlikely that a random group of $n+1$ people will contain two people who share a birthday.
3. It is unlikely that a random group of 366 people will contain two people who share a birthday.

By the pigeon-hole principle, we know that the probability of a random group of 366 people containing two people who share a birthday is 1. No event having a probability of 1 is an unlikely event, so the conclusion of the above argument is false. Although we know that events with a probability of 1 are unlikely, the vagueness of 'unlikely' prevents us from specifying the highest probability an unlikely event can have. This vagueness also prevents us from specifying a counter-example to step 2. Finally, the base step seems clearly true because it is natural to assign a probability of about $23/365$ to the event of two people in a random group of 23 sharing a birthday. So the above argument appears to be a standard sorites exploiting the vagueness of 'unlikely'. However, the base step of the argument is false. The correct probability of a common birthday is not $23/365$, but rather:

$$1 - [364/365 \times 363/365 \times 362/365 \times \ldots \times 343/365] > 0.5$$

No event with a probability of greater than 0.5 is unlikely, so the base step of the argument is surprisingly false. Proponents of the epistemological approach can maintain that the prediction paradox is only a sorites paradox in the same way that the 'birthday sorites' is a sorites paradox. Whereas normal sorites are not solvable through a denial of the base step, these are. Furthermore, those in the epistemological tradition can then explain away the gradualistic intuition as an illusion generated by a false analogy between normal sorites and the prediction paradox. Thus the sorites assimilators' insight can be appropriated by their competitors.

One of the chief difficulties of Smith's position is that most of the commonly discussed examples of the sorites and the prediction paradox only require the elimination of finitely many alternatives. Indeed, one may be inclined to doubt whether mathematical induction is ever essential to a variation of the prediction paradox. However, this temptation should be resisted in the light of a new variation of the prediction paradox constructed by Martin Hollis.[10] Two individuals, A and B, pick two positive integers. They whisper the numbers to a trusted authority, C, who informs them that they have picked different numbers and that neither A nor B can figure out which of them picked the larger number. A picked 157 and wonders which number B picked. A reasons thus: 'B did not pick 1. For had he, he would know that I picked the larger number. Since this piece of reasoning is also available to B, he knows that I could not have picked 1 either. Since 1 is eliminated, it can now be seen that B could not have picked 2. For he would know that I have the larger number. This consideration also assures B that I could not have picked 2. Similar reasoning eliminates 3, 4, and 5. Indeed, persistent application of this reasoning eliminates the possibility that 157 was the picked number.' Admittedly, A's argument only involves a finite number of alternatives and so can be formulated without mathematical induction. This is due to the fact that A knows that he picked 157 which places a cap on the number of alternatives that must be examined to obtain a contradiction. However, Hollis's puzzle can be modified to include the viewpoint of an outsider, D, who is ignorant of the numbers picked but is otherwise well-informed of the situation. Since D only knows that B picked some number, he will only be able to derive a contradiction by showing that B picked *no* number. To show that no number has the property of being picked by B, infinitely many alternatives must be eliminated. So D will have to employ a mathematical induction whose base step is the assertion that B did not pick 1, and whose induction step

---

[10] Hollis presents the variation in 'A Paradoxical Train of Thought', *Analysis*, 44/4 (Oct. 1984), 205–6.

is that B did not pick the successor of an unpicked number.

But to show that some variations of the prediction paradox essentially involve mathematical induction is not to show that they all do. Clearly the popular variations do not require mathematical induction. Smith's suggestion that these popular variations should therefore be regarded as entirely different paradoxes is *ad hoc*. For Smith is using his proposed resolution of the paradoxes as a classification principle which rules out the alleged counter-examples on the grounds that they are not genuine variations of the prediction paradox because they resist his solution.

The most serious objection to Smith's position is the high price that must be paid for his solution. As Smith concedes, the rejection of mathematical induction would put mathematics in a 'crisis'. It is doubtful that the sorites and the prediction paradox could ever warrant the outright rejection of mathematical induction. By the principle of minimum mutilation, we would be obliged to check whether the mathematical induction could be restricted to arguments employing only precise terms. Even if we were to find that approximation theory makes essential use of vague terms, we could retrench by only permitting mathematical induction in the remaining portions of mathematics. To avoid the appearance of gerrymandering, it would be tempting to instead classify approximation theory as 'merely' applied mathematics and require that full-fledged mathematics be completely precise. Yet it is likely that this controversial issue of demarcation can be avoided by attacking Smith's claim that vague terms are essential to approximation theory. The question of how to solve practical problems mathematically is not a mathematical question. For the answer to the practical problem depends on a host of pedagogical, psychological, and economic factors. These factors form the basis for practical advice such as 'If you do not require high precision, use $22/7$ instead of pi.' The version of Stirling's Formula cited by Smith is really a tip as to when the formula should be applied. Reference works describing Stirling's Formula often go on to supply information about the expected error one will have to tolerate depending on one's choice of n. Since the information about expected error is completely precise, Stirling's Formula can be stated without vagueness. So it is doubtful that the formula is evidence against the feasibility of restricting mathematical induction to mathematics should the need arise.

9
Consequential Blindspots and the Existential Premiss

THIS chapter is devoted to the construction and destruction of an analysis that I formerly believed to be a comprehensive solution to the prediction paradox.[1] A difficulty in extending this analysis to other defective mathematical inductions finally convinced me that I too had a parochial proposal. This difficulty is in no way peculiar to the approach I took. It is a problem that undercuts virtually all that has been written on the prediction paradox. So one reason for detailing the rise and fall of my theory is the generality of the cause of its demise. A second reason is that the theory I will ultimately offer in its stead purports to salvage much of what is worthwhile in its predecessor.

1. CONSEQUENTIAL BLINDSPOTS AND THE PREDICTION PARADOX

Crucial to this preliminary analysis is the concept of a consequential blindspot. Recall that a proposition is a *consequential blindspot* for a (at t) if and only if it is not a blindspot but is equivalent to a conditional whose consequent is a blindspot. For example,

(1) If Ralph survived, he is the only one who knows it,

is a consequential blindspot for everyone except Ralph.

Given that a proposition is a consequential blindspot to you, it is possible for you to know the proposition and it is possible for you to know its antecedent. However, it is impossible to know both the consequential blindspot and its antecedent. To see this, recall the proof for the unknowability of knowledge blindspots and let 'r' be 'Bob is drugged' and 'q' be 'It is raining'.

---

[1] Portions of this chapter are taken from 'Conditional Blindspots and the Knowledge Squeeze: A Solution to the Prediction Paradox', *Australasian Journal of Philosophy*, 62/2 (June 1984) 126–35; 'The Bottle Imp and the Prediction Paradox', *Philosophia*, 15/4 (Jan. 1986) 421–4, and 'A Strengthened Prediction Paradox', *Philosophical Quarterly*, 36/145 (Oct. 1986), 504–13.

The Existential Premiss

1. Kbr & Kb(r ⊃ (q & −Kbq))   Assumption
2. Kbr ⊃ Kb(q & −Kbq)   1, TF, Knowledge distributes over conditionals
3. Kb(q & −Kbq)   1, 2 TF

Since it has already been shown that a contradiction can be derived from the supposition that Kb(q & −Kbq), we can see the inconsistency of 'Bob knows he is drugged and knows that if he is drugged, it is raining but he does not know it.'

Once one realizes that the teacher's announcement for the $n+1$ day case is a consequential blindspot for the students (but not non-students), a solution to the prediction paradox begins to emerge. For the sake of simplicity, consider the two-day case of the teacher's announcement involving only one student, Dave,

(2) Either the test will be given Thursday or Friday but in neither case will Dave know in advance.

By letting 'p_4' stand for 'The test is given Thursday' and letting 'p_5' stand for 'The test is given Friday' while 'd' denotes Dave, the announcement can be symbolized as

(3) $(p_4 \& -Kdp_4) \vee (p_5 \& -Kdp_5)$.

To see that (3) is a consequential blindspot for Dave, note that (3) is equivalent to

(4) $-(p_4 \& -Kdp_4) \supset (p_5 \& -Kdp_5)$.

Since the announcement is only a consequential blindspot for Dave, nothing prevents him from knowing it on the basis of the teacher's authority. However, once Dave learns that no test has been given Thursday, he knows the antecedent of (4) and so cannot continue to know the announcement. The announcement and the antecedent of (4) are semi-blindspots. Dave's friend Fred could continue to know (4) and the antecedent of (4) since it is not a consequential blindspot to Fred. Thus the teacher can inform Dave with announcement (2) and give the test on Friday.

One might object that in the event of only one day remaining, Dave would be more likely to believe a test (albeit unsurprising) will be given on the remaining day than not at all. This may be the case since, empirically, most (but not all) teachers would prefer to make this part of the announcement true than to give no test at all. However, Dave does not have this extra psychological information about his teacher's preferences. It would be pointless to grant Dave this extra information since it would only serve to undermine the clever student's argument against the possibility of a Friday test.

The consequential blindspot analysis can be extended to all of the variations of the prediction paradox so far considered. All $n+1$ step variations involve a knowledge squeeze, that is, a situation in which one's knowledge of a consequential blindspot comes into conflict with one's knowledge of its antecedent. The general pattern of a prediction paradox argument runs as follows. First, one describes a situation in which a person or group, a, appears to know a proposition which is a consequential blindspot for a. In the above case, this is done by describing how Dave's trustworthy teacher tells him that the conditional blindspot is true. Second, one describes a contingency in which a appears to learn that the antecedent of the consequential blindspot is true. This is exemplified by Dave observing that no test has been given on Thursday. Third, one asks 'Is this contingency really possible?'. If this question is interpreted as 'Is it really possible for a to know both his consequential blindspot and its antecedent?', the correct answer is 'No'. If the question is interpreted as 'Is it really possible for both the consequential blindspot and its antecedent to be true?', the correct answer is 'Yes'. But due to unfamiliarity with the peculiar epistemic behaviour of consequential blindspots, victims of the paradox confidently concede that the contingency really is not possible and accept the consequences that follow from a negative answer to the second reading of the question. The consequence is that the contingency is eliminated and the negation of the consequent is added to our background 'knowledge'. Thus, we agree that Dave can eliminate the possibility of a Friday test, and allow Dave to use this pseudo-knowledge in his examination of other contingencies. Fourth, one shows how this derived 'knowledge' of the negation of the consequent puts a in a position to eliminate another contingency. This domino effect results from the fact that the conjunction of the consequential blindspot with the negation of its consequent is either a blindspot or a new consequential blindspot. If the conjunction is a blindspot, one asks 'Is this really a contingency?' Once again, the question has two readings: 'Is it possible for *a* to know that his blindspot is true?' and 'Is it possible for the blindspot to be true?' And once again, unfamiliarity with knowledge blindspots leads the victim of the paradox to incorrectly rule out this last possibility and conclude that the announcement cannot be fulfilled. This is what happens in the case of Dave. After eliminating the possibility of a test on Friday, he is faced with the blindspot that the test is on Thursday but he does not know the test is on Thursday. The victim of the paradox reasons that since one cannot surprise someone as to when something will happen if one tells him when it will happen, Dave cannot be surprised by a Thursday test. On the other hand, if the conjunction of the consequential blindspot and the negation of its consequent is a new consequential blindspot, then the process of deriving the negation of the consequent of a consequential blindspot is repeated on this new consequential blindspot.

As illustrated by the three recalcitrant variations of the prediction paradox discussed in the previous chapter, the knowledge squeeze can be set up in a number of ways by varying the number and kind of epistemic opportunities and by varying the nature of blindspots contained in the consequential blindspots. In the paradox of the undiscoverable position, there are four possible base steps and a large number of ways of reducing the initial consequential blindspot to a blindspot. So here, unlike the traditional variations of the prediction paradox, there is no rigid order of elimination. In the designated student paradox, the initial consequential blindspot contains individual blindspots for each of the students. The order of elimination is dictated by the increasing perceptual knowledge enjoyed by the students at the rear of the line. In the sacrificial virgin paradox, consequential blindspots come into play as universal instantiations of the general description of how a ceremony will take place. Epistemic opportunities to eliminate contingencies arise from a signalling system and the ability to feel whether one has a neighbouring virgin.

Despite this variety, there is a single feature shared by all of the variations of the prediction paradox under discussion. This feature provides the basis for a general solution. All variations of the paradox turn on fallacious reasoning about blindspots or conditional blindspots. In the one-step cases, for example the one-day case of the surprise examination paradox, one becomes a victim of the paradox only if one falsely assumes that blindspots can be known by their holders. In the $n+1$ step cases, consequential blindspots are used to set up a knowledge squeeze. Here, one becomes a victim only if one fallaciously infers the negation of a consequential blindspot's consequent from the impossibility of knowing both the consequential blindspot and its antecedent.

Although the above point is most easily made if 'surprise' is defined as an absence of knowledge, it also holds if the definition is in terms of the absence of justified belief. On Friday, the students cannot justifiably believe 'The test is on Friday but we do not justifiably believe it.' But at the week's beginning they can justifiably believe the announcement 'There will be a test on a day such that you cannot beforehand justifiably believe it is on that day.' So the announcement will evolve from an informative to an uninformative announcement should the test be delayed until the last day.

Whether the analysis runs in terms of knowledge blindspots or justified belief blindspots, the verdict on the paradoxical mathematical inductions remains the same. All of them have false base steps. This ensures that their induction steps are *vacuously* true. In this respect, they resemble unsound arguments such as:

1. Two is a prime number having three distinct factors.
2. If n is a prime number having three distinct factors, then $n+1$ is a prime number having three distinct factors.
3. All of the positive integers greater than one are primes having three distinct factors.

A positive integer is a prime if and only if it has exactly two factors, one and itself. Thus the base step of the mathematical induction is false. The induction step is vacuously true. In order to be false, there would have to be a value for n that made the antecedent true and the consequent false. But since substitutions always yield a false antecedent, there are no counter-examples to the generalization. Likewise, there are no counter-examples to the generalization 'If the students can know that the test will not occur on day n, then the students can know that the test will not occur on day $n-1$'. Although both of the generalizations are true, it would be misleading to assert them without signalling their vacuousness.

Thus the clever student in the surprise test version is vulnerable to two criticisms. First, the base step of his mathematical induction is false. Second, unqualified assertion of the induction step is inappropriate because the generalization is vacuous.

II. REDUCTION OF THE BOTTLE IMP

Given that the above analysis constitutes a comprehensive solution to the prediction paradox, it should also constitute a solution to any paradox which is reducible to the prediction paradox. The natural candidates for reduction are paradoxes that can be expressed as mathematical inductions involving epistemic terms. Richard Sharvey's bottle imp puzzle is such a paradox.[2] In Sharvey's paradox there is a bottle containing an imp who can grant almost any wish. The catch is that one must eventually sell the bottle for a price lower than one paid for it to someone who is rational and who is informed of the conditions associated with ownership of the bottle. The penalty for not selling is hell. This catch gives rise to an argument that the bottle is worthless. For no rational well-informed buyer will purchase the bottle for one penny. Since the imp cannot grant wishes that will undermine the paradox, such as changing the currency, anyone who paid one penny for the bottle would be unable to sell and would therefore go to hell. Knowing this, no rational well-informed buyer would purchase the bottle for two pennies. For one would be without customers once one acquired the bottle. Likewise, it would be unwise to buy the bottle for three pennies, four pennies, and so on. So the bottle is worthless. But intuitively, the bottle does seem worth, say, $1,000. It seems that a rational well-informed person might take the risk of hell in the hope of there being another rational well-informed person who would buy the bottle in the hope of there being yet another rational well-informed buyer disposed to reasonable risks.

The striking resemblance between the bottle imp and the prediction paradox invites a reduction through the construction of bridge paradoxes. Let us consider the first of these bridge paradoxes, the last buyer. Art, Bob, Carl, Don, and Eric are self-

[2] Richard Sharvey presents his paradox in 'The Bottle Imp', *Philosophia*, 12 (Mar. 1983), 401.

interested traders who are also ideal thinkers; that is, they are perfect logicians who do not forget and who do not overlook important facts. These traders are brought together by an experimental economist. The economist explains to them that he wants to test a prediction about risk. Towards this end, he is offering a hot potato for sale at $100. Anyone who in turn sells the potato for $100 to one of the other traders will be paid $1,000,000 for the sale by the economist. Thus a given trader could become a millionaire by first purchasing the potato for $100, then selling it in turn for $100, thereby earning $1,000,000 for his sale from the experimental economist. Side payments are forbidden and since the traders will never meet again, there is no chance that any of their future behaviour will affect each other. In addition, one can only sell to someone whose name is alphabetically lower than the seller's. Thus Art can sell to any of the other traders, but Bob cannot sell to Art, only Carl, Don, and Eric. The economist tells them that he predicts that at least one of the traders will buy the hot potato. One of the traders objects. 'Eric will not buy the hot potato because he would then be certain to be the last buyer. Don is a perfect logician, so he knows that Eric, his only potential customer, will not buy the potato. So Don realizes that if he buys the potato, he will be the last buyer. So neither Don nor Eric are possible purchasers of the potato. Being a perfect logician, Carl knows that Don and Eric are eliminated, so he will not buy. The same reasoning rules out Bob and Art, so it is impossible that anyone will buy the potato.'

Of course, this argument can be extended to any larger number of traders. But it seems to be clear, especially as the number of traders grows, that someone would risk $100 and buy the potato in the hope of selling it to someone else.

This variation has several advantages over the bottle imp. There is no need to worry about the distraction of the imp granting wishes that might undermine the puzzle. More importantly, Pascalian issues of infinite disvalues are avoided. Further, there is the advantage of simplification. The last buyer avoids the disadvantages of the bottle imp while preserving its spirit.

The last buyer can be formalized in the following way. Let 'p_1' stand for 'Art is the last buyer', 'p_2' for 'Bob is the last buyer', and so on. Also, let 'a' denote Art, 'b' denote Bob, etc. Then 'Kap_1' reads 'Art knows that he is the last buyer.' The announcement of

The Existential Premiss

the economist's prediction combined with other information available to the traders implies

(A) $[(p_1 \supset -Kap_1) \& (p_2 \supset (-Kbp_2 \& Kb-p_1)) \& \ldots \& (p_5 \supset (-Kep_5 \& Ke-(p_1 \vee p_2 \vee p_3 \vee p_4))] \& (p_1 \vee p_2 \vee p_3 \vee p_4 \vee p_5)$.

Now (A) is intended to reflect the fact that a trader buys only if he does not know that he is the last buyer, that he knows that his purchase eliminates the preceding traders from being the last buyer, and (A) also represents the economist's prediction that there will be a last buyer.

If (A) is a faithful representation of the crucial information available to the traders, then a strong argument can be made for the thesis that the last buyer is a variation of the prediction paradox. For (A) is merely a reinterpretation of the crucial information made available to the students in the designated student variation of the prediction paradox. Let 'p_1' stand for 'Mr Monday is the designated student', 'p_2' for 'Mr Tuesday is the designated student', and so on. (A) can thus be reinterpreted to represent the crucial information available to the students.

In both the last buyer and the designated student paradoxes, the crucial information is common knowledge. That is, everyone knows the information and further, everyone knows that everyone knows the crucial information. The fact that the information is public information seems to force us to represent the situation as '$(x)Kx(y)Ky(A)$'. However, as was shown in the previous chapter, '$(x)Kx(y)Ky(A)$' is inconsistent in any quantified normal modal analysis of epistemic logic. Thus we can provide a formal reconstruction of the sceptical arguments used in both the last buyer and the designated student.

The task for the reductionist is to show that the bottle imp paradox is a variation of the prediction paradox. This seems to have been achieved with the help of two bridge paradoxes. From the bottle imp we moved to the last buyer, from the last buyer we moved to the designated student, and finally, from the designated student we move to the prediction paradox.

III. A STRENGTHENED PREDICTION PARADOX

Although I believe that the attempted reduction succeeds in pointing out the resemblances between the prediction paradox and the bottle imp, it masks a crucial disanalogy. The disanalogy is best exposed indirectly through another paradox inspired by one of Gregory Kavka's puzzles.

Kavka's toxin puzzle is a puzzle about intention.[3] It exploits the distinction between having a reason to intend to do x and having a reason to do x. Suppose you have been offered $1,000,000 to intend to drink a vial of toxin tomorrow afternoon. Since the toxin will only make you ill for a day, you would drink it if the offer were $1,000,000 for *drinking* it. However, the deal is that you receive $1,000,000 if you *intend* to drink it at, say, midnight. Whether you actually drink it the following afternoon is irrelevant. Offhand, it sounds like an easy million, for one need only form the intention at midnight (whereupon the money is immediately given to you) and then not carry out the intention. The catch is that it is impossible to intend that which one knows one will not do. Once you have the money, it would be stupid to go on to drink the toxin and suffer the day of misery. Since you know that you are not stupid, you know that you will not drink the toxin. The surprising conclusion is that you cannot form the $1,000,000 intention even though you are strongly motivated to do so.

Various objections can be raised to this conclusion. Perhaps you could create a reason for carrying out the intention (like hiring a hit man to kill you if you do not). Perhaps you could make yourself forget certain key facts about the deal (like the irrelevance of actually drinking the toxin). Perhaps you could hire a hypnotist to implant the intention. Kavka patiently stipulates these suggestions away by supposing that the fine print of the offer rules out such tricks. Janice Thomas suggests that you might have independent reasons for wanting to drink the toxin; curiosity, desire for fame as the toxin drinker, and so on.[4] But Kavka is free to stipulate these independent reasons away in the same manner he stipulated the above suggestions away. Kavka will make sure that you are a person with a reason to intend to drink the toxin but without a reason to drink it.

[3] This article appears in *Analysis*, 43/1 (Jan. 1983), 33–6.
[4] Her article, 'The Toxin, the Blood Donor, and the Bomb', appears in *Analysis*, 43/4 (Oct. 1983), 207–10.

The Existential Premiss

Kavka's observation that one cannot intend to do what one knows one will not do discloses a resemblance between intention and surprise. Both concepts imply types of ignorance. In order to be surprised that p, I must lack foreknowledge of p. In order to intend to bring about p, I must lack foreknowledge of the fact that I will not bring about p. As many commentators on the prediction paradox have noted, the paradox seems to work by converting ignorance into knowledge. Whether we get the ignorance through an analysis of 'surprise' or 'intention' is irrelevant. At a syntactic level this is clear from the fact that formal reconstructions of the prediction paradox do not require 'surprise' operators. Followers of the epistemological approach only use epistemic operators: 'know', 'justifiably believe', and 'believe'. Self-referentialists only use deducibility relations. These considerations suggest that the prediction paradox could just as well be formulated in terms of 'intend'.

Suppose Indy's wealthy teacher makes him the following offer. Starting next week, Indy will be paid $1,000 if at midnight he intends to take an unpleasant test the following Monday afternoon. Indy hates tests but loves money. Although Indy is only being paid for his intentions, he has an apparent incentive for actually taking the test. For if he carries out his intention, he has earned an opportunity to have the offer renewed for the next day. However, there is a maximum of four renewals. And once Indy fails to carry out an intention, there are no more offers. Indy quickly calculates that he stands to make $5,000 by carrying out his midnight intentions on all five days of the week. But then he realizes that he will have no reason to take the Friday test since he will have already exhausted his renewals. The last offer is equivalent to the single offer situation described by Kavka. The last offer and the offer made to Kavka are equally worthless because one cannot form the required intentions. Given that the Friday offer is worthless, does Indy have a motive for taking the Thursday test? His only apparent motive is to gain the Friday offer. But since he realizes that the Friday offer is worthless, he has no reason to take the Thursday test and so will not be able to form the intention to take the Thursday test. Thus the Thursday offer is as worthless as the Friday offer. In a like manner, it can be shown that the earlier offers are also worthless. Thus, it has been 'proved' that Indy cannot make any money from the teacher's offer. This intentional variation of the prediction paradox is more disturbing than Kavka's toxin puzzle because it is clear that Indy could make some money from the teacher's offer. This becomes even clearer once we consider versions having a larger number of maximum renewals. For example, if the number of maximum renewals was 1,000, it is clear that Indy could make a very comfortable living from the teacher's deal. Yet we once again have an apparently impeccable mathematical induction to demonstrate the worthlessness of the teacher's offer.

(A) Indy cannot intend to take the Friday test.
(B) If Indy cannot intend to take test n, then he cannot intend to take test $n-1$.
(C) Indy cannot intend to take any of the tests.

Premisses (A) and (B) are justified in much the same way as the premisses (A) and (B) in the surprise test version. If Indy is to intend to take a test, he must not know that he will not take it. So given that Indy retains his knowledge of the teacher's offer and knows that he is not stupid, it is impossible for him to intend to take the Friday test. So (A) is established. To establish (B) we need only add the assumption that Indy realizes that (A) holds and that he follows out the consequences of this realization to eliminate the possibility of having the intention on the preceding day. The assumptions suffice for the general result that any predecessor of an eliminated day can also be eliminated.

One might object that the assumptions supporting (A) and (B) might fail to hold because of Indy being forgetful, illogical, or just suspicious of the teacher's offer. Likewise, one could object to the surprise test version on the grounds that the students might forget the announcement, not realize that a test has not been given in the past four days, fail to make the available inferences, or just have doubts about the teacher's announcement. Just as these objections are red herrings in the case of the surprise test variation, they are red herrings in the case of the intentional variation of the prediction paradox. We are to assume that the students and Indy are ideal agents in an ideal epistemological environment. A solution to the paradoxes should show the paradoxical arguments fail even under these idealizations, for the conclusions of the arguments are unacceptable even under idealization assumptions.

The crucial disanalogy between the paradoxes is that the teacher's announcement of the offer in the intentional variation does not imply an existential proposition. In the surprise test version, the teacher announces that 'There will be a surprise test next week', which implies the existence of a test. But in the Indy version, the announcement does not imply

(5) Indy will intend to take a test.

In the intentional version, the key event is entirely hypothetical. The teacher only says that *if* Indy forms test-taking intentions, he will receive the rewards. Thus the teacher cannot be construed as saying something that might become incredible or unknowable. Without the existential proposition, the proponents of the epistemological approach cannot show that believing the offer would ever force the believer into the Moorean bind they describe for believers in the surprise test announcement. Nor can the teacher be construed as saying that an undeducible event will occur on one of the five days, since all the factual commitments of the teacher's announcement are satisfied with or without the occurrence of the event. In short, the standard approaches to the surprise test version have no purchase on the intentional variation of the prediction paradox.

Of course, there is a simple way to make the standard approaches applicable. Simply have the teacher include (5) in his announcement of his offer to Indy. The self-referentialists can interpret (5) as saying that Indy will not be able to deduce that he will abstain from taking a test. Since (5) is part of the amended announcement, this amounts to saying that Indy cannot make the deduction from the conjunction of the announcement and any background information he acquires. The amended announcement is also grist for the epistemic mill. For proponents of the epistemological approach can interpret (5) as saying that Indy's abstention from a test is inaccessible, that is, cannot be believed, justifiably believed, or known (depending on the subvariation). This will make the announcement inaccessible to Indy just at the point where it seems to imply that Indy will abstain. So I grant that the amended version poses no threat to the dominant approaches.

However, I deny the legitimacy of the amendment. We want our paradoxes lean and mean. Proponents of the dominant approaches should draw no comfort from the fact that they can solve a fattened version of a recalcitrant paradox. Compare this situation with the introduction of the strengthened liar paradox. Many philosophers believed that they could solve the liar by denying that 'This statement is false' has a truth value. However, critics pointed out that the truth-value gap approach does not solve the strengthened liar: 'This statement is not true'. The truth-gapper should take no comfort in the fact that he can handle the amended strengthened liar: 'This statement is not true; it's false'.

Proponents of the dominant approaches might deny that the intentional variation of the prediction paradox is a *genuine* variation of the prediction paradox. One might take the inapplicability of the mainstream solutions as evidence that we are dealing with an essentially different paradox. Although this might be some evidence, we cannot individuate paradoxes by their proposed resolutions. We could hardly fail to solve our problems if the problems are defined in terms of what our attempted solutions actually solve. As far as I can see, past proposals can only help to define their problems in two ways. First, they can provide information about the structure of the problem in the form of the goals the proposals are intended to achieve. And second, the proposals can be diagnostic data. Often, new proposals treat their predecessors as clues to the nature of the problem by maintaining that the old proposals rest on errors induced by tricky features of the problem. So past proposals can point us toward the key features of the problem. In the case of the prediction paradox, the obvious goal of past proposals is to reveal the defect of the paradoxical argument. Various subgoals, or constraints, have been formulated.[5] All of the adequacy conditions that hold for the surprise test version also hold for the intentional variation. So we cannot reject the genuineness of the intentional variation on that score. However, it might be objected that counting the Indy puzzle as a genuine variation of the prediction paradox would foist a foreign constraint upon us; do not assume the existential implication. But this objection begs the question since any strengthened variation of a paradox must introduce a new adequacy condition.

[5] For example, Crispin Wright and Aidan Sudbury begin their discussion of the paradox with a long list of adequacy conditions in 'The Paradox of the Unexpected Examination', quoted in ch. 7.

Otherwise, it would not be a *strengthened* variation. Nor can we object to the genuineness of the intentional variation of the prediction paradox by maintaining that it fails to suggest a diagnosis of the failure of past proposals. As a strengthened variation, it naturally suggests that the past attempts fail because they concentrate on an inessential feature of the paradox.

Given that the inapplicability of past proposals fails to disqualify the intentional version as a genuine variation of the prediction paradox, one might try to disqualify it on the grounds of an undermining disanalogy with the surprise test version. Such a disanalogy was found in the case of the Pseudo-Scotus interpretation of the prediction paradox. However, the analogy between the Indy version and the traditional surprise test paradox is quite strong. Both can be formulated as mathematical inductions. Both support the premisses of the inductions with the same epistemic principles. Both exploit an analytical connection between a propositional attitude and ignorance. The disanalogies are few. In one paradox, the key propositional attitude is 'surprise', while the other's key propositional attitude is 'intend'. I have already minimized the significance of this disanalogy by arguing that the role of these attitudes is to induce types of ignorance. Formal reconstructions of the paradoxical reasoning lend credence to this claim of functional equivalence. A second disanalogy is that the intentional version involves the notion of agency. Indy must have self-knowledge of his prudence. He must know that he will not act stupidly, irrationally, or incontinently. The students in the surprise test version, however, need only have self-knowledge of their acquisition, retention, and use of the information that becomes available to them. Like Indy, they must know that they will not be 'epistemically imprudent' but apart from talk of mental acts of inference and so forth, the notion of agency does not fit into the surprise test situation as well as it fits into Indy's. Once again, this disanalogy does not seem significant especially under idealization assumptions. The third disanalogy is the presence of the existential implication in one paradox and its absence in the other. This is a significant disanalogy. If it could be combined with other significant disanalogies, their cumulative weight might warrant the claim that the intentional paradox is not really the same kind of paradox as the surprise test paradox. But in view of the lack of other significant disanalogies, the absence of the existential implication can only be an undermining disanalogy if it is an essential feature of the prediction paradox. But its claim to being essential has to be compared to the claims that can be made on behalf of other features which are generally regarded as inessential. Many commentators have assumed that the prediction paradox essentially involves the 'temporal retention' principle, the KK principle, a rigid order of elimination, and knowledge of the number of alternatives to be eliminated. But we have encountered variations of the paradox that show that each of these conditions is inessential. There is only one respect in which the claims that these conditions are essential are weaker than the claim that the existential implication is essential, and that is in the number of proposals that are undercut by denying the claim.

Our pre-theoretical response to the story of Indy is that it is a variation of the prediction paradox. Furthermore, a reasoned defence of this gut reaction can be developed from the intuitions underlying this response. We can articulate the judgement of overall similarity by constructing an analogical argument from their shared features (same argument form, same supporting principles for the premisses, convertibility of the intentional variation into a standard variation by the addition of a single existential statement, and so on). We can point to precedents. First, the precedent of the strengthened liar. Second, the precedent of features that were formerly thought to be essential to the prediction paradox but were later revealed to be inessential. This puts the burden of proof on those who deny that the intentional version is essentially the same paradox as the surprise test version. It is *ad hoc* and question-begging to support the denial merely on the basis of the fact that the dominant approaches cannot be successfully applied to the intentional version. It is *ad hoc* because one is avoiding an ostensible counter-example by means of an auxilliary classificatory hypothesis tailored to this restricted end. The defence is question-begging because it assumes the adequacy of the dominant approaches in order to defend their adequacy.

The proper response to the intentional variation is our initial, intuitive response. It is a variation of the prediction paradox that must be solved along with the remaining variations. For an adequate solution must be a comprehensive solution. Since the intentional variation does not have the existential implication, and its absence renders almost all of the past work on the paradox inapplicable, the intentional version is a strengthened prediction paradox akin to the strengthened liar.

IV. THE REDUCTION OF THE BOTTLE IMP RECONSIDERED

In the aftermath of this counter-example, the inadequacy of the 'reduction' of the bottle imp to the prediction paradox becomes apparent. In the last buyer, there is an experimental economist who announces that there will be a transaction. This announcement supplies the existential implication necessary for the applicability of the standard approaches. However, this existential implication is not present in the original bottle imp puzzle. So the bottle imp more closely resembles the strengthened prediction paradox than the last buyer as far as the existential implication is concerned. Thus the reduction fails because it slips in an assumption not made by the bottle imp.

In addition to sharing a freedom from existential implication, the bottle imp and the strengthened prediction paradox are akin in that they involve the notion of agency. However, they differ in that the strengthened prediction paradox appeals to the nature of rational intention, the bottle imp turns on properties of rational choice. Whereas only a modest amount of philosophical literature has been generated by the study of the rationality of intention, the concept of rational choice has been a focus of intense study in a variety of fields. This interdisciplinary research has uncovered a number of paradoxes which we are now in a position to examine.

10
Agency, Super-games, and Blindspotting

THE bottle imp, the modified last buyer, and the Indy puzzle are not the only variations of the prediction paradox free of existential implication.[1] First of all, there is an entire family of 'super-games' possessing this feature. After discussing this family of paradoxes, I will begin the business of salvaging the blindspot analysis. The key move will be to argue that agents other than the announcer of a prediction paradox situation can introduce the elusive existential implication. For the existential implication can be introduced by actions which make the implication true. The introduction of this information can take place as a strategic move akin to deception. For by making the implication true, one can force one's opponent or even oneself to lose knowledge. I call this process 'blindspotting'. Although blindspotting requires the blindspotter to have an opportunity to manipulate his victim's evidence, I shall show that the analysis can even be extended to the booth paradox in which the participants cannot manipulate each other's evidence.

I. THE SUPER-GAMES

When game theorists set up a particular pay-off matrix, they are usually interested in determining the proper strategy under the assumption that it will be played just once. But since many strategic situations involve repeated interactions, the matrix is sometimes presented with the understanding that the game will be played many times. Game theorists use the term 'super-game' to cover such situations of repeated play. Game theorists have discovered some super-games which bear a striking resemblance to the prediction paradox. After presenting the super-games that have received commentary, I will present several more paradoxical super-games with a view to characterizing the class of paradoxical super-games.

[1] Portions of this chapter are taken from 'Blindspotting and Choice Variations of the Prediction Paradox', *American Philosophical Quarterly*, 23/4 (Oct. 1986), 337–52.

A. *The Iterated Prisoners' Dilemma*

The prisoner's dilemma is probably the most intensively studied of all games. For it appears to capture the structure of many social conflicts ranging from littering to the arms race. The game is usually presented with a pay-off matrix such as the one in Table 10.1.

TABLE 10.1

		Column Confess	Don't confess
Row	Confess	(−5, −5)	(0, −20)
	Don't confess	(−20, 0)	(−1, −1)

If both prisoners confess, they will both be convicted of their crime but will receive some leniency in the light of their confessions and receive five years in prison. If neither confesses, there will only be enough evidence to send each to prison for one year. However, if one confesses while the other does not, the confessor will be set free while the 'sucker' receives twenty years in prison. The question is 'Given that a prisoner's choice will have no further influence on his interests, what should a rational, self-interested prisoner choose?' Almost all game theorists answer 'Confess', on the grounds that the alternative of confessing dominates the alternative of not confessing. An alternative x dominates an alternative y if and only if the outcomes associated with x are not worse than the outcomes associated with y. A prisoner that confesses will receive 0 if his partner does not confess, and −5 if he does. On the other hand, if a prisoner does not confess, he receives −1 if his partner does not confess, and −20 if his partner does confess. Since confessing guarantees outcomes that are better in every case, confessing (strongly) dominates not confessing. Some people who are persuaded by this argument nevertheless find the conclusion paradoxical because it is a counter-example to the thesis that a group behaves rationally if its members do.[2]

Of course, the above defence of confessing holds only if the

[2] The prisoners' dilemma is not the only apparent counter-example to this thesis. Condorcet's paradox of cyclical majorities shows that the social aggregation device of majority rule can yield intransitive group preferences from transitive individual preferences. So there appears to be a common source for some of the puzzlement generated by the different paradoxes.

prisoners are certain that their choices are independent of one another and do not have any further impact on their welfare. If, for example, the prisoners belonged to the Mafia, a group which makes efforts to heavily penalize confessors, it may be irrational to confess. In effect, these 'external' penalties would change the pay-off matrix so that the players were no longer in a prisoner's dilemma. One may doubt that real-life prisoners can ever be certain that their choices will have no extra influence on their interests, but one should be willing to grant such certainty as a logical possibility in order to acquire a better understanding of the principles underlying rational choice.

In addition to there being a persuasive argument in favour of confessing, Lawrence Davis has produced an interesting argument in favour of not confessing.[3] Given that it is common knowledge amongst the prisoners that they are rationally self-interested agents faced with the same decision problem, they have an excellent argument by analogy to the conclusion that they will make the same choice. Thus each prisoner realizes that it is impossible for one to confess and the other not to confess. So both will realize that the only possible outcomes are that they both confess or that both do not confess. Since joint non-confession is preferred over joint confession, rationally self-interested prisoners will not confess.

So the prisoners' dilemma is also paradoxical by virtue of the fact that there is a strong argument that a rationally self-interested prisoner will confess and a strong argument that he will not confess. To solve this paradox, one must disarm at least one of the arguments.

Davis supplements his main defence for the cooperative solution by appealing to the iterated prisoners' dilemma. The iterated prisoners' dilemma is a 'super-game' in which the prisoners' dilemma is played repeatedly. For example, suppose that two rationally self-interested agents are faced with the matrix in Table 10.2. Here, Row and Column play for dollars rather than years in prison. But this does not significantly alter the paradox since the arguments for confessing and not confessing apply to competing and co-operating. Now suppose the prisoners are certain that they

---

[3] Lawrence Davis presents his argument in 'Prisoners, Paradox, and Rationality', *American Philosophical Quarterly*, 14/4 (1977), 319–27.

TABLE 10.2

	Column	
	Cooperate	Compete
Row Cooperate	(100, 100)	(0, 101)
Compete	(101, 0)	(1, 1)

will be playing this second game exactly 100 times, each being informed of the other's move after each play. Since it now seems possible that one prisoner's choice will influence the choices of his partner, it seems that the prisoners will try to influence each other by co-operating. If the prisoners competed on all 100 plays, we would be inclined to regard them as irrational. Those impressed by the dominance argument might argue that a one-play prisoners' dilemma differs from a $n + 1$ play prisoners' dilemma because the dominance principle only applies when one is sure that one's choice will not have any further influence on one's interests. If there are $n + 1$ plays, then this requirement is not met; one must take into account the possibility of future retaliation and reward. So the co-operation displayed by players in an iterated prisoners' dilemma does not show that co-operation will occur in the one-play prisoners' dilemma.

However, the prisoners are certain that their choice on the last play of the prisoners' dilemma is equivalent to a one-play prisoner's dilemma. So if the argument from dominance is correct, the prisoners will compete on the last play. But given that the prisoners know that they will compete on the last play regardless of the previous course of the game, they should also compete on the second to last play. And given that they will compete on the second to last play, they should compete on the third to last. The same reasoning requires competition on the fourth to last, fifth to last, and so on. We are thus driven to the conclusion that rationally self-interested players will compete on every move of the iterated prisoners' dilemma.

The paradox of the iterated prisoners' dilemma can be compactly expressed as an apparently sound mathematical induction leading to an absurd conclusion.

1. The players know they will compete at play 100.
2. If the players know they will compete at play n, then they know they will compete at play $n - 1$.

3. The players know they will compete on every play.

Davis points out that his position on the single play prisoners' dilemma provides a simple solution to the paradox: deny the base step. Thus Davis's supplemental defence of his co-operative solution to the prisoners' dilemma can be expressed as an argument whose premisses are (2) and the negation of (3) and whose conclusion is the negation of (1). The chief difficulty with this argument is that there is another paradox which casts doubt on (2).

B. *The Chain Store Paradox*

The chain store paradox is sometimes discussed in conjunction with the iterated prisoners' dilemma.[4] In the chain store paradox, we are to consider a fictitious market situation. A chain store has twenty branches in twenty towns. In each town there is a potential competitor. The potential competitors are accumulating capital which will eventually permit them to compete with the branch of the chain store in their town (call this the 'In' option). However, they are accumulating capital at different rates so that their opportunities to compete emerge sequentially. If a given potential competitor foregoes his opportunity to actually compete (call this the 'Out' option), he does not receive another opportunity. When confronted with an actual competitor, the chain store has two options: a co-operative response and an aggressive response. The pay-off matrix is depicted in Table 10.3.

TABLE 10.3

	In	Out
Co-operative	(2, 2)	(5, 1)
Aggressive	(0, 0)	(5, 1)

It seems clear that the chain store should take the co-operative option if the last competitor chooses the In option since it is better to have two rather than none. Knowing this, the last potential competitor will choose the In option. Since the last potential

---

[4] The chain store paradox is given a detailed description in Reinhold Selten, 'The Chain Store Paradox', *Theory and Decision*, 9/2 (Apr. 1978), 128–59.

competitor is sure to choose the In option, the chain store cannot hope to deter his choice by adopting the aggressive response should the nineteenth competitor choose the In option. Thus, the chain store is sure to adopt the co-operative option if the nineteenth competitor chooses the In option. Knowing this, the nineteenth competitor will choose the In option since he prefers two to one. So once again, the chain store has no hope of affecting its future welfare by the short-term loss involved with the aggressive option. So the chain store will co-operate in response to an In choice by the eighteenth competitor. In a like manner, it can be argued that the chain store will adopt the co-operative option throughout the course of the game, accumulating a total of forty. But intuitively, the chain store can do better than that by making aggressive choices early in the course of the game. For the potential competitors will realize that the chain store has a long-term interest in deterring later competitors from exercising their In option. By accepting the short-term losses involved in choosing aggressively when an early competitor takes the In option, the chain store can profit in the long run by exploiting the fear of later players that they will be used for demonstration purposes.

C. *Hodgson's Paradox of Punishment*

In *The Consequences of Utilitarianism* D. H. Hodgson attempts to refute utilitarianism by arguing that its universal adoption would lead to disaster. Hodgson argues that truth-telling, promising, and punishment are useful institutions that cannot be justified within a utilitarian framework. His general objection is that such a framework cannot produce certain kinds of expectations necessary for these institutions. I shall focus on the case of punishment.

Punishment poses an immediate problem for the utilitarian. On the one hand, utilitarianism counsels us to maximize the well-being of all. On the other hand, punishment requires the infliction of harm. The conflict is standardly resolved through a deterrence theory of punishment. According to this theory, punishment is indeed intrinsically bad but it can be extrinsically good as a deterrent. By harming the offender now we can discourage him and others from committing future crimes. This discouragement consists of an expectation that future offences will also be punished.

Hodgson's difficulty for utilitarianism is introduced by the question of what would happen if it were common knowledge that the utilitarian punisher only had a given number of opportunities to punish. The essence of the problem can be cast in game-theoretical terms by means of the matrix in Table 10.4

TABLE 10.4

	Commit crime	Refrain from crime
Punish	(1, 2)	(3, 1)
Don't punish	(2, 4)	(4, 3)

The numbers record each party's preference rankings, from best = 4 to worst = 1. Most of the pay-off assignments are straightforward. The citizen would most prefer committing the crime without being punished. Second best would be to refrain from the crime without being punished. Third best is being punished with the consolation of having committed the crime, and worst is to be punished without this consolation. The utilitarian punisher, of course, most prefers the absence of both crime and punishment. What is worst in his eyes is having society harmed by the crime and the criminal harmed by punishment. The remaining alternatives are harder to rank. I have assumed that the punisher would prefer punishing an innocent man over failing to punish a guilty one, on the grounds that criminals inflict more overall harm than the punishment of innocent people. But others could equally well argue for the reverse preference, while still others could argue for a tie. However, controversy as to whether the punishment of innocents should rank second or third is needless. For any of the three assignments yields the crucial result that not punishing dominates punishing. So if the utilitarian punisher knew that he was to play the punishment game exactly once, he would refrain from punishment regardless of the citizen's choice. Since the citizen knows this, he realizes that committing crime gives him his highest pay-off. Thus the punisher cannot deter crime in a one-play punishment game. But at first blush it does seem that the punisher could deter in a hundred-play punishment game. For the punisher could accept the short-term losses of punishing in response to offences in order to achieve the long term gains associated with deterring offences. However, the hundredth game is equivalent to the one-play punishment game. So the punisher could not deter at the hundredth play. Since this is common knowledge, the punisher could not deter at play ninety-nine. For he is resigned to not punishing at play one hundred and so realizes that punishment at play ninety-nine would not frighten the citizen into refraining from crime at play one hundred. Given inevitable non-punishment at plays ninety-nine and one hundred, the citizen can also be sure that there will be no punitive response to the crime choice at play ninety-eight. Similar reasoning appears to demonstrate that the punisher will never punish.

D. *Iterated Chicken*

Chicken is a game made famous by California teenagers in the 1950s. The game proceeds by having two players drive their cars toward each other at great speed on a collision course. If neither veers off, they have a disastrous crash which is the worst outcome for both parties. Second worst is to veer off while one's opponent does not since this is thought to reflect poorly on one's courage, because it shows that you are 'chicken'. What is most preferred is to humiliate one's opponent by having him be the sole compromiser. Second best is a draw in which both parties compromise. Chicken can thus be described with the aid of Table 10.5.

TABLE 10.5

	Compromise	Don't compromise
Compromise	(3, 3)	(2, 4)
Don't compromise	(4, 2)	(1, 1)

Chicken is played at lower stakes amongst some middle-aged drivers. At four-way intersections most drivers prefer others to stop while they drive through. So especially when right of way is unclear, drivers are tempted to count on the other fellow's caution and drive through. If you can convince your opponent that you will not compromise, he is forced to compromise in order to avoid the worst case. By appearing drunk, reckless, or careless one can gain a first move advantage, thereby winning the game. Let us now suppose that Column always moves first in a supergame of Chicken whose length is known to be one hundred plays. Just as

Row must compromise in a one-play Chicken given that Column has the first move, Row must also compromise at the hundredth play of iterated Chicken. Since this is common knowledge, Row has no motivation to refrain from compromise at move ninety-nine. As before we are led to rule out anything but Row compromising for play ninety-eight and all of its predecessors.

E. *The Iterated Pricing Game*

The Pricing game features a merchant who has the options of demanding a high price or a low price for his goods and a customer who has the options of buying or not buying as represented in Table 10.6.

TABLE 10.6

	Buy	Don't buy
Price high	(3, 1)	(0, 0)
Price low	(2, 2)	(0, 0)

Since the merchant moves first, he can force the customer into a take it or leave it situation by pricing high. So the customer is helpless in the single play version of the Pricing Game. But it would seem that the customer would fare better in the hundred-play version. For the customer would be in a position to reward and penalize the merchant's pricing behaviour. Nevertheless, the familiar backwards induction tells us differently.

F. *Super-games and Emergent Threat Potential*

Common to our five examples of paradoxical super-games is the phenomenon of emergent threat potential. The base step of each puzzling mathematical induction is supported by the principle that rationally self-interested agents only fulfill threats for the sake of future gains. For the fulfilment of a threat entails a sacrifice on the part of the threatener. If the fulfilment of the threat were in the interest of the threatener, rational self-interest would make the given action inevitable. The person threatened would be able to foresee the threatener's action without the threat. Threats are always expressible as non-trivial conditionals of the form: if x

happens, then penalty y is inflicted. Given that the conditional expresses a threat rather than a warning, the infliction of the penalty costs the threatener something. Prudence dictates that sacrifices be for the prospect of compensating gain. At the last play, there is no future to justify sacrifice. So we are led to the common-sense conclusion that the threat cannot be fulfilled in the absence of future interactions. Although belief in the possibility of future interactions is a necessary condition for the rational fulfilment of threats, it is not a sufficient condition. The future interactions must be ones in which the fulfilment of threats is credible to the person threatened. If I am certain that you will not fulfil your threat, then your threat is without efficacy.

Threats can only arise when the interest of the threatener and the person threatened neither completely converge nor completely diverge. Thus the class of paradoxical super-games is contained in the class of *partial* conflict games. Since the base step of the corresponding mathematical induction invariably concerns the last play, the super-game must be of finite length.

II. CRITICISMS OF DAVIS AND HARDIN

The strong resemblance between the chain store paradox and the iterated prisoners' dilemma produces the expectation that they are to be solved in the same way. However, Davis's position on the iterated prisoners' dilemma frustrates this expectation. Davis's denial of the base step is founded on the excellent analogy holding between the players in the iterated prisoners' dilemma. But there is no such analogy in the chain store paradox. For the chain store is faced with a *sequence* of opponents each having more information than his predecessor and who all possess a first-move advantage along with options and pay-offs which differ from the chain store's. Without the analogy Davis is forced by standard game-theoretical reasoning to accept the base step of the chain store paradox. Davis must also run with the crowd in rejecting the conclusion of the mathematical induction. For the conclusion that the chain store will make exclusively co-operative moves is no less repugnant than the conclusion that the participants in the iterated prisoners' dilemma will make exclusively competitive moves. Thus Davis will be forced to reject the induction step of the chain store paradox.

But then we should ask why the induction step of the iterated prisoners' dilemma is true while the induction step of the chain store paradox is false. In the absence of a relevant difference between the two, Davis's supplemental defence of the co-operative solution to the prisoners' dilemma should be rejected.

Those who believe that the prediction paradox has been solved naturally view the resemblance between it and the iterated prisoners' dilemma as a reason for extending the solution. So it is not surprising to find Russell Hardin attempting such an extension given his acceptance of Quine's analysis of the prediction paradox. Hardin's strategy for extending Quine's analysis to the iterated prisoners' dilemma is clear. Both paradoxes rest on strong knowledge assumptions. If Quine is right in questioning whether those assumptions hold for the prediction paradox, Hardin should be right in questioning whether they hold for the iterated prisoners' dilemma. Like Quine, however, Hardin must provide grounds for rejecting the assumptions that do not lead to unacceptable sorts of scepticism.

Hardin maintains that there are two sources of uncertainty.[5] First, the players cannot be certain of the exact length of the supergame. Hardin points out that even if Jehovah himself assured the players that the supergame was composed of exactly 100 plays, the players would be faced with the epistemological problem of determining that their authority was Jehovah rather than some impostor. The second source of uncertainty is that of predicting what the other player will do. Either one of these two types of uncertainty would suffice to undermine the paradoxical mathematical induction. Thus Hardin concludes that the paradox is 'doubly resolved'.

However, neither one of these candidates for uncertainty can be supported without embracing scepticism about knowledge assumptions which are standardly employed by game theorists. This is especially apparent in the case of Hardin's objection to the possibility of the players knowing the length of the game. Hardin accepts the standard dominance argument for competition in the one-play prisoners' dilemma. But this argument assumes that the players know that the length of the game equals one play. If the players can know that a game is composed of one play, why should we be sceptical about the possibility of them knowing that a game is

[5] The gist of Hardin's argument appears in *Collective Action* (Baltimore: Johns Hopkins University Press, 1982), 148.

composed of 100 plays? This reply to Hardin should not be construed as a mere *tu quoque* argument. Were Hardin to regain consistency by simply retracting his assent to the standard dominance argument, his position would no longer be a live option for the vast majority of game theorists. These game theorists are interested in a conservative resolution of the iterated prisoners' dilemma: one that preserves the standard result for the prisoners' dilemma while demonstrating the possibility of co-operation in the iterated prisoners' dilemma. Thus a conservative resolution of the puzzle requires acceptance of the base step of the mathematical induction and a rejection of the induction step.

Hardin's second sort of scepticism, concerning knowledge about what one's opponent's choices will be, is also too strong. Were we to say that it is *impossible* to know the decision-making tendencies of rationally self-interested players, we would have to abandon the concept of a solution to a game. The whole point of idealizing the players as rationally self-interested is to form the basis for predictions as to how they will choose. The centrality of the assumption that we can predict the behaviour of rationally self-interested agents makes it no surprise that we can find material for another *tu quoque* argument against Hardin. Indeed, Hardin's position on the iterated prisoners' dilemma itself will serve this purpose. For Hardin's commitment to a strategy of at least some co-operation in the supergame is based on the possibility of at least limited knowledge of how one's opponent will react.

III. BLINDSPOTTING

Prior to reflection on the choice variations of the prediction paradox, it seemed that all variations of the paradox involve a disjunction of knowledge blindspots. The crucial information given by the teacher in the test announcement can be interpreted as:

(A) (There is a test on Monday but the students do not know it beforehand) or (There is a test on Tuesday but the students do not know it beforehand) or . . . or (There is a test on Friday but the students do not know it beforehand).

The essential flaw in the clever student's argument is that it assumes that their initial knowledge of (A) can be combined with knowledge of the falsity of the first four disjuncts of (A). Although each of the two propositions are knowable, they are not co-knowable. The pair are semi-blindspots. Should an examination not occur by Thursday, the students would be placed in a 'knowledge squeeze'. They could have knowledge of (A) or knowledge that the first four disjuncts were false, but they could not have knowledge of both. So I concluded that an examination could be given on Friday.

The teacher can get away with a Friday examination because he would have 'blindspotted' his students. By delaying until the last day, the teacher undermines his students' knowledge by allowing them to accumulate other knowledge which, as it were, competes for scarce epistemic space; one bit of knowledge crowds out the other. One might be tempted to say that the teacher is allowing the students to accumulate misleading evidence. But I think this temptation should be resisted in the light of the fact that the evidence is not at all misleading to nonsurprisees. Outsiders, say the students' parents, could know that the examination must occur on Friday on exactly the same evidence that the students have. There is no contradiction in a *parent* knowing 'The examination is on Friday but the students do not know it beforehand'; the proposition is a blindspot for students, not parents. The parents cannot pass their knowledge on to the students because the two groups have fallen into a simple blindspot disagreement. Their disagreement is irresolvable. So if the blindspotter is a misleader, he is a misleader of a peculiar sort. He achieves his end without polluting his victim's evidence. He does not exploit any *remedial* defect of his victim's epistemological equipment. The blindspotter exploits a necessary limitation of his victim. Every knower has a unique set of knowable propositions. When confronted with evidence supporting propositions outside that set, the thinker's blindspots prevent him from treating the evidence as a non-blindspotee would. So the explanation of the epistemic breakdown must be in terms of the nature of the thinker, not of the nature of the evidence.

The choice variations of the prediction paradox differ from the traditional variations in that the announcer of the initial conditions is not a potential blindspotter. In order to extend the blindspot analysis to the choice variations, the agents themselves must be shown to be potential blindspotters. So I will attempt to salvage the epistemological analysis by arguing that the participants in the choice variations can blindspot others and even themselves. In other words, I shall be arguing that the missing disjunctions are provided by other parties.

To solve the iterated prisoners' dilemma, we have to ask 'What would happen if Row were to co-operate?' If the mathematical induction is sound, then Column appreciates its soundness. Column would then take Row's co-operative move as conclusive evidence that some of the announced conditions of the game do not really hold. In other words, Column could no longer know the apparently known list of propositions containing members such as 'Row is rationally self-interested', 'Row knows that it is common knowledge that Column is rationally self-interested', 'Row and Column are correctly informed of each other's moves', 'The pay-off matrix is accurate', and 'Row knows that Column will not influence his welfare after the game.' In short, the co-operative move would plunge Column into doubt. So if the paradoxical argument is sound, each of the players has an opportunity to undermine the other's knowledge of the game situation. Yet the soundness of the paradoxical argument also requires that the players forego this opportunity. To determine whether the players really would forego this opportunity, we have to determine whether it would ever be in the interest of one of the parties to exercise this option. For if it is sometimes in their interest, the fact that the players maximize their self-interest will ensure that they take advantage of the opportunity. This in turn would show the paradoxical argument to be unsound.

Row could benefit from Column's doubts about Row's rational self-interest. If, for instance, Column acquired the impression that Row was a tit for tat player, Column would be inclined to sometimes co-operate. Of course, this would hold only if the play in question were not the last play. Column's choice for the last play is not influenced by his opinion of Row's choice-making tendencies. If Column had doubts about the length of the game or the accuracy of the pay-off matrix, however, he might even co-operate on the last play. On the other hand, Column's inclination to co-operate would not increase if he believed that the moves of the players were being misreported or if he believed Row was irrationally indifferent to Column's choices. So the question of whether Row's interests might be served by a co-operative choice is dependent on how Column would revise his beliefs in the light of that co-operative move. Under the most probable revision of Column's beliefs, Row's interests are served. For Column is most likely to regard Row's co-operation as probably a reputation-building ploy. The longer the expected length of the game, the more it is in Column's interests to play along with the ploy in order to obtain long sequences of co-operative moves from Row. The expected utility of playing along sharply decreases as the remaining moves near one. So the co-operation should eventually break down. But this is just as common sense predicts. Interestingly, Row could recognize that Column would probably regard his co-operation as a ploy that it is worthwhile to play along with, and thus make the co-operative move without strong deceptive designs.

A defender of the paradoxical argument might object that a co-operative move by Row could not force any revision of Column's beliefs because Column would realize that Row might be merely trying to manipulate Column's opinions. This objection is self-defeating. If Column believes that Row might be trying to manipulate his opinion, then Column believes that a rationally self-interested agent might try to influence the opinion of another rationally self-interested player in the situation described in the paradox. Yet Column knows that rationally self-interested people do not try to do what they know to be impossible. So in order for Column to suspect opinion manipulation, opinion manipulation must be possible, which is contrary to what the objector alleges.

The key point is that neither Row nor Column can exclude the possibility of co-operative moves. One cannot predict another's behaviour with certainty if he has the motive and the means to disconfirm the prediction. In summary, the basic problem for the proponent of the paradox is that each player is able to introduce the missing disjunction 'There are some co-operative moves', which makes the puzzle a standard variation of the prediction paradox.

All of the preceding is contingent on the ability of the players to influence each other. If we required the participants to play in total ignorance of each other's moves, there would be no co-operation.

For the only value they attach to co-operation is the extrinsic value of reputation manipulation.

The chain store paradox can be solved in the same manner as the iterated prisoners' dilemma. If the players really knew that a rationally well-informed chain store would always co-operate, the chain store would be able to achieve an instant propaganda victory by competing. So the supposition that the players know that the chain store will always co-operate must be abandoned. Thus we have another illustration of the fact that one cannot foresee the choices of an equally well-informed ideal agent if that agent has the means and the motive to undermine the prediction. Similar reasoning accounts for Hodgson's punishment problem, iterated chicken, and the iterated pricing game.

Whereas the iterated prisoners' dilemma and the chain store paradox involve blindspotting others, the Indy puzzle involves self-blindspotting. Indy seems to know too much about himself. He cannot form the requisite intention because he knows that he is rationally self-interested and well-informed, and knows that such agents refrain from inflicting pointless suffering on themselves. If Indy could lose this self-knowledge, he would be able to form some of the lucrative intentions. So Indy is motivated to lose knowledge of his prudence. Suppose that Indy, as a result of accepting the paradoxical argument, knows that a prudent man would not take any of the noxious tests. He would then be able to persuade himself that he was not prudent by taking one of them. Since it is in the interest of Indy to be so persuaded, he will take advantage of the opportunity by taking some tests. Since the test-taking would be intentional, Indy would earn some money from his teacher's offer. Thus the supposition that Indy knows that a prudent man would not take any tests leads to the conclusion that he would take some. Therefore we must reject the supposition.

Once again, someone might object that Indy would detect the possibility that his test-taking is just a ploy to undermine his self-knowledge. Thus Indy cannot rule out the possibility that he really is prudent on the basis of his test-taking. The critic is correct in pointing out that noxious test-taking is insufficient evidence for the conclusion that the test-taker is imprudent. But by maintaining that test-taking and prudence are compatible, the critic has undermined his position. For the objection is made in defence of the thesis that a prudent man would know that he would not take any noxious tests. Since the objection is sound only if the thesis is false, the objection is self-defeating.

Let us now return to the bottle imp. Even if we ignore the defects which inspired the last buyer, the bottle imp is vulnerable to the strategy applied in the above paragraphs. For early purchasers of the bottle can influence the judgement of later customers. Ideal thinkers realize that similar choosers choose similarly. There is no significant difference between purchasing the bottle for one million pennies and purchasing it for 999,999 pennies or 999,998 pennies. Someone who knows that the previous one hundred people have purchased the bottle at one penny decrements from an original price of one million pennies is entitled to make the inductive inference that he will be able to sell the bottle to someone else at an insignificantly lower price. So the purchase will be a reasonable risk. The original million-penny purchaser realizes that his purchase will count as favourable evidence for those worried about future customers. The original purchase is evidence because it is a sample of the population's decision tendencies. One buys the bottle only if one believes that others will buy. So one's purchase is a reliable sign of this belief. The initial purchase prompts further purchases which increases the size of the sample.

As the price falls, the degree of similarity between the decision problems diminishes. The difference between purchasing the bottle for one million pennies and purchasing it for 999,999 pennies is an insignificant difference. However, there is a significant difference between purchasing the bottle for five pennies and purchasing it for four pennies. As in a chain letter, the sample becomes more biased as it grows larger. Eventually, the bias becomes too great and purchases are no longer justified. It is impossible to specify the exact point at which the purchase becomes unjustified because of the vagueness of 'justified'. This is a common situation. Suppose it would be prudent of you to sell your car to me for one million pennies. After I point out that a penny difference is insignificant, you also agree that 999,999 pennies is a prudent selling point. But lest you wind up selling the car for a single penny, you must insist that there is some number of pennies at which you would be unjustified in selling me your car. Your inability to precisely specify this number is due to the vagueness of the terms involved. Although this situation is philosophically interesting (indeed it is just a variation of the sorites paradox), we need not linger over it in order to appreciate the intuitive result of this solution. Our first reaction to the bottle imp is that those who can purchase the bottle for a large number of pennies are justified in doing so, those who can only purchase it for a very small number of pennies are unjustified, and that there is a substantial borderline interval in which we are uncertain as to whether the purchase would be justified. These intuitions are vindicated through a line of reasoning which emphasizes the vagueness of 'justified', a vagueness rooted in the vagueness of the similarity relation.

IV. ISOLATED AGENTS AND COMMON CAUSES

It is now appropriate to consider an important objection to the blindspotting analysis. The iterated prisoners' dilemma, the chain store paradox, the Indy puzzle, and the bottle imp, are susceptible to a conservative resolution because the parties can manipulate the evidence and are motivated to do so. This potential for propaganda can be eliminated.

In the booth paradox, there are one thousand rationally self-interested agents: Mr 1, Mr 2, Mr 3, . . . Mr 1000. Each is placed in a booth whose number corresponds to the agent's name. Although each agent knows the number of the booth in which he has been placed, he cannot communicate with the other booth-members and knows that he will never interact with them once they leave their booths. Over the intercom comes a public announcement from Mr Reliable. It is common knowledge that Mr Reliable always tells the truth and always keeps his promise. He says 'In each of your booths there is a dollar and a teletype machine. You may either keep the dollar or exchange the dollar for an opportunity to type the sentence "There is someone with a booth number less than mine who has also typed a token of this sentence." If the statement so produced is true, you receive one million dollars. If false, you receive nothing. All those who choose to type, will do so at noon.' Note that Mr Reliable has made no prediction as to whether anyone will part with a dollar or will produce any true or false statements. So Mr Reliable will have broken no promise nor told a falsehood if none of the booth-members types a truth. And indeed it seems that none of the booth-members will type anything. For Mr 1 can plainly see that he has no hope of typing a truth. So he will be content with his dollar. Mr 2 realizes that Mr 1 will not type anything, and so Mr 2 will type nothing. In a like manner, the remaining 998 booth-members can be shown to be non-typers. Of course, the argument is unaffected by increasing the prize for a true statement or increasing the number of ideal agents. Yet intuitively, it seems that some true statements would be typed. However, this intuition cannot be defended by an appeal to tacit communication. The booth-members are isolated from each other. None can influence another's decision through his own decision. Without this opportunity to manipulate each other's opinions, there appears to be no way to apply our previous approach to the booth paradox.

But consider the situation from the vantage point of a high booth-member, say, the fellow in booth 900. Mr 900 has the choice of obtaining one dollar with certainty or obtaining one million dollars with a probability of m. As long as m exceeds 0.000001, he should type. The paradoxical argument suggests that the probability is 0. Does Mr 900 assign a non-zero probability to successful typing? He reasons as follows: 'If I try for the million, then I will know that there is at least one booth-member who is a typer: me. Although this would refute the paradoxical position that there will be no typers, it remains to be seen whether the probability of my actually becoming a millionaire would be non-zero. Unless the probability exceeds zero, I will not try for the million in which case the paradoxical position would not be refuted by me. After making my choice, what evidence would I have that other booth-members are typers? Well my own choice would be evidence. After all, I am trying to predict the behaviour of booth-members. I am a booth-member. So my behaviour is an admittedly small sample of the relevant population. But is my choice a biased sample of the choices of the remaining population? The only difference between me and Mr 899 is that the size of his group of predecessors is 898/899 the size of mine. This is an insignificant difference. Indeed, there is little difference between me and Mr 898, Mr 897, and so on for a considerable distance down the sequence. Of course, the insignificant differences accumulate into significant difference eventually. But before this happens we must

pass through a large neighbourhood of agents who are quite similar to myself. Therefore, it is safe to assume that many of them are thinking much the same thoughts that I am now thinking. So my choice is not a significantly biased sample of the choices of the booth-members in my neighbourhood. Therefore, the probability of 'There is someone with a booth number less than mine who also types a token of this sentence' is greater than 0. Once my neighbours realize that the probability need only be slightly greater than 0 in order to justify exchange of the dollar for the typing option, they will realize others realize it; and so many of them will be emboldened to make the exchange, thereby dramatically increasing the probability. It is necessarily the case that one of the exchanges will be unfruitful. But since the risk is so small, we cannot conclude that the unfruitful exchange lacked justification. In conclusion, it is best to take my chances and type the sentence.'
The above argument exploits the self-affectivity of the booth-member's decision problem. His choice is evidence about what his choice should be. This phenomenon has a precedent in Newcomb's problem.

Newcomb's problem features a chooser and a predictor. The chooser is presented with a transparent box containing $1,000 and an opaque box containing $1,000,000 if and only if the predictor has predicted that the chooser will pick only the opaque box (even though the chooser is free to take both). The chooser knows that the predictor made his prediction a week ago and on that basis has either placed the $1,000,000 in the opaque box or placed nothing. The chooser further knows that the predictor is very reliable. The question is 'Should the chooser pick both boxes or just the opaque box?' Since the two-box option dominates the one-box option, it seems clear that both boxes should be taken. Yet the expected utility of taking only one box exceeds the expected utility of taking both boxes. So we also have a powerful argument for taking only one box. The key feature of Newcomb's problem is that although the chooser's decision in no way causes the money to be in the box, his decision is correlated with the presence of the money. The correlation is due to a common cause responsible for both the decision and the presence of money in the opaque box.

In the booth paradox, a similar common cause situation obtains. Although each booth-member has no causal influence over other booth members, each is aware that an albeit weaker correlation between their decisions exists by virtue of their similar constitutions as ideal choosers and the (gradated) similarity of their decision problems. As in Newcomb's problem, the correlation makes the decision evidence about the fruitfulness of the decision.

At this point, it might be objected that my common cause argument for seeking $1,000,000 in the booth paradox can be counterbalanced with a common cause argument for not seeking the million. My choice to seek $1,000,000 is extra evidence that my choice will be fruitful. Likewise, if I choose to keep the dollar and type nothing, my choice is also extra evidence in favour of the non-typing decision. For my choice is evidence that others have also chosen to not type. Self-support cuts both ways. So, the objector concludes, the self-supportive nature of the decision to seek the million fails to show that it is the best choice.

This objection neglects the fact that the decision to seek the million is self-supportive with respect to differential expected utility as well as mere probability. This point can be illustrated with a co-ordination problem. Suppose two clones are led into separate rooms containing one lever each. They are to choose between pushing the lever up, pushing it down, or doing nothing. Their pay-off matrix is presented in Table 10.7.

TABLE 10.7

		Column		
		Up	Do nothing	Down
	Up	(2, 2)	(0, 0)	(0, 0)
Row	Do nothing	(0, 0)	(1, 1)	(0, 0)
	Down	(0, 0)	(0, 0)	(2, 2)

Since it is common knowledge that the clones are quite similar, each is confident that the other will make the same choice he does. This makes the Up and Down options better than doing nothing. By choosing Up, Row gains the good news that Column also chose Up yielding a pay-off of two rather than zero. But why is choosing to do nothing irrational? It too brings good news; the news that Column also did nothing rather than something, yielding a pay-off of one rather than zero. Row would not wish to alter his choice after learning Column's. Nevertheless, his choice is irrational because it failed to bring about the *best* available news. Since it is common knowledge that the clones are so similar that they will almost certainly make the same choice, all of the options are self-supportive. Row's Up choice increases the probability that the Up choice is the fruitful one. For it is extra evidence that Column choose Up, and so evidence that he is better off.

Just as a choice to seek the million does not guarantee that there is a lower typer, the choice to not seek the million does not exclude the possibility that there is a lower typer. Thus a choice to not type could leave the expected utility of typing higher than $1. Of course I also concede that a choice to type need not raise the expected utility of that choice above $1. Indeed this certainly holds for the agent in booth one! My position is that agents in high-numbered booths will have expected utilities of greater than $1 for their choices to type. So, a non-typing decision by a high-numbered agent is self-supportive in the sense that the decision is itself extra evidence in favour of the hypothesis that the decision will be fruitful. For a non-typing decision increases the probability that there are no lower typers. However, a non-typing decision is not self-supportive in the sense of providing evidence that makes the expected utility of non-typing exceed the expected utility of typing. Since the key sense of 'self-supportive' is this latter sense, the objection fails.

This objection leads us to a more obvious and serious objection. The agents in high-numbered booths agree that Mr 1 will not type. And they agree that Mr 2 realizes this and so will decline the opportunity to type as well. Similar reasoning seems to rule out indefinitely many higher booth-numbers. In general, there is no n at which the higher booth members can claim certainty that the agent in booth $n - 1$ will not type and uncertainty as to whether the agent in booth number n will type. So what prevents the certainty of Mr 1 not typing from being passed upwards? In short, exactly where does the paradoxical argument for universal non-typing go wrong?

V. THE VAGUENESS OF 'KNOWLEDGE'

Our inability to specify the value for n does not license the mathematical induction to the conclusion that no one will type. For our inability to specify the value is due to vagueness. It is generally agreed that mathematical inductions involving vague predicates are defective. Of course there is disagreement over the nature of the defect, but the sorites paradox makes it clear that something is wrong.

As with most of our vocabulary, 'know' is vague. To show that 'know' is vague, it suffices to produce borderline cases of knowledge. One method of producing borderline cases of knowledge is to gradually vary the degree of complexity of the object of knowledge. For example, I know that $1 + 1 = 2$, that $2 + 2 = 4$, and that $3 + 3 = 6$. But as n increases, I become less sure of what the sum of $n + n$ is. Clearly, if n is a billion-digit number, then I fail to know the sum of $n + n$. Yet I cannot specify an n such that I know the sum of $n + n$ and fail to know the sum of $(n + 1) + (n + 1)$. The similarity of each pair of addition statements is evidence that either both are known or both are unknown propositions. For if I am ignorant of one, it is likely that I am ignorant of the other. If I could be mistaken about one, it is very likely that I could be mistaken about the other. Should I get one of the sums right and the other wrong, then the best explanation for the difference is luck. And if I got one of the sums right by luck, I did not know the sum.

Of course, the complexity of propositions is relative to the epistemic equipment of the knower. Since the booth-members are ideal thinkers, none of their ignorance should be explained in terms of their computational limits. Nevertheless, ideal thinkers can be affected by other sources of vagueness. One such source is simply the vagueness of the predicates used to express the proposition. For instance, suppose a list is passed amongst a group of one thousand people with the instructions 'Add your name to this list if and only if the list contains only a small percentage of the people in the group.' Those who sign early know that they are following instructions. As the list grows, so does reason for doubt. Yet the ground for doubt grows too slowly to enable us to decide where to draw the line between those who know they are following instructions and those who do not.

The list situation resembles the booth paradox situation insofar as the booth members, like the list readers, have gradually varying objects of judgement. The list readers make judgements about propositions of the form '$x\%$ is a small percentage'. Since x grows slowly, the propositions resemble each other. In the booth situation, each proposition encompasses its predecessor:

> 0. No one lower than Mr 1 types.
> 1. Mr 1 knows (0).
> 2. Mr 2 knows (1).
> 3. Mr 3 knows (2).
> .
> .
> .
> 1000. Mr 1000 knows (999).

To answer the objection that knowledge gets passed up the entire chain of agents, one must provide an account of how the links in the chain can weaken even if the agents are epistemically ideal. In short, how could one of the above propositions be false?

If Mr 900 were to type, proposition (901) would be false. Since propositions (902)–(1000) each imply (901), they would also be false. Of course, this observation does not meet the objection. For the objector wants to know why (900) would thereby be falsified. After all, if (900) is true, Mr 900 would be typing with the knowledge that he had no chance of getting the million. The falsity of (900) would follow because of the similarity between Mr 900's higher neighbours and Mr 900's lower neighbours. The epistemic state of Mr 899 is insignificantly different from the epistemic state of Mr 901. Yet the objector is committed to maintaining that Mr 899 knows (898) while Mr 901 would not know (900). If Mr 899 has a true belief in (898) it would be a matter of luck. For Mr 901's false belief shows that Mr 899 could have been wrong. By typing, Mr 900 would be showing that an agent in a quite similar position could have typed. This possibility ensures that Mr 899 does not know that none of his predecessors are typers. So if Mr 900 types, then (900) is false. Indeed, many of the propositions lower than (900) are false. Of course, I can no more specify the first false proposition than can I specify the first large integer.

Vagueness is a virtue of my account rather than a vice. For it enables us to reconcile our belief in (1) and some of its successors with our disbelief in the high-numbered propositions. Without the element of vagueness we would be obliged to support this position by specifying the first false proposition in the sequence. Having introduced an element of vagueness through the use of the similarity relation, we can properly dismiss the request to specify the first false proposition in the same way that we dismiss the request to specify the first moment of adulthood, the earliest time at which it is noonish, and the minimum number of pennies a rich man must have.

VI. BLINDSPOTTING IN THE BOOTH PARADOX

In the iterated prisoners' dilemma, the chain store paradox, and the bottle imp, the participants' abilities to manipulate each other's evidence provides the basis for blindspotting possibilities which undermine each of the paradoxical arguments. But in the booth paradox, the participants are isolated. Their inability to cause others to acquire evidence precludes blindspotting others. If any blindspotting occurs, then it must be self-blindspotting as exemplified by the Indy puzzle. I now turn to the question of how blindspotting takes place in the booth paradox.

I argued that Mr 900 could rightly construe his decision to type as evidence that some of his predecessors have also typed. By typing, Mr 900 ensures that he does not know whether his predecessors have typed by creating evidence that they did type. Since it is likely that there are lower typers, Mr 900's typing is unlikely to be the cause of his ignorance of whether there are lower typers. The likely cause of his ignorance is the unfortunate first typer. Given that this first typer occupies a very low numbered booth, we can say that he would have known that he had no lower typers had he not typed. Let's call him Mr Premature. Mr Premature is the cause of his own ignorance. He blindspots himself. For Mr Premature gives himself evidence for a set of compossible but not co-knowable propositions.

(i) Mr 1 knows there is no lower typer than 1.
(ii) If Mr 1 knows there is no lower typer than Mr 1, then there is no typer near Mr 1.
(iii) Booth members type only if they don't know that there are no typers lower than them.
(iv) Mr Premature is near Mr 1.
(v) Mr Premature is a booth member who types.

If Mr Premature had not typed, he would have known (i)–(iv). By typing, Mr Premature learns that (v) and thus cannot also know the conjunction of (i)–(iv).

Mr Premature blindspots himself only because his typing makes the crucial difference between knowing and not knowing (i)–(iv). If the first typer does not occupy a very low booth, he need not be blindspotting himself because his typing does not make the crucial difference between knowing and not knowing. The reason why their typing does not make the crucial difference is that they must take account of *possible* self-blindspotting on the part of lower typers.

VII. APPEALS TO THE SIMILARITY PRINCIPLE

In order to solve the booth paradox, I appealed to the similarity principle: similar choosers choose similarly. Since the choosers have been idealized, differences in their choices have to be explained in terms of differences in their decision problems. And since the differences between the decision problems of neighbouring high booth-members are slight, similar choices can be expected. So a high booth-member can use his decision to type (or whatever inclines him to so decide) as part of his justification.

In light of this appeal to the similarity principle, one may wonder how Davis and I could arrive at such different conclusions. Davis's appeal to similarity leads him to support purely cooperative solutions to the prisoners' dilemma, the iterated prisoners' dilemma, and even the 'opaque' super-game in which the players are not informed of each other's moves. I, on the other hand, favour the purely competitive solution to both the prisoners' dilemma and the opaque super-game, and favour a 'mixed' solution to the 'transparent' super-game. For I find it most probable that a long stretch of co-operation will eventually give way to competition as the transparent super-game nears its end. In general it will be found that Davis and I diverge whenever the similarity principle appears to conflict with a dominant strategy. Davis resolves these conflicts by maintaining that the similarity principle generates expected utilities which override the dominance principle. I maintain that these override arguments, such as we find in Newcomb's problem, are flawed. Although I shall defer detailed discussion of Newcomb's problem until the next chapter, my main objection to the one-boxer's expected utility argument can be briefly summarized.[6] A rational agent under the sway of the expected utility argument could not form a final decision to take only one box. For such a decision would make the decider sure that the million is indeed in the opaque box. And if he is sure the million is in the opaque box, he cannot raise his expected utility by taking only the opaque box. Likewise, an agent in either a prisoner's dilemma or an opaque super-game cannot form a final decision to co-operate. For such a decision would be information which raises the probability of the desired event to a level which cannot be enhanced by acting on the decision. The presence of a dominant option forces recalculations of the expected utility of taking one box.

Although the foregoing criticism is too sketchy to constitute a refutation of Davis's main argument for co-operation in the prisoners' dilemma, it does convey my rationale for accepting some appeals to similarity and rejecting others. Davis's appeals to the similarity principle are objectionable because they are blocked by the presence of a dominant strategy. Since there is no dominant strategy in the booth paradox, the appeal to similarity is legitimate. So expected utility calculations can lead to stable, final decisions to type, solving the paradox.

[6] My criticism of the expected utility argument as it arises for Newcomb's problem appears in 'Newcomb's Problem: Recalculations for the One-Boxer', *Theory and Decision*, 15/4 (Dec. 1983), 399–404.

11
Stability and Anti-expertise

THIS chapter is devoted to a defence of the stability requirement used in the previous chapter.[1] This principle tells us that rational choosers do not wittingly take inferior options. After exhibiting its role in analyses of Newcomb's problem, I will concentrate on the strongest ostensible counter-examples to the principle: 'instability cases'. These are situations in which the decision maker is an anti-expert. Someone is an anti-expert about p if and only if he is reliably wrong about p. Although it will be conceded that anti-expertise is possible, I will deny that a rational decision-maker can be aware of his own anti-expertise. That is, 'anti-expert' is a personal blindspot predicate. Since self-predication of 'anti-expert' is a necessary ingredient of a fully-fledged instability situation, I shall exclude these scenarios as logically impossible.

I. NEWCOMB'S PROBLEM

One reaction to Newcomb's problem is to view it as a counter-example to the sort of decision theory epitomized by Richard Jeffrey's *The Logic of Decision*. Jeffrey defines the expected utility of an option in terms of the probability of *indicative* conditionals. The resulting decision theory is an evidential one, roughly counselling us to maximize 'good news'. The chooser in Newcomb's problem must ask himself whether he would be more pleased to learn that he chose one box or two boxes. Since the one-box choice is a strong sign that he is a millionaire, he should take only the opaque box. Causal decision theorists claim that the two-box choice is the correct solution to Newcomb's problem. They maintain that expected utility should be calculated by means of *subjunctive* conditionals, so that we produce the maximum 'real gain'. Although learning that you have taken both boxes is bad news, causal decision theorists point out that one can take solace

[1] Portions of this chapter have been taken from 'Anti-Expertise, Instability, and Rational Choice', *Australasian Journal of Philosophy*, 65/3 (Sept. 1987), 301–15.

in the fact that you would have been worse off if you had taken only one box.

Since the question of whether one box or two boxes should be taken is a controversial question, causal theorists have appealed to less controversial decision problems to garner intuitive support for their thesis. All theorists agree that the principle of dominance does not apply if one's decision has a causal influence on the states of affairs in question. Let C stand for 'I get cancer' and S stand for my choice to smoke. By letting 1 to 4 represent my ordinal preferences from lowest to highest, we can read off the situation from Table 11.1.

TABLE 11.1

	C	−C
S	2	4
−S	1	3

Given my belief that smoking causes cancer, it would be sophistical of me to conclude that I should smoke because smoking dominates not smoking. But suppose I instead believed that the correlation between smoking and cancer was due to a common cause, say, a gene that caused both cancer and a craving for cigarettes. Now the appeal to dominance seems valid. My choice to smoke would be bad news since it is a sign of eventual cancer but it would be silly to forego the pleasures of smoking on that account. Causal decision theorists then complain that this valid appeal to dominance is counted as invalid in Jeffrey's theory. For Jeffrey restricts the dominance principle to contexts in which the options are *probabilistically* independent of the states of affairs.

Jeffrey and Ellery Eells have used the 'tickle defence' to support their view that evidential decision theory does not have the consequences ascribed to it by causal decision theorists. Upon noticing that I crave cigarettes (the tickle), the probability that I have smoker's gene rises. The decision to smoke produces no further increase in the probability. The information about my craving 'screens off' the information derived from my decision. Thus the expected utility of the smoking option will be higher than not smoking. Jeffrey and Eells agree that the decision-maker in Newcomb's problem will receive information that screens off the information about whether one or two boxes have been taken.

However, they offer different accounts of what this information is. Jeffrey seems to believe that it is the chooser's final decision. If one box is chosen, the individual will be sure that there is a million in the box even before opening it. So as he reaches for it, he should feel some regret that he did not take both boxes. This shows that the one-boxer's decision is not *ratifiable*. A ratifiable decision is one that I 'can live with', that I can 'see as rational, once I have made it'. Since only the two-box decision is ratifiable, Jeffrey concludes that it is the correct one. One might object that since the screening-off takes place at the end of the deliberative process, it is of no practical value because it happens too late. Jeffrey's remarks about ratifiability suggest that he does not think that decision theory should be required to be action-guiding. Rather, it need only give us verdicts about which decision is correct, i.e. has the highest expected utility at the time at which the decision is made. Eells, on the other hand, suggests that the individual's beliefs and desires provide the screening-off information. The act of taking both boxes will not be bad news because it will be old news. Whenever I believe there is a common cause for my decision and a state of affairs, the news value of my decision is discounted by news of the causal antecedents of my decision. Since rational decisions require knowledge of how much I value the states of affairs and the probabilities I assign to obtaining those outcomes, the rational decision maker has epistemic access to a causal ancestor of his decision. So evidential decision theory will give us the same results as causal decision theory for the crucial common cause cases.

Jeffrey and Eells have had their candidates for screening-off information criticized. Rather than defend their candidates, I want to argue that there isn't any need for them to specify this information. For the tickle defence is better used negatively than positively. It should be used as a *reductio* of the one-box position.

One-boxers maintain that the one-box decision is the rational choice. If they are right, then *they* will have specified the screening-off information for us. The screening-off information will be the evidence demonstrating that an ideal chooser will take one box. This evidence is available to the ideal chooser. So he can be sure that he will take one box. But if he is sure that he will take one box, he is sure that the million is in the opaque box even before he executes his decision. But if he is sure that the million is there, then he will take both boxes. After all, the point of making the box opaque was to introduce uncertainty about its contents. Now it is as if the box were transparent. Once the deliberator is sure that the money is there, the two-box choice is the obvious choice. Thus from the supposition that the one-box position is correct, it follows that it is not correct. Therefore, the one-box position is not correct. So given that there is a correct choice, evidential decision theory rules that the two-boxers are right.

The above argument exploits the fact that the one-box option is *unstable*. An option is unstable if a decision to take that option is evidence against that decision's fruitfulness. One-box options are unstable because a decision to take one box is evidence that you are better off taking two boxes. A two-box option, on the other hand, is stable. Indeed, all dominant options are stable because the definition of 'dominance' ensures that you are never better off taking a dominated option.

One might object that the *reductio* overlooks the possibility that the ideal chooser's decision is a blindspot to him prior to execution of that decision. However, there are a couple of considerations which make this possibility a poor prospect for the one-boxer. First of all, he would be claiming that the rational choice is unknowable and yet, all the same, gets made. Are we to suppose that the decision-making process is submerged in the unconscious? Second, if the one-boxer's expected utility argument is sound, what prevents the ideal chooser from appreciating its soundness? We would have to suppose that the ideal choosers go about knowing that the one-box choice is always made and yet they lose this knowledge when they themselves are faced with the decision problem. Year after year, they make the one-box choice and observe others make it. Yet even when this inductive evidence is supplemented with a theoretical demonstration of the fact, their conviction evaporates when the decision must be made. Even allowing them to confer with those who are outside the spell of the blindspot fails to reawaken the old knowledge. Why buy into this epistemological morass when the two-boxer has an alternative free of these complications? In order to make this blindspot hypothesis a contender, the one-boxer must show that the two-boxer has serious complications of his own.

II. THE CASE OF THE INFALLIBLE PREDICTOR

A tried and true method for stirring up trouble for two-boxers is to ask what should be done when faced with an infallible predictor. Here, the one-box choice seems the obviously correct one. For if the predictor's chance of being right is 1.0, taking one box guarantees a million while taking two boxes guarantees a thousand.

Compromisers concede that a one-box solution is correct when the predictor's probability is 1 and yet insist that at any lower probability the two-box solution is correct. But this seems *ad hoc*. Why should a tiny difference in probabilities yield opposite solutions? One might reply that tiny differences in probability are crucial to other decision problems. For example, if one knows that the probability of a prize being behind one door is just slightly greater than it being behind the remaining doors, one ought to choose the slightly more probable one. However, the perfect predictor case is not a situation in which slight probability tips a balance. Ellery Eells describes an alternate explanation offered by James H. Fetzer: 'if the agent takes seriously the premise that the predictor will make the correct prediction in every case, then the agent should not list among the possible outcomes of his action his getting $1,001,000 or his getting $0. [And so] dominance reasoning is not applicable,'[2] This reply answers the charge of *ad hocness* by showing how the small quantitative change in probability gives rise to a qualitative difference. If we conceive of Newcomb's problem as a puzzle about how to reconcile the principle of dominance with the expected utility principle, we can maintain that the puzzle does not really arise for the infallibility case because there is no conflict when the dominance principle is silent.

Although Eells agrees that assigning a probability of 0 to the predictor being incorrect would make the dominance principle inapplicable, he regards such a probability assignment as irrational. Eells agrees with David Lewis' view that assigning a 0 probability to a proposition

is tantamount to a firm resolve never to change your mind, and that is objectionable. However much reason you may get to think that option A will not be realized if K holds, you will not if you are rational lower

---

[2] Ellery Eells, *Rational Decision and Causality* (New York: Cambridge University Press, 1982), 207–8.

[P(K & A)] quite to zero. Let it by all means get very, very small; but very, very small denominators do not make utilities go undefined.[3]

Lewis does not supply an argument supporting his view that such a probability assignment is dogmatic. The only argument I know of for this conclusion bears a defeating resemblance to Harman's paradox of dogmatism mentioned in chapter 8. Lawrence Davis expresses his doubts about Lewis's argument as follows:

> I have not firmly resolved never to change my mind about the proposition 'Zeus will strike me dead unless I beg him to spare me within the next 30 seconds.' I (think I) can even imagine evidence that would persuade me of its truth. Yet I simply do not consider it in deliberating what to do. Nor is this a matter of assigning it a *low* probability. I assign it a *zero* probability. I *have* entertained the proposition (and so, now, have you), but I *do not consider it at all* in planning my actions (and nor will you, if you are rational).[4]

Allan Gibbard and William Harper maintain that the two-boxer need not make any compromise when confronted with the infallible predictor. They maintain that the 'obvious' wisdom of the one-box choice is illusory. To support their position, they first consider the case where the agent knows whether he will take one or two boxes. If the agent knows that he will take one box, he knows that there is $1,000,000 in the opaque box. But given there is $1,000,000 in the opaque box, it follows that even if he were to have chosen both boxes, there would be a million in the opaque box. So he would be better off taking both boxes. On the other hand, if he knows that he will take both boxes, he knows that the opaque box is empty. So he is also better off taking both boxes in this situation.

Now suppose that the agent does not know what he will do. He then knows the following disjunction:

(i) Either I shall take one box and be a millionaire, or I shall take both boxes and be a non-millionaire.

But this disjunction does not imply the conjunction of the subjunctive conditionals:

---

[3] David Lewis, 'Causal Decision Theory', *Australasian Journal of Philosophy*, 59/1 (Jan. 1981), 5–30.

[4] Lawrence Davis, 'Is the Symmetry Argument Valid?', in Richmond Campbell and Lanning Sowden (eds.), *Paradoxes of Rationality and Cooperation* (Vancouver: The University of British Columbia Press, 1985), 257.

(ii) If I were to take one box, I would be a millionaire.
(iii) If I were to take both boxes, I would be a non-millionaire.

For (ii) and (iii) are mutually exclusive. (ii) is true if and only if the opaque box contains $1,000,000. And (iii) is true if and only if it does not contain a million. So if the agent knew (ii), he would know that there is a million in the opaque box. And if he knew (iii), he would know the opaque box to be empty. In either case the agent would know what he was going to choose. But since we are supposing that he does not know, neither (ii) nor (iii) follows from what the agent knows. What the agent does know is that regardless of whether the opaque box contains $1,000,000, he would receive $1,000 more by taking both boxes. Since the agent wants as much as he can get, it would therefore be irrational of him to forego both boxes even if he knows that the predictor is infallible.

One-boxers have basically two responses to the Gibbard–Harper analysis. First, insist that infallibility does indeed support the conjunction of (ii) and (iii).[5] For it could be maintained that the subjunctive conditionals are back-tracking conditionals which require us to alter suppositions about the past in order to accommodate suppositions about a changed present. Thus, as we observe someone take one box we should say 'If he had taken both boxes, the predictor would have predicted it and left no money in the opaque box.' Critics of this view complain that back-tracking interpretations deviate from the standard way of resolving the vagueness of counter-factuals. For the standard interpretation ensures that counter-factual dependence is asymmetric; the present depends on the past but not vice versa. Some contexts, such as time-travel speculation, make back-tracking interpretations appropriate. Reason for thinking that Newcomb's problem is not such a context is provided by the fixity constraint: the choice has no influence over the contents of the boxes. Posers of the puzzle emphasize that the prediction was made long ago, that there are no false bottoms to the boxes, that there are no tricks involved. Adoption of the back-tracking interpretation conflicts with the fixity constraint. It is inappropriate in the same way that

---

[5] Terence Horgan takes this position in 'Counterfactuals and Newcomb's Problem', *Journal of Philosophy*, 78/6 (June 1981), 331–56.

the introduction of reverse causation is unacceptable. Insisting on a back-tracking interpretation creates an inconsistent set of puzzle conditions. So as long as we wish to view Newcomb's problem as a possible decision problem, we have to drop the back-tracking interpretation.[6]

The second objection to the Gibbard–Harper analysis focuses on the stability requirement. Gibbard and Harper point out that if you know that you will take only one box, you know that there is $1,000,000 in the opaque box even if you take both boxes. Hence the one-boxer would have to knowingly choose an inferior alternative. But this violates the stability requirement. Some one-boxes, such as Reed Richter, respond by rejecting the requirement. The basis for the challenge is an appeal to 'instability cases'.

III. INSTABILITY CASES

An early example of an instability situation can be found in Robert Nozick's seminal article 'Newcomb's Problem and Two Principles of Choice'.

To get the mind to really boggle, consider the following.

	S1	S2
A:	10	4
B:	8	3

Suppose that you know that either S1 or S2 already obtains, but you do not know which, and you know that S1 will cause you to do B, and S2 will cause you to do A. Now choose! ('Choose?')[7]

Usually choices reveal a preference for the chosen alternative. In the case of arbitrary choices, there is at least indifference between the alternatives. But here the chooser appears destined to choose a dispreferred alternative. That is, if he chooses A, he prefers B. And if he chooses B, he prefers A.

We ought to be more specific about what is mind-boggling about

---

[6] Don Hubin and Glenn Ross argue that the mere supposition of an infallible predictor conflicts with the fixity constraint in 'Newcomb's Perfect Predictor', *Nous*, 29/3 (Sept. 1985), 439–46.

[7] Robert Nozick, 'Newcomb's Problem and Two Principles of Choice', in Nicholas Rescher (ed.), *Essays in Honor of Carl G. Hempel* (Dordrecht: D. Reidel, 1970), 141.

this situation. One suggestion is that the situation is puzzling because it is an apparent counter-example to the principle that rational agents minimize regret. However, this principle only rules out cases where one knows which decision is better. As I. L. Humberstone points out, there are ordinary situations in which regret is inevitable.[8] Consider horse bets. If the horse wins, the better will regret not betting more. If the horse loses, he will regret betting at all. But this type of inevitable regret does not show that the decision is irrational. For the better does not know which decision is superior until after it is too late.

In the light of the betting case, the suggested diagnosis of our puzzlement should be revised to include the epistemic element. That is, we are puzzled because we have an apparent counter-example to the principle that rational agents do not choose an alternative they recognize to be inferior to a rival option. Reed Richter formulates the jeopardized principle as follows:

'(R) If options A and B are both available to agent x and if x knows that were he to do A he would be better off in every respect than were he to do B, then in the strictest sense of rational self-interest rationality requires x to do A over doing B.'[9]

This principle requires that decisions be *stable*; that they remain choiceworthy upon being chosen. As Richter points out, (R) underlies defences of the two-box solution to Newcomb's problem. The solution depends on the point that a one-boxer will have to choose knowing that he would have been better off taking both boxes. Were (R) to be rejected, the one-boxer would escape the central objection to his choice. Since Richter views this as an attractive consequence, he appeals to several other 'instability' cases designed to show that (R) is indeed false.

Richter first considers a case introduced by Gibbard and Harper in their defence of causal decision theory.[10] Here we are to consider the dilemma of a traveller who knows he has an appointment with Death. Death's schedule is fixed weeks in advance, on the basis of virtually infallible predictions as to the

[8] Humberstone makes this point in 'You'll Regret It', *Analysis*, 40/3 (June 1980), 175–6.

[9] Reed Richter, 'Rationality Revisited', *Australasian Journal of Philosophy*, 62/2 (Dec. 1984), 392.

[10] Allan Gibbard and William Harper discuss the Death case in 'Two Kinds of Expected Utility', in William Harper et. al. (eds.), *Ifs* (Dordrecht: D. Reidel, 1981), 184–7.

victims' locations. Thus the man knows that, although his choice as to where to be does not cause Death to join him at the place in question, his choice to be in a certain place is excellent evidence that Death will turn up at that place. The traveller also knows that Death cannot be foiled by randomizing tactics. For the sake of simplicity, we shall also assume that the man can only be in one of two places: Aleppo or Damascus. Given the man's beliefs and his aversion to meeting Death, the man's decision is unstable. For his decision is evidence against itself. According to the story, the man can decide to remain in Damascus only if he realizes that he would have been better off going to Aleppo. On the other hand, if the man chooses to go to Aleppo, he knows he would have been better off staying in Damascus. Application of (R) to this situation yields the conclusion that the man's decision will be inevitably irrational. For the man will be choosing an alternative which he knows leaves him worse off. Thus Gibbard and Harper deny that 'ought' implies 'can' in the context of rational prescriptions.

Richter objects that no decision problem ensures such inevitable irrationality. In order to preserve 'ought' implies 'can', he urges that we reject (R). A common intuition in the Death case is that neither option is better than the other. However, Richter maintains that the Death case can be modified to provide an example of an instability case in which there is a uniquely rational choice. Let us suppose that the traveller's mother lives in Damascus, so that the Damascus option has the bonus of a last visit. Richter claims that this bonus makes the decision to stay in Damascus the rational choice even though the man knows that he would be better off going to Aleppo. So Richter also concludes that causal decision theory wrongly classifies some rational choices as irrational.

Richter's objection can be amplified by modifying an instability case discussed by Brian Skyrms.[11] Here you are to choose exactly one of two opaque boxes, A and B. A mean demon has put $1,000 in the box he predicted you would not take and nothing in the other. Since you know that the predictions are quite reliable, you can be sure you will pick the wrong box. So far the situation corresponds to the Death Case, and so one could maintain that

---

[11] Skyrms analyses the case of the mean demon in his 'Causal Decision Theory', *Journal of Philosophy*, 79/11 (Nov. 1982), 695–711.

either option is rational. The counterpart to the Modified Death Case is where we add a small bonus for taking box B. Some of us are now inclined to say that this modification renders the A option irrational. For it seems that the bonus tips the balance that previously existed between two equally good choices. If taking box A is as rational as taking box B, then the package deal of taking B plus the bonus must be more rational than taking box A. Yet loyalty to (R) forces us to say that the bonus is immaterial. If the bonus makes taking B the uniquely rational choice, then you would know that the money was in box A. This knowledge would force you to change your mind in favour of taking box A. Perhaps this reply has some persuasiveness when the bonus is small. But now suppose that the bonus is almost as great as the prize itself, say $900. Wouldn't it be irrational to forego a sure $900 by taking box A?

Wlodzimierz Rabinowicz agrees with Richter in so far as both reject stability as a necessary condition for choiceworthiness.[12] Like Richter, he adds unpleasant co-ordination problems to the list of apparent counter-examples. Rabinowicz has us suppose that Row and Column are isolated from each other in separate rooms equipped with a lever. They must choose between moving the lever upwards or downwards in accordance with Table 11.2.

TABLE 11.2

		Column	
		Up	Down
Row	Up	(0, 0)	(1, 1)
	Down	(1, 1)	(0, 0)

We are to further suppose that it is common knowledge that the players are very similar to each other. Since randomization is forbidden, this similarity gives them strong evidence that they will make the same choice. So as Row makes his final choice, he will have strong evidence that he would be better off doing elsewise. This constitutes another apparent counter-example to (R).

---

[12] Rabinowicz presents his position in 'Ratificationism without Ratification: Jeffrey meets Savage', *Theory and Decision*, 19/2 (Sept. 1985), 171–200.

IV. ANALOGUES

Since beliefs have morally significant consequences, a utilitarian can face self-referential difficulties in arriving at some value judgements. For suppose that the utilitarian learns that an erroneous value judgement would have the best consequences. His utilitarianism would preclude any rational judgement about the situation. As Marcus Singer points out, Moore, Sidgwick, and Dewey display at least partial awareness of this peculiar predicament.[13] Frederick Kroon illustrates the problem by having us suppose that he is a rational utilitarian on the verge of assessing the moral status of an act of cruelty. Normally, he would judge the act to be wrong. However, this situation is unusual in that others

> who in some ways are superior to me (they can directly intuit, by a kind of mental telepathy, a person's emotional responses, including his moral approval or disapproval of actions), will learn from my moral stance: if I evaluate A as wrong, that will reinforce their hatred of such acts . . . while if I evaluate A as right, that will reinforce their admiration of such acts. . . . Suppose I know that there are no other morally relevant consequences, and suppose I cannot communicate with these 'witnesses'. Suppose, in fact, that this is the final moral 'training' that I, or anyone else, can provide for these witnesses, who are due to spend the rest of their lives on a desert island, applying the moral lesson they will presently learn from me. . . .[14]

The utilitarian cannot judge the act of cruelty as wrong because then the act would have had enormously beneficial consequences (through the edifying effect of his condemnation of it). On the other hand, the utilitarian cannot approve of the act because the approval will set a disastrous precedent. Lastly, suspending judgement will also set a bad precedent, so it too is wrong. Thus the utilitarian under observation is unable to correctly evaluate the situation. Given that act-utilitarianism is required to be an action guiding theory, it will be ruled inadequate. By permitting one's moral judgement to be part of the consequences to be evaluated by the judgement, act-utilitarianism (and perhaps some forms of rule-utilitarianism) becomes vulnerable to self-referential difficulties.

---

[13] Singer makes this point in 'The Paradox of Extreme Utilitarianism', *Pacific Philosophical Quarterly*, 64/2 (Apr. 1983), 242–8.
[14] Frederick Kroon, 'A Utilitarian Paradox', *Analysis*, 41/2 (Mar. 1981), 107.

Earl Conee has responded to Kroon's paradox by first pointing out that the self-referential problem also occurs outside moral contexts. He gives the example of a thirtieth century brain physiologist who knows that all of a person's N-fibres fire if and only if he does not believe it. The brain physiologist then considers the hypothesis that all of his N-fibres are firing. As in Kroon's case, paradox arises. In general, Conee believes that the paradox arises for any theory allowing the following sort of case:

> Knowledge of the theory and of what the consequences of certain mental acts would be gives knowledge that evaluating something implies that evaluation to be incorrect, and that failing to evaluate the thing implies a particular evaluation to be correct. Basically the same problem would remain even if all such theories were counted false. Knowledge is not actually crucial. Justified belief in the theory seems as plausibly to be capable of rendering a rational subject unable to form, or withhold, the relevant judgements. Thus in order to block the paradoxes by faulting the theories we would have to go to the extreme of claiming that they are all insufficiently coherent to be the basis for rational belief in the problematic implications.[15]

As Conee emphasizes, any theory that implies 'p if and only if it is not judged that p' possesses a self-referential peculiarity paralleling the one Kroon uses to object to utilitarianism. The 'theory' in question need not be much more than a description. For example, it might be observed that a particular student passes when and only when he studies and studies if and only if he is not sure whether he will pass. This description implies that he will pass if and only if he is not sure that he will pass. How should the student react to the observation?

Essentially the same problem is behind E. V. Milner's paradox of Dives and Lazarus named after the characters in the New Testament parable (St Luke, chap. 16).[16] In this parable, a rich man and a beggar, Lazarus, both die. Although Lazarus enters heaven, the rich man is condemned to hell. It is explained that 'thou in thy lifetime receivedst thy good things, and likewise Lazarus evil things: but now he is comforted and thou art tormented.' Having given up hope for himself, the rich man asks that Lazarus be sent to warn his rich brethren of what lies in store

[15] Earl Conee, 'Utilitarianism and Rationality', *Analysis*, 42/1 (Jan. 1982), 57.
[16] E. V. Milner, 'The Paradox of Dives and Lazarus', *Mind*, 76/303 (July 1967), 441.

for them for fear that they too will wind up in hell. This request is denied. Milner argues that a paradox would arise if the request were granted.

For if I *knew* that the unhappiness which I suffer in this world would be recompensed by eternal bliss in the next world, then I should be happy in *this* world. But being happy in this world I should fail to qualify, so to speak, for happiness in the *next* world. Therefore, if there were such a recompense awaiting me, its existence would seem to entail that I should at least be not wholly convinced of its existence.[17]

M. E. Williams objects that knowing one is bound for heaven need not make one happy.[18] John O'Connor raises the same objection but offers an amendment intended to preserve the paradox.[19] O'Connor points out that news about one's heavenly destination may provide some temporary cheer but terrestrial troubles might eventually draw one back into unhappiness. O'Connor's amendment to Milner's paradox is to instead assume that knowledge of one's future bliss makes one happy *on the whole* with one's life. When this more plausible assumption is conjoined with knowledge of one's earthly condition, Milner's puzzle is reinstated. For the amendment yields a situation in which a proposition is true if and only if it is not believed (or perhaps justifiably believed or known).

How do we avoid the extreme of declaring incoherent theories and descriptions having consequences of the form '*p* if and only if it is not judged that *p*'? Conee's answer is to deny that rationality requires thoroughness. He suggests that Kroon's utilitarian could rationally refuse to accept a consequence of what he knows to be true. In particular, the utilitarian could believe both the premisses of the following valid argument without believing the conclusion.

If I suspend judgement about whether the act is wrong, then it is wrong.
I suspend judgement about whether the act is wrong.
The act is wrong.

---

[17] Ibid.
[18] M. E. Williams, 'On the Dissolution of the Paradox of Dives and Lazarus', *Mind*, 79/314 (Apr. 1970), 253.
[19] John O Connor, 'A Note on the Paradox of Dives and Lazarus', *Mind*, 79/314, (Apr. 1970), 251–2.

Kroon's criticism of this position is that it rests on an impoverished notion of rationality.[20] After all, Conee is committed to rejecting the following principle even when restricted to ideal thinkers:

$$[Kp \,\&\, K(p \supset q)] \supset Bq$$

Kroon emphasizes that this principle is not controversial even amongst epistemologists who profess scepticism about the principle that knowledge is closed under known logical consequence:

$$[Kp \,\&\, K(p \supset q)] \supset Kq$$

Kroon further points out that unless Conee also denies that knowledge is closed under known logical equivalence, he is even committed to denying:

$$K(p \,\&\, q) \supset Bp$$

For as Nozick has shown, the conjunction of this principle and closure under logical equivalence implies $[Kp \,\&\, K(p \supset q)] \supset Bq$.[21] Were we to follow through on Conee's commitment to reject these modest principles, Kroon finds it difficult to see what kind of a priori constraints *would* apply to rational knowers. Kroon concludes that the implications of Conee's position are

> counterintuitive, and reinforce my suspicions of Conee's way out and the general theoretical position on which it rests: a 'low' conception of rationality according to which rationality does not make various absolute demands, but is instead a matter of compunctions and incentives that can be safely overridden by other compunctions and incentives (but what, then, explains their hold on us in cases where they are *not* overridden?) I incline, instead, to an absolutist 'high' conception of rationality, and incline also to the view that in certain situations we cannot do what we rationally ought to do. It is not the rational acceptability of utilitarianism which stands threatened by this possibility, I now acknowledge, but only the supposition that for utilitarianism to be rationally acceptable, fully

---

[20] Kroon's response appears in 'Rationality and Paradox: A Reply to Conee', *Analysis*, 43/3 (June 1983), 156–60.
[21] See Nozick, *Philosophical Explanations* (Cambridge: Harvard University Press, 1981), 692, n. 63.

informed and rational utilitarians must always be able to judge in accordance with the demands of their theory.[22]

Kroon's acceptance of the possibility of inevitable irrationality parallels the Gibbard–Harper rejection of (rational) 'ought' implies 'can'. His contrast between low and high conceptions of rationality may be objectionable to those who seek to establish epistemic principles in terms of compunctions and incentives. Nevertheless, the basic diagnosis of the disagreement in terms of weak versus strong conceptions of rationality seems correct. Kroon is also correct in conceding to Conee the generality of the paradox. Indeed, its generality is what makes it relevant to the instability cases discussed in the Newcomb literature. Whereas standard instability cases concern prudence, Kroon's utilitarian paradox concerns morality. Since utilitarianism treats morality as group prudence, this does not constitute a structural difference.

It might be suggested we can find a structural difference in the fact that the instability situations discussed in the Newcomb literature do not actually imply the omissive 'p if and only if it is not judged that p'. They instead imply the commissive 'If it is judged that p then $-p$; and if it is judged that $-p$ then p.' This divergence is significant in that the latter implication seems to offer an unproblematic stance toward p: suspending judgement. Nevertheless, the omissive offshoots of common instability cases pose essentially the same challenge to two-boxers. For example, if Skyrm's mean demon has placed the thousand in box A just in case you do not believe it is in A, we get essentially the same puzzle as the original. The stability requirement implies that the chooser of A will not believe that B is the better option. Yet his knowledge of the demon's predictive powers assures that he would believe it. Since this knowledge also enables the chooser of B to deduce that A is better, this alternative is also ruled out. So once again, we appear to have a counter-example to the stability requirement.

V. ANTI-EXPERTISE AND MOORE'S PROBLEM

A. *The Hidden Moorean Implication*

Recall that in the Death case, Death meets victims on the basis of

---

[22] Frederick Kroon, 'Rationality and Paradox: A Reply to Conee', *Analysis*, 43/3 (June 1983), 159–60.

virtually infallible predictions. Furthermore, the traveller knows that he is scheduled to meet Death at either Aleppo or Damascus, and that he must go to exactly one of these two places. So the traveller is persuaded that

> (1) If I choose to go to Aleppo, then I will meet Death at Aleppo; and if I choose to go to Damascus, I will meet Death at Damascus.

Since the traveller knows that he is rational, he realizes that he will not choose to go to Aleppo if he believes that Death will meet him there.

> (2) If I choose to go to Aleppo, then it is not the case that I believe that I will meet Death at Aleppo; and if I choose to go to Damascus, then it is not the case that I believe I will meet Death at Damascus.

Although he does not seem to have better grounds for picking one over the other, we do know that he will make a choice. But upon making his choice, he will be aware of it. So given that he chooses to go to Aleppo, the traveller believes

> (3) I choose to go to Aleppo.

The conjunction of (1), (2), and (3) is consistent. Perhaps some of the traveller's companions even believe the conjunction. However, the traveller cannot rationally believe the conjunction. For if he believes the conjunction, his commitment to (2) and (3) requires him to believe

> (4) It is not the case that I believe that I will meet Death in Aleppo.

Yet the traveller's commitment to (1) and (3) also requires him to believe

> (5) I will meet Death in Aleppo.

Thus the traveller's belief in the conjunction of (1), (2), and (3) commits him to believing the Moorean sentence

> (6) I will meet Death in Aleppo, but it is not the case that I believe it.

As is typical with Moorean sentences, the proposition expressed by (6) is consistent but 'unbelievable'. The sense in which (6) cannot be believed has been specified in Chapter 1. For present purposes, it will suffice to observe that the properties standardly assumed for ideal agents prevent them from consistently believing Moorean sentences. For their inferential thoroughness ensures that belief in (6) leads to logically necessary error. One would have to believe Death will be met in Aleppo and believe that one lacked this belief, making it impossible for both beliefs to be correct. Since we are assuming that the traveller is ideally rational, we must conclude that he avoids the inconsistency of believing (6) by not accepting the conjunction of (1), (2), and (3).

We ought not to ask 'What would he do if he believed the conjunction?' For that would be like trying to answer 'What happens when an irresistible force meets an immovable object?' without denying the presupposition that such a confrontation is possible. This is the problem with the answer provided by Gibbard and Harper. In effect, they accept the supposition that the traveller can know the conjunction and deduce that the traveller's choice will be irrational. Since they are deducing from inconsistent premisses, their deduction is valid but unsound. Instead of attributing the strangeness of their conclusion to the strangeness of the situation, they should deny the possibility of the situation.

Given that the conjunction of (1), (2), and (3) cannot be accepted, it is natural to wonder whether a particular conjunct would be rejected. As illustrated by the Preface and Lottery paradoxes, belief in the members of the conjunction does not require belief in the conjunction itself. Rejection of a conjunct is only required if it threatens the coherency of one's probability judgements. Since the number of conjuncts is small, one can show that a particular conjunct would not be accepted if the remaining conjuncts were shown to warrant a sufficiently high joint probability. Thus arguments to the effect that a particular conjunct would be rejected under the pressure of inconsistency should be understood as assigning high probabilities to the remaining conjuncts. Although it would be difficult to build a case for the non-acceptance of a particular conjunct if the agent were an ordinary one, we have the good fortune of working with an ideal agent. So we can ignore the distractions of forgetfulness, inattentiveness, wishful thinking, and so on.

My thesis is that the traveller in the Death case would not believe (1). In order to give a point to viewing the traveller as an ideal thinker, we must suppose that he is aware of his choices. We postulate ideal thinkers to study the ways in which beliefs and desires give rise to choices. So ignorance about one's choice requires ignorance about the associated beliefs and desires. But to the extent that the ideal thinker is ignorant of his beliefs and desires, he lacks the data necessary for an ideally rational choice. Yet by definition, ideal agents make the best choice available given their beliefs and desires. So given that the traveller chooses to go to Aleppo, he will believe that he has made that choice. Thus (3) will be believed by virtue of the self-intimating nature of (ideally rational) choice. The traveller's belief in (2) follows from (R), the principle that rational agents do not wittingly pick inferior alternatives. So only (1) remains as a candidate for non-acceptance.

Although Richter would agree that the traveller will believe (3), his view that the instability cases are counter-examples to (R) would lead him to say that the traveller would not believe (2). For if Richter is right in maintaining that ideal agents will wittingly choose an inferior alternative in an instability situation, this truth would be as evident to ideal agents as it is to Richter. But since Richter wishes to conclude that (R) is false on the basis of situations like the Death case, he cannot assume the falsehood of (R) in describing the situation. He must instead maintain that the conjunction of (2) and (3) would be more plausible to the traveller than the conjunction of (1) and (3). This is a formidable task in view of his concession that denying (R) is highly counter-intuitive and the fact that (R) implies the negation of (2) given awareness of one's choice. Recall that belief in (1) is belief in a remarkable pair of conditionals:

(1) If I choose to go to Aleppo, then I will meet Death at Aleppo; and if I choose to go to Damascus, I will meet Death at Damascus.

Why should the traveller believe this? It is especially doubtful in view of the fact that it cannot be consistently believed given acceptance of a highly intuitive principle about rational choice and awareness of one's choice. Of course, it would be question-begging of Richter to merely point out that the traveller has been stipulated to have this knowledge or to claim that (1) is known by authority. The only non-question-begging reason for thinking that (1) could be accepted by the traveller lies in the possibility of his being convinced by strong empirical evidence. My position is that no amount of empirical evidence could rationally convince the traveller of (1).

B. *Overshadowed Hypotheses*

My position is supported by examples of consistent hypotheses that cannot be rationally believed regardless of the available evidence. For instance:

(7) It is raining but it is not the case that I believe it.
(8) My memory is completely unreliable.
(9) Perpetual motion machines are impossible but I am trying to build one.
(10) The successor of the largest number ever conceived is 8,392,192,043.
(11) Sentience is impossible.
(12) The world popped into existence five minutes ago complete with fossil records, 'memories', and so on.

Although (7) simply records an omissive error, I can never acquire evidence that will justify belief in it. Suppose, for example, I can simultaneously observe the rain falling outside and the output of a reliable belief-reading machine. What happens if the machine says that I do not believe it is raining? According to Arthur Collins, I would then be justified in believing (7). But as Collins notes, this is impossible. He therefore maintains that we must reject the supposition which implies the impossibility, namely, the assumption that such belief-reading machines are possible. Since brain-reading machines would be possible if beliefs were internal representations in the brain, Collins concludes that beliefs cannot be internal representations in the brain.[23] However, the fact that a belief-reading machine could not make (7) convincing fails to show such machines to be impossible. Simultaneous observation of rainy weather and the machine would only prompt a Duhemian response. The observer will avoid the inconsistency of believing (7) by revising background beliefs. Instead of believing (7), he will suspect that the machine is either being misread, or is malfunctioning, or is a fake, or that something he cannot yet identify has gone awry. For him, evidence in favour of (7) is like evidence in favour of $2 + 2 = 3$. Rather than accept such 'evidence' at face value, we will try to explain the evidence away. The hypothesis that (7) is true will always be *overshadowed* by some other hypothesis.

A hypothesis is overshadowed (in the eyes of an individual *a*) just in case *a* must always regard one of the hypothesis's rivals as a superior explanation of the available evidence. Since appeals to explanatory dominance seek to rule out the possibility of overshadowed hypotheses becoming acceptable by accumulating evidence, they attract the charge of dogmatism. In order for this charge to be effective, it must be shown that the appeal involves an *irrational* insensitivity to evidence. Merely pointing out that new evidence will not change someone's mind does not suffice to convict him of dogmatism. Assuming so begs the question against the proponent of explanatory domination.

The dogmatism charge is especially dubious when it amounts to the claim that someone refuses to let new evidence lead him to a position that he cannot consistently hold. Given that it is the *irrationality* of dogmatism that we are trying to avoid, we hardly succeed by embracing any of (7)–(12). Just as our ideal traveller cannot believe (7)–(12), he cannot believe

> (13) It is best to go to Damascus but I choose to go to Aleppo.

Although a weak-willed person might believe (13), an ideally rational agent cannot. Yet (13) does follow if the traveller believes (1) and (3) and views the avoidance of Death as best. The spirit of the stability requirement is embodied in the intuition that belief in (13) implies a defective decision. This intuition gains support from

---

[23] Collins advances his argument in 'Could Our Beliefs Be Representations in Our Brains?', *Journal of Philosophy*, 76/5 (May 1979), 225–43.

the resemblance between (13) and (7)–(12). For these examples show how consistent propositions can be as rationally repulsive as inconsistent ones. Since we are warranted in making costly revisions to our background assumptions to escape acceptance of an inconsistent proposition, we are also justified in paying a high price to avoid positions which cannot be consistently accepted.

C. *'Anti-expert' as a Personal Blindspot Predicate*

A general solution to the instability cases can be gleaned from the peculiar nature of 'anti-expertise'. Someone is a commissive anti-expert about p if and only if his belief that p is strong evidence that $-p$ and his belief that $-p$ is strong evidence that p. Someone is an omissive anti-expert about p just in case p is true if and only if it is not the case that he believes it. All instability cases require that the decision-maker predicate 'anti-expert' of himself. My objection is that decision-makers cannot do this. For this type of self-predication is as illegitimate as self-predication of 'modest', 'dead', and 'popular solipsist'. Thus my complaint is that commentators on the instability cases have overlooked the fact that 'anti-expert' is a personal blindspot predicate.

It's all right to believe that *someone else* is anti-expert. For example, some people who speculate in the stock-market, 'contrarians', ascribe anti-expertise to the consensus view. Other speculators view odd-lot traders as anti-experts. Still others profess confidence in the anti-expertise of physicians and dentists. It is also all right to believe that you *were* an anti-expert. Indeed, developmental psychology suggests that we all go through periods of anti-expertise. To test for comprehension of the distinction between active and passive sentences, T. G. Bever asked young children to act out the following sentences.[24]

(a) The alligator chases the tiger.
(b) The tiger is chased by the alligator.

Children between two and two and a half years old performed only slightly better than chance, suggesting that they were using word

[24] The following results are discussed in T. G. Bever's 'The Cognitive Basis for Linguistic Structures', in J. R. Hayes, *Cognition and the Development of Language* (New York: Wiley, 1970), 279–362.

order to infer the underlying sentence structure. Those older than two and a half did increasingly better with active sentences but not with passives. Indeed, performance on passives grew worse, bottoming out at about three and a half when it was significantly worse than chance. The explanation is that the children had acquired the Subject-Verb-Object rule but were over-generalizing it to Noun-Verb-Noun sentences. Since the child is doing worse than chance, an outsider can do better than chance by betting in favour of the negation of the child's answer. Over-generalization is a pervasive side-effect of learning. It is likely that everyone is an anti-expert about some (almost invariably trivial) issues. So it is reasonable to believe that you are now an anti-expert about some proposition or other. What is unreasonable is to believe that you are now an anti-expert about a specified proposition.

An anti-expert is as useful as an expert since you can convert anti-expert beliefs into expert beliefs by accepting their negations. Well almost as useful. An anti-expert's beliefs aren't useful to himself. For given that the anti-expert follows out the consequences of his beliefs, he cannot realize that he is an anti-expert and also be aware of his beliefs about p. Belief that p would commit him to believing $-p$ and vice versa. Could suspending judgement help? Certainly not in the case of omissive anti-expertise. As Kroon's utilitarian paradox illustrates, when suspended judgement about p implies p, self-awareness precludes neutrality.

Conee, in effect, tries to save self-predication of 'anti-expertise' by denying thoroughness. In addition to the defects cited by Kroon, Conee's proposal fails to reflect the tight connection between inference and belief. Recall that Conee asserts that a rational agent can fail to believe the conclusion of the argument even though he believes the conjunction of the premises and realizes that the argument instantiates a valid argument form. My objection is that we cannot distinguish between the person who believes the conclusion of the argument and the fellow who recognizes that a conclusion follows from an accepted conjunction. The recognition constitutes belief. To believe p is to regard p as true, and vice versa. If I recognize that p follows from true premises, I believe p. So if I recognize that p follows from (collectively) believed premises, I believe p. A second objection is that even if the belief/recognition distinction can be sustained, the basic problem is left unresolved. For the puzzle can be revived by reformulating it in terms of recognition rather than belief.[25]

Given dissatisfaction with Conee's proposal, one might instead deny that the agent is aware of his doxastic states. Like the notion that an ideal agent can be ignorant of his own choice, the suggestion that he is ignorant of his beliefs and non-beliefs undermines the point of invoking ideal thinkers. The point is to see how belief and desires give rise to rational choice. Once the agent is denied access to his beliefs, his decision problem is underdetermined. A second problem is that it is unclear how such ignorance can be sustained. The agent's incoming information about his behaviour and inclinations would give him doxastic clues. Even if this ignorance could be sustained, there would remain a problem concerning the rationality of the agent's beliefs. The rationality of a doxastic state is at least partly determined by its coherence with other doxastic states. Ignorance of these states prevents coherence verdicts.

Since we cannot plausibly deny thoroughness or self-awareness, we should conclude that self-predication of *omissive* anti-expertise is impossible for the sort of ideal agents that interest decision theorists and epistemologists. Although this conclusion would handle puzzles such as Kroon's and Milner's, what about cases involving *commissive* anti-expertise? Suspending judgement seems like a viable option for someone who credits himself with this sort of reverse competence.

The first difficulty with saying that the (commissive) anti-expert suspends judgement is that it commits him to a type of dogmatism. For he must discount any evidence for propositions within his field of expertise as misleading evidence. For if he believed that the evidence for p was not misleading, he would be inclined to believe p and so his neutrality would be breached. The anti-expert cannot accept the testimony of others, he cannot believe his eyes if he sees Death settle in Damascus, nor can he believe any refutation of the case for him being an anti-expert. He can only sustain his suspended judgement by becoming insensitive to new information. But this is dogmatic and ideally rational choosers are not dogmatic.

As a corollary to the dogmatism charge, it should also be noted

---

[25] I owe this second objection to Frederick Kroon (personal correspondence 1986).

that the anti-expert will not be able to recognize his own choice. For given belief in (1) and (2), he cannot believe (3). So if he goes to Aleppo, what entitles us to say that he *chose* to go? Rejecters of the stability requirement do agree that the traveller will choose one destination or the other. In order to make their case that there has been a choice, they must attribute some means-end reasoning to the travel. But this sort of reasoning can only take place if the traveller is in a position to make predictions about the consequences of choosing one way or the other. Since some of the essential predictions are within his field of anti-expertise, they constitute beliefs that breach his assumed neutrality.

A second difficulty with the suspended judgement position is that it leaves the anti-expert no way of verifying that he is still an anti-expert. For he cannot observe the reliability of his beliefs within his field of anti-expertise (for he has none).

The problem of verifying whether one is still an anti-expert is related to a third, logically prior difficulty of explaining how one could learn that one was an anti-expert. It would be illegitimate to just stipulate that the anti-expert acquired overwhelming evidence or that he knows it by authority. Presumably he learned it from past trials. For example, one might suppose that he has witnessed one hundred previous victims of Death.

The first shortcoming of this answer is the representativeness of the traveller's sample. Death's first victim could not have realized that he was an anti-expert because he did not have the benefit of a previous sample. Death's second victim only had a sample of one. In general, each victim differs from his predecessor in having a larger sample. If there is a sample sufficient to warrant the conclusion that one is an anti-expert, then there is a first such sample. This sample must warrant the conclusion without containing any members who are warranted in believing themselves to be anti-experts. The conclusion will be warranted by the sample only in so far as one resembles the members of that sample. But to the extent that the resemblance is strong, you have evidence that you, like they, are unwarranted in concluding that you are an anti-expert. So since there cannot be a first self-acknowledged anti-expert, there cannot be any at all.

One reaction to this argument is to dismiss it as a variety of the sorites paradox. It might be insisted that the vagueness of 'warranted' produces borderline cases of 'anti-experts warranted in believing themselves to be anti-experts'. However, the appeal to borderline cases provides no refuge. A person who has borderline warrant would be neither clearly warranted nor clearly unwarranted in believing he is an anti-expert about p. Yet he would also believe p. But if he is not clearly unwarranted in believing himself to be an anti-expert, then he is not clearly warranted in taking p to be clearly more likely that $-p$. But a necessary condition for having rational belief in p is having clear warrant for believing p is more likely than $-p$. So the appeal to borderline cases fails because of the link between suspected anti-expertise about p and belief that p.

Further support for the view that 'anti-expert' cannot be justifiably self-ascribed comes from cases where it is plainer that anti-expertise should not be assumed. Suppose that you are to choose between receiving $100 and $10. Prior to choosing you have an opportunity to sell your right to take the larger sum of money for $10. A predictor who you know to be 90 per cent reliable, tells you that he predicts you will not take the $100. Thus the expected value of selling out is $20 and of not selling out is ($100 × 0.1) + ($10 × 0.9) = $19. Rather than acting in accordance with this expected utility calculation, the agent should be sceptical about his anti-expertise and not sell out.

VI. CONCLUSIONS ABOUT INSTABILITY CASES

I have portrayed the problem raised by instability cases as akin to the question 'If you believe "It is raining but you do not believe it", should you bring an umbrella?' Someone who takes the question at face value might be puzzled. On the one hand, he should take an umbrella because it is raining. On the other hand, he should not take the umbrella since he does not believe it is raining. Such puzzlement would be the product of a false presupposition. You cannot believe 'It is raining but you do not believe it', so it is pointless to speculate as to how your desires would link with your beliefs about the situation to generate a decision.

The instability cases are sophisticated variants of the above question. Their power to puzzle us emanates from the fact that we fail to detect the fact that they are inconsistent suppositions. By attending to part of the supposition, we are led to one conclusion. Attending to another part leads us to its negation.

We fail to detect the inconsistency of the supposition because we overestimate the epistemic access of agents. As Moore's problem shows, there are consistent propositions that cannot be consistently, correctly, and thoroughly believed. Hence, the agents in question cannot discover the truth of those propositions. Others can be in a position to discover these truths just as others can believe 'It is raining but you do not believe it' despite the fact that you cannot. Outsiders can know I am an anti-expert about p. My scepticism about anti-expertise is epistemological not metaphysical. Indeed, even I can know that I am anti-expert about some proposition or other. I only deny the possibility of knowing that I am anti-expert about a specific proposition. The impossibility of recognizing one's own anti-expertise makes it impossible for agents to know what describers of instability situations stipulate they know. Therefore fully-fledged instability situations (those requiring awareness of one's anti-expertise) are impossible. So they are not counter-examples to the stability requirement. Therefore, two-boxers remain free to appeal to the requirement in their analysis of Newcomb's problem.

12
The Slippery Slope Fallacy

HAVING presented support for my solutions to the defective mathematical inductions individually, I now wish to support them in a collective manner. That is, I wish to supplement the piecemeal analyses with a background theory that explains why these analyses should work. The point is to persuade the reader that the best way of accounting for the separate merits of the analyses is by the hypothesis that the analyses are fundamentally correct. I will cultivate this belief through a general study of slippery slope arguments. For I take the sorites, the prediction paradox, and the super-game puzzles to be just sophisticated instances of the slippery slope fallacy. The puzzles that have held centre stage in this book lie on a continuum with more elementary slippery slope arguments. Study of blindspots reveals the nature of this continuum and suggests a recipe for concocting 'mendacious mathematical inductions'. In addition to accounting for the old inductions it can be used to cook up novel slippery slope arguments. Some of those found in the sample batch are comparable in power to the familiar examples. So, besides confirming the blindspot theory about the structure of the initial list of paradoxes, the new puzzles constitute further obstacles for rival accounts of the old puzzles. They also narrow down the competition for the title of 'best account of the slippery slope fallacy'. For only accounts centring on blindspots can offer a unified explanation, free of radical bifurcations between classically fallacious and deviantly fallacious slippery slope arguments.

I. HYPOTHETICAL V. CATEGORICAL SLIPPERY SLOPE ARGUMENTS

It has been observed that what is known as mathematical induction within mathematics is known as the slippery slope fallacy outside it. (As Bernard Le Bovier Fontenelle remarked, 'Mathematicians are like lovers. . . . Grant a mathematician the least principle, and he will draw from it a consequence which you must also grant him, and from this consequence another.') We need not strain to see the similarity between mathematical induction and informal slippery slope arguments. First consider the form of hypothetical slippery slope arguments:

S_1 leads to S_2
S_2 leads to S_3
.
.
.
S_k leads to S_{k+1}
―――――――――
S_1 leads to S_{k+1}

Categorical slippery slope arguments are obtained by adding S_1 as a premiss and changing the conclusion to S_{k+1}. In both cases, the arguer intends 'leads' to be read as some relation he takes to be transitive such as 'causes', 'is a precedent for', or 'implies'. Some slippery slope arguments are homogenous with respect to the relation, assigning only one reading of 'leads' throughout the argument. Frequently, they are heterogenous. Heterogenous relata are sometimes found in their wake. Thus S_1, S_2, . . . can consist of a mixture of propositions, states, or events.

Since the material conditional is well understood and propositions are more familiar to logicians than events, states, and so on, the cause of clarity is usually served by recasting slippery slope arguments into a form suitable for analysis in terms of standard sentential and predicate logic. The sanitized slippery slope will then be found to be a large scale version of hypothetical syllogism. How long must the slippery slope argument's chain of hypothetical statements be? Our confidence in calling something a slippery slope argument increases with increases in its number of premisses. Many might therefore think that we must settle for the vague answer 'Slippery slope arguments must have many premisses'. But whatever arbitrariness there is in answering, 'At least three' seems to be of the warrantable sort that we find in good precisifying definitions. For in addition to bringing about a tidy classification, it avoids resistance from those unwilling to countenance vague argument forms. In any case, my remarks apply equally to the ordinary notion of slippery slope reasoning and its (perhaps) precisified counterpart.

Mathematical inductions can be shown to be categorical slippery slope arguments by interpreting $S_1, S_2, \ldots$ as propositions and 'leads to' as the material conditional.

1. S_1
2. If S_k then S_{k+1}.

For all n, S_n.

Since the induction step merely abbreviates the chain of hypotheticals, mathematical induction is just a species of categorical slippery slope arguments.

Hypothetical slippery slope arguments are the rule in deliberative contexts. For here the point of exhibiting a slippery slope is to influence a decision. Usually this is done by presenting a slope that has a bad bottom. The arguer tries to dissuade us from taking the first step that will send us tumbling to the bottom. In order for there to be the possibility of someone heeding the warning, a slide down the slope cannot be a foregone conclusion. Hypothetical slippery slope arguments dissuade by convincing the audience that an apparently acceptable state will lead (by degrees) to an obviously unacceptable state. Once the audience assents to this consequence, the choice becomes an all or nothing affair. Were it not for the popularity of this pattern of persuasion, De Quincey's objection to murder would go unappreciated:

> For, if once a man indulges himself in murder, very soon he comes to think little of robbing, and from robbing he comes next to drinking and Sabbath-breaking, and from that to incivility and procrastination. Once begin upon this downward path, you never know where you are to stop. Many a man dated his ruin from some murder or other that perhaps he thought little of at the time.[1]

More rarely, the bottom of the slope is pictured as good. 'Supply side' economists (or is it supply side 'economists'?) argued this way. Cutting taxes will lead to more productivity, which leads to larger incomes, which generates a larger tax base, which in turn yields about the same revenue that would have been obtained at

---

[1] Thomas De Quincey, 'Of Murder, Considered as one of the Fine Arts' in *De Quincey's Works* (Edinburgh: Adam and Charles Black, 1863), 4.

The Slippery Slope Fallacy

the higher tax rate. Result: a more prosperous public without a loss of tax revenue. A similar slide into prosperity is envisioned by the following proponent of land reform for famine-prone countries:

> With effective land redistribution, many more farmers get a homestead. Thus, rural unemployment (commonly 30 per cent) tends to disappear. With land (and thus money) of their own, the former poor buy more food and become stronger; hence the quantity and the quality of labor force simultaneously increase.
>
> Moreover, the labor force now has reason to work hard and to seek out new ways to improve yields. Output improves, and because it is more evenly distributed, so do health and education, which in turn further improve output. Farm demand leads now to appropriate industrialization—shoes, hammocks, roofs (not El Dorados)—which in turn leads to greater demand for farm goods, and so on.[2]

A third example of an optimistic slippery slope can be drawn from Confucius in *The Great Learning*:

If there be righteousness in the heart,
there will be beauty in the character.
If there be beauty in the character,
there will be harmony in the home.
If there be harmony in the home,
there will be order in the nation.
If there be order in the nation,
there will be peace in the world.

To insist that slippery slopes can never have bottoms that are judged good would make the argument form relative to the speaker. Consider the 'domino' argument concerning the spread of communism. In the eyes of the capitalist, the slippery slope has a bad bottom. In the eyes of the communist, it has a good bottom. Are we to say that the argument in the mouth of the capitalist is a slippery slope, but that it is not when in the mouth of the communist?

Given that the arguer has indeed chosen a transitive reading of 'leads', the argument is valid. So the widespread suspicion that slippery slope arguments are fallacious cannot be explained in

---

[2] Nick Eberstadt, 'Myths of the Food Crisis', in James Rachels (ed.), *Moral Problems*, 3rd edn., (New York: Harper & Row, 1979), 311.

terms of their invalidity. David White has argued that we must also rule out explanations that claim that these arguments are unpersuasive or characteristically contain a false premiss.[3] White then draws the heterodox conclusion that slippery slope arguments are not fallacious.[4]

Other commentators hold a mixed position. Some separate the good from the bad by emphasizing differences in the empirical support for the premisses.[5] Other holders of the mixed position place more emphasis on form. For example, Trudy Govier maintains that there are several argument forms subsumed under the label of 'slippery slope argument'. Some of the forms are fallacious, some are not. She lists three fallacious versions. The first sort commit the 'fallacy of assimilation' which is a matter of inferring 'that differences in degree cannot cumulate into a significant difference simply on the grounds that they *are* differences of degree'.[6] According to Govier, this explains the sorites:

> Logicians have not been interested in *sorites* primarily for its possibilities for generating fallacious assimilations. What has traditionally interested them is its revelation of the imprecise boundaries for the application of terms in ordinary language, and the prospect that this imprecision may leave truth value gaps and how such gaps, once postulated, should be handled by logical theory, are not issues which I can presume to treat here. In any case, their resolution is not required for the explanation of that fallacy of assimilation which some have called 'slippery slope'.[7]

Slippery slope arguments of the second sort are guilty of inconsistent premisses while the third sort assume a false 'all or nothing' dilemma. But in addition to these bad kinds of argument. Govier presents the following kind as a good sort:

1. Case (a) is prima facie acceptable.
2. Cases (b), (c), . . . (n) are unacceptable.

---

[3] White's analysis is presented in 'Slippery Slope Arguments', *Metaphilosophy*, 16/2–3 (Apr.–July 1985), 206–13.

[4] White notes that he is not the first to draw this conclusion. L. S. Stebbing endorses slippery slope arguments in *Thinking to Some Purpose* (Harmondsworth: Penguin, 1939), 200–4.

[5] This is one of Frederick Schaur's themes in 'Slippery Slopes', *Harvard Law Review*, 99/2 (Dec. 1985), 361–83. This article contains an excellent collection of legal examples of the argument.

[6] Trudy Govier, 'What's Wrong with Slippery Slope Arguments?', *Canadian Journal of Philosophy*, 12/2 (June 1982), 307.

[7] Ibid., 308.

3. Cases (a) ... (n) are assimilable, as they differ from each other only by degrees, and are arrangeable as a spectrum of cases.
4. As a matter of psychological fact, people are likely to assimilate cases (a)–(n).
5. Case (a), if permitted, will be taken as a precedent for the others, (b)–(n).
6. Permitting (a) will cause the permission of (b)–(n).
7. Case (a) should therefore not be permitted.[8]

Govier maintains that someone could avoid the variety of pitfalls associated with this argument and thereby provide a good slippery slope argument.

Govier does not provide a 'real life' example of a good slippery slope argument. Scepticism about our talent for psychological predictions provides grounds for doubting that her schema will help fill the gap. For the schema embodies three psychological predictions at premises 4, 5, and 6. Govier does provide examples of fallacious slippery slope arguments. Standard worries about charitable interpretation may lead some to doubt whether the examples really instantiate the forms she describes. For the errors she attributes are not subtle. Is it probable that the likes of Bertrand Russell and W. V. Quine are guilty of the fallacy of assimilation? Contrary to what Govier suggests, the literature on the sorites does not primarily concern the intricacies of truth-value gaps. Truth-value gaps are only a means to the end of revealing a flaw in sorites arguments. Virtually everyone agrees that insignificant differences can add up to a significant difference. The problem is to translate this observation into a *specific* objection to the sorites. As it stands, the observation does not tell us that a particular premiss is false or whether the argument is invalid. Thus the fallacy of assimilation does not explain what is wrong with slippery slope arguments of the sorites variety.

Govier's remaining subfallacies are special instances of two other general fallacies: inconsistent premises and false dilemma. So we are left with a hodgepodge.

II. JOINT PROBABILITIES

The blindspot analysis of the defective mathematical inductions suggests that our craving for generality can be satisfied. For it

[8] Ibid., 315.

suggests that the widespread suspicion of slippery slope arguments is correct, and that it is correct because of a standard malfunction. The central function of an argument's premises is to support the conclusion. Premises support a conclusion only when they make the conclusion significantly more assertible. Unless the argument has redundant premises, support is lent only when the premises have a high joint probability.[9] Most examples of slippery slope arguments fail to satisfy this necessary condition for support. Slippery slope arguments are in fertile ground for this failure because they have a large number of premises. Often the insufficient support passes undetected because people focus on the individual probabilities of the premises rather than on their collective probability. This accounts for the frequency with which people can be puzzled by an argument such as the following:

1. If the die does not yield a six in one roll, then it will not yield a six in two rolls.
2. If the die does not yield a six in two rolls, then it will not yield a six in three rolls.
3. If the die does not yield a six in three rolls, then it will not yield a six in four rolls.
4. If the die does not yield a six in four rolls, then it will not yield a six in five rolls.
5. If the die does not yield a six in one roll, then it will not yield a six in five rolls.

Slippery slope arguments tend to look better than they are because people tend to estimate the strength of support by a measure other than joint probability. Some seem to operate by averaging the probabilities. Others seem to use an acceptance rule. They believe each premiss because each has a high probability. Still others go by the least probable premiss. This procedure is encouraged by standards of argumentative sportsmanship. Given that you accept the validity of the argument, refusal to accept the conclusion is felt to obligate the rejection of a particular premiss. Thus a valid

---

[9] An argument has redundant premises if and only if deletion of one of its premisses leaves the argument valid. For a general study of the conditions under which the joint probability requirement fails to be satisfied, see Ernest W. Adams and Howard P. Levine, 'On the Uncertainties Transmitted from Premises to Conclusions in Deductive Inferences', *Synthese*, 30/3–4 (Apr.–May 1975), 429–60.

argument is thought to be as compelling as its weakest premiss. A second reason for measuring the strength of an argument this way is the belief that a chain is as strong as its weakest link. However, an argument containing a chain of interlocking conditionals is normally weaker than its weakest link. For example, each premiss of the above argument has a probability of ⅚ but their joint probability is only (⅚)^4 which is less than ½. So although the argument is valid and has highly probable premisses, it fails to make its conclusion probable.

The joint probability requirement states that a cogent argument with no redundant premisses must have premisses with a high joint probability. Most bad slippery slope arguments are bad because they fail to satisfy this necessary condition for being a good argument. Slippery slope arguments that do not run foul of this requirement come in three varieties.

A. *Improbable Antecedents and Vacuous Slopes*

The first group is comprised of arguments that have a conditional conclusion whose antecedent is highly improbable. Suppose you know that I spend much of my spare time playing tennis and that I am heavily insured against personal injury. You may hear me argue as follows:

1. If I lose all of my limbs, then I will receive a million dollars from my insurance company.
2. If I receive a million dollars, then I will be rich.
3. If I become rich, I will have more leisure time.
4. If I get more leisure time, I will play more tennis.
5. If I lose all of my limbs, I will play more tennis.

Since the conclusion is a material conditional, it is only false if the antecedent is true and the consequent false. Since the probability of the antecedent is extremely low, it is extremely unlikely that the conditional is false. This means that the probability of the conclusion is indeed high. So the deflationary effect of the joint probability requirement is not responsible for the argument's unacceptability.

The argument is nevertheless a poor one. Despite the conclusion's high probability, it is not assertible. As commentators on conditionals have noted, the assertibility of 'If A then B' goes by the conditional probability of B given A, not the probability of the conditional. The function of an argument's premises is to make the conclusion assertible. Making the conclusion probable is a necessary condition for the execution of this function, not a sufficient condition. So when the conclusion is a conditional, as is the case for hypothetical slippery slope arguments, the arguer needs a way of propounding his premises that will raise the conditional probability of the conclusion. The premises will confer a high conditional probability on the conclusion if one employs 'restricted' conditionals whose antecedents incorporate all the antecedents of the preceding conditionals. Thus restricted slippery slope reasoning does ensure that the conditional probability of the conclusion is high given that the joint probability of the premises is high.[10]

1. If S_1 then S_2.
2. If S_1 and S_2, then S_3.
3. If S_1 and S_2 and S_3, then S_4.
  .
  .
  .
k If S_1 and S_2 and . . . and S_k, then S_{k+1}.
k + 1. If S_1 then S_{k+1}.

The argument about the limbless tennis player does not fit this form because we cannot restrict the last premiss's antecedent:

(i) If I lose all my limbs and receive a million dollars from the insurance company and get more leisure time, then I will play more tennis.

The restricted slippery slope reflects the practice of accumulating past suppositions when judging the acceptability of new suppositions.

The probability of a conditional is never lower than the conditional probability, and is almost always significantly higher.

---

[10] Restricted slippery slope arguments are the large scale version of Ernest Adam's restricted hypothetical syllogism discussed in *The Logic of Conditionals* (Dordrecht: D. Reidel, 1975), 22–3.

The two are only equal when both have a probability of 1 or the antecedent has a probability of 1. When the probability of the antecedent is 0, the material conditional obviously has a probability of 1 but calculating the conditional probability is problematic. Some commentators suggest that the value be 1, others leave it undefined. In either case, the argument is bad. For in either case the premises have not *raised* the conclusion's degree of assertibility. Thus arguments with vacuous slopes are defective even though there is no violation of the joint probability requirement.

B. *Redundant Slopes*

The second group consists of redundant arguments. Consider, for instance, an argument composed of distinct chains of interlocking premises. It would then suffice that only one of the chains held. Since this sort of argument would be a complex slippery slope argument composed of intertwined slopes leading to the same conclusion, its strength is equivalent to the probability that at least one of the corresponding simple slippery slope arguments has entirely true premises. A redundant slippery slope argument need not have distinct slopes. There might be a single slope containing branches. Indeed, a slippery slope argument can have a number of chains each with its own branches. Charitably interpreted, the domino argument about communist expansion contains a large number of chains whose branches blend into each other before they reach the bottom of world communism. This significantly enhances the argument's redundancy and hence its strength.

Although the various sorts of redundancy sometimes yield an argument that is even stronger than its strongest link, they can also fail to be as strong as their weakest link. Nevertheless, the redundancy will usually be beneficial. The question is whether it will be of sufficient benefit. The errors responsible for the high frequency with which the joint probability requirement is violated will also increase the frequency with which arguments are left insufficiently redundant. The ones with sufficient redundancy will be good slippery slope arguments. The ones without will be bad for much the same reason as those that violate the joint probability requirement. Since there is no special theoretical problem with detecting the sufficiently redundant examples, we could systematically produce good slippery slope arguments.

C. Certain Slopes and the Statistical Concept of Fallacy

The third group of slippery slope arguments are those whose premises enjoy a non-vacuous probability of 1. Since the joint probability remains 1 regardless of the number of premises, use of erroneous measures of support will never lead us to overestimate the degree of support. This explains why the slippery slope fallacy is harmless in mathematical and logical contexts. We are saved by the hospitality of the environment. Some of us enjoy similar good fortune with allergies, improperly wired homes, and clogged sprinkler systems. As long as the air is free of pollen, my allergy is harmless. As long as I do not run many appliances, my improperly wired home will not ignite. And as long as my warehouse is free of flames, a clogged sprinkler system is as useful as a functional one. Yet these considerations do not alter the fact that allergies, improper wiring, and clogged sprinkler systems are disorders. Likewise, the harmlessness of slippery slope arguments in cases where the premises enjoy a probability of 1 does not alter the fact that the argument *form* is fallacious. Bad argument types typically have some good argument tokens. One reason why people tend to think otherwise is a failure to observe the process/product ambiguity of such terms as 'argument', 'reasoning', and 'explanation'. The same ambiguity can be observed with 'spit', 'rip', 'statement', 'perception', 'distribution', and 'election'. The distinction is worth drawing because the process can be defective without the product being lamentable. Distributing an equally-owned pie by the height of the distributees is unjust. Here we are objecting to the distribution process. The product of distribution will be just if it so happens that the distributees are of equal height. In this lucky eventuality, there is no cause to redistribute since the product of the distribution is equivalent to the one that would have arisen through a just process of distribution. The product is fine. Likewise, the fallacious argument form of composition sometimes produces good arguments.[11]

> (i) All of the parts of this chair are brown, therefore, the chair is brown.

[11] The following examples are taken from William Rowe, 'The Fallacy of Composition', *Mind*, 71/281 (Jan. 1962), 87–92.

(ii) All of the parts of this desk are made of metal, therefore, this desk is made of metal.
(iii) All of the parts this object are located in space, therefore, this object is located in space.

But since valid instances of the compositional form are rare, and the instances are usually presented as deductive arguments, the compositional form is fallacious. The only arguments that can be determined invalid by form are those with only logically true premisses and a logically false conclusion. The remaining argument forms only provide a sufficient condition for validity, never a sufficient condition for invalidity. So if we were to require an adequate theory of fallacy to always predict invalidity by form, we could conclude that an adequate theory of fallacy is impossible. Rather than abandon the pursuit of a theory of fallacy we should question the proffered adequacy condition. Once we recognize that our criteria for what counts as a good argument go well beyond validity, we can cheerfully drop the demand for a purely formal means of identifying invalid argument tokens. The adjusted expectations pave the way for a statistical concept of fallacy. Under this view, fallacies are *types* of arguments which have an unusually high proportion of bad tokens. Thus fallacies are interesting to logicians in the same way that poor production schemes are of interest to quality control analysts. Comparisons between output populations can make it clear that something is wrong with the production process. Knowledge that a product was produced by a defective mechanism permits inferences about probable defects of that product. Likewise, knowledge that an argument token was produced in accordance with a fallacy permits inferences about its probable defects.

The foregoing was intended to make way for the concession that some slippery slope arguments are good arguments. However, it must be further conceded that good slippery slope arguments can be produced *systematically*. In such cases, the fallacy operates like a partially functional tool or machine. Pens that skip, fans stuck at low speed, and dictionaries with missing pages are all defective but do as well as their fully operational counterparts under special conditions. A person familiar with these narrowed conditions of utility can make these tools serve his ends without mishap. The same goes for the slippery slope fallacy. Although the form is defective, it can be applied in special circumstances to systematically yield non-fallacious argument tokens. Those aware of the nature of the malfunction can still apply the argument form in mathematics, logic, and even to certain empirical contexts. Teachers usually introduce mathematical induction with the empirical example of dominoes. Having lined up your dominoes, you can assign a very high probability to each conditional of the form 'If domino n falls over, then so does domino $n + 1$.' This will ensure that the joint probability requirement is satisfied as long as 'you don't go too far'. This constraint is recognized in domino-toppling competitions in Japan. For there are standard penalties for the number of dominoes that fail to topple when world records are being sought.

An argument form only qualifies as a fallacy if its population of tokens has a higher proportion of bad arguments than the average of other forms. The higher the proportion, the better the fallacy performs as a predictor. Often there are subpopulations with low ratios of bad to good arguments. By redefining the fallacy so as to exclude these subpopulations, one can enhance its value as a predictor. However, there are sometimes disadvantages to these redefinitions. If the amended definition specifies the topic of the argument, the fallacy loses its status as a topic-neutral means of appraising arguments. Second, simplicity and 'naturalness' may have been sacrificed. Lastly, the goal of the redefinition can usually be achieved at the level of application rather than theory. When there are no narrower reference classes to consider, we proceed with a simple statistical syllogism:

1. Most tokens of fallacy F are bad arguments.
2. <u>Token t is an instance of fallacy F.</u>
3. Token t is a bad argument.

When there are narrower reference classes to consider, information about them can be added as a premiss. This will alter the strength of the statistical argument. For example, learning that a slippery slope argument is of a psychological sort will enhance the strength of the meta-argument, while learning that it is mathematical will weaken it. Thus sensitivity to narrower reference classes can be reflected at the application stage instead of being directly incorporated into the theory. Adopting this strategy preserves the analogy with partially functioning machines. If a typewriter produces lower-case letters perfectly but cannot be coaxed into printing legible upper-case letters, we don't bother to distinguish between it as a good lower-case typewriter but a poor upper-case typewriter. It's just broken. But this is not to deny that it will do just fine in the e. e. cummings fan club.

D. *Explanation, Chain Reaction, and Speculation*

Environmental considerations also account for the fact that good slippery slope *explanations* are easier to construct than good slippery slope arguments. Explainers have two advantages. First, the proposition to be explained is not in controversy. Thus the explainer only has to provide reasons for something we already believe. The second advantage is that these reasons can be descriptions of the recent past. Since the recent past is easier to know than the future, reasons can be given with the benefit of hindsight. Consider the following explanation of how an individual became addicted to cigars: 'I smoked my first cigar at my sister's wedding. This led me to smoke cigars at social occasions. From there I wound up smoking a few privately at home. This made me crave them at work so I started smoking there too. All that smoking made any period without cigars uncomfortable. Thus my addiction to cigars can be traced back to my sister's wedding.' Here cigar addiction is explained by a long chain of events, the first being a remote cause of the last. Since phenomena such as addiction, repression, and bankruptcy often arise in a gradual manner, appeal to slippery slopes often constitutes an acceptable genetic explanation. The success of such explanations assures us that future phenomena will also arise in a slippery slope fashion. However, this does not provide much help in constructing good slippery slope predictions. Smoking one cigar rarely leads to addiction. Only hindsight gave the cigar smoker knowledge of how the causal chain would unfold.

Our knowledge of chain reactions enables us to make predictions that appear to be the conclusions of slippery slope arguments. For example, I know that if I turn the ignition of my car, the engine will start. I also know that this is due to a long sequence of intermediate events. Suppose I present the conditionals describing this sequence as the premisses of an argument having the prediction as a conclusion. Is the result a good slippery slope argument? If it is, it will not be hard to show that we are in a position to propound many good slippery slope arguments about empirical matters. The reason why our familiarity with chain reactions fails to provide a rich source of slippery slope arguments is that the premisses are not *raising* the assertibility of the conclusion. In normal arguments, each premiss is asserted on the basis of a separate piece of evidence (which explains why we list them separately).[12] But here our evidence for the conclusion is the basis for each premiss.

Scepticism about slippery slope arguments is compatible with the view that some of them have cautionary value. Given that the bottom of the speculated slope is highly undesirable even a small increase in the probability of reaching it can make the first step unacceptable. Recall early fears among physicists that splitting the atom would create a giant chain reaction destroying the world. The fear did not arise from their attaching a high probability to the conclusion of the slippery slope argument. They thought the conclusion improbable but they were not sure that the conclusion was improbable enough to warrant taking the first step, in view of the magnitude of the possible harm. This, incidentally, is the only value of slippery slope arguments against the construction of a 'ladder' of nuclear deterrence. The ladder consists of a range of nuclear alternatives designed to give the decision-maker the option of a proportional response rather than an all-or-nothing choice. At one end lies the explosion of an atomic bomb over an uninhabited area as a 'warning shot'. At the next rung, we find strikes against isolated military targets, such as fleets of enemy ships at sea. Higher up lie somewhat messier attacks against military establishments. Up further are nuclear attacks against the military's infrastructure (weapon manufacturers, transportation and communication centres, and so on). Purely civilian targets complete the ascent. The worry is that the availability of the ladder will incline leaders to take the first small step on the ladder, and then climb to the top by degrees, past steps serving as precedents for the successors.

---

[12] By 'separate' I mean that they are robust with respect to the negation of any of the remaining premisses. That is, the probability of the premiss given the negation of another premiss is high — you'd continue to assert it.

E. *Validity Illusions*

The joint probability requirement also explains why some invalid slippery slope reasoning looks valid. For ignorance of the requirement makes some intransitive relations, such as 'makes likely', look transitive. A more controversial candidate for pseudo-transitivity is 'causes'. E. J. Lowe urges that the following nursery rhyme reveals the non-transitivity of causation.[13]

> For want of a nail the shoe was lost,
> For want of a shoe the horse was lost,
> For want of a horse the rider was lost,
> For want of a rider the battle was lost,
> For want of a battle the kingdom was lost,
> And all for the want of a horseshoe nail.

Agreement with Lowe is influenced by one's views about the proper analysis of causation. Agreement should be expected from those who analyse 'cause' probabilistically. Disagreement should issue from those who identify causes with necessary or sufficient conditions. A mixed reaction can be expected from those who favour a counter-factual analysis. But regardless of whether one agrees with Lowe, one's misgivings about causal slippery slope arguments will emanate from the same source. Those who reject the causal arguments as invalid will diagnose the invalidity as arising from an illusion about the transitivity of causation. For they take causation to require that a minimum degree of something obtain between cause and effect. Since effects can themselves be causes, it is possible for this requirement to be satisfied between pairs of neighbouring events without being satisfied between more distant neighbours. Those who believe that 'causes' is transitive will of course grant the validity of the causal slippery slope argument. Nevertheless, they will object that the fact that we can say of each pair of neighbouring events that they probably stand in the relation of cause and effect does not imply that it is also probable that all of the neighbouring pairs stand in this relation.

Some of those who deny the transitivity of causation base the denial on the non-transitivity of similarity. For example, many analyses of causation in terms of counter-factuals evaluate these

[13] E. J. Lowe, 'For Want of a Nail', *Analysis*, 40/1 (Jan. 1980), 50–2.

conditionals in terms of the similarity between possible worlds. It is also plausible to analyse 'is a precedent for' in terms of a close similarity between cases. So causal and precedence slippery slope arguments may be invalid as they stand. However, the charge of invalidity can be avoided by sanitizing them. Suppose, for example, that I have cornered the market on water and defend myself by arguing that the permissibility of owning n litres of water is a precedent for owning $n + 1$ litres. In response to the objection that 'is a precedent for' is not transitive, I recast my argument in terms of material conditionals.

1. It is permissible for me to own one litre of water.
2. If it is permissible for me to own n litres of water, then it is also permissible for me to own $n + 1$ litres of water.
3. It is permissible for me to own all the water.

Since material implication is transitive, the objectors can no longer doubt the validity of my argument. Their doubts about the transitivity of precedence cannot be easily redirected to the truth of the induction step. For I have arranged the cases too closely to permit the specification of a counter-example.

III. COUNTER-EXAMPLE RESISTANCE AND MENDACIOUS GENERALIZATIONS

The point of taking small steps in constructing a slippery slope is to make each step undeniable. Often, slippery slope reasoners are too hasty. They succumb to the temptation of taking larger steps in order to reach their conclusion with fewer strides. Such impatience spoils the sophistry by rendering some individual premisses open to challenge. Greater patience remedies the flaw. High-grade fallacies require patient application of the slippery slopers' slogan: small is slow but sure. For only then does one obtain a 'slick' slippery slope, that is, an argument with undeniable premisses.

Mathematical induction counts amongst the slippery slopers' modern conveniences. For it produces top-grade slopes without time consuming 'manual construction'. For the conditionals constituting the slope are all neatly encapsulated in the induction step. All that is necessary is a special type of generalization that resists refutation by counter-example. Sorites paradoxes are distinguished by the fact that they satisfy this condition through the vagueness of the inductive predicate. The predicate ensures that all of the counter-examples to the induction step are blindspots. Thus none of the counter-examples can be used for the purpose of refuting the generalization.

A. *Recipe for Mendacious Mathematical Inductions*

The blindspot analysis of the defective mathematical inductions which have held centre stage in this book suggests a recipe for cooking up new slippery slope puzzles. The key to the procedure is to find a universal generalization that has four properties.

The first property is a type of counter-example resistance. A generalization is counter-example-resistant to an individual just in case he cannot refute the generalization with a counter-example. In the case of the sorites, the counter-example resistance is universal because all of the counter-examples are symmetrical blindspots to everyone. But since there are personal blindspots, one can also imagine the resistance being limited to just one individual. For example, I cannot think of a counter-example to the generalization that I will at some time think of every integer. Other generalizations will only be counter-example-resistant to members of certain schools of thought. Those who believe that universals exist may disagree about whether every universal has a corresponding predicate. The realist who wishes to reject this generalization will not be able to refute it by counter-example. Since nominalists deny the existence of universals, they can simply dismiss the generalization as vacuously true. In addition to the question of who is resisted, there is a second question of how strong the resistance is. At one extreme, 'cannot refuse' reads 'is logically impossible to refute'. At the other extreme, 'cannot refuse' amounts to a mild inconvenience. Slippery slope arguments are persuasive only when the degree of resistance is high enough to invite the inference that there are no counter-examples. So although we need not demand absolute counter-example resistance, the generalization must place a serious obstacle in the path of those who wish to construct a counter-example.

In addition to counter-example resistance, the generalization must appear to be non-vacuous. Since a categorical slippery slope argument takes as its base step an instance of the generalization's antecedent, suspected vacuity will make this premiss improbable. As we learned from traditional variations of the prediction paradox, persuasive categorical slippery slope arguments can have false base steps as long as they appear to be true. The important thing is not to get caught. Upon first hearing the surprise test version, virtually everyone grants that *obviously* the test cannot be given on the last day. This leads them to focus on the induction step of the argument which is in reality, vacuously true. For the generalization runs 'If the students can know that the test will not take place on day n, then the students can know that the test will not take place on day $n - 1$'. Since the antecedent is false for every n, the conditional is vacuously true. Nevertheless, this generalization makes for a fine slippery slope argument because it *looks* non-vacuous and is absolutely counter-example-resistant (indeed, its vacuous truth guarantees that it has no counter-examples).

To exploit the convenience of mathematical induction, our generalizations must also be sequential so that they can take the form of an induction step. With a bit of ingenuity, most of the generalizations satisfying the first two conditions can also be rearranged to satisfy the sequentiality requirement. As illustrated by the undiscoverable position paradox, a unique order is unnecessary. Given a multiplicity of slopes, we need only choose one of the paths to reach our destination. Let us call generalizations that satisfy the foregoing three conditions 'slippery generalizations'. The name is appropriate because sequential counter-example-resistant generalizations that appear to be non-vacuous suffice for the construction of categorical slippery slope arguments. For the apparent non-vacuousness of the generalization lays the groundwork for acceptance of the base step. And counter-example resistance ensures that each increment along the slope will go unchallenged.

However, we have yet to separate the good mathematical inductions from the bad. For the slippery generalization might owe the foregoing properties to the fact that it is well-supported and non-vacuously true. To filter these cases out, we must require that the generalization *cloak* any counter-examples it might have. Whether it actually has counter-examples is irrelevant. The truth of a generalization is a sufficient condition for counter-example resistance. Since there are other sufficient conditions, irrelevant to truth value, some counter-example resistance is overdetermined. Such is the case with true but cloaked generalizations. Cloaked generalizations that are false will not be overdetermined but will none the less resist refutation by counter-example. Without independent knowledge of the truth value of a cloaked generalization, we cannot figure out whether the resistance is of the overdetermined sort. So even if a generalization owes its resistance to its truth, it can still qualify as a cloaked generalization.

The mechanics of cloaked generalizations are most easily illustrated by concentrating on falsidical counter-example resistance. Should the cloaked generalization be false, it must have counter-examples, each of which is a blindspot. Given that the generalization has the form '$F_k \supset F_{k+1}$', this happens when every true statement of the form '$F_k \& -F_{k+1}$' is a blindspot. Any consistent conjunction containing a belief blindspot is itself a belief blindspot. So if every counter-example contains at least one blindspot, every counter-example will be a blindspot. This is a sufficient condition for counter-example resistance but not a necessary condition. For the conjuncts could be semi-blindspots where each conjunct is accessible but not co-accessible. Remember that we call such conjunctions 'holistic blindspots'. Also recall that consistent conjunctions containing blindspots are termed 'super-blindspots', while the blindspots they contain are called 'sub-blindspots'. These reminders will help us classify types of falsidical counter-example resistance.

First of all we have the pure cases, where all the counter-examples are holistic blindspots or all of them are super-blindspots. Purely holistic resistance is illustrated by

(1) If someone believes that p, then someone believes that someone believes that p.

Counter-examples to this generalization have the form 'Someone believes that p but no one believes that someone believes that p', which are universal Moorean sentences. Although each conjunct is believable, the conjunction is not believable. To see that there must be counter-examples, note that the generalization implies the existence of infinitely iterated beliefs about p given that someone believes p.

Purely super-blindspot resistance comes in two forms. First there is the regular form, where the antecedent is always a sub-blindspot or the negation of the consequent is always a sub-blindspot. Examples of antecedent resistance include:

(2) If everyone shares n permanent false beliefs, then everyone shares $n + 1$ permanent false beliefs.

In order to refute the conditional, we need to find a case where the antecedent is true and the consequent is false. However, we cannot detect cases where the antecedent is true. Since the antecedents are all blindspots, the generalization is counter-example-resistant. The reverse difficulty is encountered with negated consequent resistance:

(3) If something weighs at least n grams, then something weights at least $n + 1$ grams.

In order to refute this generalization we must find a case where the consequent is false. But the negation of the consequent places a maximum weight on everything that has or will ever exist. Since our access to the universe is too limited to fix the limit, the negation of the consequent is a blindspot. Yet we are reluctant to accept the generalization, because it implies the existence of things having arbitrarily high weight. Notice that if F is either a blindspot predicate or the complement of one, all propositions of the form 'F_k & $-F_{k+1}$' are blindspots. Hence regular resistance will be achieved. When the corresponding existential generalization, $(\exists x)Fx$, is also plausible, one will have the base step for an induction. Thus blindspot predicates are especially useful in the construction of slippery slope arguments.

In addition to the regular cases, one can envisage the resistance being due sometimes to the antecedent and sometimes to the negated consequent. Lastly, there are mixed cases where some of the counter-examples are holistic blindspots and the remainder are super-blindspots.

Since cloaked but true generalizations cannot have counter-examples, we must instead speak of their *potential* counter-examples. Potential counter-examples can be defined syntactically as conjunctions of each conditional's antecedent and the negation of its consequent. A true generalization has only false potential counter-examples. A false generalization has some true potential counter-examples. When the generalization is cloaked, any true potential counter-example is hidden from view by its blindspot status. When faced with a cloaked generalization, the search for counter-examples is pointless. For the search will be fruitless regardless of the generalization's truth value. This method cannot exclude the possibility that some of the potential counter-examples are blindspots and true. Any confirmation or refutation of the generalization must issue from another source. In short, cloaked generalizations are those which a search for counter-examples cannot test because the search cannot rule out the possibility that counter-example resistance is falsidical.

Having explained the mechanics of cloaking, I can now state the structure of the most sophisticated instances of the slippery slope fallacy. In essence, they are mathematical inductions containing 'mendacious' generalizations as their induction steps. A generalization is *mendacious* just in case it is:

(a) apparently nonvacuous,
(b) sequential, and
(c) either false or a cloaking generalization.

Thus a mendacious mathematical induction can be a sound argument. Consider the following argument:

1. Some object has endured for at least one year.
2. If some object has endured at least n years, then some object has endured for at least $n + 1$ years.
3. No object is oldest (in *total* years).

A person who already doubts that there are oldest objects will believe that the argument is sound. Nevertheless, he should be reluctant to propound this argument because the induction step is a cloaking generalization. The induction step is counter-example-resistant because the negation of the consequent is a blindspot. For we can only know that the consequent is false if we can know the maximum age anything has ever or will ever attain. Since our access to the universe is insufficient to allow the discovery of this span, the generalization cannot be refuted by counter-example.

Nevertheless, this is a poor basis for inferring that there are no counter-examples and concluding that no objects are oldest. For it does not give us enough information to decide whether the counter-example resistance is veridical or falsidical. So given that a believer in immortal objects wishes to *rationally* persuade unbelievers, he will not use this argument.

When the counter-example resistance is of the strongest sort, the semantic anti-realist cannot allow for the possibility that the generalization is false. For semantic anti-realists deny that there are unknowable truths. Thus they are especially vulnerable to mendacious mathematical inductions.

B. *Universally Resistant Slopes*

We can confirm the theoretical expectation that the recipe works by using it to cook up a variety of novel slippery slope arguments. These divide into two groups: those having generalizations that are universally resistant and those with only locally resistant generalizations. Since the former are simpler, we shall begin with them.

1. *The Idealist's Slippery Slope*

Idealists say that only thinkers and their thoughts exist. One of Bertrand Russell's objections to this view is that there must be unthought of numbers. For surely there is an integer n such that it is the largest integer that ever will be thought of. It then follows that $n + 1$ is an integer that will never be thought of. One of the interesting features of this number is that no one can specify it. Indeed, there is an infinite class of unspecifiable numbers composed of the successors of n.

An idealist might try to turn the tables on Russell by offering the following argument in reply:

1. At some time someone thinks of the integer one.
2. If at some time someone thinks of the integer n, then at some time someone thinks of the integer $n + 1$.
3. All of the integers are at some time thought of by someone.

Since 'thought of' is vague, one might suspect that the idealist's argument is a sorites. However, borderline cases do not play an essential role. The reason why counter-examples to the induction

The Slippery Slope Fallacy

step are blindspots is that the objection has to think about the numbers. Like a boy chasing his shadow, the objector's quarry is always moved out of reach by the attempt to grasp it. Agent self-reference explains why all of the following are blindspots:

1. At some time someone thinks of 1 but at no time does someone think of 2.
2. At some time someone thinks of 2 but at no time does someone think of 3.
3. At some time someone thinks of 3 but at no time does someone think of 4.

.
.
.
.

No reasonable precisification of 'think of' will make any of these propositions knowable. So vagueness is not the culprit. Although each potential counter-example is a contingent proposition, every potential counter-example *that we consider* has a probability of 0. For in considering the candidate, we think about the number it claims to be unthought of. Also notice that the second conjunct of each member of the list is a blindspot, but none of the first conjuncts are blindspots. Thus the mendacious generalization in this argument clearly illustrates negated consequent resistance.

It may also be possible to illustrate this point with sentential self-reference. Consider sentence tokens that express propositions of the form 'Generalization G is refuted by n and $n + 1$'. For example, 'The generalization that every pair of integers has a sum greater than 3 is refuted by 1 and 2'. Call such sentence tokens 'refuters'.

1. There is a refuter specifying 1.
2. If there is a refuter specifying n, then there is a refuter specifying $n + 1$.
3. Every number is specified by some refuter.

In order to specify a counter-example to the induction step, the objector must produce a sentence token that specifies an integer and its successor that refutes the generalization. But since it follows that this sentence token would qualify as a refuter for those numbers, the token would express a false proposition.

Our inability to specify counter-examples to the induction steps of the last two mathematical inductions does not persuade us there are none. The reason is that we can readily see that the counter-example resistance is best explained by an hypothesis not implying the truth of the generalization. The preferred hypothesis is that the resistance is an artifice of counter-example presentation. We know that there are preconditions of cogent refutation by counter-example beyond the generalization's falsehood. The sentence token expressing the counter-example must be true, probable, non-question-begging, and comprehensible. The objector must have tried to refute the generalization, and hence must have thought about it and the counter-example, and he must be sentient, exist, and so forth. Thus a counter-example that implies that one of the preconditions of cogent refutation fails to obtain, cannot be used in a cogent refutation by counter-example. By crafting a generalization in such a way that its only counter-examples are of this inaccessible sort, one creates a counter-example-resistant generalization.

Since everyone recognizes this sort of artificial irrefutability, one can solve the sorites by showing that our inability to refute the induction steps by counter-example is best explained by the hypothesis that their counter-example resistance is a species of this phenomenon. I have followed this strategy in my analysis of the sorites by maintaining that the counter-examples to the induction step are useless because they are too improbable for refutational purposes. On my account, sorites arguments are just sophisticated instances of the slippery slope fallacy. They arise from the same recipe as the previous two. All three exhibit falsidical counter-example resistance. In the case of the sorites, the resistant generalizations concern the micro-applicability of vague predicates.

(4) Any rich man who loses a penny remains a rich man.
(5) The parent of any mammal is itself a mammal.
(6) If n minutes after noon is noonish, then $n + 1$ minutes after noon is noonish.

These generalizations are especially effective because their resistance to counter-examples is not an obvious artifice. This encourages people to assign a probability of 0 to every potential counter-example. One could justify this if it could be shown that each potential counter-example is a contradiction. But this would commit one to the claim that (4)–(6) are analytically true.

Perhaps one reason why there are so few defenders of this view is the contemporary climate of scepticism about analyticity and sympathy to fallibilism. However, it is more likely that the critics of classical logic have just overlooked the importance of the joint probability requirement. Only sorites arguments that satisfy the joint probability requirement pose a problem for classical logic. The critics have displayed little interest in showing that there are such sorites. The best explanation is that they have not felt the need to do so. And they have not felt the need to do so because of the tendency to overlook the joint probability requirement.

2. *The Measurement Slippery Slope*

Consider the predicate 'has an irrational length (in metres)'. Due to inevitable measurement error, we can never know whether lengths of particular objects are rational or irrational. Nevertheless, it is plausible that some object or other has an irrational length. This puts us in a position to argue as follows:

1. Some page has an irrational length.
2. If a page has an irrational length, then pages which are nearest to it also have irrational lengths.
3. All pages have irrational lengths.

Anyone who tries to refute the induction step by counter-example faces two impossible tasks. First he must show that a particular page has an irrational length. Second, he must show that its immediate neighbours have rational lengths. Since neither can be done, the generalization exhibits both antecedent resistance and negated consequent resistance.

Some may find the last example murky. Calculating the probability of a page having an irrational length is problematic. They may prefer to concentrate on the following version.

1. One of the first hundred mystery numbers is even.
2. If n of the first hundred mystery numbers is even, then $n + 1$ of the first hundred mystery numbers is even.
3. All of the first hundred mystery numbers is even.

Whereas one can never know whether the length of a page is rational or irrational, one can sometimes be sure that a number exceeds the number of even integers amongst the first hundred mystery numbers.

3. *The Sense Data Slippery Slope*

The idealist's slippery slope neatly illustrates counter-example resistance because it achieves its pseudo-irrefutability in an obvious way. For this reason, the argument is not as powerful as the one it was designed to illuminate. But given that the recipe I have suggested is accurate, one should expect that it can be used to cook up a variety of novel slippery slope arguments, and that some of the batch should rival the sorites in power.

To show that this expectation goes unfrustrated, I need slippery generalizations whose mendacity is controversial. The natural place to shop for these is in the literature devoted to misgivings about the law of excluded middle or bivalence.

Let us first consider discussions of the speckled hen problem as it arose fifty years ago for phenomenalism. Sense data were supposed to be incorrigible. Yet one can be uncertain as to how many speckles are contained in one's image of a speckled hen. You can be sure that there are between, say, ten and one hundred but unsure about their exact number, so you might be wrong if forced to guess. The case of mental images is of interest to slippery slopers because there is no way to obtain narrower intervals that will provide a refutation by counter-example to:

(6) If the image has n speckles, then it has $n + 1$ speckles.

No one can know the exact number of speckles. Subsequent inspection of the hen can tell us how many speckles the hen has. For it is a public, stable object. However, the privacy and ephemerality of mental images makes inner inspection problematic. Even if the number of speckles is small enough to make counting feasible, how can one be sure that the image has not been subtly altered by the counting effort? For given that one could not initially detect the exact number, indiscernible changes in the image could occur. These indiscernible changes sometimes accumulate into discernible differences allowing recognition of a change. But why suppose they always do so? Perhaps if you had held the image a little longer, the gradual shift would have become discernible.

Having sown the seeds for doubting that any counter-example to the generalization can serve to refute it, the slippery slope is ready to use:

1. The image has at least one speckle.
2. If the image has at least n speckles, then it has at least $n + 1$ speckles.
3. The image has a billion speckles.

Although the argument uses vague predicates, the inductive generalization does not resist counter-examples by exploiting their vagueness. This is clear from the fact that precisification of the predicates does not yield a counter-example.

The slippery slope argument might prompt some to search harder for a refutation by counter-example—or at least the possibility of it. For example, one might argue that since sense data accurately match the viewed surface, the number of speckles on the viewed surface is equal to the number of speckles possessed by the image of the surface. However, this belief would not help in the case non-representational sense data such as after-images or the sensaton of 'seeing stars before your eyes'.

One might maintain that the number of speckles could be known by appealing to the possibility of an image-reading machine. The machine takes a 'snapshot' of your mental image, so that we can do the counting at our leisure. But now the question becomes how would we establish the reliability of the snapshots. The obvious response is that we could have the subject compare his mental image with the snapshot of the image. But even if the subject finds them indistinguishable, he could be mistaken. Given that his zone of uncertainty is large, a large number of distinct mental images could be possessed by him. We could be sure that our snapshot is pretty close to the actual image but we could not fine tune our picture-taking beyond the subject's threshold of discernibility.

Another suggestion rests on optimism as to how well a skilled subject could count. If there were no upper limit on how well, we might insist that the subjects *could* have reliably summed them up no matter how many items and no matter how disorganized the items were. But how would we check their reliability?

In addition to arithmetic problems, there are geometrical ones. Can a patch in your subjective visual field be known to be *perfectly* circular? Just as we can never be sure that a physical object is a perfect cube because of the possibility that the deviation from perfection is below our threshold of detection, isn't it impossible to know that one's imagined circle fails to deviate from perfection? Here native ability and skill don't matter. Physics may give us reasons to doubt the existence of a perfect physical cube (though I do not think it entirely excludes it). But these reasons don't extend to images. Suppose I look at a piece of paper containing two stripes lying side by side for easy comparison. They *look* the same length but we know that sophisticated measuring devices could demonstrate the inequality. But aren't these devices irrelevant to the question of which of the two imaged stripes is longer? I might be uncertain as to whether the left stripe is longer than the right, so I could be wrong about it. And if they are of equal length, how could I ever know?

It is interesting to note that the problem of the speckled hen led some phenomenalists to suggest solutions that parallel those found in the sorites literature. A. J. Ayer writes:

> If the sense-data do not appear to be enumerable, they really are not enumerable.... For a group of sense-data can be said to be enumerable only if it is in fact enumerated. And to say that it might have been enumerated, though actually it was not, is not to say that it had any undetected property, but only that some other group, which would have been enumerable, might have occurred in its place.[14]

As Chisholm notes, there are two ways to interpret Ayer.[15] First, we can take Ayer to be denying that the law of excluded middle applies, that is, it is neither true nor false to say that the image has forty-eight speckles. After noting the general inadvisability of departures from this law, Chisholm criticizes the move as ineffective. Since we can be certain in cases where the number of speckles is small, we would have to maintain that the law holds for low numbers but not high ones. Chisholm dismisses this as *ad hoc*.

---

[14] A. J. Ayer, *The Foundations of Empirical Knowledge* (New York: St Martin's, 1940), 124–5.

[15] Roderick Chisholm analysed Ayer's proposal in 'The Problem of the Speckled Hen', *Mind*, 51/204 (Oct. 1942), 368–73.

The alternative to this truth-value gap interpretation is attributing to Ayer a belief in indefinite numbers. Under this interpretation, Ayer agrees that there are many speckles, and assuredly more than three, four or five, but there is no answer to exactly how many speckles there are. As H. H. Price notes, this would commit Ayer to the view that an entity can exist with only a generic characteristic.[16] Unlike the gappy interpretation, Ayer would be read as saying that it is *false* that the image has forty-eight speckles. Chisholm deems this as analogous to saying that victory will come next year, but not in January, February, or any other particular month of the year.

Regardless of which interpretation is adopted, Chisholm maintains that Ayer's position is defeated by some cases in which one does enumerate the speckles. Ayer admits that the speckles are enumerable if they have in fact been enumerated. However, the fact that one has enumerated the speckles is compatible with the enumeration being erroneous.

Further evidence that there is a definite number of speckles is afforded by the fact that relations beyond 'greater than', 'equal', and 'less than' can hold for sense data. Consider the visual image caused by Figure 12.1.

FIGURE 12.1

. . . .
. . . .

Although you cannot tell how many dots are in either the top row or the bottom row, you can know that there is an equal number in each by noting the one to one correspondence. Indeed, knowledge of mathematical relationships can enable one to calculate the exact number in circumstances where simple enumeration fails, as with Figure 12.2.

FIGURE 12.2

* * * *
* * * *
* * * *
* * * *

---

[16] Price makes this point in his critical notice of Ayer's *The Foundation of Empirical Knowledge* in *Mind*, 50/199 (July 1941), 280–93.

Knowing that the length of the square array is four allows those acquainted with multiplication to figure that the array is composed of sixteen items. Greater mathematical sophistication permits one to cope with more challenging images, like the one caused by Figure 12.3.

FIGURE 12.3

```
 $    $
$$    $$
$$$$$$
$$$$$$
$$    $$
 $    $
```

Notice that one might temporarily forget or fail to apply the mathematical principles that permit the calculation. After the image has vanished you might then recall the basic mathematical features of the image and apply the principles to deduce the image's composition. Your later confidence would be entirely misconceived if it were not assumed that there was a fact of the matter. Thus there must have been a definite but unknown number of items prior to reflection. Since the discovery might never have taken place, it follows that the number could have remained forever unknown. If well-organized images can have this epistemic property, higgledy-piggledy ones can as well. This leads us to the conclusion that certain highly complex and disorganized images have *unknowable* numbers of components. Successful application of mathematics to images requires basic input that cannot be gathered from such images. Thus a quick glance at the night sky or a vigorous bop on the head might create a vast reservoir of unknowable facts.

4. The Fictional Slippery Slope

My next example is drawn from the literature on fictional incompleteness. How many hairs did Sherlock Holmes have on his head when he first met Watson? Answers such as 'Sherlock Holmes has 97,463 hairs on his head' are generally thought to be neither true nor false, even though it is true that 'Sherlock Holmes had some hair on his head'. Only precision is denied. Furthermore, this incompleteness is thought to be non-epistemic; there just is no fact of the matter. Arguments in defence of non-epistemic incompleteness are rare. However, J. Heintz offers one.

> My reasoning is this: authors are not foreign correspondents, reporting, sometimes incompletely, on events they witness in some far-flung corner of the world. They create (most of) the events they write about. What they fail to tell us, either explicitly or by implication, simply does not exist. To believe otherwise is to posit a multiplicity of pre-existing fictional worlds to some of which authors have some kind of special access which, in principle, non-authors might come to share.
>
> ... I accept the more natural view that writers make up their stories, and that what they write down is, as far as the fiction goes, the way it is. When nothing in the text supports either 'Fa' or '−Fa', neither is true of that fictional world.[17]

Heintz goes on to assert that although fictional discourse illustrates failures of bivalence, the law of excluded middle, 'Fa v −Fa', still holds because it asserts nothing about a.

Whether or not one adopts a deviant logic, refutation by counter-example does not work against the generalization running the following argument:

1. Sherlock Holmes had more than one hair on his head.
2. If Sherlock Holmes had more than n hairs on his head, then he had more than $n + 1$ hairs on his head.
3. Sherlock Holmes had more than a billion hairs on his head.

As with a normal sorites, we are tempted to reject the induction step, (2). But rejecting the inducton step is equivalent to accepting the negation of the induction step. And the negation is equivalent to the assertion that there is a precise maximal number of hairs on Holmes' head.

As with the previous versions, the fictional slippery slope argument does not seem to turn on vagueness. For although 'hair' and 'head' are vague, the paradox survives any precisification of those predicates. Notice that the paradox does not get off the ground if 'Jimmy Carter' is substituted for 'Sherlock Holmes'. Jimmy Carter has a definite number of hairs on his head (at least given precisification of 'head' and 'hair'). Fictionality seems to be the key.

---

[17] J. Heintz, 'Reference and Inference in Fiction', *Poetics*, 8 (1979), 92.

C. Local Resisters

The foregoing examples illustrate how the recipe works when the sequential generalization appears non-vacuous and enjoys universal counter-example resistance. In the next examples, the generalizations only satisfy the slipperiness condition when we restrict ourselves to the members of certain schools of thought. For it is the deviant doctrines of these schools that prevent them from refuting the generalization by counter-example and prevent them from dismissing the generalization as vacuous.

1. *The Future Contingents Slippery Slope*

Ever since Aristotle we can find philosophers denying the law of excluded middle to escape logical fatalism. It is now true that I will either have a child or not. Given that it is now true that I will have a child, there is nothing I can do to prevent it. And given that it now true that I will not have a child, there is nothing I can do to produce one. So it follows that I have no control over whether this future event comes to pass. The laws of logic reveal that the apparently contingent statement 'I will have a child' is either necessarily true or necessarily false. Since the same reasoning applies to all 'future contingent' statements, everything is fated.

Aristotle and others have suggested that future contingents must be rescued by denying them truth values. That is, it is now neither true nor false that I will have a child. Nevertheless, the necessary statement about the future 'Either I will have a child or it is not the case that I will have a child' is assigned a truth value.

Those who hold this position are precluded from offering a counter-example to the generalization that I will have $n + 1$ children given that I will have n children. For they cannot find an n for which the antecedent is true and consequent is false. All concerned will agree that the number of children I will father equals some non-negative integer (for it is a necessary statement about the future). So we can then present them with the following slippery slope argument:

1. I will father at least 0 children.
2. If I will father at least n children, then I will father at least $n + 1$ children.
3. I will father at least a million children.

Since most philosophers are willing to assign truth values to statements about future contingencies, the induction step is not counter-example-resistant to them. Without biographical details they will admit that they do not *know* the specific n for which the generalization fails. But they will go on to point out that a patient wait-and-see policy will provide the answer. And if certainty was urgently needed, they could suggest several ways of altering my body that would remove all doubt.

Those unwilling to assign standard truth values to future contingents, on the other hand, would have to agree that there is no n at which the antecedent is true and the consequent false. Since they accept the base step, their options are limited to deviations from classical logic. These deviations parallel those found in the case of the sorites. The truth-value gap analysis suggested by Aristotle has been refined into a supervaluationist treatment by van Fraassen. Here it would be maintained that the consequent of the conditional lacks a truth value for $n = 0$, and that this ensures that the conditional itself lacks a truth value.[18] Interestingly, Lukasiewicz first introduced many-valued logic to cope with logical fatalism. In his three-valued system, conditionals with true antecedents and indeterminate consequents receive an indeterminate truth value. Although there is no n at which the induction step is false, either approach will cite the $n = 0$ case as showing that it is not true. The Kneales can serve as our parallel to the view that vague predicates fall outside the scope of logic. For they maintain that logic does not apply to future contingent sentences.[19] As in the case of the sorites, they could maintain that our mistake was to suppose that logic applies to the second premiss.

2. *The Arbitrary Object Slippery Slope*

Prior to Frege, it was common to hold that there were arbitrary objects. Arbitrary objects have those properties that are common to the individuals in the class to which they are associated. Thus an arbitrary penguin is mortal because all penguins are mortal. An arbitrary penguin also has weight and height. However, it does not

---

[18] Aristotle's treatment is in *De Interpretione*, while van Fraassen's is in 'Presupposition, Implication and Self-Reference', *Journal of Philosophy*, 65/5 (1968), 136–52.

[19] They take this position in *The Development of Logic* (Oxford: Oxford University Press, 1962), 51.

have any particular weight and height because there is no weight or height shared by all penguins. Contemporary scepticism about arbitrary objects was largely anticipated by Berkeley's criticism of Locke's theory of abstract ideas. After Frege developed a theory of quantification that made arbitrary objects unnecessary in the eyes of virtually all logicians, the sceptical position has become nearly unanimous. Only with Kit Fine's recent *Reasoning with Arbitrary Objects* has the new orthodoxy been challenged. At any rate, it should be clear that arbitrary objects satisfy the requirements for slippery slope construction:

1. An arbitrary penguin does not have a height between 0 and 1 decimetres.
2. If an arbitrary penguin does not have a height between n and $n + 1$ decimetres, then neither does it have a height between $n + 1$ and $n + 2$ decimetres.
3. An arbitrary penguin does not have a height within any interval of decimetres.

Since anything lacking a height within some interval of decimetres lacks a height, the conclusion denies that an arbitrary penguin has a height. However, arbitrary penguins must have some height because all penguins have in common the property of height.

Metaphysical scepticism about arbitrary objects rids the generalization of slipperiness. For given that there are no arbitrary objects, the generalization is vacuously true. As in the case of the traditional variations of the prediction paradox, the proper response is to reject the base step.

Had this slippery slope argument been in circulation prior to Frege, it would have been a puzzle with a higher victimization rate. For logicians prior to Frege had neither the quantification theory nor the sophistication in deviant logics that their successors enjoy.

3. *The Quantum Mechanics Slippery Slope*

Some interpretations of quantum mechanics also set the groundwork for counter-example-resistant generalizations. Heisenberg's uncertainty principle states that it is impossible to know both the *exact* position and momentum of a subatomic particle. Under the weakest reading, the principle merely states that we cannot *now* know both. A stronger epistemological reading maintains that it is physically impossible to know both the position and the momentum of a particle. Unlike the weaker reading, it rules out the possibility that future scientists could learn how to determine both. In effect, the stronger reading states that position statements and momentum statements about the same particle are relative blindspots. Since Heisenberg's principle does not preclude knowledge of the *rough* position and velocity, we have the familiar contrast between the possibility of rough knowledge and the impossibility of exact knowledge. This provides the key ingredient for counter-example resistance.

To obtain the corresponding slippery slope argument, suppose that we have an exhaustive list of propositions about the state of a subatomic particle's momentum, $M_0, M_1, \ldots, M_m, \ldots$ ascribing momenta of increasing magnitude. Now suppose that it is determined that the particle has position 3, making the statement P_3 known. We could then infer

(Q1) P_3 & $(M_0 \vee M_1 \vee \ldots \vee M_m \vee \ldots)$

because it merely conjoins a known position with something that follows from the particle having some momentum or other.[20] In turn, (Q1) is equivalent to the base step of the following argument because 'at least 0' is equivalent to an alternation of all the possible values.

1. The particle with position P_3 has at least a momentum of 0.
2. If the particle with position P_3 has at least a momentum of n, then it has at least a momentum of $n + 1$.
3. The particle with position P_3 has an infinite momentum.

In order to specify a counter-example to the induction step, an exact state of momentum of the particle would be required — at

[20] Although (Q1) has the advantage of being a standard, simple formulation, it has been an object of complaint in P. F. Gibbins, 'Why the Distributive Law is sometimes False', *Analysis*, 44/2 (Mar. 1984), 64–7. For as Gibbins notes, (Q1) misleadingly suggests denumerability and the possibility of a 0 momentum. However, the continuous nature of position-momentum uncertainty and the impossibility of a 0 value does not preclude slippery slope problems. Having a (proper) height requires a non-zero value and heights are continuous. But that does not block sorites reasoning about 'tall'. David Sanford addresses the continuity point in 'Infinity and Vagueness', *Philosophical Review*, 84/4 (Oct. 1975), 520–35.

least n but less than $n + 1$. Since the epistemic interpretation of Heisenberg's principle precludes knowledge of such a counter-example, the generalization is counter-example-resistant. Under this interpretation, we are to escape the absurd conclusion by appealing to an unknowable counter-example.

In contrast to the conservatism of the epistemic interpretation, ontological interpretations make the indefiniteness 'real'. Sometimes there are calls for 'quantum logic' or at least a revision or restriction of classical logic reminiscent of responses to the sorites. We find Reichenbach suggesting a three-valued logic.[21] Destouches-Fevrier suggests that classical logic is only appropriate to the larger world and offers her own version of many-valued logic as appropriate to subatomic reality.[22] Reichenbach attributes to Bohr and Heisenberg the view that certain quantum mechanical sentences are meaningless. Karel Lambert promotes a super-valuational approach.[23] Lambert also suggests that Isaac Levi's views about quantum mechanics may commit Levi to a non-classical logic akin to intuitionism.[24] Many of the deviant responses will follow the strategy of conceding that the generalization is free of counter-examples while refusing to accept its truth or the validity of the argument. Others are in a position directly to challenge the induction step. For instance, Hilary Putnam deviates from classical logic by denying that (Q1) implies

(Q2) ($(P_3$ & $M_0)$ v $(P_3$ & $M_1)$ v . . . v $(P_3$ & $M_m)$ . . .)

Since (Q1) implies (Q2) given the principle of distribution, (A & (B v C)) ⊃ ((A & B) v (A & C)), Putnam argues that quantum theory requires the rejection of this portion of classical logic.[25] His

---

[21] Reichenbach presents his system in his *Philosophical Foundations of Quantum Mechanics* (California University Press, 1944).

[22] Destouches-Fevrier takes her position in 'Les relations d'incertitude du Heisenberg et la logique', *Comptes rendus de l'Académie des Sciences*, 204 (1937).

[23] Lambert makes this proposal in 'Logical Truth and Microphysics', in Karel Lambert (ed.), *The Logical Way of Doing Things* (New Haven: Yale University Press, 1969), 93–117.

[24] Ibid., 107. Levi's views are found in 'Putnam's Three Truth Values', *Philosophical Studies*, 10/5 (Oct. 1959), 65–9.

[25] Putnam takes this position in 'The Logic of Quantum Mechanics', in his *Mathematics, Matter and Method*, I (Cambridge: Cambridge University Press, 1979).

objection to the slippery slope would be that although the base step is true, the induction step fails when $n = 0$. For when $n = 0$, the consequent eliminates a possible value for the particle. And the uncertainty relation is taken to forbid such eliminations for particles having precise positions. Hence Putnam's view shows that the generalization does not achieve universal counter-example resistance.

There are also those who would reject the base step of the quantum slippery slope argument. Jonathan Harrison, for example, suggests that those who take quantum indefiniteness seriously should reject (Q1).[26] The reason is that we should distinguish between a particle having a disjunction of determinate momenta and it having an indeterminate momentum. The distinction is akin to the one drawn by Frank Jackson in a comment on the speckled hen problem:

> If I look at a speckled hen, no doubt it will appear to have more than ten speckles; but there will be a number, depending of course on the particular hen, which will be such that I hesitate, indeed am unable, to say whether the hen appears to have more or less than this number of speckles. The obvious explanation for this is not that the hen looks to have a definite number of speckles which I am unable to specify, but that the hen does not look to have a definite number of speckles at all.[27]

Instead of analysing indeterminacy in terms of a disjunction of determinacies, we can construe the indeterminacy as basic. The goal is to avoid the implication that there is a hidden truth of the matter without revising logic. Thus Harrison maintains that those who wish to reject (Q2) can reject (Q1) rather than the distribution principle. He can then claim that the base step *looks* true because of our tendency to confuse indeterminacy with disjunctive determinacy. Once the two are untangled, the base step is revealed as false and the induction step as *vacuously* true. The burden of such an approach is to respond to Chisholmian objections to the effect that the logical conservatism of this distinction is illusory.

---

[26] Jonathan Harrison, 'Against Quantum Logic', *Analysis*, 43/2 (Mar. 1983), 83–5.
[27] Frank Jackson, 'Is There a Good Argument against the Incorrigibility Thesis?', *Australasian Journal of Philosophy*, 51/1 (Jan. 1973), 51–62.

IV. DEVIANCY V. UNITY

According to the classicist, a generalization is true if and only if it is free of counter-examples. Deviants deny this. Deviant solutions to the mendacious mathematical inductions rest on the thesis that some generalizations lacking counter-examples are not true. How do we tell which counter-example free generalizations fail to be true?

The preceding section was intended to convey the quantity and variety of mendacious mathematical inductions. In the face of this quantity and variety, no deviant should wish to adopt a deviant approach to all the examples. He will pick and choose. In doing so, he assumes an explanatory burden. The deviant will have to provide grounds for the differential treatment. Should he succeed in overthrowing suspicions of arbitrariness, he will nevertheless be left with a position that treats some slippery slopes deviantly and some not.

In contrast, the classicist can offer a unified analysis of all slippery slope arguments. At one end of the continuum lie hastily formulated slippery slope arguments whose conditionals can easily be refuted. Gradually increasing the difficulty of refuting the conditionals leads us to arguments that benefit from the joint probability illusion. The conditionals are too probable to deny. This puts us in a terrain where we frequently malfunction. For most people do not act in accordance with the joint probability requirement. If the antecedent of the beginning conditional is improbable, another sort of illusion may arise. Although such arguments satisfy the joint probability requirement, we are apt to take the high probability conferred on the concluding conditional to be a high conditional probability. Within this intermediate range of slippery slope arguments, it is never doubted that new empirical evidence could falsify one of the conditionals. By further increasing the degree of resistance, one arrives at slippery slope arguments that do raise this doubt. It is at this point that alternative approaches to slippery slope arguments will bifurcate the fallacy. They will postulate a qualitative change where the classicist only admits a quantitative change. For alternative approaches will claim that some of the mendacious mathematical inductions are fallacies of a radically different *type*. Whereas hasty slippery slopes and those occupying an intermediate position on the continuum can be handled by conventional means, selected mendacious mathematical inductions require departures from classical logic. So in addition to showing that such a drastic measure is more effective than more moderate responses, the deviant faces the objection that his account is unparsimonious.

The classicist offers an account free of this dualism. According to him, there is just one slippery slope fallacy and all of the bad arguments can be handled within the confines of classical logic. Although bad slippery slope arguments can be bad for a variety of reasons, there is one necessary condition that most of the bad ones will violate. An argument is good only if its premises have a high joint probability that significantly enhances the assertibility of the conclusion. All slippery slope arguments are equivalent to arguments composed of many interlocking conditionals. This makes them tricky in two ways. First, the scale of the argument is deceptive because we tend to overestimate the likelihood of all the premises holding. Second, the conditionals constituting the slope are treacherous in the myriad of ways that logicians have charted in journal articles. These two tricky features of slippery slope arguments conspire to bring about frequent violations of the necessary conditions for good arguments. This explains why most instances of the slippery slope argument form are bad arguments. Thus the diagnosis supports a statistical syllogism:

1. Most instances of the slippery slope argument form are bad argument tokens.
2. Argument token t is an instance of the slippery slope argument form.
3. Argument token t is a bad argument.

As with inductive reasoning in general, the strength of the argument can be affected by adding a premiss.

Knowledge of fallacies is useful to the appraiser of arguments in the same way that knowledge of structural flaws is useful to the appraiser of buildings. Such knowledge guides the appraiser by informing him of promising areas for inspection. Knowledge of the slippery slope fallacy makes us suspicious of instances of this argument form. Deeper investigation vindicates our suspicions in the case of the sorites, the prediction paradox, and the super-game puzzles. With the help of the blindspot analysis of mendacious mathematical inductions, each comes to occupy a position in a larger constellation of conundrums.

In surveying any large collection of objects such as pebbles in a stream or stars in the sky, one wonders whether one is faced with a random distribution or the product of some natural ordering. Theories that permit us to predict new elements in the distribution while explaining the old resolve one's wonder. What holds for concrete objects holds for the abstract. The recipe for mendacious mathematical inductions reveals an underlying order to the slippery slope puzzles which seem to make a higgledy-piggledy appearance in philosophical literature.

The order takes the form of a pre-condition. Sophisticated slippery slope reasoning emerges only where the ground is fertile for mendacious generalization. History scatters the seeds of scholarship widely but thinly. So mendacious mathematical inductions have sprouted here and there, providing a few wild specimens. Since the blindspot analysis cannot predict where the seeds will land, it cannot provide a sufficient condition for their historical occurrence. However, it does provide a necessary condition, information that enables us to cultivate selected plots. Domestication of the species increases the size and variety of our sample.

Reasoning about puzzles is largely an inductive affair: noting analogies, common elements, exceptions, correlations, residual effects. Increases in the representativeness of our sample are therefore crucial to a fine-grained understanding of the population. The blindspot analysis of mendacious mathematical inductions thus offers more than piecemeal solutions. It feeds us the details necessary for constructing an accurate big picture. It is a picture worth constructing. For it exhibits a path of thought that gently draws us down to a dazed surrender of our most central beliefs.

Bibliography

ADAMS, ERNEST W., *The Logic of Conditionals* (Dordrecht: D. Reidel, 1975).
—— and LEVINE, HOWARD P., 'On the Uncertainties Transmitted from Premises to Conclusions in Deductive Inferences', *Synthese*, 30/3–4 (Apr.–May 1975), 429–60.
ALDRICH, VIRGIL, 'Some Meanings of "Vague" ', *Analysis*, 4/6 (Aug. 1937), 89–95.
ALSTON, WILLIAM, 'Self-Warrant: A Neglected Form of Privileged Access', *American Philosophical Quarterly*, 13/4 (Oct. 1976), 257–72.
ANSCOMBE, G. E. M., 'The First Person', in Samuel Guttenplan (ed.) *Mind and Language* (Oxford: Oxford University Press, 1975), 45–65.
ARMSTRONG, DAVID M., *A Materialist Theory of Mind* (London: Routledge and Kegan Paul, 1968).
—— *Belief, Truth and Knowledge* (Cambridge: Cambridge University Press, 1973).
AUSTIN, A. K., 'On the Unexpected Examination', *Mind*, 78/309 (Jan. 1969), 137.
—— 'The Unexpected Examination', *Analysis*, 39/1 (Jan. 1979), 63–4.
AYER, A. J., *The Foundations of Empirical Knowledge* (London: Macmillan, 1940).
—— 'On a Supposed Antinomy', *Mind*, 82/325 (Jan. 1973), 125–6.
BEARDESMORE, R. W., *Moral Reasoning* (New York: Schocken Books, 1969).
BENACERRAF, PAUL, 'What Numbers Could Not Be', in Paul Benacerraf and Hilary Putnam (eds.), *Philosophy of Mathematics*, 2nd edn. (Cambridge: Cambridge University Press, 1983), 47–73.
BENNETT, JONATHAN, 'Review', *The Journal of Symbolic Logic*, 30/2 (June 1965), 101–2.
BEVER, T. G., 'The Cognitive Basis for Linguistic Structures', in J. R. Haynes (ed.) *Cognition and the Development of Language* (New York: Wiley, 1970), 279–362.
BLACK, MAX, 'Vagueness', *Philosophy of Science*, 4/4 (Oct. 1937), 427–55.
—— 'Saying and Disbelieving', *Analysis*, 13/2 (Dec. 1952), 28–31.
—— 'Reasoning with Loose Concepts', *Dialogue*, 2/1 (Jan. 1963), 1–12.
BOER, STEPHEN and LYCAN, WILLIAM, *The Myth of Semantic Presupposition* (Bloomington, Ind.: Indiana University Linguistics Club Publications, 1976).

Boos, William, 'A Self-Referential *Cogito*', *Philosophical Studies* 44/2 (Sept. 1983), 269–90.

Bosch, Jorge, 'The Examination Paradox and Formal Prediction', *Logique et Analyse*, 59–60 (Sept.–Dec. 1972), 505–25.

Bunch, Bryan, *Mathematical Fallacies and Paradoxes* (New York: Van Nostrand, 1982).

Campbell, Keith, *Body and Mind* (Garden City, N.Y.: Anchor Books, 1970).

Cargile, James, 'Review', *The Journal of Symbolic Logic*, 30/2 (June 1965), 102–3.

—— 'The Surprise Test Paradox', *Journal of Philosophy*, 64/18 (Sept. 1967), 550–63.

—— 'The Sorites Paradox', *British Journal for the Philosophy of Science*, 20/3 (Oct. 1969), 193–202.

—— *Paradoxes: A Study in Form and Predication* (New York: Cambridge University Press, 1979).

Carnap, Rudolph, *Logical Foundations of Probability* (Chicago: University of Chicago Press, 1950).

Casullo, Albert, 'Reid and Mill on Hume's Maxim of Conceivability', *Analysis*, 39/4 (Oct. 1979), 212–19.

Champlin, T.S., 'Quine's Judge', *Philosophical Studies*, 29/5 (May 1976), 349–52.

Chapman, J. M., and Butler, R. J., 'On Quine's "So-called Paradox" ', *Mind*, 74/295 (July 1965), 424–5.

Chisholm, Roderick, 'The Problem of the Speckled Hen', *Mind*, 51/204 (Oct. 1942), 368–73.

Clarke, D. S., 'The Addressing Function of "I" ', *Analysis*, 38/2 (Mar. 1978), 91–3.

Cohen, L. Jonathan, 'Mr. O'Connor's "Pragmatic Paradoxes" ', *Mind*, 59/233 (Jan. 1950), 85–7.

Cole, David, 'Meaning & Knowledge', *Philosophical Studies*, 36/3 (Oct. 1979), 319–21.

Collins, Arthur, 'Could Our Beliefs Be Representations in Our Brains?', *Journal of Philosophy*, 74/5 (May 1979), 225–43.

Conee, Earl, 'Utilitarianism and Rationality', *Analysis*, 42/1 (Jan. 1982), 55–9.

Davidson, Donald, 'On the Very Idea of a Conceptual Scheme', *Proceedings and Addresses of the American Philosophical Association* 47 (1973–4), 5–20.

Davis, Lawrence, 'Prisoners, Paradox, and Rationality', *American Philosophical Quarterly*, 14/4 (1977), 319–27.

—— 'Is the Symmetry Argument Valid?', in Richmond Campbell and Lanning Sowden (eds.) *Paradoxes of Rationality and Cooperation* (Vancouver: University of British Columbia Press, 1985), 255–62.

DESTOUCHES-FEVRIER, P., 'Les relations d'incertitude du Heisenberg et la logique', *Comptes rendus de l'Académie des Sciences*, 204 (1937).

DEUTSCHER, MAX, 'Bonney on Saying and Disbelieving', *Analysis*, 27/6 (June 1967), 184–6.

DUHEM, P., *The Aim and Structure of Physical Theory*, trans. P. P. Wiener (Princeton: Princeton University Press, 1954).

DUMMETT, MICHAEL, 'Wang's Paradox', *Synthese*, 30/3–4 (Apr.–May 1975), 301–24.

—— 'What is a Theory of Meaning (II)?' in Gareth Evans and John McDowell (eds.) *Truth and Meaning* (Oxford: Clarendon Press, 1976), 67–137.

EDGINGTON, DOROTHY, 'The Paradox of Knowability', *Mind*, 94/376 (Oct. 1985), 557–68.

EELLS, ELLERY, *Rational Decision and Causality* (New York: Cambridge University Press, 1982).

ELLIS, BRIAN, *Rational Belief Systems* (Totowa, N.J.: Rowman and Littlefield, 1979).

—— 'Truth as a Mode of Evaluation', *Pacific Philosophical Quarterly*, 61/1–2 (Jan.–Apr. 1980), 85–99.

—— 'Reply to Sorensen', *Journal of Philosophical Logic*, 19/4 (Nov. 1982), 460–2.

FAIN, HASKELL, and GRIFFITHS, PHILLIPS A., 'On Falsely Believing that One Doesn't Know', in Nicholas Rescher (ed.) *Studies in the Philosophy of Mind* (Oxford: Basil Blackwell, 1972), 10–23.

FINE, KIT, 'Vagueness, Truth and Logic', *Synthese*, 30/3–4 (Apr.–May 1975), 265–300.

FINEMAN, MARK, *The Inquisitive Eye* (New York: Oxford University Press, 1981).

FLEW, ANTHONY, 'Parapsychology: Science or Pseudo-Science', *Pacific Philosophical Quarterly*, 61/1–2 (Jan.–Apr. 1980), 100–14.

FORBES, GRAEME, *The Metaphysics of Modality* (Oxford: Clarendon Press, 1985).

FOREST, TERRY, 'P-Predicates', in Avrum Stroll *Epistemology* (New York: Harper & Row, 1967), 88–97.

FRASER, J. T., 'Note Relating to a Paradox of Temporal Order', *Voices of Time* (New York: George Braxiller, Inc., 1966), 524–6.

FREEMAN, DEREK, *Margaret Mead and Samoa: The Making and Unmaking of an Anthropological Myth* (Cambridge: Harvard University Press, 1983).

GIBBARD, ALLAN, and HARPER, WILLIAM, 'Two Kinds of Expected Utility', in William Harper et. al. (eds.) *Ifs* (Dordrecht: D. Reidel, 1981), 152–90.

GIBBINS, P. F., 'Why the Distributive Law is Sometimes False', *Analysis*, 44/2 (Mar. 1984), 64–7.

GINET, CARL, 'Can the Will be Caused?', *Philosophical Review*, 71/1 (Jan. 1962), 49–55.
GOGUEN, J., 'The Logic of Inexact Concepts', *Synthese*, 19/3–4 (Apr. 1969), 325–73.
GOLDSTICK, D., 'Methodological Conservatism', *American Philosophical Quarterly*, 8/2 (Apr. 1971), 186–191.
GOVIER, TRUDY, 'What's Wrong with Slippery Slope Arguments?', *Canadian Journal of Philosophy*, 12/2 (June 1982), 303–16.
GRIM, PATRICK, 'What Won't Escape Sorites Arguments', *Analysis*, 42/1 (Jan. 1982), 38–43.
—— 'Some Neglected Problems of Omniscience', *American Philosophical Quarterly*, 20/3 (July 1983), 265–76.
HALDANE, J. B. S., *The Inequality of Man* (London: Chatto and Windus, 1932).
—— *Science and Life: Essays of a Rationalist* (London: Pemberton, Barrie & Rockliff, 1968).
HARDIN, RUSSELL, *Collective Action* (Baltimore: Johns Hopkins University Press, 1982).
HARMAN, GILBERT, *Thought* (Princeton: Princeton University Press, 1973).
HARRISON, JONATHAN, 'Against Quantum Logic', *Analysis*, 43/2 (Mar. 1983), 83–5.
HART, W. D., 'The Epistemology of Abstract Objects', *Aristotelian Society Supplementary*, 53 (1979).
HEINTZ, J., 'Reference and Inference in Fiction', *Poetics*, 8/1 (Jan. 1979), 86–97.
HINTIKKA, JAAKKO, *Knowledge and Belief* (Ithaca: Cornell University Press, 1962).
HOLLIS, MARTIN, 'A Paradoxical Train of Thought', *Analysis*, 44/4 (Oct. 1984), 205–6.
HOLMAN, L., 'Continuity and the Metaphysics of Dualism', *Philosophical Studies*, 45/2 (Mar. 1984), 197–204.
HORGAN, TERENCE, 'Counterfactuals and Newcomb's Problem', *Journal of Philosophy*, 78/6 (June 1981), 331–56.
HUBIN, DON, and ROSS, GLENN, 'Newcomb's Perfect Predictor', *Nous*, 19/3 (Sept. 1985), 439–46.
HUMBERSTONE, I. L., 'You'll Regret It', *Analysis*, 40/3 (June 1980), 175–6.
HUME, DAVID, *A Treatise of Human Nature*, ed. L. A. Selby-Bigge (Oxford: Clarendon Press).
—— *An Inquiry Concerning Human Understanding* (London, 1809, orig. 1748).
JACKSON, FRANK, 'Is There a Good Argument Against the Incorrigibility Thesis?', *Australasian Journal of Philosophy*, 51/1 (Jan. 1973), 51–62.

JEFFREYS, H., *Theory of Probability* (Oxford: Oxford University Press, 1961), 3rd edn.
JOHNSON, OLIVER, 'Aesthetic Objectivity and the Analogy with Ethics', in Godfrey Vesey (ed.) *Philosophy and the Arts* (New York: St Martin's Press, 1973), 165–81.
KAMP, HANS, 'The Paradox of the Heap', in Uwe Monnich (ed.) *Aspects of Philosophical Logic* (Dordrecht: D. Reidel, 1981), 225–77.
KAPLAN, DAVID, and MONTAGUE, RICHARD, 'A Paradox Regained', *Notre Dame Journal of Formal Logic*, 1/3 (July 1960), 79–90.
KATZ, STUART, and WILCOX, STEPHEN, 'Do Many Private Worlds Imply No Real World?', *Journal for the Theory of Social Behaviour*, 9/3 (Oct. 1979), 289–301.
KAVKA, GREGORY, 'The Toxin Puzzle', *Analysis*, 43/1 (Jan. 1983), 33–6.
KEELING, S. V., *Descartes* (London: Oxford University Press, 1968).
KEENE, G. G., 'Self-referent Inference and the Liar Paradox', *Mind*, 92/367 (July 1983), 430–3.
KIEFER, JAMES, and ELLISON, JAMES, 'The Prediction Paradox Again', *Mind*, 74/295, (July 1965), 426–7.
KING, JOHN L., 'Bivalence and the Sorites Paradox', *American Philosophical Quarterly*, 16/1 (Jan. 1979), 17–25.
KNEALE, W. and M., *The Development of Logic* (Oxford: Oxford University Press, 1962).
KOHL, M., 'Vagueness', *Australasian Journal of Philosophy*, 4/1 (Jan. 1969), 31–41.
KRAEMER, ERIC, and SAYWARD, CHARLES, 'Dualism and the Argument from Continuity', *Philosophical Studies*, 37/1 (Jan. 1980), 55–9.
KROON, FREDERIC, 'A Utilitarian Paradox', *Analysis*, 41/2 (Mar. 1981), 107–12.
—— 'Rationality and Paradox: A Reply to Conee', *Analysis*, 43/3 (June 1983), 156–60.
LAMBERT, KAREL, 'Logical Truth and Microphysics' in Karel Lambert (ed.) *The Logical Way of Doing Things* (New Haven: Yale University Press, 1969), 93–117.
LEHRER, KEITH, 'When Rational Disagreement is Impossible', *Nous*, 10/3 (Sept. 1976), 327–32.
LEHRER, KEITH, and WAGNER, CARL, *Rational Consensus in Science and Society* (Dordrecht: D. Reidel, 1981).
LEMMON, E. J., 'If I Know, Do I Know that I Know?', in Avrum Stroll (ed.) *Epistemology* (New York: Harper & Row, 1967), 54–82.
LEVI, ISAAC, 'Putnam's Three Truth Values', *Philosophical Studies*, 10/5 (Oct. 1959), 65–9.
LEVIN, MICHAEL, 'Quine's View(s) of Logical Truth', in Robert W. Shahan and Chris Swoyer (eds.) *Essays on the Philosophy of W. V. Quine* (Norman: University of Oklahoma Press, 1979), 45–68.

—— 'Yes, Our Beliefs Could Be . . .', *Journal of Philosophy*, 77/4 (Apr. 1980), 233–7.
LEWIS, DAVID, 'Truth in Fiction', *American Philosophical Quarterly*, 15/1 (Jan. 1978), 37–46.
—— 'Causal Decision Theory', *Australasian Journal of Philosophy*, 59/1 (Jan. 1981), 5–30.
LINSKY, BERNARD, 'Factives, Blindspots and Some Paradoxes', *Analysis*, 46/1 (Jan. 1986), 10–15.
LINSKY, LEONARD, 'On Interpreting Doxastic Logic', *Journal of Philosophy*, 65/17 (Sept. 5, 1968), 500–2.
LOCKE, DON, *Memory* (New York: Doubleday & Company, 1971).
LORIE, JAMES H., DODD, PETER, and KIMPTON, Mary Hamilton, *The Stock Market* 2nd edn. (Homewood, Il: Irwin, 1985).
LOWE, E.J., 'For Want of a Nail', *Analysis*, 40/1 (Jan. 1980), 50–2.
LUNDBERG, GEORGE, 'The Postulates of Science and Their Implications for Sociology', in M. Natanson (ed.) *Philosophy of the Social Sciences* (New York: Random House, 1963), 33–72.
LYCAN, WILLIAM G., *Logical Form in Natural Language* (Cambridge, Mass.: MIT Press 1984).
—— 'Epistemic Value', *Synthese*, 64/2 (Aug. 1985), 137–64.
LYON, ARDON, 'The Prediction Paradox', *Mind*, 67/272 (Oct. 1959), 510–17.
MACHINA, KENTON, 'Truth, Belief, and Vagueness', *Journal of Philosophical Logic*, 5/1 (Jan. 1976), 47–78.
MACINTOSH, J. J., 'Some Propositional Attitude Paradoxes', *Pacific Philosophical Quarterly*, 65/1 (Jan. 1984), 21–5.
—— 'Fitch's Factives', *Analysis*, 44/4 (Oct. 1984), 153–8.
MACKAY, D. M., 'On the Logical Indeterminacy of Free Choice', *Mind*, 69/1 (Jan. 1960), 31–40.
MACKIE, J. L., 'Truth and Knowability', *Analysis*, 40/2 (Mar. 1980), 90–2.
MACLAUGHLIN, ROBERT, 'Necessary Agnosticism?', *Analysis*, 44/4 (Oct. 1984), 198–202.
MAKINSON, D. C., 'The Paradox of the Preface', *Analysis*, 25/6 (June 1965), 205–7.
MALCOLM, NORMAN, 'The Conceivability of Mechanism', *The Philosophical Review*, 77/3 (Jan. 1968), 45–73.
—— *Ludwig Wittgenstein: A Memoir* (Oxford: Oxford University Press, 1984).
MALKIEL, BURTON G., *A Random Walk Down Wall Street* (New York: Norton & Company, 1985).
MARTIN, MICHAEL. 'The Philosophical Importance of the Rosenthal Effect', *Journal for the Theory of Social Behavior*, 7/1 (Apr. 1977), 81–97.
MARTINICH, A. P., 'Conversational Maxims', *Philosophical Quarterly*, 30/120 (July 1980), 215–28.

MASSEY, GERALD, 'Are there any Good Arguments that Bad Arguments are Bad?', *Philosophy in Context*, 4/1 (Jan. 1975), 61–7.
—— 'The Fallacy Behind Fallacies', in Peter A. French. Theodore E. Uehling, and Howard K. Wettstein (eds.) *Midwest Studies in Philosophy*, IV (Minneapolis: University of Minnesota Press, 1981).
MCGEE, VANN, 'A Counterexample to Modus Ponens', *Journal of Philosophy*, 82/9 (Sept. 1985), 462–71.
MCLELLAND, J., 'Epistemic Logic and the Paradox of the Surprise Examination', *International Logic Review*, 3/1 (Jan. 1971), 69–85.
MCLELLAND, J., and CHIHARA, CHARLES, 'The Surprise Examination Paradox, *Journal of Philosophical Logic*, 4/1 (Jan. 1975), 71–89.
MCMULLEN, W. A., 'Censorship and Participatory Democracy: A Paradox', *Analysis*, 32/6 (June 1972), 207–8.
MCTAGGART, J. E., *Philosophical Studies* (London: Routledge & Kegan Paul, 1934).
MEDLIN, BRIAN, 'The Unexpected Examination', *American Philosophical Quarterly*, 1/1 (Jan. 1964), 66–72.
MELTZER, B., 'The Third Possibility', *Mind*, 73/291 (July 1964), 430–3.
MELTZER, B. and GOOD, I. J., 'Two Forms of the Prediction Paradox', *British Journal for the Philosophy of Science*, 14/61 (May 1965), 50–1.
MILL, JOHN STUART, *A System of Logic* (Toronto: University of Toronto Press, 1974), orig. 1843.
MILNER. E. V., 'The Paradox of Dives and Lazarus', *Mind*, 76/303 (July 1967), 441.
MOORE, G. E., *Principia Ethica* (Cambridge: Cambridge University Press, 1903).
—— *Philosophical Studies* (London: Routledge & Kegan Paul, 1922).
—— *Some Main Problems of Philosophy* (London: Allen & Unwin, 1953).
NERLICH, G. C., 'Unexpected Examinations and Unprovable Statements', *Mind*, 70/280 (Oct. 1961), 503–13.
NISBETT, RICHARD, and ROSS, LEE, *Human Inference* (Englewood Cliffs, N.J.: Prentice-Hall, 1980).
NOZICK, ROBERT, 'Newcomb's Problem and Two Principles of Choice', in Nicholas Rescher (ed.) *Essays in Honor of Carl G. Hempel* (Dordrecht: D. Reidel 1970), 114–46.
—— *Anarchy, State and Utopia* (Cambridge, Mass.: Harvard University Press, 1974).
—— *Philosophical Explanations* (Cambridge, Mass.: Harvard University Press, 1981).
OAKLEY, I. T., 'An Argument for Scepticism Concerning Justified Belief', *American Philosophical Quarterly*, 13/3 (July 1976), 221–8.
O'CARROLL, M. J., 'Improper Self-Reference in Classical Logic and the Prediction Paradox', *Logique et Analyse*, 10/38 (June 1967), 167–72.

O'CONNOR, D. J., 'Pragmatic Paradoxes', *Mind*, 62/227 (July 1948), 358–9.

O'CONNOR, JOHN, 'A Note on the Paradox of Dives and Lazarus', *Mind*, 79/314 (Apr. 1970), 251–2.

ODEGARD, DOUGLAS, 'Alston and Self-Warrant', *Analysis*, 39/1 (Jan. 1979), 42–4.

OLIN, DORIS, 'The Prediction Paradox Resolved', *Philosophical Studies*, 44/2 (Sept. 1983), 225–33.

OLIVER, J. WILLARD, 'Formal Fallacies and Other Invalid Arguments', *Mind*, 76/304 (Oct. 1967), 463–78.

PARFIT, DEREK, *Reasons and Persons* (New York: Oxford University Press, 1984).

PETERS, DOUGLAS, and CECI, STEPHEN, 'Peer-review Practices of Psychological Journals', *The Behavioral and Brain Science*, 5/2 (June 1982), 185–6.

PITCHER, GEORGE, *A Theory of Perception* (Princeton: Princeton University Press, 1971).

POPPER, KARL, and ECCLES, JOHN C., *The Self and its Brain* (New York: Springer-Verlag, 1977).

PRATT, JAMES B., *Matter and Spirit* (New York: MacMillan Company, 1922).

PRICE, G. R., 'Science and the Supernatural', *Science*, 122/3165 (Mar. 1955), 359–67.

PRIEST, GRAHAM, 'The Logic of Paradox', *Journal of Philosophical Logic*, 8/2 (1979), 219–41.

PRIOR, ARTHUR, *Objects of Thought* (Oxford: Oxford University Press, 1971).

PUTNAM, HILARY, 'The Logic of Quantum Mechanics', *Mathematics, Matter and Method*, 1 (Cambridge: Cambridge University Press, 1979).

—— 'Vagueness and Alternative Logic', *Erkenntnis*, 19/2 (Mar. 1983), 297–314.

QUINE, W. V., 'On a so-called Paradox', *Mind*, 62/245 (Jan. 1953), 65–7.

—— *Word and Object* (Cambridge, Mass.: MIT Press, 1960).

—— 'Epistemology Naturalized', *Ontological Relativity and Other Essays* (New York: Columbia University Press, 1969).

—— *The Ways of Paradox*, (Cambridge, Mass.: Harvard University Press, 1976).

RABINOWICZ, WLODZIMIERZ, 'Ratificationism without Ratification: Jeffrey meets Savage', *Theory and Decision*, 19/2 (Sept. 1985), 171–200.

READ, STEPHEN, 'Self-Reference and Validity', *Synthese*, 42/2 (Oct. 1979), 265–74.

REGAN, DONALD, *Utilitarianism and Cooperation* (Oxford: Clarendon Press, 1980).

REICHENBACH, HANS, *Philosophical Foundations of Quantum Mechanics* (Los Angeles: California University Press, 1944).

RESCHER, NICHOLAS. 'Philosophical Disagreement', *Review of Metaphysics*, 32/1 (Sept. 1978), 217-51.

RICHTER, REED, 'Rationality Revisited', *Australasian Journal of Philosophy*, 62/2 (Dec. 1984), 392-403.

ROBINSON, RICHARD, 'Arguing from Ignorance', *Philosophical Quarterly*, 21/83 (Apr. 1971), 97-108.

ROLF, BERTIL, 'A Theory of Vagueness', *Journal of Philosophical Logic*, 9/3 (Sept. 1980), 315-25.

ROSENKRANTZ, R., *Inference, Method and Decision* (Dordrecht: D. Reidel, 1977).

ROWE, WILLIAM, 'The Fallacy of Composition', *Mind*, 71/281 (Jan. 1962), 87-92.

RUNYON, RICHARD. *How Numbers Lie* (Lexington, Mass.: Lewis Publishing Company, 1981).

RUSSELL, BERTRAND, 'Vagueness', *Australasian Journal of Philosophy*, 1 (1923), 297-314.

RYLE, GILBERT, 'Heterologicality', *Analysis*, 11/3 (Jan. 1951), 61-9.

SANFORD, DAVID, 'Borderline Logic', *American Philosophical Quarterly*, 12/1 (Jan. 1975), 29-39.

—— 'Infinity and Vagueness', *Philosophical Review*, 84/4 (Oct. 1975), 525-35.

—— 'Competing Semantics of Vagueness: Many Values versus Supertruth', *Synthese*, 33/2, 3 and 4 (Sept. 1976), 195-210.

SCHAUR, FREDERICK, 'Slippery Slopes', *Harvard Law Review*, 99/2 (Dec. 1985), 361-83.

SCHEDLER, GEORGE, 'The Argument from Ignorance', *International Logic Review*, 9/1 (June 1980), 66-71.

SCHEFFLER, ISRAEL, *Science and Subjectivity* (Indianapolis: Bobbs-Merrill, 1967).

SCHLESINGER, GEORGE *The Range of Epistemic Logic* (Aberdeen: Aberdeen University Press, 1985).

SCHMIDT-RAGHAVEN, MAITHILI, 'On "I" as an Index', *Pacific Philosophical Quarterly*, 61/4 (Oct. 1980), 39-46.

SCHOENBERG, JUDITH, 'A Note on the Logical Fallacy in the Paradox of the Unexpected Examination', *Mind*, 75/297, (Jan. 1966), 125-7.

SCRIVEN, MICHAEL, 'Paradoxical Announcements', *Mind*, 60/239 (July 1951), 403-7.

SELTEN, REINHOLD, 'The Chain Store Paradox', *Theory and Decision*, 9/2 (Apr. 1978), 128-59.

SHARPE, R. A. 'The Unexpected Examination', *Mind*, 74-294, (Apr. 1965), 255.

SHARVEY, RICHARD, 'The Bottle Imp', *Philosophia*, 12/3-4 (Mar. 1983), 401.

SHAW, R., 'The Paradox of the Unexpected Examination', *Mind*, 67/267 (July 1958), 382-4.

SIDGWICK, HENRY, *Methods of Ethics* (London: Macmillan, 1907), 7th edn.
SINGER, MARCUS, 'The Paradox of Extreme Utilitarianism', *Pacific Philosophical Quarterly*, 64/2 (Apr. 1983), 242–8.
SKYRMS, BRIAN, 'Causal Decision Theory', *Journal of Philosophy*, 79/11 (Nov. 1982), 695–711.
SLATER, B. H., 'The Examiner Examined', *Analysis*, 15/4 (Dec. 1974), 505–25.
SLEZAK, PETER, 'Descartes' Diagonal Deduction', *British Journal for the Philosophy of Science*, 34/1 (Mar. 1983), 13–36.
SMITH, JOSEPH WAYNE, 'The Surprise Examination on the Paradox of the Heap', *Philosophical Papers*, 13 (May 1984), 43–56.
SMULLYAN, R. M., 'Languages in which Self-Refererence is Possible', *The Journal of Symbolic Logic*, 22/1 (Jan. 1957), 55–67.
—— *What is the Name of this Book?* (Englewood Cliffs, N.J.: Prentice-Hall, 1978), 185–6.
SORENSEN, ROY A., 'Disagreement Amongst Ideal Thinkers', *Ratio*, 23/2 (Dec. 1981), 136–8.
—— 'Epistemic and Classical Validity', *Journal of Philosophical Logic*, 9/4 (Nov. 1982), 458–9.
—— 'Recalcitrant Variations of the Prediction Paradox', *Australasian Journal of Philosophy*, 60/4 (Dec. 1982), 355–62.
—— 'An "Essential Reservation" about the EMH', *The Journal of Portfolio Management*, 9/4 (Summer 1983), 29–30.
—— 'Newcomb's Problem: Recalculations for the One-Boxer', *Theory and Decision*, 15/4 (Dec. 1983), 399–404.
—— 'Uncaused Decisions and Pre-decisional Blindspots', *Philosophical Studies*, 45/1 (May 1984), 51–6.
—— 'Conditional Blindspots and the Knowledge Squeeze: A Solution to the Prediction Paradox', *Australasian Journal of Philosophy*, 62/2 (June 1984), 126–35.
—— 'An Argument for the Vagueness of "Vague" ', *Analysis*, 27/3 (June 1985), 134–7.
—— 'Pure Moorean Propositions', *Canadian Journal of Philosophy*, 15/3 (Sept. 1985), 489–506.
—— 'The Bottle Imp and the Prediction Paradox', *Philosophia*, 15/4 (Jan. 1986), 421–4.
—— 'A Strengthened Prediction Paradox', *Philosophical Quarterly*, 36/145 (Oct. 1986), 504–13.
—— 'Blindspotting and Choice Variations of the Prediction Paradox', *American Philosophical Quarterly*, 23/4 (Oct. 1986), 337–52.
—— 'Vagueness, Blurriness, and Measurement', *Synthese*, forthcoming.
—— 'Anti-Expertise, Instability, and Rational Choice', *Australasian Journal of Philosophy*, 65/3 (Sept. 1987), 301–15.

STALNAKER, ROBERT, *Inquiry* (Cambridge, Mass.: MIT Press, 1984).
STEINER, MARK, 'The Causal Theory of Knowledge and Platonism', *Journal of Philosophy*, 70/3 (8 Feb. 1973), 57–66.
STICH, STEPHEN, 'Do Animals Have Beliefs?', *Australasian Journal of Philosophy*, 57/1 (Mar. 1979), 15–28.
STRAWSON, P. F., *Logico Linguistic Papers* (London: Methuen, 1971).
TAYLOR, RICHARD, 'Deliberation and Foreknowledge', *American Philosophical Quarterly*, 1/1 (Jan. 1964), 73–80.
THOMAS, JANICE, 'The Toxin, the Blood Donor, and the Bomb', *Analysis*, 43/4 (Oct. 1983), 207–10.
TYLER, BURGE, 'Buridan and Epistemic Paradox', *Philosophical Studies*, 39/1 (Jan. 1978), 21–35.
—— 'Epistemic Paradox', *Journal of Philosophy*, 81/1 (Jan. 1984), 5–29.
UNGER, PETER, *Ignorance* (Oxford: Clarendon Press, 1975).
—— 'There are no Ordinary Things', *Synthese*, 4/2 (June 1979), 117–54.
—— 'I Do Not Exist', in Graham Macdonald (ed.) *Epistemology in Perspective* (London: Macmillan Press, 1980), 235–51.
—— *Philosophical Relativity* (Minneapolis: University of Minnesota Press, 1984).
VAN FRAASSEN, BAS, 'Presupposition, Implication and Self-Reference', *Journal of Philosophy*, 65/5 (1968), 136–52.
—— 'Epistemic Semantics Defended', *Journal of Philosophical Logic*, 19/4 (Nov. 1982), 463–4.
VENDLER, ZENO, 'A Note to the Paralogisms', in Gilbert Ryle (ed.) *Contemporary Aspects of Philosophy* (Stocksfield: Oriel Press, 1977), 111–21.
WAISMANN, F., 'How I See Philosophy', in H. D. Lewis (ed.) *Contemporary British Philosophy* (New York: Macmillan Company, 1956), 447–90.
WARMBROD, KENNETH, 'Epistemic Conditionals', *Pacific Philosophical Quarterly*, 64/3 (July 1983), 249–65.
WARNOCK, G. J., 'Every Event Has a Cause', in Anthony Flew (ed.) *Logic and Language*, 2nd ser. (Oxford: Basil Blackwell, 1959).
WASSERMAN, WAYNE, 'What is Fundamental Ethical Disagreement?', *Analysis*, 45/1 (Jan. 1985), 34–9.
WEISS, PAUL, 'The Prediction Paradox', *Mind*, 61/242 (Apr. 1952), 265–9.
WEISS, STEPHEN, 'The Sorites Fallacy: What Difference does a Peanut Make?', *Synthese*, 33/2, 3, and 4 (Sept. 1976), 253–72.
WHEELER, SAMUEL, C., 'Reference and Vagueness', *Synthese*, 30/3–4 (Apr.–May 1975), 367–80.
—— 'On That Which is Not', *Synthese*, 41/2 (June 1979), 155–94.
WHITE, DAVID, 'Slippery Slope Arguments', *Metaphilosophy*, 16/2 and 3 (Apr./July 1985), 206–13.
WILLIAMS, J. N., 'Moore's Paradox: One Or Two?', *Analysis*, 39/3 (June 1979), 141–2.

WILLIAMS, M. E., 'On the Dissolution of the Paradox of Dives and Lazarus', *Mind*, 79/314 (Apr. 1970), 253.
WILLIAMSON, T., 'Intuitionism Disproved?', *Analysis*, 42/4 (Oct. 1982), 203–7.
WINTERS, BARBARA, 'Believing at Will', *The Journal of Philosophy*, 76/5 (May 1979), 243–56.
—— 'Sceptical Counterpossibilities', *Pacific Philosophical Quarterly*, 62/1 (Oct. 1981), 30–8.
WOLGAST, ELIZABETH H., *Paradoxes of Knowledge* (Ithaca: Cornell University Press, 1977).
WOODS, JOHN, and WALTON, DOUGLAS, 'The Fallacy of "Ad Ignorantiam" ', *Dialectica*, 32/2 (Apr. 1978), 87–99.
WREEN, MICHAEL, 'Vagueness, Values, and the World/Word Wedge', *Australasian Journal of Philosophy*, 63/4 (Dec. 1985), 451–64.
WRIGHT, CRISPIN, 'On the Coherence of Vague Predicates', *Synthese*, 30/3 and 4 (Apr./May 1975), 325–66.
—— and SUDBURY, AIDEN, 'The Paradox of the Unexpected Examination', *Australasian Journal of Philosophy*, 55/1 (May 1977), 41–58.
—— and READ, STEPHEN, 'Hairier than Putnam Thought', *Analysis*, 25/1 (Jan. 1985), 56–8.
WRIGHT, J. A., 'The Surprise Exam: Prediction on the Last Day Uncertain', *Mind*, 76/301 (Jan. 1967), 115–17.
ZIFF, PAUL, 'The Number of English Sentences', *Foundations of Language*, 11/4 (Oct. 1974), 519–32.
—— *Epistemic Analysis* (Dordrecht: D. Reidel, 1984).

Subject Index

abstraction principle 54
absolute terms 178–84, 201
acceptance 82–4
analogy 118, 151–9, 183–4, 217–18, 361–70
analyticity 234–5, 423
anarchism (epistemological) 103–7
anti-experts 12, 114, 386–97
anti-realism 122–59, 244–6
argumentum ad ignorantiam 8, 129–59
  falsity form 140–2, 262
  gappy form 143–4
  simple form 130–40
  unbreakable tie form 144–59
arbitrary objects 431–2
assertibility 18, 404–8

BB principle 34
belief
  blindspots 53–4, 63
  de se 72–4
  scepticism about 70–4
bias 104–7
bivalence
blindspot
  antecedential 78
  belief blindspot 53–4, 63
  conditional 76–84, 200, 328
  compared with Moorean proposition 53–4
  consequential 78–80, 328–33
  characterized 1–4
  defined 52
  for various propositional attitudes 53–5
  generic 82–4
  holistic 93, 417–19
  knowledge blindspot 52–3, ch. 4, 332
  personal 10, 95, 160
  relative 93, 433
  semi-blindspot 12, 92–5, 108, 329, 356, 417–19
  sub-blindspots 93, 417–19
  superblindspots 93, 417–19
  symmetrical 9, 151–4, 199–216

blindspotting 12, 355–60
blurry predicates 9–10, 199–213
booth paradox 361–8
borderline cases 200–6
bottle imp 333–5, 343

causation 185–6, 191–4, 361–4, 371–2, 413
censorship 115–16
charity 18–19, 27, 132–3, 173–7
cogito 31, 75, 309
common cause 361–4
common sense 168–9
commitment 35–40
completeability 37–8
compositionality 228–9, 408–9
conceptual schemes 174–7
conditionals
  back-tracking 377–9
  conditional blindspots 8, 76–84, 200, 328
  indicative v. subjunctive 371–8
conversational implication 19–20
counter-example resistance 415–35
criticism 39–42

decision 190–9
Death case 379–80, 386–96
democracy 115–16
determinism 104–6, 180, 190–9, 260–1, 430–1
dogmatism 315, 375–6, 391, 394
dominance 6, 345–6, 372–4
disagreement
  basic 88–91, 115–16
  complex blindspot 92
  ethical 88–9
  indirect 98–9
  interminable 92, 116
  irresolvable 88–116
  simple blindspot 8, 92, 356
doxastic logic 20–3, 34, 43–4, 52–3

EMH (efficient market hypothesis) 109–14
entailment 201–4

epistemic semantics 66–84
error theories 96–114
essentially contested concepts 99
excluded middle 260–1
experts 87–8
explanation 163–8, 411–12

fallacy
  ad ignorantiam 129–59
  ad populum 138–9
  compositionality of ignorance 161–2
  post hoc 138–9
  proportionality 251–2
  proving invalidity 181
  slippery slope 12–13, ch. 12
  statistical notion of 8, 13, 137–40, 408–11
  v. myth 99–100
fiction 54–5, 144, 428–30
forgetting 53–4

game theory 6–7, 280–2, 322–3, 344–54
generalizations
  cloaked 418–20
  mendacious 414–20
Godel's theorem 269–71, 273
guess 47
gullibilism 21–3

hypertasks 151–6

'I' 29–33, 45–7, 73–4
imagination 54, 60–5
inconsistency
  direct 26–8, 37–8
  indirect 26–8, 49
  patent 26–8, 37–8
incorrigibility 29–33, 34
infallible predictor 375–8
instability cases 12, 378–81
intuitionism 128–9, 230
iterated prisoners' dilemma 5–7, 345–7

KK principle 131–2, 242–3, 290–2, 312–17

liar paradox 301–3, 307
limits
  agent 188–9
  impersonal 121–8
  personal 118–21
  temporal 186–8
lottery paradox 25–6, 93–4, 161, 239–40, 288–9, 388
luck 186–8

many-valued logic 233–6, 261
mean demon 380–1
measurement 142, 152–5, 182
methodological conservatism 90–1
miracles 162–8
misjudgement theories 96–116
modesty 9, 67–8, 120–1
Moorean propositions
  addressee 46
  defined 42–3
  grades of 43, 46–7
  impure 33–4
  user 45–6
Moore's Problem
  and anti-expertise 390
  and truth 58–9
  formulated 15
  pure Moorean proposition 42–3, 55
  and the prediction paradox 284–9
mystery numbers 9–10, 154–9

Newcomb's problem 12, 363, 369–70, 371–7
negative sorites 217–18
nonstandard sorites 217–19

ontology 213–16
optimism (epistemological) 118
other minds 118–20
overshadowed hypotheses 390–1

Paradox of Dives and Lazarus 382–3
parapsychology 135–6, 169–71
positive sorites 217–19
possible worlds 66–7
pragmatic paradox 17–18, 256–8
predicates (blindspot) ch. 5, 392–5
prediction paradox 4–5, 10–12
  see also variations of the prediction paradox
preface paradox 23–5, 93–4, 161, 388
presupposition 219, 230–1
prisoners' dilemma 5–6, 345
privileged access 172–3
probability 48–50, 89, 168–71, 235–6, 239–42, 403–13, 375–6
pseudo-science 112, 169–71
punishment 349–51

quantum mechanics 432–5

Subject Index

ratifiability 372–4
rational belief systems 66–76
realism 122
reduction 211, 301–3
referential transparency of 'I' 29–33
regret 379
relative likelihood 163

scale effect 25
scepticism 57–8, 103, 118–20, 123–4, 164
self-blindspotting 359
self-intimation 33–4
self-reference
 belief *de se* 72–4
 Buridanean 268–9
 contingent 32–3, 303
 game-theoretic 280–3, 322–4, 382–6
 indirect 302, 306
 misjudgement theories 102–7
 sentential 264–80, 298–310
 sophisticated preface paradox 23–4
semantic anti-realism 122–59
sensitivity 10, 209, 246–52
sense data 424–8
simplicity 214–15
slippery slope arguments
 categorical v. hypothetical 398–400
 fallacy 12–13
 optimistic 400–1
sorites paradox 4, 10, 150, 215–16, 292–4, ch. 6, 324–7, 360–8, 395–6, 415, 431
stability 12, 374, 378–97
stock market 109–14, 392
subjective properties 100–2
super-games
 and the prediction paradox 12
 chain store 348–9
 Hodgeson's paradox of punishment 349–51
 iterated chicken 351–2
 iterated prisoners' dilemma 5–7
 iterated pricing game 352–3
super-valuationism 236–39, 430

temporal retention 286–7
toxin puzzle 336–7
thoroughness 36
tickle defense 372–4
time travel 170–1, 322–3
truth-value gap 144–5, 402–3, 426, 430–1

unanchored predicates 201–5
understanding 29, 183–4
utilitarianism 91, 349–51, 382–3

vacuous slopes 405–7
validity
 epistemic v. classical 7–9, 65–74
 gaps 224–5
 illusions 413–14
 logical analogy 151–9
 proving invalidity 140, 181, 221–4
 Pseudo-Scotus' paradox of 299–310
 vagueness of 234–5
vagueness 101, 200–16
 counterparts to 206–13
 defined 199
 higher order 242–3
 non-compositionality of 228–9
 of 'Moorean sentence' 48–50
 of 'knowledge' 365–8
 of 'vague' 227–8
variation of the prediction paradox
 ace of spades 311
 bottle imp 333–6, 360–1
 booth paradox 361–5
 class A blackout 256–7
 designated student 335
 hangman 262, 267–9, 310–11
 Hollis's 326–7
 Indy puzzle 337–43
 last buyer 333–5
 undiscoverable position 320–1
 sacrificial virgin 322–4
 surprise egg 262
 surprise test 4–5, 260
verificationism 58, 126–7

Name Index

Adams, Ernest W. 404 n., 406 n.
Aldrich, Virgil 227 n.
Alexander, Peter 257–8
Alston, William 172–3
Anderson, Alan Ross 96
Anscombe, G. E. M. 29 n.
Aristotle 121, 188, 260, 430–1
Armstrong, David M. 77 n., 147–8
Austin, A. K. 278
Ayer, A. J. 279, 426–7

Bacon, Francis 130
Beardesmore, R. W. 88
Benacerraf 145, 148, 150, 157, 212–13
Bennett, Jonathan 273–5
Berkeley, George 58–65, 432
Bever, T. G. 342–3
Binkley, Robert 284–6, 311
Black, Max 19 n., 225 n., 230–3
Boer, Stephen 231 n.
Boos, William 309 n.
Bosch, Jorge 285–6
Bradley, Francis Herbert 141
Brouwer, L. E. J. 153–4
Bunch, Bryan 253
Burge, Tyler 268–9
Buridan, Jean 268–9, 276
Butler, R. J. 275–6

Campbell, Keith 148–50, 158
Campbell, Richmond 239, 243–4
Cargile, James 232, 239, 243–4, 275–7, 280–3, 322–4
Carnap, Rudolph 224
Casullo, Albert 64 n.
Ceci, Stephen 106–7
Champlin, T. S. 284
Chapman, J. M. 276–8
Chihara, Charles 291–3, 312
Chisholm, Roderick 426–7
Churchland, Paul 70, 102
Cohen, L. Jonathan 17–19, 257
Cole, David 51–2
Collins, Arthur 189–94, 390–1
Conee, Earl 383–6, 392–4
Copi, Irving 130, 133–6

Danto, Arthur 314
Davidson, Donald 48, 107–8, 174–7
Davis, Lawrence 346–8, 353–4, 369–70
Descartes, René 31, 86, 109, 147, 169, 309
Destouches-Fevrier 434
Deutshcer, Max 23–6, 32
Dewey, Thomas 87, 382
Dietl, Paul 295, 325–7
Driver, Julia 120 n.
Duhem, Pierre 67
Dummett, Michael 122, 226 n., 294–5

Eccles, John C. 105 n.
Edgington, Dorothy 127–9
Edman, Martin 279
Eells, Ellery 372–4
Ekbom, Lennart 253
Ellis, Brian 65–74, 77, 79–80, 185–6
Ellison, James 277
Epicurus 104
Eubulides 217, 226, 299

Fain, Haskell 21–2
Fetzer, James H. 375
Feyerabend, Paul 103
Fine, Kit 238, 432
Fitch, Frederic 124–9, 273
Forbes, Graeme 251
Forest, Terry 123
Frege, Gottlob 431–2
Fraser, J. T. 262, 318
Freeman, Derek 167–8
Freud, Sigmund 60, 108–9

Gardner, Martin 253, 272–3
Gettier, Edmund 97
Gibbard, Allan 376–8, 379, 386, 388
Gibbins, P. F. 433 n.
Ginet, Carl 191–4
Godel, Kurt 185, 253, 269–72
Goethe 60
Gogueun, J. 247
Goldstick, D. 90–1
Govier, Trudy 402–3
Grice, H. P. 20

Name Index

Griffiths, A. Phillips 21–2
Grim, Patrick 225, 309 n.

Haack, Susan 224
Haldane, J. B. S. 105
Hanson, Norwood Russell 133 n.
Hardin, Russell 264 n., 354–5
Hare, R. M. 88
Harman, Gilbert 97, 145–6, 315
Harper, William 376–8, 379, 386, 388
Harrison, Craig 289
Harrison, Jonathan 435
Hart, W. D. 124–9
Hegel, George 26
Heintz, J. 429
Heisenberg, Werner 143, 432–5
Hintikka, Jaakko 20–2, 50–1, 285, 315
Hodgson, D. H. 349–51
Hollis, Martin 326–7
Holman, Emmet L. 149 n.
Horgan, Terence 377–9
Hubin, Don 378
Humberstone, I. L. 379
Hume, David 9, 22, 58, 64, 162–8, 311

Jackson, Frank 435
Jaynes, E. T. 89
Jeffrey, Richard 371–4
Jeffreys, H. 89 n.
Johnson, Oliver 61–5

Kamp, Hans 247
Kant, Immanual 58, 86, 102, 104–5
Kaplan, David 267–9
Katz, Stuart 147
Kavka, Gregory 336–8
Keeling, S. V. 86
Keene, G. B. 301 n.
Kiefer, James 277
King, J. L. 232, 244–6
Kneale, M. 431
Kneale, W. 431
Kraemer, Eric Russert 148 n.
Kroon, Frederick 382–6, 393
Kuhn, Thomas 89–90
Kvart, Igal 285
Kyburg, Henry 161

Lambert, Karel 434
Lehrer, Keith 87–8
Laing, R. D. 177
Lemmon, E. J. 54, 313–14
Levi, Isaac 434

Levin, Michael 174, 176, 190–2
Levine, Howard P. 404 n.
Lewis, David 54–5, 128, 186, 375–6
Linsky, Bernard 125–6
Linsky, Leonard 21 n.
Locke, Don 107
Locke, John 130
Lowe, E. J. 413–14
Lukasiewicz 261, 431
Lundberg, George 70, 102
Lycan, William 76, 91, 231 n.
Lyon, Ardon 266–7, 275, 310

MacKay, D. M. 195–9
Machina, Kenton 234–6, 239–40
MacIntosh, J. J. 24 n., 124–5
Mackie, J. L. 102, 126–7
Makinson, D. C. 24 n., 161
Malcolm, Norman 1 n., 105
Martins, Michael 106 n.
Martinich, A. P. 19–20
Marx, Karl 108–9
Massey, Gerald 181, 223–4
McCracken, Charles J. 86
McGee, Vann 71 n.
McLaughlin, Robert 133 n.
McLelland, J. 293–4, 315–17
McMullen, W. A. 115
McTaggart, J. E. 141
Mead, Margaret 167
Medlin, Brian 273–6
Meltzer, B. 261
Mill, John Stuart 252
Milner, E. V. 383–4
Montague, Richard 267–9
Moore, G. E. 1, 61–2, 168–9, 382

Nerlich, G. C. 269–72, 298
Nisbett, Richard 252
Nozick, Robert 165–6, 378, 383 n.

Oakley, I. T. 103
O'Carroll, M. J. 278
O'Connor, D. J. 256–8
O'Connor, John 384
Odegard, Douglas 172
Olin, Doris 288–9
Oliver, J. Willard 223 n.

Parfit, Derek 148 n., 250–1
Peirce, C. S. 29 n., 87, 114
Peters, Douglas 106–7
Pitcher, George 146

Name Index

Plato 86, 121
Popper, Karl 105, 272–3
Pratt, James B. 140–1
Price, George R. 9, 169–71
Price, H. H. 427
Priest, Graham 27
Prior, Arthur 309
Protagoras 103
Pseudo-Scotus 299–309
Putnam, Hilary 230, 434–5

Quine, W. V. 9, 122–3, 145–6, 173–7, 226 n., 262–4, 276, 283–7, 309, 310–12, 354

Rabinowiwcz, Wlodzimierz 381
Radford, Colin 314
Ramsey, Frank 77–84
Read, Stephen 230, 300–1
Regan, Donald 264 n.
Reichenbach, Hans 434
Reid, Thomas 64
Rescher, Nicholas 109
Richter, Reed 378–81, 389–90
Robinson, Richard 130 n.
Rolf, Bertil 226 n., 229 n.
Rosenthal, Robert 105 n.
Ross, Glenn 378
Ross, Lee 252
Rowe, William 408 n.
Russell, Bertrand 135, 224–5, 420
Runyon, Richard 179–80
Ryle, Gilbert 29 n., 308–9

Sanford, David 232–4, 433 n.
Sayward, Charles 148 n.
Schaur, Frederick 402 n.
Schedler, George 131 n.
Scheffler, Israel 106
Schiffer, Stephen 46
Schmidt-Raghavan, Maithili 29 n.
Schlesinger, George 128 n.
Schoenberg, Judith 277–8
Scriven, Michael 133 n., 258–9, 264
Selten, Reinhold 346 n.
Sharpe, R. A. 280–1, 322
Seneca 103
Sharvey, Richard 333–6
Shaw, R. 264–6, 270
Singer, Marcus 382
Sidgewick, Henry 61, 91, 382
Skyrms, Brian 380–1, 386
Slater, B. H. 283–4

Slezak, Peter 309 n.
Smith, Joseph Wayne 219–20, 293–5, 325–7
Smullyan, Raymond M. 26, 273
Stalnaker, Robert 77, 81–4
Stebbing, L. S. 402 n.
Steiner, Mark 185
Stich, Stephen 148 n.
Strawson, Peter 58, 230–1
Sudbury, Aiden 286–7, 311–12, 318, 340 n.
Swinburne, R. G. 126

Taylor, Richard 192–3
Thomas, Janice 336

Unger, Peter 75, 103, 178–9, 226–9, 246, 248
Unterecker, John 103

van Fraassen, Bas 70–4, 431
Vendler, Zeno 30 n.
Voltaire 104

Wagner, Carl 87–8
Waismann, Frederick 149–50, 158
Walton, Douglas 130–3, 138
Warmbrod, Kenneth 77 n.
Warnock, G. J. 180
Wasserman, Wayne 89 n.
Watkins, J. W. N. 152
Weiss, Paul 260–2, 318
Weiss, Stephen 221–4
White, David 402
Wheeler, Samuel 226–9
Wilcox, Stephen 147
Williams, J. N. 20
Williams, M. E. 384
Williamson, T. 128–9
Windt, Peter 279
Winters, Barbara 97, 105
Wittgenstein, Ludwig 1, 29 n., 58–60, 75–6, 149–50
Wolgast, Elizabeth H. 59–60, 65, 77
Woods, John 130–3, 138
Wreen, Michael 100–2
Wright, Crispin 145–6, 230, 286–7, 311–12, 318, 340 n.
Wright, J. A. 279–80
Wu, Kathleen Johnson 285

Ziff, Paul 220, 224